# INSIDERS' GUIDE® TO

# FAIRFIELD COUNTY

TRISHA BLANCHET

**INSIDERS'**GUIDE®

GUILFORD, CONNECTICUT
AN IMPRINT OF THE GLOBE PEQUOT PRESS

The prices and rates in this guidebook were confirmed at press time. We recommend, however, that you call establishments before traveling to obtain current information.

To buy books in quantity for corporate use or incentives, call **(800) 962–0973, ext. 4551,** or e-mail **premiums@GlobePequot.com.**

Text design by LeAnna Weller Smith
Maps by XNR Productions, Inc. © The Globe Pequot Press

ISSN 1552-7247
ISBN 0-7627-2727-6

Manufactured in the United States of America
First Edition/First Printing

*Wolfe Park beach with flowers, Monroe.*
TRISHA BLANCHET

*Brookfield town center.* HOUSATONIC VALLEY TOURISM/KEN KAST

**[Top]** *Statue of Jonathan Trumbull in front of Trumbull town hall.* TRISHA BLANCHET
**[Bottom]** *Putnam Cottage, Greenwich.* TRISHA BLANCHET

**[Top]** *Ives Concert Park, Danbury.* HOUSATONIC VALLEY TOURISM/KEN KAST
**[Bottom]** *Richter Park Golf Course, Danbury.* HOUSATONIC VALLEY TOURISM/KEN KAST

*A hidden stream in Wolfe Park, Monroe.* TRISHA BLANCHET

*Midtown Campus gate at WCSU, Danbury.* PEGGY H. STEWART, COURTESY OF WESTERN CONNECTICUT STATE UNIVERSITY

*WCSU's Westside Athletic Stadium, Danbury.*
PEGGY H. STEWART, COURTESY OF WESTERN CONNECTICUT STATE UNIVERSITY

**[Top]** *Longshore Sailing School, Westport.* COURTESY OF LONGSHORE SAILING SCHOOL
**[Bottom]** *Norwalk Harbor.* CONNECTICUT'S COASTAL FAIRFIELD COUNTY CONVENTION & VISITOR BUREAU

**[Top]** *Boats along the shoreline.* CONNECTICUT'S COASTAL FAIRFIELD COUNTY CONVENTION & VISITOR BUREAU
**[Bottom]** *Rowing on Norwalk Harbor.* CONNECTICUT'S COASTAL FAIRFIELD COUNTY CONVENTION & VISITOR BUREAU

*Lakeside Pottery, Stamford.* LAKESIDE POTTERY LLC/MORTY BACHAR

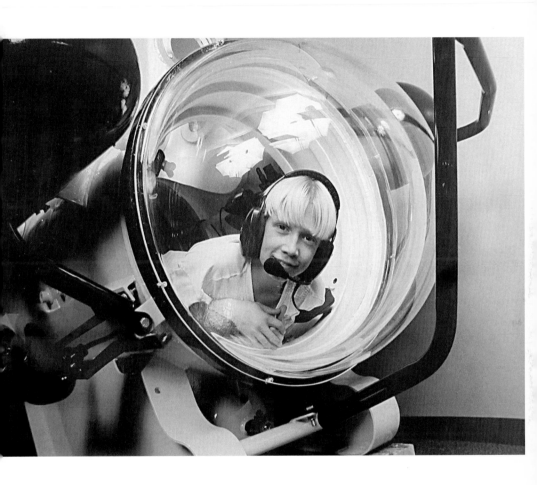

*Discovery Museum, Bridgeport.* THE DISCOVERY MUSEUM

*Connecticut Audubon Birdcraft Museum, Fairfield.* TRISHA BLANCHET

*Fairfield Hall at WCSU, Danbury.* PEGGY H. STEWART, COURTESY OF WESTERN CONNECTICUT STATE UNIVERSITY

*Squantz Pond State Park, New Fairfield.* HOUSATONIC VALLEY TOURISM/KEN KAST

# CONTENTS

Preface . . . . . . . . . . . . . . . . . . . . . . . . . . . . . . . . . . . . . . . . . . . . . . . . . . . . . . . . . xxv

Acknowledgments . . . . . . . . . . . . . . . . . . . . . . . . . . . . . . . . . . . . . . . . . . . xxvii

How to Use This Book . . . . . . . . . . . . . . . . . . . . . . . . . . . . . . . . . . . . . . . . . 1

Area Overview . . . . . . . . . . . . . . . . . . . . . . . . . . . . . . . . . . . . . . . . . . . . . . . . 3

Getting Here, Getting Around . . . . . . . . . . . . . . . . . . . . . . . . . . . . . . . 21

History . . . . . . . . . . . . . . . . . . . . . . . . . . . . . . . . . . . . . . . . . . . . . . . . . . . . . . 32

Accommodations . . . . . . . . . . . . . . . . . . . . . . . . . . . . . . . . . . . . . . . . . . . . 38

Restaurants . . . . . . . . . . . . . . . . . . . . . . . . . . . . . . . . . . . . . . . . . . . . . . . . . 48

Nightlife . . . . . . . . . . . . . . . . . . . . . . . . . . . . . . . . . . . . . . . . . . . . . . . . . . . . 78

Shopping . . . . . . . . . . . . . . . . . . . . . . . . . . . . . . . . . . . . . . . . . . . . . . . . . . . 90

Attractions . . . . . . . . . . . . . . . . . . . . . . . . . . . . . . . . . . . . . . . . . . . . . . . . . 111

Kidstuff . . . . . . . . . . . . . . . . . . . . . . . . . . . . . . . . . . . . . . . . . . . . . . . . . . . . 129

The Arts . . . . . . . . . . . . . . . . . . . . . . . . . . . . . . . . . . . . . . . . . . . . . . . . . . . . 140

Annual Events . . . . . . . . . . . . . . . . . . . . . . . . . . . . . . . . . . . . . . . . . . . . . . 156

Beaches, Parks, and Recreation . . . . . . . . . . . . . . . . . . . . . . . . . . . . . . 175

Golf . . . . . . . . . . . . . . . . . . . . . . . . . . . . . . . . . . . . . . . . . . . . . . . . . . . . . . . . 200

Spectator Sports . . . . . . . . . . . . . . . . . . . . . . . . . . . . . . . . . . . . . . . . . . . . 206

Day Trips and Getaways . . . . . . . . . . . . . . . . . . . . . . . . . . . . . . . . . . . . . 209

Nonprofits and Volunteering . . . . . . . . . . . . . . . . . . . . . . . . . . . . . . . . . 224

Real Estate . . . . . . . . . . . . . . . . . . . . . . . . . . . . . . . . . . . . . . . . . . . . . . . . . 231

Relocation . . . . . . . . . . . . . . . . . . . . . . . . . . . . . . . . . . . . . . . . . . . . . . . . . . 239

Education . . . . . . . . . . . . . . . . . . . . . . . . . . . . . . . . . . . . . . . . . . . . . . . . . . . 247

Child Care . . . . . . . . . . . . . . . . . . . . . . . . . . . . . . . . . . . . . . . . . . . . . . . . . . 257

Health Care . . . . . . . . . . . . . . . . . . . . . . . . . . . . . . . . . . . . . . . . . . . . . . . . . 266

Media . . . . . . . . . . . . . . . . . . . . . . . . . . . . . . . . . . . . . . . . . . . . . . . . . . . . . . . 272

Worship . . . . . . . . . . . . . . . . . . . . . . . . . . . . . . . . . . . . . . . . . . . . . . . . . . . . . 278

## CONTENTS

Index . . . . . . . . . . . . . . . . . . . . . . . . . . . . . . . . . . . . . . . . . . . . . . . 280

About the Author . . . . . . . . . . . . . . . . . . . . . . . . . . . . . . . . . . . . . . 292

## Directory of Maps

Connecticut Area Overview . . . . . . . . . . . . . . . . . . . . . . . . . . . . . . . xix

Fairfield County . . . . . . . . . . . . . . . . . . . . . . . . . . . . . . . . . . . . . . . xx

Downtown Stamford . . . . . . . . . . . . . . . . . . . . . . . . . . . . . . . . . . . . xxi

Downtown Danbury . . . . . . . . . . . . . . . . . . . . . . . . . . . . . . . . . . . . xxii

SoNo Area, Norwalk . . . . . . . . . . . . . . . . . . . . . . . . . . . . . . . . . . . . xxiii

Downtown Bridgeport . . . . . . . . . . . . . . . . . . . . . . . . . . . . . . . . . . . xxiv

# Connecticut Area Overview

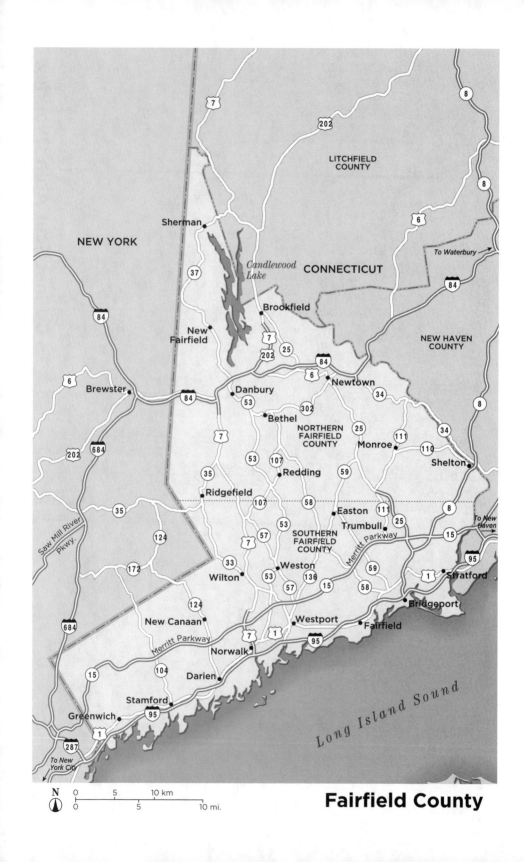

# Fairfield County

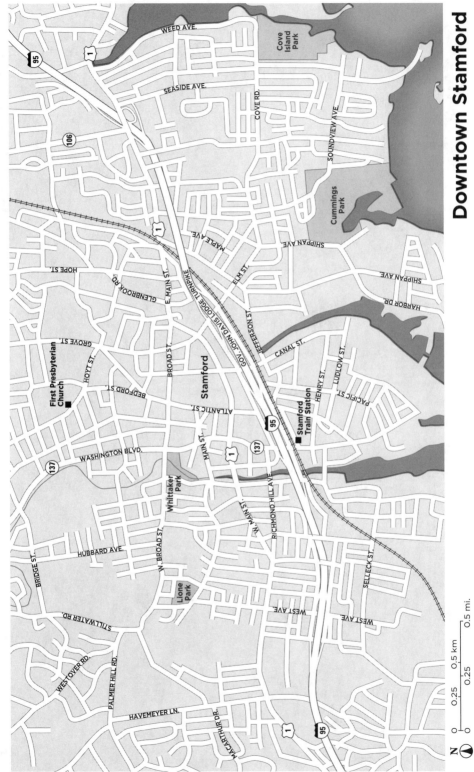

# Downtown Stamford

Downtown Danbury

84

NEWTOWN RD.

OLIVE ST.

FEDERAL RD.

202
7
6
84

OSBORNE ST.
JAMES ST.
Western Conn.
State University
WHITE ST.

37
37

BALMFORTH AVE.

53

Danbury

FRANKLIN ST.

Danbury
City Hall

TOWN HILL AVE.
53

MAIN ST.

GRAND ST.

DEER HILL AVE.

WEST ST.

GOLDEN HILL RD.

39

KOHANZA ST.

Ridgewood
Country Club

GREGORY ST.

S. KING ST.

FRANKLIN ST. EXT.

LAKE AVE.

PARK AVE.

SOUTH ST.

COAL PIT HILL RD.

MEMORIAL DR.

Rogers
Park

MOUNTAINVILLE RD.

SOUTHERN BLVD.

53

302

RESERVOIR ST.

53

Bethel

PLUMTREES RD.

302

58

Danbury
Fair Mall

7

Danbury
Municipal
Airport

BACKUS AVE.

6
202
84

N

0      0.5      1 km
0    0.5      1 mi.

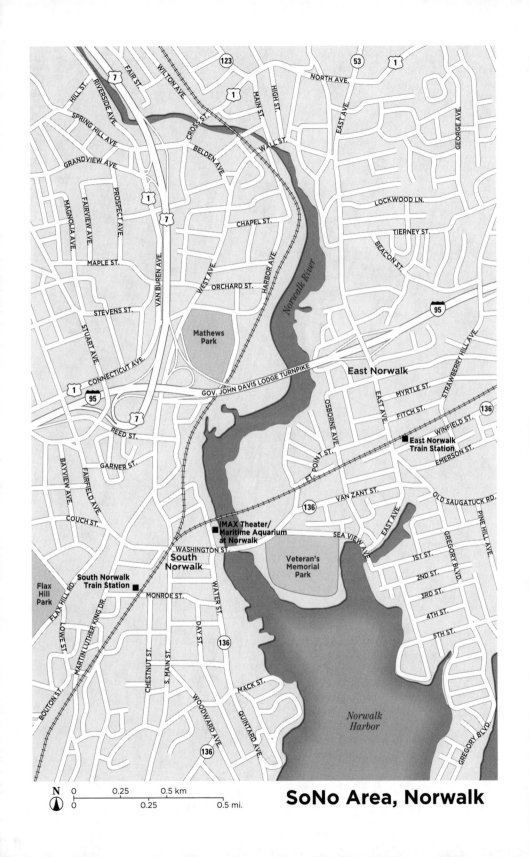

**SoNo Area, Norwalk**

# Downtown Bridgeport

**N**

| 0 | 0.25 | 0.5 km |
| 0 | 0.25 | 0.5 mi. |

Newfield Park
NEWFIELD AVE.
SEAVIEW AVE.
SEAVIEW AVE.
HAMILTON ST.
Yellow Mill Pond
130
E. MAIN ST.
KOSSUTH ST.
STRATFORD AVE.
Pleasure Beach Park
Ferry to Port Jefferson
Pequonnock River
Bridgeport Harbor
95
MAIN ST.
Water St.
CONGRESS ST.
Bridgeport Train Station
Bridgeport City Hall
MAIN ST.
FAIRFIELD AVE.
BROAD ST.
JOHN ST.
Bridgeport Bus Terminal
Arena at Harbor Yard
Ballpark at Harbor Yard
LINDEN AVE.
N. GROVE RD.
8
25
WASHINGTON AVE.
GREGOR ST.
ATLANTIC ST.
Seaside Park
JAMES ST.
PEQUONNOCK ST.
COLEMAN ST.
PARK AVE.
Bridgeport
IRANISTAN AVE.
WALDEMERE AVE.
BARNUM BLVD.
PARK AVE.
BENHAM AVE.
WOOD AVE.
LAUREL AVE.
NORMAN ST.
130
130
SOUTH AVE.
AVE.
STATE ST.
FAIRFIELD
RAILROAD AVE.
GOV. JOHN DAVIS LODGE TURNPIKE
PINE ST.
LAUREL AVE.
NORTH AVE.
MAPLEWOOD AVE.
BEECHWOOD AVE.
HOWARD AVE.
HANCOCK AVE.
BOSTWICK AVE.
Captain's Cove Seaport
59
BRIARWOOD AVE.
DEWEY ST.
1
VILLA AVE.
58
95
WOODIN AVE.
FAIRFIELD AVE.
130
ELLSWORTH ST.

# PREFACE

Trying to categorize Fairfield County is like trying to eat ice cream with a fork: At first everything goes well. But the longer you keep at it, the more the good stuff seems to slip through those pesky prongs. This is a place that reaches both ends of nearly every spectrum, from downtown apartments to waterfront mansions, hot-dog stands to French bistros, and herb-education centers to private universities. One day you're searching for hidden worms at a pick-your-own apple orchard; the next you're sampling fine wines at a local vineyard. Outdoor enthusiasts can relax with a rowboat and a fishing pole on the lake or cruise Long Island Sound in a schooner. Shoppers can find bargains at a flea market or diamonds at Tiffany's. Fairfield County is sometimes overwhelming, sometimes cozy, and sometimes a combination of the two. But it's never boring.

And let's face it: It's not exactly subtle, either. In fact, a reputation for extravagance and exclusivity—deserved or not—often precedes us. As a newcomer, or perhaps even a longtime resident, you probably have questions about these and other things you have seen or heard about Fairfield County. This guide is designed to remove the guesswork by sorting through the myriad options for dining, housing, recreation, shopping, commuting, and living in this diverse and popular region of Connecticut.

Despite our best efforts to neatly catalog it, our region remains ripe with quirks and unanswerables. (Why, for example, is the Westporter Diner located in Norwalk?) In many ways, that's what makes this corner of New England—the lower, left-hand corner—such a wonderful and interesting place to live. Locals sometimes consider themselves more as New Yorkers than New Englanders; Yankee and Mets T-shirts here far outnumber those sporting a Red Sox logo. And that only makes sense, considering that New York City is just a short train ride away and many residents commute to jobs in the Big Apple or visit there on a regular basis.

On the other hand, Fairfield County retains the best "New Englandy" qualities, as well. Most towns have quaint greens and churches, historic homes, and fascinating local lore documenting colorful characters of the past. Agriculture still plays a role in the local economy, and farmland dots the landscape in places like Easton and Sherman. The coast of Long Island Sound supports fishermen, marinas, and recreational boaters. We have crisp white snow in winter (bring your sled), fiery orange and red leaves in fall, delicate hues of purple and pink in spring, and flat-out splendor in summer. Even during the height of winter, the skies are typically sunny and blue.

The county is conveniently located, blessed with miles of shoreline, and filled with employment opportunities, excellent public school systems, and great shopping and restaurants. All of these qualities make the region desirable—they also, unfortunately, make it an expensive place to live. Some areas are far more costly than others; in general, the closer you get to New York City and/or the coastline, the more you can expect to pay for homes, services, and even gasoline. Towns like Greenwich, Darien, and Westport are famous for housing celebrities like Paul Newman, David Letterman, Martha Stewart, Harry Connick Jr., and Rosie O'Donnell; but you're more likely to run into a CEO than a movie star. There is another side to the story of Fairfield County life, as staffers at local food pantries and nonprofits will tell you. Recent immigrants, recent college grads, newlyweds, newcomers from other areas of the country—even longtime residents—are often shell-shocked by the high costs and struggle to make ends meet. Rumors imply that everyone here is well-to-do, and, yes, many families are. But many are not.

Whether you fall into the former category or the latter, *Insiders' Guide to Fairfield County* is designed to help you navigate the complex, intriguing, and usually fun Fairfield County way of life. If you are visiting the area or plan to relocate here, this guide can serve as an invaluable tool in finding the restaurants, attractions, and services that best suit your needs. If you already live in Fairfield County, this book will hopefully give you insight into lesser known corners of the region and places that you might not have had a chance to explore—yet. Read on to learn about the intriguing opportunities that Fairfield County has to offer.

# ACKNOWLEDGMENTS

I would like to extend my gratitude to Catherine Brashich, Executive Director of the Housatonic Valley Tourism District, and to Mary L. Woods, Director of Communications for the Coastal Fairfield County Convention and Visitor's Bureau. Both were extremely generous with their time and resources, helping to make this book possible.

Thank you also to golf guru John Barton for lending his expertise about Fairfield County's courses, and to my editor, Michael Urban, who offered invaluable guidance and insights. In addition, I am grateful to the countless historians, librarians, business owners, and local residents who provided opinions, photos, and information that helped to complete this picture of county life. And as always, thank you to Scott, whose support makes my life and work better every day.

# HOW TO USE THIS BOOK ?

This guide offers the practical information that you need to enjoy Fairfield County, including details about lodging, restaurants, and attractions. If you're new to the area, *Insiders' Guide to Fairfield County* provides the basics— where to get your driver's license, how to secure day care, where to find the best housing for your price range—and assists with the other, equally pressing concerns of finding great sushi, hiking trails, and golf courses. For those who are considering a move to Fairfield County, the Area Overview, Real Estate, Relocation, and Education chapters are a good place to start: What is each community's personality? Will you fit in there? Someone looking for a plethora of country clubs, for example, probably wouldn't be happy in Shelton. Likewise, if your priority is affordable housing, you should probably steer clear of Westport or Darien. You'll find the good, the bad, and the ugly in our town-by-town breakdowns. The History chapter can also provide insight into how the region's convoluted and colorful past shaped our cities into the diverse places you find today.

Getting Here, Getting Around gives newcomers and locals a glimpse at the workings of Fairfield County transportation, whether you want to find the quickest route to work or you need to catch a plane outta here. Airport shuttles, ferry schedules, highways and byways, and the Metro-North Railroad commuter line are all essential aspects of living and moving around southeastern Connecticut. The Child Care, Health Care, Media, and Worship chapters provide specifics about day-to-day necessities.

If you're planning a visit (or if you're expecting the in-laws), the Accommodations chapter includes a variety of options, including swanky hotels, economical motels, and homey bed-and-breakfasts. The eateries in the Restaurants chapter are listed alphabetically by town or city. Craving Thai? Want a quick deli sandwich, or maybe a five-course Italian dinner? The listings make it easy to satisfy even the pickiest palate, wherever you might be in the county.

The Nightlife, Shopping, Attractions, Arts, Annual Events, and Beaches, Parks, and Recreation chapters detail the many boutiques, bars, museums, county fairs, art galleries, beaches, orchards, sports fields, festivals, and other attractions that stretch from border to border. Kidstuff concentrates on hot spots and activities for the younger set. Spectator Sports provides information about cheering on the favorite local teams. As hard as it might be to believe, there are occasions when you might want to venture out of our fair region for a while. Day Trips and Getaways provides itineraries for visiting the city, seashore, or countryside, none of which are too far away.

Readers of other Insiders' Guides will recognize many of those chapters and sections as hallmarks of the series. This book also contains chapters that are unique to Fairfield County. Golf, for example, pays homage to one of the region's most popular activities with detailed information about local courses and clubs, both public and private. The Nonprofits and Volunteering chapter lists and describes the numerous organizations dedicated to helping people in need, improving the environment, supporting educational or medical causes, or sheltering homeless animals.

Throughout this book we give you Insiders' tips (indicated by ▇) for quick insights, and more lengthy Close-ups with information that is particularly interesting, unusual, or helpful to know.

Every guidebook is, by definition, subjective, and *Insiders' Guide to Fairfield County* is no exception. Although every attempt was made to achieve accuracy and parity, you may nevertheless disagree with some of the viewpoints expressed or the descriptions presented. If you spot an error, or if you think any essential information has been omitted, please let us know. After all, we Fairfield County residents aren't known for keeping our opinions to ourselves—and we wouldn't have it any other way.

You may e-mail us at editorial@Globe Pequot.com or write to us at:

The Globe Pequot Press
Reader Response/Editorial Department
P.O. Box 480
Guilford, CT 06437-0480

# AREA OVERVIEW

Fairfield County can be roughly divided into two areas: the southern, coastal region, and the northern towns and cities. These areas are distinct in personality as well as geography; some residents in either place would even be surprised to learn they share the same county designation. Generally speaking, it's a long way from one end to the other, and most locals tend to stay in their own region when searching for restaurants, activities, stores, parks, and even jobs.

In the south, Greenwich, Westport, New Canaan, Easton, Weston, and Darien perpetuate the Fairfield County reputation for affluence; these are some of the most scenic, in-demand, and exclusive towns in the United States. The southern region is also home to large cities like Norwalk, Stamford, and Bridgeport, where residents can experience museums, shopping, sporting events, theater, and diverse and lively populations. The city of Danbury anchors the northern area of the county, providing jobs and attractions for the residents of nearby quiet suburbs like Brookfield, Newtown, Ridgefield, and New Fairfield. Whether glitzy or laid-back, each community contributes in its own way to the unique fabric of Fairfield County life.

The largest Fairfield County town is Newtown, with an area of 60 square miles. Greenwich comes in a close second with 50.6 square miles. In terms of population, Bridgeport is the largest, with more than 140,000 residents, followed by Stamford with 117,000 and Danbury with almost 75,000. Sherman has just less than 4,000 residents, making it by far the town with the smallest population; Easton's population of around 7,000 is the second smallest. The town with the tiniest geographic area—just 12 square miles—is Darien, followed by Bethel at 17 square miles.

New England weather is unpredictable, and this is no exception in Fairfield County.

Winters can be harsh, with mountains of snow persisting from November to March, or mild, with hardly a flake hitting the ground. Most years, however, fall somewhere in between those two extremes. The towns along the coastline tend to see less snow and slightly warmer temperatures throughout the year than the towns in the northern areas. Throughout the region, average temperatures for January range from 22 to 36 degrees; average July temperatures are between 66 and 82 degrees. Precipitation averages out at about 3 to 4 inches each month; this isn't an unusually rainy region, but it never hurts to carry an umbrella just in case.

## SOUTHERN FAIRFIELD COUNTY

## Bridgeport

All Fairfield County had reason to cheer in 1998 when Bridgeport invested $19 million in a baseball stadium for its new Atlantic League team, the Bridgeport Bluefish. The Ballpark at Harbor Yard, which allows a great view from every seat—not to mention reasonably priced tickets and hot dogs—was an instant hit, as was the popular team. The baseball stadium was quickly followed by the Arena at Harbor Yard, home to a new hockey team, the Bridgeport Sound Tigers. The 10,000-seat arena also hosts ice-skating competitions, concerts, and basketball games. Both venues draw crowds from around Fairfield and New Haven Counties and are sure to become even more popular when the disruptive I-95 highway renovations (located just next to the sports complex) wrap up in 2004 or 2005.

But there's more to this city than sports. Bridgeport residents are also proud of their most famous son, circus entrepreneur-turned-mayor P. T. Barnum. In addition to an annual parade and festival in his honor, the city is also home to the Barnum Museum, where you can ogle remnants of the early days of his famous circus. Visitors at Captain's Cove in Black Rock Harbor can tour the HMS *Rose,* a replica of a Revolutionary War ship, or stroll on the boardwalk past shops, restaurants, and outdoor music concerts on summer Sundays.

Two excellent hospitals, St. Vincent's and Bridgeport Hospital, serve city residents and those living in the neighboring towns of Trumbull, Stratford, Fairfield, and Monroe. Tucked into the downtown area, the city manages to support not one but two high-caliber theaters: Playhouse on the Green and the Downtown Cabaret Theater. The Bridgeport & Port Jefferson Steamboat Company provides a daily ferry between Connecticut and Long Island—a nice shortcut for day or weekend trips to wine country.

Despite its strides in many areas, however, Bridgeport has been dogged by recent political scandals, high-profile crimes, and a sometimes dreary cityscape. As a result, its reputation within the county is still less than stellar. This is, after all, a big city, with typical big-city problems. But the turn of the new century has brought a spirit of revitalization among Bridgeport's 140,000 residents, and the "Park City" is quickly becoming more attractive for locals and visitors alike.

## Darien

With a prized location on the Metro-North commuter line, this waterfront community has become a desirable home for those who want to work in New York City but live in a scenic, coastal, suburban town. About 20,000 people live within Darien's (pronounced *der-ee-en*) 12 square miles. Though geographically small, the community supports three thriving country clubs, a beach club, a yacht club, and a hunt

club. The average home price is $1 million, though many reach the $10-million mark or higher.

Most exclusive of all is the fabled Tokeneke (pronounced *toe-ken-ek-ee*) section of Darien, where mansions dot tree-lined, winding roads in quiet neighborhoods. Other distinct neighborhoods within the town include Noroton and Noroton Heights. Residents can learn all about their hometown at the Darien Historical Society, located in a 1736 saltbox known as the Bates-Scofield House. The well-staffed society maintains a research library and art gallery devoted to preserving the town's past.

This is largely a bedroom community with little industry, although bagel shops, boutiques, bistros, and specialty stores do well in downtown and along the busy Post Road. Darien also supports several historic businesses, including Ring's End Lumber (more than 100 years old) and the family-owned Nielsen's Florist & Garden Shop (more than 60 years old). The town's proximity to Long Island Sound makes it a natural for fish markets and seafood restaurants. Darien is also home to 2 beaches and 12 parks, including Cherry Lawn, Pear Tree Park, and Tilley Pond Park. Three volunteer fire departments are headquartered in Noroton, Noroton Heights, and Darien proper; hospitals are located nearby in Stamford and Norwalk. Busy, insulated, and historically minded, Darien welcomes newcomer, in-town residents but remains guarded with outsiders.

## Easton

Easton seems to have managed the impossible: Though close to metropolitan centers, it has truly retained the rural, countrified character that defined the region in earlier centuries. Here you'll still see cows, chickens, and plots planted with lettuce and rhubarb, along with apple orchards, pumpkin patches, and cut-your-own Christmas tree farms. Easton's 7,000 residents cherish their unusual oasis, prizing its quiet charm while also appreciating its proximity to the grocery stores, shopping malls, and hospitals in nearby towns.

Still, even Easton couldn't escape the housing and development boom of the 1980s, 1990s, and early 21st century. Contemporary homes have increasingly sprouted alongside historic farmhouses and colonials, bringing a more modern feel to this town's 28 square miles. All development adheres to Easton's strict zoning requirements of one- to three-acre lots. Many residents have even larger plots, and pastures filled with horses are not an unusual sight here. The town is within close commuting distance of Danbury, Stamford, Bridgeport, and the Metro-North train stations leading into New York City. Home prices in Easton are within the region's upper ranges.

The town is almost exclusively residential, with the exception of several small businesses such a general store, a restaurant, a car-repair shop, veterinarians' offices, and a few farm stands. In addition to a country club, a golf club, and a riding academy, Easton is also home to three scenic reservoirs, 7,500 acres of protected forestland, several parks, and plenty of open space for cross-country skiing, hiking, and horseback riding. The town was incorporated from neighboring Weston in 1845. Today half the town land is owned by the Bridgeport Hydraulic Company, which manages the reservoirs as a major source of Fairfield County's drinking water.

# Fairfield

Early settlers found the area along the Long Island Sound coastline to be full of desirable—or fair—fields, thus providing a name for this town and the county that eventually grew up around it. Of course the Fairfield of today hardly resembles the sleepy agricultural town it was at the time of its settlement in 1639. Modern Fairfield has nary a farm field in sight: Instead, visitors will find a citylike atmosphere in some spots and a suburban-style setting in others, all of it filled with a diverse population and plenty to see and do.

Fairfield has one of the area's best selections of restaurants, ranging from romantic trattorias to rollicking brewpub grills and Mexican eateries. Many of the ethnic restaurants are owned and run by immigrants who serve the real thing, so aficionados are not likely to be disappointed. The food and bars are appreciated by the town's many college students, who live in dorms or nearby apartments while attending one of the town's two higher education schools: Fairfield University and Sacred Heart University. The colleges and dining scene provide a sense of liveliness not found in many of the more staid, family-centered suburbs nearby.

But Fairfield is more than food and fun. Commuters appreciate its location on the Metro-North line, while homebuyers and apartment-hunters value housing that is often more affordable than elsewhere along county's coastline. Of course the town's prime location, services, and school system make it nevertheless susceptible to the laws of supply and demand, and certain neighborhoods fall more into the price range of towns like Westport and Easton (to the west) than those in Bridgeport and Trumbull (to the east). In the Southport section, for example, historic buildings and waterfront homes command top dollar; likewise, the stately mansions and rural quality of the Greenfield Hill district make it one of the most sought-after neighborhoods in the county.

Recreation in this 30-square-mile town is hard to beat. The array of opportunities includes 7 beaches, 2 marinas, 27 open-space preserves, 10 tennis courts, 17 parks, 4 baseball fields, 2 football fields, and 6 soccer fields. (Parking permits for beaches and marinas are available to Fairfield residents for $25 and to nonresidents for $100.) Within just a few miles, shoppers will find lingerie boutiques, bike shops, big-box hardware stores, grocery and health-food stores, kids' clothes, sporting goods, jewelry, office supplies, and virtually anything else you could need. Community clubs and organizations are numerous and varied, ranging from kennel clubs and Girl Scouts to arts associations and sailing clubs. The town even offers an excellent historical society with its own library and rotating exhibits. If it's possible to have something for everyone, Fairfield manages to do just that.

# Greenwich

There aren't too many communities in America where the local chamber of commerce lists "Feng Shui" as a category in its business directory. But Greenwich isn't like most other communities. Undoubtedly the most famous town in Fairfield County, Greenwich (pronounced *gren-itch*) calls to mind images of towering mansions, security fences, exclusive country clubs, ladies-who-lunch, and Range Rovers—and with good reason. You'll find all these things, and more, in this haven for celebrities, Wall Streeters, modern-day business titans, and old-money inheritors. But you might be surprised to learn that Greenwich also has more than a few everyday-looking streets lined with ranches, cozy cottages, apartments, and duplexes. Not everyone here trades stocks or signs autographs: Some toss pizza, cut hair, or teach geometry. Still, it's hard to get around the reputation for exclusivity that seems to follow Greenwich around like a puppy—well, more like a best-in-show purebred poodle.

And then there's Greenwich Avenue. (If you have to ask, you can't afford it.)

Few places provide more fun for window-shopping or even actual shopping, depending on your inclination: Tiffany & Company, Kate Spade, Cadeaux, Saks Fifth Avenue, Chancy D'Elia, Richards of Greenwich. On "the Avenue" you can people-watch from a sidewalk cafe, order custom-made children's clothing, choose ceramic tile, or find the perfect little black dress. The intersections here don't have traffic lights; they have real, live traffic cops, one on each corner, each doing a complicated dance routine of waves and whistles designed to keep pedestrians and cars out of each other's way. It's one of the best shows around. The town's local government has hinted that budget woes have led them to consider replacing the beloved cops with—gasp!—plain old stoplights. Say it isn't so. We can only hope the proposal will be shelved indefinitely.

But forget shopping for a moment: Greenwich also has some of the best views in the county—you can even see the Manhattan skyline on a clear day. Greenwich Point, a 147-acre peninsula park with a beach, a boathouse, gardens, picnic areas, restrooms, and trails for walking and jogging, is truly a gem and is usually packed on warm days. The park was also the subject of a recent controversy when a lawyer sued the town in protest of its residents-only policies regarding the beach. Today nonresidents have access to the Point—but for a hefty fee: $10 per person plus $20 per car to park. Residents can still park and access the area free of charge.

The town, which includes Cos Cob, Byram, Old Greenwich, and Riverside, has more than just the Point to offer outdoorsy types. Residents will also run across myriad other parks, beaches, playgrounds, ponds, golf courses, tennis courts, boat launches, and marinas. Indoor pleasures include the Bruce Museum, the Greenwich Symphony Orchestra, the Greenwich Arts Center, and the expansive Greenwich Library. The town also supports no fewer than 13 yacht and country clubs, many of which have their own golf courses, tennis courts, swimming pools, and gourmet restaurants. Just another day in Greenwich.

# New Canaan

After the Revolutionary War, many New Canaan residents worked in the town's shoe-making factories. Today's residents are more likely to be special-ordering Manolo Blahnik's than making them, thanks to family fortunes made in long-ago business ventures and more recent dot-com gambles. The first mansions were built here in the late 1800s, when well-to-do New Yorkers constructed summer homes in the bucolic hills. Modern New Canaan estates are designed with year-round good living in mind. Still, not every resident lives in a lavish mansion. Town houses, duplexes, and modest ranches can also be found in some neighborhoods.

The 22.5-square-mile town has one of the most popular downtowns in Fairfield County, filled with upscale gift shops, architects' and Realtors' offices, antiques dealers, clothing boutiques, lunchtime delis, and gourmet restaurants. (Locals call it the "golden triangle.") Home to about 20,000 people, New Canaan also supports larger businesses like nurseries and fuel-oil companies. The town also shares a border with the charming Silvermine arts district in Norwalk.

Like Greenwich, this town is often home to celebrities—some of whom are only temporary residents while staying at New Canaan's Silver Hill Hospital, a well-known substance-abuse treatment and psychiatric facility. Another town landmark is the New Canaan Nature Center, an environmental education center with walking trails, a summer camp, a gift shop, after-school workshops, and adult programs covering such topics as wildlife identification, gardening, and flower arranging. And residents can always learn more about their town at the New Canaan Historical Society, which has been guarding the community's artifacts since 1889. New Canaan newcomers are attracted to the town's top-notch schools, luxury lifestyle, scenic surroundings, and open space areas like the 300-acre Waveny Park. It doesn't look as though those shoe factories will be coming back any time soon.

# Norwalk

If Fairfield County were a dinner party, Norwalk would be the one guest you'd just *have* to invite. The city brings an appreciated shot of vitality to its largely suburban and sedate neighbors with annual festivals, museums, art galleries, nightclubs, diverse neighborhoods, children's events, beaches, a lighthouse, specialty shops, and restaurants offering nearly every cuisine you could imagine. Norwalk's 83,000 residents—accountants, waitresses, engineers, shopkeepers, CEOs, fishermen—come from a wide variety of ethnic and educational backgrounds, but most share a love for their hometown and a friendly spirit that welcomes others to enjoy all the city has to offer.

South Norwalk, known locally as SoNo, is usually the center of the action. College students, singles, and young couples take full advantage of the downtown district's ultracool martini bars, trendy restaurants, art galleries, and unique shops, most of which are housed in historic buildings. SoNo also has a movie theater showing new releases, the recently expanded Maritime Aquarium and IMAX Theater, New York–style pizzerias, delis, apartments, home-furnishing stores, and waterfront seafood eateries. Though it's popular year-round, the area draws the largest crowds during two annual outdoor events: the SoNo Arts Celebration, usually held in August, and the Oyster Festival, usually held in September. The city's International In-Water Boat Show, also usually held in September, attracts browsers and buyers from around New England, New York, and even farther locales.

The city's other sections, including East Norwalk, Cranbury, and Norwalk Center, are a bit more residential, offering parks (Calf Pasture Park and Cranbury Park are Norwalk's largest), golf courses, tennis courts, playgrounds, cross-country skiing trails, and boat launches. For the adventurous, Sheffield Island and the Norwalk Islands chain, including the Stewart B. McKinney Wildlife Refuge, provide seafaring destinations. Chain retail stores, restaurants, and grocery stores line the busy U.S. Route 1 corridor. Large companies such as AT&T, CISCO, Citibank, J. P. Morgan, and Martha Stewart Living Omnimedia provide employment opportunities. Many residents commute to jobs in New York City as well; the train ride to Grand Central Station takes about 45 minutes. The facilities at Norwalk Hospital, including a same-day surgery center and a cancer center, admirably serve the community's health needs.

One of Norwalk's most charming sections is the quaint corner of Silvermine along the New Canaan border, where the Silvermine River flows past private, tucked-away homes. The Silvermine Guild Arts Center houses popular exhibitions and galleries, and visual and performance-art classes are taught at the Silvermine College of Art. The historic Silvermine Tavern is one of the best known accommodations in Fairfield County, offering guest rooms and fine dining, all overlooking a waterfall.

Norwalk's Rowayton district looks less like a section of the city and more like the suburban towns that surround it. Residents here are more likely to give Rowayton as their hometown address than Norwalk, reinforcing the notion that this coastal neighborhood is an insulated world unto itself. Like many other places in Fairfield County, Rowayton has changed in recent years. The waterfront community is secluded, homey, and surrounded by impressive views—nothing different there. But as land prices climb and more people discover the community's charms, the smaller Victorians, colonials,

and cottages are increasingly giving way to bulldozers as new residents demolish older homes to build larger, new ones. Where simple fishermen's boats once lined the harbor, now, for the most part, grand sailboats and yachts have taken their place. Some longtime residents bemoan the changes, but others say the neighborhood—which includes fish markets, ice-cream shops, and general stores—is still as friendly and quaint as ever. Whatever your opinion, there's little doubt that Rowayton will continue to be one of the county's most unique and desirable spots. Likewise, historical rehabilitation, a sense of fun, and that unavoidable "hipness factor" will probably keep Norwalk's appeal on an upward climb for the foreseeable future.

# Stamford

If you're on a first date, Stamford is the place to go. From brewpubs to comedy shows to restaurants and clubs, there's always something to do downtown. Or let's say you're married with 2.5 kids. No problem: Stamford's the place for you, too. Suburban-style neighborhoods, concerts, libraries, theater, shopping, and children's activities are as plentiful as the nightlife is hopping. From babies to bikers and everyone in between, this city serves up opportunities and advantages that are seemingly unparalleled anywhere in Fairfield County—or in Connecticut, for that matter.

At 37.3 square miles, Stamford is big, but not too big. Job seekers find this city of 117,000 people especially attractive. Located only about 25 miles from New York City, it also hosts its own cadre of big companies and small businesses that help keep the unemployment rate at an impressive 2.5 percent. The population is diverse and interesting, ranging from recent immigrants to college students and professionals. Housing is diverse, too, whether you're looking for an urban loft or a four-bedroom estate on two acres. None of it comes cheap, of course, but

Stamford residents still pay slightly less for real estate than their suburban next-door neighbors in New Canaan, Darien, and Greenwich.

Stamford is a patchwork quilt of varied neighborhoods: You'll find sections like Shippan, Waterside, Glenbrook, and Downtown to the south near Long Island Sound; busy spots like Springdale, Westover, and Belltown in the center; and more suburban neighborhoods north of the Merritt Parkway in North Stamford. Though it would be tempting to categorize all the southern sections as "urban" and all the northern regions as "suburban," the reality is much more complicated. Indeed, many of Stamford's waterfront communities are considerably more affluent and spread out than the inner-city neighborhoods located nearby.

Downtown is the place that out-of-towners are most likely to see on a visit. The Palace Theater and the Rich Forum, both part of the Stamford Center for the Arts, lead the pack of entertainment options by hosting big-name entertainers and productions. But they are far from the only shows in town: The Crown Majestic, the Crown Theater, the Stamford Symphony Orchestra, and Stamford Theater Works also keep things lively. A shopping mall and smaller independent stores along the sidewalks sell everything from shoes to ski gear to fine art. Locals can also choose from more than 65 restaurants and bars, along with 7 nightclubs. And as if all that wasn't enough, the Stamford Downtown Special Services District promotes the area with outdoor art exhibits and concerts, events calendars, beautification programs, and other activities throughout the year.

Beyond the reaches of Downtown, Stamford residents can enjoy city-owned beaches, picnic areas, parks, bird sanctuaries, ice-skating rinks, and nature trails. The most popular is 83-acre Cove Island Park, which offers a beach, a marina, a snack bar, walking paths, tennis courts, and playgrounds. Independent organizations and attractions include the Stamford Museum and Nature Center, Soundwaters Environmental Education Center, the Bartlett Arboretum, the Stamford Historical Society Museum, two public golf courses, and a yacht club. That should be more than enough activities to fill that first date—and if everything works out, it should be more than enough to keep those 2.5 kids busy for a long time.

# Stratford

"We're in Fairfield County, too!" could be the rallying cry of Stratford's 50,000 residents, who often report feeling unfairly separated from the rest of the Fairfield County community—especially when many people assume that the county's southeastern border ends at Bridgeport. But the town's low profile has been in many ways an advantage, allowing this beautiful and historic waterfront community to maintain its relaxed and quiet personality in the midst of the county's recent population explosion.

Bordered by the Housatonic River to the east and Long Island Sound to the south, Stratford provides a nearly ideal home base for boaters, anglers, joggers, wildlife-watchers, and those who simply enjoy nice views. Public boat launches, fishing piers, five marinas, and two beaches are all open to the public. The 18.7-square-mile town also has a 250-acre protected forest, one of the largest salt marshes in New England, and a section of the Stewart B. McKinney National Wildlife

*On September 11, 2001, much of Connecticut's emergency rescue personnel arriving at Ground Zero left from Sikorsky Memorial Airport in Stratford. The Black Hawk helicopters that carried them also were invented and built in Stratford. The town has long been recognized as the "birthplace" of American helicopter technology.*

Refuge. Stratford's famous Shakespeare Festival Theater, a major tourist attraction in the '60s, '70s, and '80s, ceased operations in 1989. At the time of this writing, however, the theater was slated for revitalization by a local nonprofit company. Another of the town's best-known attractions is Boothe Memorial Park, which houses elaborate rose gardens and restored historic buildings.

The home of Sikorsky Aircraft, Stratford has a proud tradition in the aviation and helicopter-manufacturing industries. Sikorsky is still the largest business in town, but there are many others—more than 2,000 others, actually. Large corporate parks join small shops, chain stores, and restaurants in providing jobs and retail shopping opportunities for locals. Housing is more affordable here than in most other coastal Fairfield County communities and provides more variety in type, size, and style as well. Town softball tournaments, a well-staffed historical society, a local theater company, a community center, and a cozy downtown area are other elements that combine to make Stratford one of the county's most appealing—if least talked-about—locations.

## Trumbull

Surrounded by five other Fairfield County towns and the city of Bridgeport, Trumbull's benefits are many: It's within commuting distance of several city centers and is located along main highway routes for easy access to all of them. The town also has a tax base that is boosted by a large shopping mall, office and medical facilities, restaurants, and several big-box chain stores. In addition, a large recreation department provides locals with sports clinics and leagues, fitness programs, summer camps, field trips, a teen center, and swimming lessons in the town pool.

If all of these characteristics make the town appealing to families, then the housing costs—lower than those in many other towns in the southern region—make it even more so. Residents also have a wide variety of housing choices, from affordable bungalows and ranches to large farmhouses, split-levels, and colonials. Trumbull's charming historic districts also offer restored Revolutionary War–era homes in friendly neighborhoods. The town's residential sections, including Long Hill, Nichols, Tashua, and the Canoe Brook Lake area, are home to about 32,000 people.

Trumbull has one public golf course, Tashua Knolls, and 20 public parks and sports fields. The most popular parks are 83-acre Twin Brooks, which has ponds, pavilions, and hiking trails; 75-acre Old Mine Park, which has trails, a bridge, pavilions, and picnic areas; and 104-acre Indian Ledge Park, which offers an amphitheater, a playground, a BMX race track, and sledding hills. Myriad garden centers, Girl Scout troops, and Little League teams reveal the town's deep suburban roots. Though perhaps not a "name-brand" town, Trumbull has proven to be a warm and comfortable home for its many satisfied residents.

## Weston

Weston perhaps personifies the notion of a bedroom community more than any other Fairfield County town. Woodsy and serene, it contains miles of country lanes lined with estates, historic colonials and farmhouses, and towering contemporary homes. With the exception of one tiny shopping center—home to the Post Office, a gas station, a hardware store, and one or two other small businesses—the town has few services and stores. And the residents hope to keep it that way, preferring to head south to busier towns like Westport to do their shopping.

Nearly one-quarter of the town's total acreage is devoted to open space, including the popular Nature Conservancy preserve known as Devil's Den, 645-acre Aspetuck Land Trust forestland, and 53-

acre Bisceglie-Scribner Park. The town's zoning requires that its 10,000 residents live on plots of two acres or more. Farmers' markets, football games, and country fairs add to Weston's old-fashioned, traditional ambience and make it a hot spot in the county's real estate market.

Despite all those features, however, Weston's primary appeal lies in its location. Most people who live in Weston work somewhere else, and commuters highly value the relatively short daily trip to Stamford, Greenwich, and even New York City. Residents are able to have the best of both worlds, living in a quiet, upscale community that's also close to employment and recreational opportunities. It's a benefit that Westonites are willing to pay top-dollar for—and a way of life they are willing to guard zealously.

# Westport

As one of Fairfield County's best-known communities, Westport is famous for... well, for being famous. Celebrities live here, as do other wealthy families and those who are attracted to the town's reputation as an arts and commerce haven. Many of the largest manors sit directly on Long Island Sound, although country estates are also tucked inland, with horse pastures, tennis courts, and ubiquitous stone walls.

But Westport has also changed dramatically in the past two decades. Former resident Martha Stewart described her distaste with the town's transformation in a published essay. The tirade irritated locals with its complaints about traffic congestion and rapid development but nevertheless contained a grain of truth. Longtime residents will attest that new housing developments and drastic home renovations—many adhering to the "knock it down and rebuild it" school of thought—have affected Westport's charm and historic flavor, not always for the better. Ironically, it is the town's own popularity

that is forcing the changes: Everyone wants to live here. And looking at the great schools, the waterfront location, the parks, the valuable real estate, the bustling downtown, and the lively arts community, who can blame them?

Westport is also a shopper's dream. Downtown is upscale, featuring clothing boutiques, jewelry stores, coffee shops, eateries, shoe stores, art-supply stores, delis, and home-furnishing showrooms. Then there's U.S. Route 1, a busy thoroughfare that is lined with every variety of bookstore, grocery store, bakery, and restaurant you could hope for. Throughout the town, renovated mills once used for manufacturing now house fitness centers, printing companies, flower shops, and other small businesses. Whether you're looking for an architect, an acupuncturist, or a publisher, you'll find it in Westport.

The town's 26,000 residents find plenty to keep themselves busy outside the stores as well. This is primarily a family-oriented place (the median age here is 41), and kids and adults take full advantage of more than 35 parks, playing fields, beaches, and greens. Westport is also home to the Levitt Pavilion for Performing Arts, the Westport Arts Center, the Westport/Weston YMCA, the Westport Country Playhouse (run by Paul Newman and Joanne Woodward), the Earthplace Nature Discovery Center, a rowing club, and numerous country clubs and golf courses. Residents may have to share all of these resources with a growing number of locals, but they nonetheless appreciate and enjoy the unique amenities of their one-of-a-kind town.

# Wilton

An interesting blend of old and new, Wilton is making an effort to preserve its past while also offering the latest commercial, technological, and educational opportunities for its residents. Many parts of the town resemble the neighboring

*Valid library cards from your hometown library can be used at any library in Connecticut. The Westport Library, overlooking the river, offers a huge selection of periodicals and reference books—not to mention some of the best views in town. Doing research? The reference librarians at the Danbury Library are renowned for their helpful, friendly service.*

Weston and New Canaan suburbs, with spacious lots, wooded streets, and historic and contemporary homes. Other areas are bustling with small and large businesses, including sporting-goods stores, cafes, grocery stores, and gas stations.

Families flock to Wilton, where the school system is well funded and admired. The town also maintains several recreational opportunities available only to residents, including the Wilton Family Y, which offers indoor and outdoor swimming pools, a fitness center, picnic areas, a pavilion, and walking trails; and Merwin Meadows Park, where visitors will find a pond, a playground, and picnic areas. Commuting from Wilton is relatively easy, with U.S. Route 7 running up into the Danbury area and south to the Merritt Parkway and I-95. Housing costs here are comparable with other in-demand southwestern Fairfield County towns.

One of Wilton's best-known landmarks is the Weir Farm National Historic Site, located on the Ridgefield border. The preserved buildings and nature trails at Weir Farm commemorate the life of J. Alden Weir, one of America's first Impressionist painters. The town's Woodcock Nature Center is another big attraction, with 146 acres of self-guided trails as well as an interpretive center with a gift shop and exhibits. And for the past 30 years, locals living in or near Wilton have celebrated the passing of summer into fall with the annual Cannon Grange Agricultural Fair and Expo, usually held on the Sunday before Labor Day Weekend. Like many other Wilton traditions, this is one that

seems to have withstood Fairfield County's rapid changes in recent decades—and will probably withstand those changes yet to come.

# NORTHERN FAIRFIELD COUNTY

## Bethel

Once part of the city of Danbury, this 17-square-mile town is one of the smallest in Fairfield County. Bethel's unusual boomerang shape has created two communities in one: The eastern end, near Newtown, is primarily residential; the western end, near Danbury, supports homes as well as a busy downtown with restaurants, ice-cream shops, banks, consignment clothing stores, bakeries, business offices, and gift shops.

Sandwiched between the city and the country, Bethel seems at times to be suffering from an identity crisis. The burgeoning population has created an increased need for housing and modern amenities; at the same time, the town struggles with an equally pressing need to preserve a sense of history and solitude. Sometimes the effort fumbles: When a historic downtown home burned down, for example, it was replaced by a 24-hour gas station. On the other hand, residents supported a recent downtown renovation program that brought new brick sidewalks, old-fashioned lamps, a new terrace for the library, and a general spiffed-up feel that made the area more cozy and inviting.

P. T. Barnum was born in Bethel and lived here for a short time as a child. You can see his former home at 55 Greenwood Avenue, still used as a private residence, and pay homage to him in the triangle-shaped section of downtown known as P. T. Barnum Square—the life-size painting of a "Greatest Show on Earth" elephant is hard to miss. You'll see other famous faces on the big screen at Bethel Cinema, one of the few remaining art-house theaters in the area. And before you end your visit, be sure to stop and ruminate in the shade of the town's famous Sycamore: Located at the corner of Greenwood Avenue and Grassy Plain, the historic tree is rumored to be more than 250 years old.

# Brookfield

This 20-square-mile, mostly residential town borders Litchfield County and is home to about 16,000 people—a number that is growing rapidly each year. Many of the residents work in the neighboring city of Danbury or commute farther to Waterbury and Hartford. Even as Brookfield grows to accommodate a burgeoning population, it manages to maintain a New England charm and small-town feel, particularly at the quaint "four corners" area that is home to many of the town's historic and newer church buildings.

That's the quiet end of town. Closer to Danbury you'll find the bustling U.S. Route 7 corridor, where megastores, supermarkets, and car dealers attract shoppers from all over Litchfield and Fairfield Counties. Commerce is nothing new in Brookfield, which has hosted taverns, hotels, farms, factories, and railroad stops since its inception in 1788. The town was named after its first permanent minister, Reverend Thomas Brooks.

Brookfield's well-received school system has long been attractive to newcomers, as are the town's outdoor attractions, including Cadigan Park, Lillinonah Woods, Domain Pond, Whalen Pond, Still River, Candlewood Lake, and the Gursky Open Space. Two of the bordering towns offer hospitals, although Brookfield also has an in-town emergency care center. Locals don't have to go far to find good food, either: Pizzarias, cafes, and fine restaurants are plentiful in Brookfield and its neighbor to the north, New Milford. One of the town's most unique and valued attractions is the Brookfield Craft Center, a school specializing in teaching such almost-forgotten crafts as metalsmithing,

weaving, ceramics, woodworking, and bookmaking. The school is tied to traditions but looking toward the future—much like the town it calls home.

# Danbury

Danbury's nickname, Hat City, alludes to its once-prominent past as the hatmaking capital of the United States—at one point around the turn of the last century, three million fashionable hats per year poured out of this 42-square-mile city. Unfortunately, the accepted hat-manufacturing method involved treating animal fur with extremely high levels of mercury. This gave the fur the feltlike look that most consumers wanted, but it also exposed the hatmakers to enough mercury to literally burn holes in their brains. This sad occurrence, a lesson learned the hard way, gave rise to the phrase "mad as a hatter." It was also the origin of the term "Danbury shakes," still used to describe the effects of mercury poisoning.

Luckily, Danbury employees today enjoy much better health and safety standards than their predecessors. Some work downtown in restaurants, shops, and small businesses; some work in one of the city's manufacturing plants or large companies; and still others work at the region's largest shopping mall, the Danbury Fair Mall. The mall, built on the site of the once-mighty Danbury Fair, draws shoppers from around Connecticut as well as New Yorkers traveling over the state line in search of bargains. Nearby, the U.S. Route 7 corridor is home to big-box stores, chain restaurants, and even unique retail outlets like Stew Leonard's, "the world's largest dairy store." A minority of commuters living here make the arduous daily journey to jobs in Hartford and even New York City.

In addition to its antique Victorians and downtown apartments, Danbury also has a large suburban-style residential community—mostly to the north—where residents take advantage of large lots, tree-lined streets, and some of the most affordable housing in the county. Danbury has a more diverse population than its neighboring suburban towns, giving rise to a good selection of Portuguese, Hispanic, and Italian-American restaurants and social clubs owned by recent immigrants. The city also maintains a well-regarded system of social services: City-managed agencies work with local nonprofits to provide assistance to hungry, elderly, and mentally retarded local residents; victims of domestic violence or child abuse; and even children in need of mentors. This is not a city where the less fortunate are left to fend for themselves.

Danbury's jewel is Candlewood Lake, a man-made body of water that's surrounded by homes, boat launches, public beaches, marinas, and forested land. On a typical summer day, the lake is packed with recreational boaters, fishermen, water-skiers, and personal-watercraft enthusiasts riding Jet Skis and Ski-Doos. For those who prefer playing on frozen water, the city's new downtown ice arena has provided another recreational venue.

The resident Western Connecticut State University also serves its city well, giving Danbury a lively shot of energy, youth, and culture. The university's performing arts centers (including one outdoor venue) often host big-name artists for summer concerts and winter theater productions, while the students keep downtown bars, restaurants, brewpubs, and dance clubs busy on Saturday night. One of downtown's only drawbacks is that it is difficult for newcomers to find: The green, along with its surrounding eateries and bars, is tucked behind a parking garage and long walls of buildings. If you're just driving by, it's easy to miss. But once you find it, you'll relish the well-lit parking, fun selection of restaurants and nightlife, and free summer concerts on the green. At times this city feels more like a small town. And that's exactly how the residents like it.

# Monroe

It seems perhaps appropriate that this smallish town was named after the country's fifth president, James Monroe: You don't hear much about Mr. Monroe, and his namesake town keeps an equally low profile in the Fairfield County community. Not that that's a bad thing. The 19,000 or so residents enjoy good schools, a variety of stores and services, recreational opportunities in-town and nearby, and a good commuting location to jobs in Bridgeport, Westport, Danbury, New Haven, and Waterbury. If Monroe seems to lack the cachet of neighboring towns like Easton and Newtown, it more than makes up for it with affordable housing prices, large lots, and a small-town feel. Caught on the border of the northern and southern regions of the county, the town is quiet and uncrowded but within a half-hour drive of most shopping malls, movie theaters, and hospitals.

One of Monroe's biggest draws is Wolfe Park, a 300-acre recreational center with a 16-acre pond, a sandy beach, hiking trails, a swimming pool, three large playgrounds, picnic areas, eight tennis courts, seven baseball and softball fields, and four soccer fields. Families are everywhere here, as they are throughout the town, flying kites, sunbathing, pushing strollers, jogging, and cheering on the home team. No one would mistake Monroe for a hot spot for singles or young professionals. From carnivals to parades, group activities here often focus on children. Still, the spotlight on kids doesn't mean that the older members of the family are neglected. The town recently completed construction of a new Senior Center near one of the Wolf Park entrances.

Most of the commercial activity is concentrated along two main roads: Route 111 and Route 25. Shoppers here will find relief from the large chains, located in larger towns several miles away. Instead they can browse hardware, paint and wallpaper, gifts, auto parts, pet food, and unfinished furniture at small, often family-owned shops. Similarly, the restaurants here are cozy and casual and tend to fill one of two categories: Chinese and pizza. Takeout is plentiful, although a few upscale Italian eateries have broadened the dining selection in recent years. The stores and restaurants are mostly spread out in shopping plazas, which too often lack the quaint feel of "downtown" areas in other towns. But the town green, surrounded by historic churches and dotted with majestic trees and a gazebo, provides a picturesque backdrop for this best-kept-secret of a town.

## New Fairfield

With one of Fairfield County's smallest populations, New Fairfield is home to about 13,000 people living on a countrified and scenic 25.3 square miles. Too far from New York City to attract most Big Apple commuters, the town is nonetheless very popular with those who work in Danbury, Waterbury, and Westchester County, New York. Part of the attraction for families is the highly regarded school system and relatively affordable housing.

Three bodies of water dominate New Fairfield. The largest is Candlewood Lake, which provides beautiful views and nearly limitless recreational opportunities. (About 2,800 acres of the lake lie within New Fairfield town boundaries.) Residents can also enjoy Ball Pond, which is largely surrounded by houses, and Squantz Pond State Park, a 172-acre park that attracts boaters, swimmers, hikers, and sunbathers. The state park is frequently crowded, especially during the summer season. For those who want to get away from the crowds, Pootatuck State Forest offers more than 1,000 acres of undeveloped land that's perfect for hiking, cross-country skiing, and bird-watching.

Homes near or on the lake or ponds are harder to come by, and often pricier,

than those located inland. At one time New Fairfield real estate consisted primarily of summer cottages for vacationers, and you'll still run across many small, seasonal homes along the shorelines today. But increased development since the 1950s has changed the face of this once-sleepy community. Though still fairly quiet, especially when compared with its neighbor to the south, Danbury, the town now has small businesses and restaurants (many of which are concentrated at the crossroads of Routes 37 and 39), professional offices, marinas, and coffee shops. This is a place where open space and development seem to have reached a healthy compromise—for now.

## Newtown

For history buffs, Newtown enjoys the dubious honor of being a British-friendly town during the Revolutionary War—one residential roadway here is even called Tory Lane. But that's just one aspect of this historic town's lore, which is evident almost everywhere you go here. A walk down Main Street feels like a trip into the past, with elegantly maintained historic homes, a general store, an inn and restaurant, a town hall, a library, gardens, and a square green known as Ram's Pasture.

This is the largest town in Fairfield County, and arguably one of the most sought after in the northern region. With easy access to I-84, numerous parks and waterways, and a school system that is respected throughout the state, Newtown has much to offer families and professionals. A 110-foot flagpole on Main Street is the town's primary landmark: "Just turn right at the flagpole and . . ." Within its 60 square miles, 25,000 residents live in distinct sections such as Sandy Hook, Dodgingtown, Hawleyville, and Botsford. You'll even find a few farms and horse pastures interspersed among the suburban housing developments.

Of course, an increasing population and the modern world has made its mark on Newtown, and the town's historic structures have been joined in recent years by shopping plazas, bike shops, office buildings, and even some small industry. More than 13 restaurants, including a diner, several Italian eateries, two inns, and a Mexican restaurant, keep residents well nourished. A hospital is close by in Danbury, and two large shopping malls—in Danbury and Waterbury—lie within a 20-minute drive on the highway.

For outdoorsy types, Newtown offers Paugusset State Forest, almost 2,000 acres of trails and waterway access along the Housatonic River, and Rocky Glen State Park, a smaller 41-acre parcel that's ideal for short forays into the woods. Bordering the town, the Housatonic River and Lake Zoar are dotted with boaters and water-skiers throughout the summer and into early fall; small cottages gather at the water's edge as witness to the ever-passing spectacles. The town also has two private country clubs, bridle clubs, and five town parks with sports fields, playgrounds, picnic areas, and tennis courts.

## Redding

Peaceful and prosperous, Redding attracts residents looking for lots of land, historic and new-construction homes, and an escape from the commercial atmosphere of more crowded towns and cities to the north and south. The town offers a handful of restaurants and small businesses but primarily consists of residential neighborhoods and horse pastures on quiet streets. Grocery stores and shopping malls, along with hospitals, are located within a 20- to 30-minute drive in either direction. The Redding section known as Georgetown saw its first European settlers in the early 1700s. Legend has it that the neighborhood was named for George Abbott, an early local mill owner. Another district, Branchville, was named for the rail line that "branched" out from the main

line between Danbury and Norwalk.

Parks and open space are plentiful here; Putnam Memorial State Park has picnic areas, paved and unpaved walking trails, a pond, and a preserved encampment where General Putnam's troops stayed during the winter of 1778–79. Visitors to the park today can see the remains of the soldiers' stone fireplaces, the indentations of cannonballs in the ground, memorials, and a re-created cabin. Collis P. Huntington State Park is popular with mountain bikers, horseback riders, canoeists, dog walkers, and joggers who make their way past meadows, ponds, pastures, and wooded areas. Topstone Park is town owned and provides swimming and boating opportunities in a 25-acre pond. Many of Redding's 8,000 residents are environmentally minded, and local preservation groups work hard to keep the town's undeveloped atmosphere intact.

Though Redding has few stores, residents and visitors will find other in-town organizations and attractions. Highstead Arboretum, located on a 36-acre land donation from a former resident family, offers a reference library, lecture space, map room, herbarium, and numerous native species preserved in forest, wetland, and meadow habitats. Perhaps the crowning historic jewel is the recently remodeled and expanded Mark Twain Public Library, originally founded with a 200-book donation from the renowned author himself, who was a Redding resident from 1908 until his death in 1910.

## Ridgefield

It's convenient but far from the hustle and bustle of larger cities. It looks to the future with modern art galleries and state-of-the-art health facilities but also preserves the past with stately Main Street homes, historic churches, and museums that chronicle the lives of the town's earliest residents. There are large grocery stores and retail chains, as well as a quaint downtown shopping district with sidewalk cafes and boutiques. The school system is well funded and respected. Is it any wonder that publications like *Connecticut Magazine* continue to rank Ridgefield as the state's No. 1 town?

For those who can afford it, Ridgefield is certainly a suburban oasis. Big enough to accommodate differing needs but small enough to be friendly, it provides residents with a strong sense of community. (When a local child fell ill with an obscure disease recently, it seemed the entire town turned out for a fund-raising walk along Main Street.) Most of Ridgefield's 22,000 residents are white-collar professionals who commute to jobs in places like Stamford, Danbury, upstate New York, and New York City. Home prices are steep, and contractors seem to be gobbling up much of Ridgefield's remaining land with new housing developments.

There is also a strong contingent of conservationists here, many of whom have found themselves embroiled in recent battles to preserve open space. While those battles rage on, residents can enjoy the parks and facilities that are already in place, including a recreation center, summer camp programs, the Graham Dickinson S.P.I.R.I.T. Skate Park for in-line skaters and skateboarders, Ballard Park, Sturges Park, Martin Park Beach, and lots of sports courts and fields. One of the town's most interesting offerings is the Aldrich Museum of Contemporary Art, which showcases current—and sometimes controversial—exhibits in its recently renovated galleries. It's not the kind of place you'd expect to see in buttoned-up Ridgefield, which is probably exactly why the residents like it so much.

## Shelton

Located on the easternmost boundary of the region, the 30-square-mile city of Shelton often seems more closely associated with its neighbor, New Haven County, than with Fairfield County. Retail stores, restaurants, and other necessities are more easily accessed to the east in busy

places like Derby and Orange than to the west. Downtown, the factories, bridges, two-family homes, and business centers call to mind other formerly industrial areas nestled in New Haven County's Naugatuck River Valley. Still, Shelton does share some qualities with its fellow Fairfield County towns, including suburban-style neighborhoods, green parks, pumpkin patches, and historic churches and homes.

Although it was settled in the early 1700s, Shelton was not incorporated as a city for another 200 years, in 1919. Today the population of about 36,000 continues the city's proud manufacturing heritage with one of the lowest unemployment rates in the state (4.6 percent). Numerous in-town businesses include Pitney Bowes, Black & Decker, the Viking Tool Company, Shelton Scientific Manufacturing, Emhart Fastening Technologies, and even the famous Wiffle Ball Company. Small family-owned camera shops, ice-cream parlors, pizzerias, bars, hobby shops, convenience stores, and shoe stores line the main roads as well.

Shelton residents get outside year-round in more than 450 acres of accessible public space, including a paved recreation path, a reservoir, miles of hiking trails, Indian Wells State Park, boat launches, and 230-acre Shelton Lakes Park. The nearest hospital is located in Derby, although the larger Bridgeport and Yale–New Haven Hospitals lie within a 30-minute drive. Playgrounds and sports fields are plentiful and often crowded with happily frantic children. Add other pluses like affordable housing, outdoor summer concerts, and a community center with a swimming pool, and Shelton begins to look like one of Fairfield County's best bargains.

## Sherman

Like Shelton, Sherman has an ambience that seems more closely associated with a neighboring county than with its own. In this case, the largely rural hillsides are reminiscent of other farming towns to the north and east in Litchfield County.

Nevertheless, this once-tiny community is growing fast—perhaps this is the town's sole common thread with other Fairfield County locales. Longtime residents, primarily farmers, often express frustration with the rapid changes they're seeing in their town, especially when developers transform formerly agricultural plots into streets lined with ubiquitous two-story colonials.

This transformation is occurring elsewhere in the county as well, but it somehow feels more dramatic in sleepy Sherman, where cows and horses are as common as cars or, at least, where they once were that common a decade ago. Driving through the scenic countryside, it's easy to see why the town has become so popular with newcomers who want access to services in Danbury, New Fairfield, and New Milford but also want a taste of an old-fashioned New England lifestyle. The population of about 3,500 residents share 23.4 square miles and a school system that accommodates children in kindergarten through eighth grade. Once children reach ninth grade, they attend high school in nearby New Milford or New Fairfield.

Candlewood Lake, located on the town's southern boundary, is a big source of recreation. Sailing lessons are available through the town's offices, as are classes in cooking, yoga, astronomy, gardening, and other subjects. The town is home to few businesses but more than 12 nonprofit organizations, an active Parks and Recreation Department, a library, a town beach, town garden plots, a pond, tennis courts, and a running track. Sherman's unmistakable triangle shape makes it stick out on a map, and the town's unique, laid-back atmosphere makes it equally distinguishable among Fairfield County's communities.

# Fairfield County Vital Statistics

## CONNECTICUT

**State tree:** White oak

**State flower:** Mountain laurel

**State bird:** American robin

**State nicknames:** The Constitution State, the Nutmeg State

**Governor:** M. Jodi Rell (R)

**U.S. Senators:** Christopher Dodd (D), Joseph Lieberman (D)

**State holidays:** New Year's Day, Martin Luther King Day, Lincoln's Birthday, Washington's Birthday, Good Friday, Memorial Day, Independence Day, Labor Day, Columbus Day, Veterans Day, Thanksgiving Day, Christmas Day

**State sales tax:** 6 percent on retail sales (Food products and prescription medications are exempt, as are clothing items priced under $50.)

## FAIRFIELD COUNTY

**U.S. Representatives:** Christopher Shays (R), District 4—Bridgeport, Darien, Easton, Fairfield, Greenwich, Monroe, New Canaan, Norwalk, Redding, Ridgefield, Shelton, Stamford, Trumbull, Weston, Westport, and Wilton. Nancy L. Johnson (R), District 5—Bethel, Brookfield, Danbury, New Fairfield, Newtown, and Sherman

**Mayors:**   Mark D. Boughton, Danbury
John Fabrizi, Bridgeport
Alex Knopp, Norwalk
Dannel P. Malloy, Stamford

**Population estimate:** 896,200

**Median age:** 37.3

**Land area:** 626 square miles

**Population density:** 1,410 people per square mile (double the state average)

**Businesses:** 28,673

**Major employers:** Cendant Mobility, Danbury Hospital, General Electric Company, Grolier Publishers, International Paper, Oxford Health Plans, Pitney Bowes, Praxair, Sikorsky Aircraft, Stamford Health Systems, Xerox Corporation

**Average temperatures:**
**Danbury:**  January (high/low) 35°F/20°F
July (high/low) 80°F/60°F
**Stamford:** January (high/low) 38°F/23°F
July (high/low) 83°F/62°F

**Major universities:** Fairfield University, Fairfield; Sacred Heart University, Fairfield; University of Bridgeport, Bridgeport; University of Connecticut—Stamford Campus, Stamford; Western Connecticut State University, Danbury

**Famous sons and daughters:** P. T. Barnum, showman; Charles Ives, composer; Joe Lieberman, senator and vice-presidential candidate; Paul Newman, actor; Joanne Woodward, actress; Kenneth Olsen, inventor; J. C. Penney, retailer; Tom Thumb, circus performer; Mark Twain, author; J. Alden Weir, Impressionist painter

**Daily newspapers:** *Connecticut Post,* Greater Bridgeport; *Danbury News-Times,* Greater Danbury; *Greenwich Time,* Greenwich; *Norwalk Hour*, Greater Norwalk; *Stamford Advocate,* Greater Stamford

**Major interstates:** I-95 and I-84

**Chambers of Commerce:**

Bridgeport Chamber of Commerce, 10 Middle Street, Bridgeport (203-335-3800)

Danbury Chamber of Commerce, 39 West Street, Danbury (203-743-5565)

Darien Chamber of Commerce, 17 Old Kings Highway, Darien (203-655-3600)

Fairfield Chamber of Commerce, 1597 Post Road, Fairfield (203-255-1011)

Greenwich Chamber of Commerce, 21 West Putnam Avenue, Greenwich (203-869-3500)

Monroe Chamber of Commerce, 477 Main Street, Monroe (203-268-6518)

Newtown Chamber of Commerce, P.O. Box 314, Newtown 06470 (203-426-2695)

Norwalk Chamber of Commerce, 101 East Avenue, Norwalk (203-866-2521)

Ridgefield Chamber of Commerce, 9 Bailey Avenue, Ridgefield (203-438-9175)

Shelton Chamber of Commerce, 900 Bridgeport Avenue, Shelton (203-925-4981)

Southwestern Area Commerce and Industry Association, 1 Landmark Square, Stamford (203-359-3220)

Trumbull Chamber of Commerce, 571 Church Hill Road, Trumbull (203-261-4533)

Westport Chamber of Commerce, 60 Church Lane, Westport (203-227-9234)

Wilton Chamber of Commerce, 211 Town Green, Wilton (203-762-0567)

# GETTING HERE, GETTING AROUND

There's no way around it: If you live in Fairfield County, you need a car. Granted, if you happen to live and work in a downtown urban area, it is possible to make do with public transportation while moving back and forth to a job or the grocery store. But the story is very different in the surrounding suburbs, where buses and taxis are a rarity and SUVs and minivans rule the roadways. For the most part, this is a community of commuters.

We county residents love our wheels almost as much as we love complaining about the traffic tie-ups they cause. Don't expect to rush anywhere during rush hour, especially on the major roadways. Despite the predictable backups, however, the region's proximity to major cities, airports, interstates, and train routes make it an unusually convenient and mobile place to live.

## GETTING HERE

# By Air

Local residents enjoy access to four nearby airports: two large hubs located in New York City and two smaller airports in White Plains, New York (just over the state line), and in Windsor Locks, near Hartford. In addition, the city of Danbury operates a small airport that attracts recreational pilots and smaller crafts.

**Bradley International Airport**
**Schoephoester Road, Windsor Locks**
**(860) 292-2000 or (888) 624-1533**
**www.bradleyairport.com**
This is New England's second-largest airport, trailing only Logan International in Boston. For those living in the northern region of the county, Bradley is the most convenient option for air travel in many cases. Located about an hour and 20 minutes from Danbury, Bradley is an easy ride on I-84 East, then north for a few minutes on I-91. Numerous large lots provide short-term and long-term parking. When the airport lots are filled, nearby privately owned parking lots make up the difference; most provide shuttles.

**Parking fees for Bradley International Airport:**
Long-term garage: $13 per day; $65 per week
Long-term lots: $11 to $13 per day; $55 to $65 per week
Economy lots: $7.50 per day; $45 per week

**Airlines serving Bradley International Airport:**

**Air Canada**
**(888) 247-2262**
**www.aircanada.ca**

**American Airlines and American Eagle**
**(800) 433-7300**
**www.aa.com**

**America West Airlines**
**(800) 327-7810**
**www.americawest.com**

**Continental Airlines and Continental Express**
**(800) 525-0280**
**www.continental.com**

**Delta Air Lines and Delta Express**
**(800) 221-1212**
**www.delta.com**

**Midwest Express and Skyway Airlines**
(800) 452-2022
www.midwestexpress.com

**Northwest Airlines**
(800) 225-2525
www.nwa.com

**Southwest Airlines**
(800) 435-9792
www.iflyswa.com

**United Airlines and United Express**
(800) 864-8331
www.ual.com

**USAirways and USAirways Express**
(800) 428-4322
www.usairways.com

**John F. Kennedy International Airport
Rockaway Boulevard, Queens Port
Authority of New York and New Jersey**
(212) 435-7000
www.panynj.gov
Usually called simply "Kennedy" or "JFK,"
this enormous airport can serve as your
connection to the entire world. More than
30 million people pass through Kennedy's
nine terminals each year; ongoing renovations and updates add to the confusion. If
you have time to kill, though, you'll find
plenty of shops and eateries to help while
away the hours. The airport recently
opened a new AirTran service with two
lines: AirTran JFK and AirTran Newark. The
service shuttles passengers to and from
terminals, parking lots, Beach Station, and
Federal Circle.

**Parking fees for John F. Kennedy
International Airport:**
Short-term lots: $5.00 for first two hours;
$3.00 for each hour thereafter
Long-term lot: $10.00 for the first day;
$5.00 for every 12-hour period thereafter

**Airlines serving John F. Kennedy
International Airport:**
Kennedy is served by all the airlines pro-
vided in the Bradley International Airport

listings (see above), in addition to more
than 45 other American and international
airlines. Some of the most popular include:

**Aer Lingus**
(800) 474-7424
www.aerlingus.com

**Aero Mexico**
(800) 237-6639
www.aeromexicovacations.com

**Air China**
(800) 982-8802
www.airchina.com.cn

**Air France**
(800) 237-2747
www.airfrance.com

**Air Jamaica**
(800) 523-5585
www.airjamaica.com

**Alitalia**
(800) 223-5730
www.alitaliausa.com

**British Airways**
(800) 247-9297
www.britishairways.com

**El Al Israel Airlines**
(800) 223-6700
www.elal.co.il

**JetBlue**
(800) 538-2583
www.jetblue.com

**Lufthansa**
(800) 645-3880
www.lufthanza.com

**Qantas Airways**
(800) 227-4500
www.qantas.com

**Swiss International**
(877) FLY-SWISS
www.swiss.com

Virgin Atlantic
(800) 862–8621
www.virgin-atlantic.com

## LaGuardia Airport
**Grand Central Parkway, Queens Port Authority of New York and New Jersey**
**(212) 435–7000**
**www.panynj.gov**

For Fairfield County residents, this airport is slightly closer than JFK, although it does not provide the huge assortment of airlines that serve its larger New York City neighbor. Most flights leave out of the Central Terminal Building, which was built in 1964 and is currently enjoying an expansion and makeover. Bus and shuttle services connect the airport's five terminal buildings, including the Central Terminal. Parking is available but can be pricey: Most travelers opt for a taxi, the subway, or a bus when getting to and from the airport.

**Parking fees for LaGuardia Airport:**
Short-term lots: $5.00 for up to two hours; $3.00 for every hour thereafter
Long-term lot: $24.00 per day for first two days; $5.00 for each 12-hour period thereafter

**Airlines serving LaGuardia Airport:**
All the major airlines mentioned in the Bradley International Airport listing (see above) also serve LaGuardia. You'll also find a few additional airlines, including:

Air Tran Airways
(800) AIR–TRAN
www.airtran.com

ATA Airlines
(800) 435–9282
www.ata.com

Colgan Air
(800) 428–4322
www.colganair.com

Comair
(800) 354–9822
www.comair.com

Frontier Airlines
(800) 432–1359
www.frontierairlines.com

Spirit Airlines
(800) 772–7117
www.spiritair.com

## Westchester County Airport
**240 Airport Road, Suite 202, White Plains**
**(914) 995–4850**
**www.westchestergov.com/airport**

Usually called the "White Plains Airport" by locals, this hub is easy to get to, especially for those living in the southern region of Fairfield County. Originally built as a military base, the airport first began serving the general flying public in 1947. It is used extensively by corporate aircraft and also provides direct service for more than one million passengers each year to such destinations as Atlanta, Martha's Vineyard, Chicago, Boston, Toronto, and Philadelphia. You'll find fewer destination options than at other, larger airports, but you can't beat the convenience. Also, it may be possible to use a connection to make White Plains your starting point and/or final destination, even it means making a connection in a larger city.

**Parking fees for Westchester County Airport:**
Short-term parking: $2.30 per half hour
Long-term parking (limited): $17.70 per day

*Before heading out to catch a scheduled flight, visit your airport's Web site. Most provide road maps, construction alerts, traffic advisories, terminal maps, arrival and departure delays, and other useful information. The JFK site, for example, provides drop-down menus and even information about other major airports to help make connections less confusing.*

*Although New York City's airports are relatively close, many local residents opt for Hartford's Bradley International Airport or Westchester County Airport. Their smaller size and ample parking appeal to travelers who dread the complications and crowds at LaGuardia and Kennedy. Bradley offers convenience and an ever-growing roster of destinations. New York City hubs, however, offer more variety and are the best choice for international travel.*

**Airlines serving Westchester County Airport:**

Air Canada
(888) 247-2262
www.aircanada.ca

American Airlines and American Eagle
(800) 433-7300
www.aa.com

ASA (Atlantic Southeast Airlines/
Delta Connection)
(404) 209-0162
www.flyasa.com

ComAir
(800) 354-9822
www.comair.com

Continental Airlines and
Continental Express
(800) 525-0280
www.continental.com

Northwest Airlines
(800) 225-2525
www.nwa.com

Pan American Airways
(800) 359-7262
www.flypanam.com

United Airlines and United Express
(800) 864-8331
www.ual.com

USAirways and USAirways Express
(800) 428-4322
www.usairways.com

**Danbury Municipal Airport**
Miry Brook Road, Danbury
(203) 797-4624
www.justplanestuff.com
Customers parking at the Danbury Fair Mall are used to small planes buzzing just overhead; the airport is located just across the street. The site serves primarily non-commercial, private pilots and FBOs (fixed base operators) who provide flight training, fuel, charter services, hangar space, sightseeing tours, and even aircraft rentals.

**FBOs serving Danbury Municipal Airport:**

Arrow Aviation
(203) 744-5010

Business Aircraft Center
(203) 748-7000
www.businessaircraftcenter.com

Condor Air
(203) 730-8436
www.businessaircraftcenter.com

Curtiss Aero
(203) 743-4007

Helicopter Service of Connecticut
(203) 778-2898

North American Aviation/Danbury
Flight School
(203) 778-4546
www.flynaa.com

Reliant Air
(203) 743-5100

Sadler Aero Center/Centennial
Helicopters
(203) 798-9632
www.sadleraero.com

## AIRPORT GROUND TRANSPORTATION

Locals have numerous options for getting to and from the area's various hubs. The New York City airports charge more for long-term parking and are trickier to navigate for those unfamiliar with city roadways. These transportation services are the best bet for travelers who would rather leave the driving to someone else.

### Advantage Limousine
### (413) 593-3600
### www.limoadvantage.com
Based out of Chicopee, Massachusetts, Advantage serves Bradley and other New England airports. Call for a rate quote.

### All County Express
### (800) 914-4223
This shuttle service travels to and from neighboring Westchester County, New York, and the city airports. If you live near the New York State border, you might find it worthwhile to make the short drive. Expect to pay between $35 and $58 one-way.

### Connecticut Limo
### (800) 472-LIMO
### www.ctlimo.com
Despite the name, most passengers of Connecticut Limo are more likely to be riding in a bus or van than a limousine. This is one of the area's busiest airport transportation companies, providing service to Bradley, JFK, LaGuardia, and even Newark. The buses stop in most major local cities, including Bridgeport, Danbury, Milford, New Haven, Norwalk, Stamford, and Waterbury. Fares vary according to pickup location and final destination; expect to pay between $75 and $128 for a round-trip.

### Executive Car Service
### (800) 392-8184
Executive Car offers regularly scheduled transportation services from numerous Fairfield County locations to Bradley, JFK, LaGuardia, Newark, and Westchester County airports. Rates vary widely depending on starting and ending points.

---

*Always check the fares from each nearby airport before purchasing an airline ticket; one hub may offer considerable savings over the others. Also be sure to factor in other costs associated with each airport, including ground transportation. If you save $50 by using a New York City airport but have to pay $80 for a shuttle to reach it, another location might prove to be a better bargain in the long run.*

---

### Lindsey Limousine
### (860) 289-LIMO
### www.lindseylimo.com
Clients can choose among stretch limos, sedans, SUVs, and other vehicles at this multiservice transportation company serving Bradley International. Call for a rate quote.

### Prime Time Shuttle
### (800) 733-8267
### www.primetimeshuttle.com
Prime Time carries passengers to and from southwestern Connecticut and LaGuardia and JFK airports. Door-to-door service is available from your home or office; prices range from $40 to $70 one-way.

### Red Dot
### (800) 673-3368
Private car services and scheduled shuttles carry passengers from coastal Fairfield County towns to JFK and LaGuardia. Limited service is available to Bradley as well. Call for a rate quote.

# By Train

**Amtrak**
**(800) USA-RAIL**
**www.amtrak.com**
Several of Amtrak's northeast routes, including the Regional, Federal, Vermonter, and Acela Express, pass through Fairfield County. Trains stop at Stamford Station (on Washington Boulevard and East State Street) and the Bridgeport Station (at 525 Water Street), depending on the route. Northeast routes reach such cities as Washington D.C., Newport News, Newark, Boston, Providence, Philadelphia, and Montpelier. Pets are not allowed on board. Call or visit the Web site to make reservations.

**MTA Metro-North Railroad**
**(888) MTA-911PD (MTA Police)**
**www.mta.info**
For many locals, this is the primary means of transportation between New York City and southwestern Connecticut. Coastal residents use the New Haven line and hop on a train at one of 18 stops along the shoreline. Those living in the northern part of the county follow the New Haven line's branch that makes seven stops on the way up to Danbury. The average trip into Grand Central Station takes about 60 to 90 minutes, depending on the day and time. Rush-hour trains make more stops and are, of course, more crowded than weekend or midday trains. Fares vary widely, depending on your starting point and destination. Most questions can be answered with a visit to the Web site. Discounts are given to seniors, children, large groups, and commuters who pay weekly or monthly fares.

# By Bus

Bus lines are another good option for getting to and from Fairfield County and major cities throughout the country. Many bus travel companies also provide service between local cities and nearby airports.

**Bonanza Bus Lines**
**(888) 751-8800**
**www.bonanzabus.com**

**Connecticut Transit**
**(860) 522-8101**
**www.cttransit.com**

**Greyhound Bus Lines**
**(800) 229-9424**
**www.greyhound.com**

**Peter Pan Trailways**
**(800) 343-9999**
**www.peterpanbus.com**

# By Ferry

**Bridgeport to Port Jefferson Ferry**
**(203) 335-2040**
**www.pagelinx.com/bpjferry**
This could easily be one of the area's best shortcuts: The scenic ferry ride between Bridgeport and Long Island can get you across the sound in less than 90 minutes. The ferry, which lands in lovely Port Jefferson, New York, is used by commuters, vacationers, day-trippers, and those just looking to avoid a drive through New York City. You can bring your car on board, as well as your pet. On-site snack bars provide food and drinks. In Bridgeport the ferry dock is located on Water Street, 1 block from the bus and train stations. In Port Jefferson you'll find the dock at the end of New York Highway 112. The company sails its ferries year-round and added a new boat to the fleet in May 2003. Those traveling with cars must be in line a half hour before the scheduled departure time. The one-way fare for a car and driver is $37.75; walk-on passengers pay $13.50. Children under six years of age ride for free. A monthly walk-on pass is also available for $209 per month.

## GETTING AROUND

# Buses

As you might expect, Fairfield County city residents will find easier access to buses than those living in the suburbs. In Stamford, for example, the private company CTTransit works in conjunction with the state to provide a fairly extensive "Stamford Route" that traverses the city as well as some areas of Norwalk and Darien. All CTTransit buses are equipped with bike racks. Local service fares are $1.00 for the Express Bus and $2.50 for "regular fare"; discounts are given to students, seniors, and those who purchase multiday passes. For schedules and more information call (860) 522-8101 or visit www.cttransit.com.

In the Danbury area, residents looking for bus transportation rely primarily on the Housatonic Area Regional Transit service, better known as HART. The company provides fixed-route bus service as well as commuter shuttles, dial-a-ride services, and even a trackless trolley throughout Danbury, Bethel, Brookfield, Newtown, Redding, Ridgefield, New Fairfield, and New Milford. Weekday routes are the busiest, although night and weekend routes are also available. Adults can expect to pay between $1.00 and $1.50 per ride; rates are lower for seniors and students. Multiday passes are also available at a discounted rate. For complete schedules call (203) 748-2034 or visit the HART Web site at www.hartct.org.

Bridgeport-area residents utilize the services of the Greater Bridgeport Transit Authority, which provides bus service in that city as well as in Fairfield, Stratford, and Trumbull. Extended service is also available into Monroe, the Shelton/Derby Railroad Station, and even Norwalk. Fixed routes are plentiful during the week, although somewhat limited on weekends. Fares are typically $1.25 for adults, slightly less for children and seniors. Complete fare and schedule information is available

*One of Danbury's most charming public transportation options is the City Center Danbury Trolley, which travels between the downtown/Western Connecticut State University area and Roger's Park every half hour. To board the trolley, simply wait at one of the red, white, and blue HART bus stop signs marked with a trolley logo. Trolley passes are $1.00 per day for adults and 50 cents per day for children. Depending on the driver, you might also enjoy a bit of sightseeing and historical information during your ride.*

at www.gbtabus.com, or you can call the transit authority at (203) 333-3031.

The city of Norwalk and its neighboring towns also enjoy comprehensive bus services; in this area they are provided by the Norwalk Transit District. In addition to local commuter shuttles and in-city, fixed routes, the company also offers a Coastal Link route from Norwalk to Milford, a Route 7 Link up to Danbury, and town-to-town routes to Westport, Greenwich, New Canaan, and Wilton. The base fare for most routes is $1.25; some longer routes cost $2.00. Call (203) 852-0000 or visit www.norwalktransit.com for complete schedule and fare information.

# Taxis

It's fairly easy to flag down a taxi near bus and train stations in Bridgeport, Norwalk, and Stamford. In most other areas of the county, however, you'll have to call and arrange a pickup with a local company. Most are available 24 hours a day, and many also provide service to airports. Fares vary greatly, depending on the pickup location and destination; be sure to clarify all charges before departing. Some taxis will accept major credit cards.

Canaan Parrish Taxi, New Canaan
(203) 966-6866

Fairfield Cab Company, Fairfield
(203) 255-5797

Greenwich Taxi and Limousine Service,
Greenwich
(800) 866-TAXI

JIN Transportation, Danbury
(203) 790-6396

Norwalk Taxi, Norwalk
(203) 855-1764

Stamford Taxi, Stamford
(203) 325-2611

Westport Star Taxi, Westport
(800) 324-7901

Yellow Cab Company, Bridgeport
(203) 334-2121

# Ferries

In addition to the Bridgeport to Long
Island Ferry (see listing under Getting
Here, above), locals can also take advantage of the Sheffield Island Ferry leaving
from Hope Dock in South Norwalk. Used
mostly by pleasure cruisers, the vessel
sails out to scenic Sheffield Island, home
of the Sheffield Island Lighthouse, for
sightseeing, picnics, and hikes. The ferry
also offers harbor tours, sunset cruises,

*Members of AAA, the popular nationwide
motor club, can find road maps, driving
directions, and even travel agents offering discounted services at one of AAA
Connecticut's Fairfield County offices:
Danbury (93 Lake Avenue), Stamford
(623 Newfield Avenue), Stratford (555
Lordship Boulevard), and Westport (20
Saugatuck Avenue).*

clambakes, and private charters. Schedules vary. In 2003, for example, an essential crew member was called into active
duty by the Coast Guard, forcing the company to temporarily suspend trips. For the
latest updates and information, call (203)
854-4656.

# Roadways

The most-traveled highways and byways
in Fairfield County are the three major
east-west routes of I-95, the Merritt Parkway (Route 15), and I-84. The north-south
routes can also fill up quickly with subur-
banites heading to these larger roads.
Although rush hour can be difficult no
matter where you are in the county, roadways in the off-hours—including midday
during the week, nights, and all weekend
long—are typically pleasant, not too
crowded, and relatively easy to navigate.

I-95 is Fairfield County's most notori-
ous highway in terms of traffic congestion
and car accidents; the road hugs the
coastline, carrying commuters between
local towns as well as travelers coming
from Boston, New York City, and other
points. Speeds are high, and the big rigs,
SUVs, small cars, and motorcycles make
for a sometimes dangerous mix. Accident
rates throughout Connecticut rose more
than 23 percent in the past decade, and
Fairfield County highways were no exception. I-95, on average, is the site of more
accidents than the other two highways
combined, according to Department of
Transportation records. The major and
minor crashes understandably cause considerable backups—and that's in addition
to the slow crawl already experienced
during many rush-hour periods. Renovation work at the Bridgeport exits has
made the situation even more tricky during the past few years, although the completion of expanded on- and off-ramps
will hopefully bring much-needed relief.

It's no wonder that many residents
avoid the interstate when they can, opting

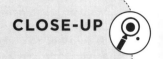

# Rush-Hour Relief

Like in many other commuter-heavy regions, peak drive times in Fairfield County (typically 7:00 to 9:00 A.M. and 3:00 to 6:00 P.M.) can be frustrating. But travelers also have numerous options for avoiding the worst of the tie-ups. A Connecticut Department of Transportation Web site (www.dot.state.ct.us/bureau/eh/maint/im/camera/8) provides real-time views of traffic, thanks to cameras set up along I-95. You can choose which camera view you'd like to see: The listings are organized by town and exit number. The site, which is updated every two minutes, also informs commuters about the latest traffic "incidents," if any. For nine-to-fivers, it's a great way to avoid making a long day even longer.

Many local radio stations also provide traffic reports every five minutes (yes, five) during rush hour. Still, unless you know the lingo of local landmarks, they can be confusing. Two of the most frequently mentioned spots are "the Sikorsky" and "The Q," both of which are actually bridges. "The Sikorsky" is shorthand for the Sikorsky Bridge, located on the busy Merritt Parkway (Route 15) in Stratford, immediately before the exit for the I-95 connector. (The moniker is a reflection of the bridge's location next to the Sikorsky Aircraft manufacturing company.) "The Q" (officially named the Pearl Harbor Memorial Bridge) is located just outside Fairfield County on the New Haven stretch of I-95. In addition, traffic reporters may simply say "the parkway" when referring to the Merritt Parkway and use the term "turnpike" when referring to I-95.

For those interested in carpooling, free state-operated lots known as Park-and-Ride Lots can help tremendously. Just meet your party at the lot, leave a car behind, and travel together to work or another destination. No matter where you're heading, one of these is likely to be on your way:

**Danbury:** U.S. Route 7 at Federal Road, Miry Brook Road, and White Turkey Road; I-84 at exits 1 and 2

**Fairfield:** Merritt Parkway (Route 15) at exits 44 and 46; and I-95 at exits 22 and 24

**Newtown:** I-84 at exits 9 and 11

**Norwalk:** Merritt Parkway (Route 15) at exit 38; I-95 at exits 15 and 16

**Stamford:** Merritt Parkway (Route 15) at exit 35

**Stratford:** Merritt Parkway (Route 15) at exit 53; I-95 at exit 30

**Trumbull:** Route 8 at Route 108; Route 25 at exits 9 and 10; Merritt Parkway (Route 15) at exit 50

**Westport:** Merritt Parkway (Route 15) at exits 41 and 42; I-95 at exit 18

**Wilton:** U.S. Route 7 at Wolfpit Road

Connecticut also operates a Rideshare program that can help you find carpool members and shuttles. For more information call (800) FIND-RIDE.

*Now you see it, now you don't: On the Danbury stretch of I–84, motorists may be surprised to discover an exit 6 (Padanarum Road/New Fairfield) on the westbound side but not on the eastbound side. (Here, the exits skip from 5 to 7.) If you're traveling eastbound and need to reach Padanarum Road, just take exit 5 and head straight through the stop signs and traffic lights.*

instead for the more scenic Merritt Parkway, completed in 1940. The road is also known as Route 15, though you'll find few locals who use this numeric moniker. Commercial vehicles aren't allowed on the Merritt, largely because of the low bridges that cross the road every few miles. These bridges, each of which was designed in a different architectural style, helped the highway achieve its listing on the National Register of Historic Places. The lack of 18-wheelers, along with roadside wildflowers and majestic oaks, can make commuting more pleasant. But the road does have some drawbacks. It has only four lanes (two lanes in each direction), which doesn't help relieve gridlock during peak drive times. The Merritt also isn't terribly convenient to many commuters' destinations, including the downtown areas of Norwalk, Stamford, Greenwich, and Fairfield, all of which are accessed more easily by I–95. In addition, the highway's so-called "no-exit zone" between Route 58 in Fairfield and Route 57 in Westport makes it impossible to escape traffic on this stretch once you're stuck on it. Despite its limitations, the Merritt remains one of Fairfield County's most beautiful and useful roadways.

In the northern region of the county, I–84 helps transport residents to jobs, stores, schools, and homes in Danbury, Newtown, Bethel, Brookfield, and New Fairfield. Heading west the interstate stretches into upstate New York; heading east it passes through Hartford and eventually makes its way to the Massachusetts Turnpike. Like all local roadways, this one can and does experience traffic tie-ups, especially during rush hour and inclement weather. But overall, I–84 is less crowded and easier to handle than the county's southern highways. In Fairfield County the road is prettiest through the Newtown area, where it passes lush forestland and the Housatonic River.

Branching off I–84 is U.S. Route 7, one of the county's most popular north-south roads. At Danbury, a highwaylike section of the road known as "Super 7" heads north toward New Milford and Litchfield County; another branch heads south into Ridgefield and eventually Norwalk. This area can be a bit confusing, as U.S. Route 7 actually merges for a short time with I–84 between exits 3 and 7. Through Ridgefield, Wilton, and Norwalk, the road is lined with large and small businesses and can become extremely congested during peak periods. This is also a popular route for northern residents trying to connect with the Merritt Parkway to the south.

Routes 25 and 8 are two other highly traveled roads connecting the northern and southern sections of the county; they actually merge into one road near Bridgeport. Route 25 traverses the suburbs of Trumbull, Monroe, and Newtown, heading eventually into Danbury. Like U.S. Route 7, much of this road is lined with businesses, and traffic lights can slow already crawling lines of cars during rush hour. But the southernmost portion of Route 25 is wide and highwaylike, with four to five lanes traveling in each direction. Due to its ample design, this part of the road is rarely slowed, even during the most crowded times of day. Route 8, which forks off from its Route 25 cousin in Trumbull, is a winding roadway that heads northeast into Shelton and New Haven County areas, including Derby, Ansonia, and Waterbury.

Other Fairfield County roads provide shortcuts and scenic alternatives to the more crowded routes. Bethel, Redding, and Easton residents, for example, can enjoy the winding beauty of Route 58 when driving north or south; the road passes reservoirs, nature preserves, and historic homes. In New Canaan, Route 124 stretches through the leafy suburbs between the Merritt Parkway and Pound Ridge, New York. Route 33 in Ridgefield, passing noteworthy churches, downtown areas, and parks, is a nice U.S. Route 7 alternative if you're not in a hurry. Roads like these permeate the county, showcasing the hidden corners and beautiful gems that Fairfield County has to offer.

# HISTORY 🏛

Long before there was a Fairfield County, Native Americans farmed, fished, and raised their families throughout the area. Native Americans in Connecticut (or *Quinnehtukqut:* "Place of the long river") are part of the Algonquin family of tribes and share similar language dialects. Although we now know them by tribal names such as Pequot, Mohegan, and Paugussett, these names were assigned by European settlers. They had no such titles for themselves.

Once they ran into each other, the contentious and distrustful relationships between Europeans and Native Americans here mirrored those in other areas. The settlers recognized the value of the rich lands of southwestern Connecticut and fought their way in, pushing the Native peoples from their homes. Although numerous Native American groups, including the Mattabesics, Schaghticokes, and Niantics, resided in the area, the best known Fairfield County tribes are the Pequot and the Golden Hill Paugussetts.

The Pequot tribe had already battled the Niantic peoples and expanded their territory considerably by the time they met up with the first Europeans in the early 1600s. The so-called Pequot War began in 1635; the two groups had already feuded numerous times, but the situation deteriorated into all-out war when the Pequots

murdered an English trader named John Oldham. The settlers declared victory after the "Great Swamp Fight" of 1637, when large numbers of Native Americans were either captured or killed in the Southport Swamp. Today the Mashantucket Pequots are best known for their Foxwoods Casino, one of the largest and most profitable in the world, in Ledyard. The Mohegan tribe currently operates the Mohegan Sun, another large casino in Connecticut.

In 1639, when the English began to expand their settlements in the Stratford and Bridgeport areas, the land they wanted was already occupied by the Paugussett tribe. The settlers seized the property and territory of the Paugussetts, who often moved from spot to spot with the seasons. The Native Americans made a formal complaint about the hostilities and received a hearing in 1659 at the General Court in Hartford. No Native Americans were allowed to testify at the hearing. Not surprisingly, the court decided that the Europeans were free to take Paugussett lands—thousands of acres—in the Bridgeport area. In exchange, the Paugussetts would live on the 80-acre Golden Hill Reservation. As a result, the Paugussetts are now known as the Golden Hill tribe or the Golden Hill Paugussetts.

Over time, even their rights to that site eroded; in 1765 the Paugussetts were forced to give up 68 of the 80 acres. Finally, in 1801 the settlers seized the last 12 acres of the reservation. The court ruled that the Paugussetts did not need the reservation land because they "earned a good living making baskets and brooms." Today the Paugussetts live on a quarter-acre plot in Trumbull, which now serves as headquarters of the tribe and the official Golden Hill Reservation. The land was bought by a Native American day laborer who saved his wages for more than 25 years to make the purchase. It is the

ℹ️ *The hysteria and paranoia of 17th-century witch hunts also reached Fairfield County. Two of the best-known victims were Goody Basset of Stratford and Goody Knapp of Fairfield, both of whom were executed. ("Goody" stands for "Goodwife," or "Mrs.") Goody Staples of Fairfield was tried after neighbor Roger Ludlow said she "was probably a witch." She was later acquitted.*

smallest Native American reservation in the United States.

The Europeans' march to settle the land throughout Fairfield County continued. Roger Ludlow founded the town of Fairfield in 1639 after personally pursuing a group of Pequots in the Great Swamp Fight. A year later, New Haven resident Captain Turner bought the territory now known as Stamford from the Native Americans living there. The natives, having realized too late that they had been swindled, revolted. But the settlers retained their hold on the Stamford-area lands, which they originally named Rippowam. Families from the Norwalk and Stamford areas then traveled north to settle the Danbury region, where they ran into similar clashes with Native Americans.

Fairfield County was officially created by a Court of Elections in Hartford on May 10, 1666. Initially only five towns were included: Fairfield, Stratford, Norwalk, Stamford, and Greenwich. Other towns were added as the population increased, leading to the 23 towns and cities we find today. Most residents were farmers or craftsmen, and many European settlers owned slaves during this period. In fact, the ports of Bridgeport were not only busy with the daily transport of food, timber, and livestock but also with the bruised and battered human cargo that would provide slave labor for years to come.

During the Revolutionary War, the people of Fairfield County were somewhat divided. Towns like Newtown were predominantly Tory, while the populace of Fairfield and Norwalk were more rebellious against the British. The coastal communities fended off frequent attacks from the British, who often approached via Long Island Sound. One of the most famous skirmishes in the area occurred in April 1777, when a handful of minutemen lined up on Compo Beach in Westport to fight more than 2,000 British soldiers led by New York Governor William Tryon.

The Patriots were badly outnumbered, and Tryon marched his men on the shore past Westport and north through Ridge-

*Local students regularly engage in archaeological digs at Putnam Memorial State Park, located in West Redding. Visitors can still see the remnants of campsites, buildings, and other evidence of the winter encampment of General Israel Putnam and his troops in 1779 during the Revolutionary War.*

field and Bethel. Once he reached Danbury, he ordered his men to burn much of the city, including the food and weapons that were stored there. On the southern march back to his ships, Tryon and his troops met resistance in Ridgefield in what became known as the Battle of Ridgefield. (General Benedict Arnold gained hero status during this battle, making a valiant effort to resist Tryon's troops.) Two years later, Tryon returned to "punish" the Connecticut rebels with more destruction: He and his men burned both Fairfield and Norwalk, and it took many years for the communities to recover.

The tendrils of the Industrial Revolution first reached Fairfield County in the early 1800s, when residents began to move away from farming and into manufacturing. This was perhaps seen most clearly in Bridgeport, a city that didn't

*The City of Stamford endured a roller-coaster ride during and after the Great Depression of the 1930s. The city's largest employer, Yale and Towne, cited rising taxation as its reason for moving to New York City and laying off more than 300 workers. Downtown, the People's National Bank went defunct. The school budget was cut dramatically, and nearly 20 percent of residents were receiving some form of welfare. But Stamford gained a few new businesses as well and pulled itself out of the Depression with the help of new mayor Alfred N. Phillips Jr. and resolute city residents.*

## CLOSE-UP

# FCI Danbury

America was in a sour mood in 1938. The Great Depression was hovering, Hitler was marching into Austria, and a freak hurricane killed more than 600 people on Long Island. In general it wasn't a year for celebration—except, perhaps, at the home of Danbury farmer Albert Ruffles, who had just come into a $77,500 windfall.

Ruffles had sold his land to an aggressive and persuasive suitor: the United States government. Not long after, the Federal Public Works Administration began to transform his high, scenic pastures into New England's first federal prison. The project was designed to create Depression-era jobs by building a short-term housing facility for prisoners. But the Bureau of Prisons also had another goal in mind; they wanted to fashion a different, "modern" kind of jail that embodied new penal philosophies of rehabilitation and compassion. Two years later, in 1940, the public got its first look at the Federal Correctional Institute (FCI) of Danbury.

Then, as now, the 400-acre site was more reminiscent of a college campus than a prison. Dormitory-style housing units had names like Concord, Providence, and Berkshire. The mess hall, housing units, and work buildings surrounded an open, flower-filled courtyard, and much of Ruffles's farmland remained intact to be tended and harvested by the inmates. Prisoners, all of whom were classified as "less serious" offenders, had

access to a variety of educational, recreational, and job-training programs.

Some called the architecture and concept innovative; others, ridiculous. Not long after FCI's completion, locals began to refer to it as "the prison without walls." Warden Edgar M. Gerlach denied the popular notions, circulated in the Connecticut press, that his prisoners were given "too many comforts and conveniences" and that his jail was nothing more than a "reform school for grown-ups."

The decades, and the prisoners, came and went. In 1994 the prison was converted into an all-female facility, and it retains its "country club" reputation to this day. On the whole, the prison's current inmates are anonymous, nonviolent convicts hoping to serve their time without incident. Their crimes didn't make headlines; their faces never appeared on the news. But that wasn't always the case at FCI, where criminal "celebrities" have often found themselves as invited guests of the federal government. Here are some of the better known prisoners to have laid their head on an FCI Danbury pillow during the past 60 years.

**The "Hollywood Ten":** In 1947 the House Un-American Activities Committee (HUAC) was on a McCarthy-style witch hunt for Americans involved in "unpatriotic behavior." HUAC members set their sights on the film industry, asserting that communists had infiltrated Hollywood. Some actors and studio execs, however,

come into its own until the "modern" era made it a viable and thriving center for trade and industry. Products like weapons, appliances, and engines were built and

shipped from Bridgeport, which didn't officially become incorporated until 1836—though it was settled almost 200 years earlier. In Danbury the manufacture of refused to answer questions. These pro-testers, who became known as the Hollywood Ten, were held in contempt of Congress and each served six months to a year at FCI Danbury.

**J. Parnell Thomas:** Thomas was instrumental in the prosecution of the Hollywood Ten: Not long after, the Republican congressman found himself jailed at
FCI right alongside them. His behavior as chairman of the HUAC angered some of his left-leaning colleagues, who began an investigation of his finances. Thomas was convicted of conspiracy to defraud the government and served his sentence at FCI.

**Horace Doyle Barnette:** On August 4, 1964, the FBI found the bodies of three missing civil rights activists buried at a farm in Neshoba County, Mississippi. In 1967 seven men were convicted: One of them, Horace Doyle Barnette, served his time at FCI Danbury. (The investigation of this crime and the trial were later immortalized in the 1988 film *Mississippi Burning.*)

**The Berrigan Brothers:** Daniel and Philip Berrigan, brothers and Roman Catholic priests, are best known for their antiwar protests during the Vietnam era. They gained the most notoriety for a 1968 break-in at the Catonsville, Maryland, draft board offices, where they stole draft records and burned them in the parking lot. Both men were paroled in 1972 after serving two years at FCI.

**George Jung:** This drug dealer's story was spotlighted in the 2001 movie *Blow,* in which Johnny Depp portrayed Jung as a clever, greedy entrepreneur. He arrived at FCI in 1972, after getting caught with 600 pounds of marijuana. Jung called the Danbury prison "a crime school," saying, "I went in with a B.A. in marijuana and came out with a Ph.D. in cocaine."

**G. Gordon Liddy:** This key player in the Watergate scandal arrived at FCI in 1975 to begin serving a 6- to 20-year sentence for burglary and other offenses. Liddy, a member of President Richard Nixon's administration, was convicted of breaking into a psychiatrist's office to plug leaks about Nixon's secret Vietnam policies.

**Sun Myung Moon:** This charismatic leader of the Unification Church religious sect (often called the "Moonies" by nonmembers) landed in trouble with the law in 1982, when he was sentenced to 18 months in jail and a $25,000 fine for failing to pay taxes on $1.7 million of his income. He served 11 months at FCI Danbury and was released in 1985.

**Leona Helmsley:** "Only the little people pay taxes." Helmsley, the billionaire real estate tycoon and poster child for tax evasion, learned how wrong she was in 1993, when Judge John M. Walker sentenced her to four years in prison, 750 hours of community service, and $7.1 million in fines. The so-called "Queen of Mean" served 18 months of her sentence at FCI.

---

hats gave the city its nickname, "Hat City," which survives today. Around this same time, the railroads brought cheap labor to Stamford and Greenwich, allowing the Stamford Manufacturing Company, the Abendroth Factory, Russell Burdsall & Ward, and the St. John Woodworking Company to grow and prosper. In Norwalk

## HISTORY

*To visit the only hardware store on the National Register of Historic Places, stop by Meeker's Hardware on White Street in Danbury. You can still get a 5-cent Coca-Cola here, although inflation has taken its toll: Your bargain liquid refreshment will be in a Dixie cup, not a bottle.*

residents depended heavily on the harvest of oysters and other seafood but also manufactured hats, pottery, and other goods to ship out of local ports.

During the Civil War years (1861–1865), Fairfield County supplied 36 regiments to the Union's efforts. Nearly all were volunteers, and many of the fighting men were armed with Sharp's rifles and Springfield muskets. The First Regiment, made up mostly of men from Danbury and Bridgeport, participated in the infamous Battle of Bull Run, in which the Union suffered heavy losses. Although the county was fortunate to have avoided any Civil War battles on its soil, the volunteer soldiers, their families, and their communities nonetheless made considerable sacrifices to the war effort.

Meanwhile, trains first started running from New York City into Fairfield County in the mid-1800s on the New York, New Haven, and Hartford Railroad. In addition to serving as the main trade routes for commerce, the trains also made it much easier for residents of the city and the county to find each other. It was around

*Bethel, which means "house of God," was incorporated in 1855 by churchgoers. But there were also vices there. In 1932 local resident Rudolph Kunett built the first American vodka distillery on South Street (where the Verdi Woodworking Company now stands). He had purchased the recipe from the Smirnoff family. He later sold the recipe to the company that still makes Smirnoff vodka to this day.*

this time that summer homes and cottages, owned primarily by wealthy New Yorkers, began to spring up around Fairfield County. Some even found that they preferred the country life to that of the city, beginning the wave of suburb-to-city commuting that continues to this day.

As the local population grew and became more mobile, it was perhaps inevitable that the development of roadways would follow. In the 1770s the New York–Boston stagecoach carved out the bumpy trail that would later become the Boston Post Road (U.S. Route 1), which was first paved in 1807. A breakthrough for its time, even that road became congested and impractical for long-distance travel by the early 1900s. The state responded to the growing need with the construction the Merritt Parkway (Route 15), Fairfield County's first highway. The first section of the road, stretching from Greenwich to Norwalk, opened to the public in 1938. Because commercial traffic was—and still is—banned on the Merritt, commerce remained at a slow crawl on U.S. Route 1 until the mid 1950s, when the massive Connecticut Turnpike (now I-95) opened. It remains the largest and most-traveled highway in the county. I-84, the major highway in the northern region of the county, was completed in the 1960s. This interstate carries Connecticut visitors and residents from the New York state line through Danbury and Newtown and eventually on to Hartford and the Massachusetts state line.

Fairfield County's population was estimated at around 20,000 in 1756; by 1810 more than 40,000 people were thought to be living in the area. The numbers continued to grow, with nearly 320,000 people calling Fairfield County home by 1920. The 1970 census revealed 792,000 county residents, and the past 30 years have seen an even more rapid growth: By the year 2000 Fairfield County had ballooned to include 882,567 people.

Today the county's considerable assets, including jobs, schools, and location-

location-location, continue to attract new residents. Summer cottages have mostly given way to permanent residences from north to south. The once-prominent role of agriculture has dwindled, leaving farms to serve a smaller, more local group of customers. Manufacturing hubs are still present, although high-tech firms, financial institutions, the publishing industry, and health-care jobs grab more headlines and workers than ever before. And even as we hurdle head-first into the future, Fairfield County's historical societies, preserved buildings, and monuments ensure that we will never forget the people and events that brought us to this unique moment in time.

# ACCOMMODATIONS

You'll find no shortage of places to hang your hat in Fairfield County. From ultradeluxe hotels to historic inns and affordable motels, the region offers a room for every type of traveler. As you might expect, the accommodations become more pricey as you head toward the southern end of the county: Hotels and inns in Greenwich, Stamford, and Westport—many of which cater to business travelers—tout their proximity to New York City and charge accordingly. Seasonal and promotional discounts are sometimes available, however, so be sure to ask about special deals when making a reservation. Whether you're hoping for a four-poster bed in a 1700s-era inn or a whirlpool bath in a high-rise hotel, the county has an accommodation to fulfill your every whim.

## PRICE CODE

The following scale is designed to help you ferret out a room in your price range. In general the rates listed here are single-night, double-occupancy. The lower end of the range is most often representative of basic rooms with double-, queen-, or king-size beds. The higher end of the spectrum typically represents the price of high-end rooms and suites. The rates do not include taxes.

*Think twice before renting a car, especially if you're planning a short-term stay. Many of the larger hotels have their own restaurants and lounges, and some provide shuttle services to nearby businesses, attractions, and airports. Others are even located within walking distance of train and bus stations.*

| | |
|---|---|
| $ | $75 to $100 per night |
| $$ | $101 to $150 per night |
| $$$ | $151 to $250 per night |
| $$$$ | $251 per night or higher |

## SOUTHERN FAIRFIELD COUNTY

### Bridgeport

**Holiday Inn Bridgeport**      **$$**
**1070 Main Street**
**(203) 334–1234**
**www.ichoicehotelsgroup.com**
Close to I-95 as well as to the Bridgeport train and bus stations, the Holiday Inn is located within convenient traveling distance of Trumbull, Fairfield, Stratford, Monroe, and even New Haven and Westport. Full-service amenities include an indoor swimming pool, a fitness center, interior corridors, a restaurant and lounge, dry cleaning and laundry services, a florist, a newsstand, wake-up calls, a rental-car desk, and airport shuttles. The hotel's 234 rooms and suites are spread out on nine floors. Business travelers can also take advantage of a limousine-for-hire service; fax, print, and photocopying services; meeting rooms; and an "executive boardroom." Pets are welcome as overnight guests.

### Darien

**Howard Johnson Inn Darien**      **$–$$**
**150 Ledge Road**
**(203) 655–3933**
**www.hojo.com**
Designed in the unique HoJo style (complete with a sharply slanting orange roof),

the Howard Johnson Inn of Darien provides visitors with affordable accommodations and a convenient location. Each of the 72 rooms has cable television, individual temperature controls, telephones, and in-room coffeemakers. Some rooms also have whirlpool baths. An outdoor swimming pool is open seasonally. The train station, with Metro-North trains heading into Manhattan, is located within walking distance of the hotel.

# Greenwich

### The Delamar                    $$$$
### 500 Steamboat Road
### (203) 661-9800
### www.thedelamar.com

The Delamar is a member of the Small Luxury Hotels of the World organization and was recently listed on the "Hot List" of *Condé Nast Traveler.* One look around the newly built accommodation will tell you why: The hotel has a waterfront location on Long Island Sound, wrought-iron balconies, a strict no-tipping policy, complimentary beach passes, and surroundings designed to mimic those of a sumptuous Tuscan villa. Apricot and green furnishings compliment the hand-knotted rugs, luxurious upholstery, and original works of art that can be found throughout the hotel. Greenwich Avenue shops and eateries are located within a short walking distance. Pets are welcome in designated rooms for an extra $20 per night; the hotel even provides a special welcome of treats and gifts for its four-legged guests.

### Harbor House Inn               $$-$$$$
### 165 Shore Road
### (203) 637-0145
### www.hhinn.com

Step into a homey atmosphere at Harbor House, a 23-room inn that is somewhat secluded but also convenient to the train station, restaurants, and shopping areas. Each guest room comes equipped with voice mail, air-conditioning, a telephone, and a TV/VCR. A daily continental break-

fast is included in the rates. If you're planning a meeting or other get-together, the inn's conference rooms can accommodate 12 to 16 people in each room. A beach and a park are located within walking distance of the inn; bicycles are also available for borrowing.

### Homestead Inn                  $$$$
### 420 Field Point Road
### (203) 869-7500
### www.homesteadinn.com

Among the most exclusive and luxurious accommodations in Fairfield County, the Homestead Inn incorporates historic architecture with European-influenced interior design, original artworks, bold colors, and furniture crafted by Brunschwig & Fils, Dana Robes, and others. The inn's 7 suites and 12 guest rooms have cable television, air-conditioning, radios, and Internet connections, plus heated bathroom floors and handpicked decorative artifacts from around the globe. Proprietors Theresa and Thomas Henkelmann also manage the on-site gourmet restaurant, Thomas Henkelmann (see the Restaurants chapter for more information). The inn is closed during the last week in February and the first week in March.

### Hyatt Regency Greenwich        $$$$
### 1800 East Putnam Avenue
### (203) 637-1234
### www.greenwich.hyatt.com

Weddings, brunches, fashion shows, expos: The Hyatt is a hot spot for special events in southern Fairfield County. The hotel's four-story atrium houses hundreds of plants and a waterfall, and the 9,600-square-foot ballroom can host up to 1,200 people. Smaller gathering can be accommodated in the Hyatt's 29 meeting rooms, which come equipped with Internet access, telephones, and individual temperature controls. Overnight guests can choose from 373 fully equipped rooms—premium movie channels, marble bathrooms, and 320-thread-count linens are standard—and enjoy access to a heated indoor swimming pool, a fitness center,

> When traveling with a pet, always bring along proof of vaccinations and a crate or kennel. Many pet-friendly hotels and inns require these, but not all will let you know beforehand.

two restaurants, a lounge, and business services.

### Stanton House Inn                    $$-$$$
**76 Maple Avenue**
**(203) 869-2110**
**www.stantonhouseinn.com**

The Stanton House Inn is an 1840s-era colonial that once served as the home of the prominent Sackett, Seaman, and Brush families. In 1937 Nora Stanton Barney opened the house as an inn and named it after her grandmother, famous American feminist Elizabeth Cady Stanton. Today the inn offers 24 rooms and suites, including one queen suite with a whirlpool bathtub and one king suite with a fireplace. Cable television, air-conditioning, and voice mail are available in all rooms. Guests also share access to a swimming pool, patio, manicured gardens, and interior gathering rooms. A continental breakfast buffet, served each day in the dining room, is included in the rates.

## New Canaan

### Roger Sherman Inn                    $$-$$$
**195 Oenoke Ridge**
**(203) 966-4541**
**www.rogershermaninn.com**

Roger Sherman, a practicing attorney in the 1700s, was the only man to sign four of his young country's most important documents: the Declaration of Independence, the Constitution of the United States, the Association, and the Articles of Confederation. Sherman's niece, Martha Sherman, lived in the home now known as the Roger Sherman Inn from 1783 to 1806. Today guests can expect to find historic

touches with all the modern conveniences, including cable television, voice mail, dataports, laundry facilities, hair dryers, irons, and ironing boards. An on-site restaurant provides contemporary cuisine (see Restaurants for more information), and guests enjoy a complimentary continental breakfast each morning. The inn also offers a two-bedroom suite, which is priced in the $$$$ range.

## Norwalk

### Courtyard by Marriott Norwalk $$-$$$
**474 Main Avenue**
**(203) 849-9111**
**www.marriott.com**

Many of the rooms and suites at this Courtyard by Marriott location have been recently renovated. The rooms are located on four floors with interior corridors, desks, satellite television, in-room movies, voice mail, free newspapers, hair dryers, coffeemakers, irons, and ironing boards. The hotel also offers a restaurant and lounge, room service, laundry facilities and a laundry valet service, an indoor swimming pool, a fitness center, and express check-in and checkout services. Business travelers will appreciate the large work desks, meeting rooms, and fax and photocopying services.

### Four Points by Sheraton
### Norwalk                             $$-$$$
**426 Main Avenue**
**(203) 849-9828**
**www.fourpoints.com/norwalk**

Primarily serving corporate travelers, this Four Points hotel is located in Norwalk's financial district. But don't let the emphasis on business fool you: The hotel is also located close to SoNo, the Maritime Aquarium, and other attractions that make it a good lodging option for leisure travelers as well. The 127 guest rooms each have air-conditioning, alarm clocks, cable television, and free Internet access. Other features include a concierge service, a car-rental service, a business center, meeting rooms, a restaurant, and a 24-hour front desk.

## Norwalk Inn & Conference Center    $$
### 99 East Avenue
### (203) 838-5531
### www.norwalkinn.com

The 71 guest rooms and suites at the Norwalk Inn & Conference Center provide comfortable furnishings, voice mail, desks, cable television, interior-corridor entrances, and individual climate controls. Visitors will also have access to a 24-hour front desk, shuttle services, an outdoor seasonal swimming pool with a large patio, a fitness center, laundry facilities, and fax and copying services. The conference and banquet facilities can accommodate 30 to 250 people with adjoining rooms of various sizes. Adams Rib restaurant (see Restaurants for more information) is also located on-site, and the inn staff can arrange summertime barbecue parties for 25 people served on the poolside patio.

## Silvermine Tavern    $$-$$$
### 194 Perry Avenue
### (203) 847-4558
### www.silverminetavern.com

One of the county's best-known landmarks, the 200-year-old Silvermine Tavern is located beside a scenic waterfall and river in the artists' community known as Silvermine. In addition to its popular restaurant (see Restaurants for more information), the inn also offers guest rooms and suites with antique furnishings, private bathrooms, four-poster beds, folk art, hardwood floors, and patios. Common areas include parlors with fireplaces, a large waterfront patio, a country store, and a bar with live jazz on Friday and Saturday nights. At check-in ask for *A Short Walking Tour of Silvermine,* a three-page guide that highlights the best sights within a 2-mile walk of the inn. Daily continental breakfasts are included in the room rate: Don't miss the Silvermine Tavern Honey Buns.

# Stamford

## Holiday Inn Select Stamford    $$$-$$$$
### 700 Main Street
### (203) 358-8400
### www.ichoicehotelsgroup.com

Walk to the train station, the shopping mall, and several large corporations from this downtown hotel, which offers 380 guest rooms and 3 suites. If you're not up for walking, the Holiday Inn Select also offers a rental-car desk, a gift shop, laundry facilities, valet dry-cleaning service, an ATM, a fitness center, an indoor swimming pool, and wake-up calls. All rooms and suites have alarm clocks, in-room movies, high-speed Internet access, work desks, irons, ironing boards, hair dryers, and coffeemakers. Manhattan is a 45-minute drive or Metro-North train ride away.

*Business travelers will be happy to know that many of the county's hotels now provide high-speed Internet access free of charge to guests. In some cases you'll have to check your e-mail in the lobby. In others you can surf the Web right in your room.*

## Sheraton Stamford Hotel    $$$-$$$$
### 2701 Summer Street
### (203) 359-1300
### www.starwood.com/sheraton

With 448 guest rooms and a location that's midway between I-95 and the Merritt Parkway, this Sheraton is set up to accommodate all types of Fairfield County visitors. For business travelers the hotel offers two-line telephones, work desks, high-speed Internet access, room service, and 22 meeting rooms—one of which can accommodate up to 1,000 people. For vacationers and other visitors, the Sheraton Stamford boasts an indoor heated swimming pool, a fitness club, a restaurant and lounge, and a convenient spot near the Rich Forum, the Palace Theater, and the Town Center Mall.

### Stamford Marriott $$$-$$$$
2 Stamford Forum
(203) 357-9555
www.marriott.com

This downtown hotel is located within a stone's throw of numerous corporations, shopping centers, restaurants, theaters, and shops. More than 500 rooms and suites are spread out on 17 floors, more than 400 of them specifically designed for business travelers. The hotel also offers three restaurants: Allie's American Grille, Vuli, and Northern Lights, along with indoor and outdoor swimming pools, a fitness center, a sauna, a rental-car desk, express check-in and checkout services, a gift shop, laundry facilities, a business center, and room service. All guest rooms have satellite television, voice mail, in-room coffeemakers, and high-speed Internet access.

### Super 8 Motel Stamford $-$$
32 Grenhart Road
(203) 324-8887
www.super8.com

If you're looking to avoid the higher costs of the downtown hotels, this Super 8 makes a good alternative. The motel's 99 rooms have been recently remodeled and offer cable television with premium movie channels, free local phone calls, laundry facilities, alarm clocks, voice mail, free daily newspapers, and complimentary continental breakfasts. Numerous restaurants are located a short drive away, as are many of Stamford's largest companies. Pets are allowed with advance permission from the general manager.

### The Westin Stamford $$-$$$$
One First Stamford Place
(203) 967-2222
www.starwood.com

Accommodations at the Westin run the gamut from standard-style double-bed rooms to ultradeluxe "club floor" suites. Overnight guests will find cable television, voice mail, minibars, coffeemakers with Starbucks coffee, work desks, and the company's trademark "Heavenly" beds and showers in every room. High-speed Internet access is also available for a fee. The hotel offers a restaurant and lounge, a gift shop, laundry and dry-cleaning services, a fitness center, valet parking, an indoor swimming pool, and fax and photocopying services. The Westin has 45,000 square feet of meeting and banquet facilities, more than any other hotel in Connecticut.

# Stratford

### Ramada Inn Stratford $-$$
225 Lordship Boulevard
(203) 375-8866
www.ramada.com

Convenient to I-95, this Ramada location is especially popular with business travelers visiting Stratford, Bridgeport, New Haven, Trumbull, and Fairfield. Inn guests can also take advantage of such amenities as in-room coffeemakers, hair dryers, alarm clocks, a game room, laundry facilities, free newspapers, a swimming pool, free daily continental breakfasts, and a 24-hour front desk. The on-site restaurant, Copperfield's, serves a seafood buffet on weekends, and the hotel lounge offers weekday happy hours.

# Trumbull

### Trumbull Marriott Merritt Parkway $$-$$$
180 Hawley Lane
(203) 378-1400
www.marriott.com

Convenience is the key word at this Marriott hotel property, where guests can simply jump onto the parkway to reach local businesses, attractions, family, and friends. (The north-south Route 25 and I-95, which runs east-west through Connecticut, are also nearby.) Five floors of rooms and suites offer voice mail, satellite television, in-room movies, two-line phones, work desks, coffeemakers, irons, ironing boards, and hair dryers. Guests can also splash in the indoor and outdoor pools, work out at the fitness center, dine in the on-site restaurant, browse in the gift shop, rent a car at the Hertz desk, or take care of necessities in the business center.

# Westport

### Inn at Longshore                    $$-$$$
**260 Compo Road South**
**(203) 226-3316**
**www.innatlongshore.com**
This former private estate-turned-country club once hosted guests like F. Scott Fitzgerald and the Rockefellers. Today well-heeled locals and visitors still frequent the waterfront property, which has been transformed into an inn, restaurant, and the Longshore Club Park golf course. Overnight guests enjoy 12 guest rooms and suites, decorated in a colonial style, and are welcome to access the 18-hole golf course, elegant common rooms, and an Olympic-size swimming pool. Locals enjoy the outdoor seating and views at the on-site eatery, which is open for lunch and dinner (see Restaurants for more information). The inn also frequently hosts weddings, conferences, and other special events.

### Inn at National Hall                $$$$
**2 Post Road West**
**(203) 221-1351**
**www.innatnationalhall.com**
Listed on the National Register of Historic Places, the 1870s-era Inn at National Hall is located within walking distance of the boutiques, restaurants, and coffeehouses of downtown Westport. The eight guest rooms include the Gold Star Room, with a canopy bed and library sitting area; the Acorn Room, with a chandelier and antique furnishings; and the India Room, which boasts a canopy bed and water views. Or choose one of the eight suites: The Henny Penny Suite is a loft with river views and a canopy bed; the Equestrian Suite has a hot tub, fireplace, and full-size living room.

*If at all possible, try to book your accommodations for the weekend. Many hotels, especially those in the southern part of the county, cater to business travelers, so you can usually find significant discounts by avoiding a weekday stay.*

### Westport Inn                        $$$-$$$$
**1595 Post Road East**
**(203) 259-5236**
**www.westportinn.com**
Conveniently located on the Post Road, the Westport Inn has a country-inn ambience with 116 rooms and suites. Some are poolside, and many have been recently renovated. The guest rooms are decorated in a "country" style with teals, whites, pinks, and blues. The heated indoor swimming pool, atrium, hot tub, and fitness center help fill downtime; the ballroom and conference rooms can host up to 120 people in each space. The on-site Tenderloin Steakhouse serves a continental breakfast, lunch, and dinner. Or you can relax by the fireplace at the inn's Piano Lounge.

## NORTHERN FAIRFIELD COUNTY
# Bethel

### Best Western Berkshire Motor Inn  $-$$
**11 Stony Hill Road (U.S. Route 6)**
**(203) 744-3200**
**www.bestwestern.com**
Located on the Bethel-Danbury border near I-84's exit 8, the Best Western Berkshire Motor Inn is convenient to Danbury's businesses and attractions but more affordable than most of the city's larger hotels. Amenities here include complimentary continental breakfast, a playground, laundry facilities, and fax and photocopying services. Guests also enjoy free use of a health club located next door. Each guest room has air-conditioning, two telephone lines, voice mail, a hair dryer, an iron and ironing board, a coffeemaker, and

cable television with premium movie channels. The hotel is family owned.

### Best Western Stony Hill Inn     $-$$
**46 Stony Hill Road (U.S. Route 6)**
**(203) 743-5533**
**www.bestwestern.com**

Don't be surprised to see newlyweds posing for wedding-day pictures at the Stony Hill Inn, which offers flower gardens, landscaped grounds, a pond, a golf driving range, and a gazebo. Meeting space for up to 275 people is also available, as is a restaurant. Guest rooms vary in size and style, although all have cable television with premium movie channels, hair dryers, coffeemakers, irons, and ironing boards. Choose from smoking and nonsmoking rooms. The Stony Hill Inn is located just down the street from its Best Western cousin, the Berkshire Motor Inn (see listing above).

### Microtel Inn and Suites     $-$$
**80 Benedict Road**
**(203) 748-8318**
**www.microtelbethel.com**

This recently built hotel offers 78 smoking and nonsmoking rooms with interior corridors. Some rooms can connect for larger parties, and all come equipped with hair dryers, cable television, irons, and ironing boards; local calls are free. The suites also have microwaves, refrigerators, and pull-out couches. All guests can take advantage of valet laundry services, fax and photocopying services, daily continental breakfast, and even a wine-and-cheese gathering on Tuesday night. Guests can purchase discount passes to a nearby gym, and a meeting room is also available for small groups. Danbury companies, shopping centers, and I-84 are just down the road.

## Brookfield

### Twin Tree Inn     $
**1030 Federal Road**
**(203) 775-0220**
**www.twintreeinn.com**

This affordable and cozy motel-style inn is located on the U.S. Route 7 corridor about halfway between Danbury and New Milford. Choose from first- or second-floor rooms with exterior corridors, cable television, air-conditioning, business services, and voice mail. Each room has wall-to-wall carpeting, colonial furnishings, and floral bedspreads and curtains. Several deluxe units offer added privacy, sliding doors leading to patios, and a view of the hillside behind the inn. Guests can also take advantage of complimentary continental breakfasts offering muffins, fruit, pastries, yogurt, cereal, coffee, and juice. The inn is located within a short driving distance of many restaurants, stores, and corporations in Danbury, Brookfield, and New Milford. Pets are welcome.

## Danbury

### Comfort Suites Danbury     $-$$
**89 Mill Plain Road**
**(203) 205-0800**
**www.comfortsuites.com/hotel/ct044**

An all-suite hotel, the modern Comfort Suites Danbury has 78 units with amenities well suited for a long-term stay or business travel. Each suite comes equipped with two telephones and two outside lines, desk, free Internet access, microwave, refrigerator, 25-inch television, cable with premium movie channels, video game console, coffeemaker, hair dryer, and iron and ironing board. Guests can also enjoy complimentary continental breakfast, laundry and dry-cleaning services, a fitness center, and free business services, including printing and photocopying. Children age 18 and younger stay in your room for free.

### Courtyard by Marriott Danbury $$-$$$
**3 Eagle Road**
**(203) 730-2228**
**www.courtyard.com**

Built in 2002, the Courtyard by Marriott is Danbury's newest hotel. Guests can choose from rooms with either a king-size bed or two queen beds. All rooms have work desks, free high-speed Internet access, free daily newspapers, extra pillows, and cable television. Some rooms also have whirlpool tubs and balconies. Other amenities include the Courtyard Cafe, laundry facilities, an indoor swimming pool, a fitness center, fax and photocopying services, and free coffee in the lobby. The new meeting rooms come equipped with Internet access, televisions, VCRs, whiteboards, and projection screens. Weary travelers will also be happy to know that a movie theater, shopping centers, and several restaurants are located within a five-minute drive of the hotel.

## Holiday Inn Danbury–Bethel      $-$$
**80 Newtown Road**
**(203) 792-4000**
**www.danburyct.holiday-inn.com**

This Holiday Inn honors its "Hat City" location with a fun theme decor of antique hats and displays honoring Danbury's history as a hatmaking capital. The 114 guest rooms all have cable television and premium movie channels, Internet access, coffeemakers, hair dryers, irons, and ironing boards. The hotel also offers free continental breakfasts, an outdoor seasonal swimming pool, a fitness center, a shuttle service, and a Kids-Stay-Free program. Pets are welcome in designated rooms and in the Pet Path dog-walking area. Guests can also let loose at the popular Teddy's Night Club (see Nightlife for more information) and the Top Hat Cafe.

## Inn at Ethan Allen      $$-$$$
**21 Lake Avenue**
**(203) 774-1776**
**www.ethanalleninn.com**

Danbury is the proud home of the headquarters of Ethan Allen furniture company, which also offers its own hotel right beside the Danbury showroom at exit 4 off I-84. The hotel, as you might expect, is furnished completely with Ethan Allen's top-quality beds, tables, sofas, chairs, desks, mirrors, and other handcrafted pieces. Most rooms have separate seating

areas, as well as cable television with premium movie channels and voice mail. Guests can also take advantage of a heated swimming pool, a cocktail lounge, a fitness center, and a restaurant serving breakfast, lunch, and dinner. Fourteen conference rooms and 15,000 square feet of banquet space accommodate even the largest celebrations.

## Sheraton Danbury Hotel      $$-$$$
**18 Old Ridgebury Road**
**(203) 794-0600**
**www.starwood.com**

The Sheraton has the largest ballroom in the area and several banquet rooms, making it a popular spot for weddings and other big events. Overnight guests can also enjoy a complimentary shuttle service to local attractions, an indoor swimming pool, a fitness center, and an on-site restaurant and bar. The smoking and nonsmoking rooms all come equipped with work desks, sleigh beds, air-conditioning, voice mail, coffeemakers, and refrigerators. The hotel also offers 19 meeting rooms, the largest of which can seat up to 700 people. The Sheraton's business travelers are often visiting such local companies as IBM, Pitney Bowes, GE Capital, and Honeywell.

## SpringHill Suites Danbury      $$
**30 Old Danbury Road**
**(203) 744-7333**
**www.springhillsuites.com**

SpringHill Suites Danbury is a four-story, all-suite property catering to those who are traveling on business, planning a long-term stay, or just looking for a little more elbow room. After a long day, guests can relax in the indoor swimming pool or work up a sweat in the fitness center. In-room amenities include voice mail, satellite television, coffeemakers, Internet access, desks, refrigerators, hair dryers, irons, and ironing boards. A complimentary continental breakfast is served each morning, and numerous restaurants and shops are located nearby.

## Super 8 Motel Danbury $
3 Lake Avenue Extension
(203) 743-0064
www.super8.com

One of Fairfield County's most affordable lodging options, this Super 8 provides no-nonsense accommodations and a convenient location off I-84 and close to numerous restaurants and the Danbury Fair Mall. Guests in the 80 guest rooms have access to free local calls, a free daily newspaper, interior corridors, and complimentary coffee and snacks. Members of the Super 8 VIP Club enjoy room discounts, express reservations and check-in, and the ability to pay room charges with a check.

## Wellesley Inn & Suites Danbury $$
116 Newtown Road
(203) 792-3800
www.wellesleyinnandsuites.com

Formerly known as the Ramada Inn Danbury, the Wellesley Inn's 181 guest rooms and suites are located in two different sections of the building on five floors. Smoking and nonsmoking rooms are available, as are wheelchair-accessible rooms, a 24-hour front desk, an indoor swimming pool, laundry facilities, and banquet rooms. Each room offers cable television with premium movie channels, video games, hair dryers, irons, and ironing boards. Located on the Bethel-Danbury border at exit 8, the Wellesley Inn is close to shopping centers, restaurants, and local corporations. The hotel's on-site Outback Steakhouse is very popular with locals and visitors alike; expect a wait on weekends.

---

**i**

*Many Fairfield County golf courses and parks are open only to members or town residents. Some accommodations provide temporary passes for guests; be sure to ask your innkeeper or hotel manager about these perks at check-in. Discount passes to local museums and other attractions are sometimes available as well.*

# Newtown

## Inn at Newtown $$
19 Main Street
(203) 270-1876
www.theinnatnewtown.com

Formerly known as the Mary Hawley Inn, this 1872 inn is located in the center of Newtown's Main Street historic district. Guests can choose one of three guest rooms: the Hawleyville Room, the Middlegate Room, or the Taunton Room. Each comes furnished with a four-poster bed and antiques. The inn is perhaps best known for its dining room, which also serves brunch on Sunday (see Restaurants for more information). The Tap Room and Proud Mary's lounge (see Nightlife for more information) are popular on weekends.

# Ridgefield

## Elms Inn $$$
500 Main Street
(203) 438-2541
www.elmsinn.com

Like other homes and buildings on Ridgefield's beautiful Main Street, the 1760s-era Elms Inn offers visitors a glimpse into New England's past. The 15 guest rooms and 5 suites vary in size and are decorated in a colonial style with four-poster beds, wallpaper, antique furnishings, and wall-to-wall carpeting. All rooms also have private baths, televisions, air-conditioning, and phones. An in-room continental breakfast is included in the rates. The on-site Elms Restaurant and Tavern (see Restaurants for more information) serves fine food and wines to guests and locals alike.

## Stone Ridge Manor $$
24 Old Wagon Road
(203) 431-8426
www.stoneridgemanor.net

This Tudor-style B&B is located within a stone manor, surrounded by woods and gardens. Guests can choose from one of two accommodations: The Victorian Suite has a queen-size bed, antique furnishings, beveled-glass mirrors, a sitting room, meadow views, and a private bath. The Sleigh Bed Room has a wooden sleigh bed, an Oriental rug, high-thread-count linens, down pillows, a private bath, robes, and slippers. The seasonal outdoor heated pool is next to a cabana and flowering trees, and the stonework in the breakfast room provides a sophisticated backdrop to the morning meal of breads, muffins, fruit salad, cereal, juice, and coffee.

**Stonehenge Inn and Restaurant  $$-$$$
U.S. Route 7
P.O. Box 667, Ridgefield 06877
(203) 438-6511
www.stonehengeinn-ct.com**
Set on 12 acres of forested land with a pond, Stonehenge Inn offers a personal touch in Fairfield County accommodations. The 16 rooms and suites are spread across the property in three buildings; amenities include four-poster beds, individualized decor, and wall-to-wall carpeting. Guests have their choice of a king-size bedroom, a four-postered master bedroom, or a king-size suite. Rates include a daily continental breakfast. Stonehenge is perhaps best known for its gourmet restaurant offering continental-French cuisine (see Restaurants), and the inn also frequently plays host to weddings, corporate retreats, and other special events.

**West Lane Inn              $$-$$$
22 West Lane
(203) 438-7323
www.westlaneinn.com**
Of the 14 smoking and nonsmoking guest rooms at West Lane Inn, two have fireplaces, two have kitchenettes, and one is actually a suite. Each has a four-poster bed (or two), cable television, voice mail, Internet access, a private bath, a hair dryer, and individual climate control. The inn fits right in with Ridgefield's historic and refined character. Built in 1849, the countrified home manages to be charming and cozy while offering all the modern conveniences for travelers. After you've

settled in, enjoy breakfast or coffee on the large front porch, or explore nearby walking trails, museums, and restaurants.

# Shelton

**Ramada Plaza Hotel Shelton    $-$$
780 Bridgeport Avenue
(203) 929-1500
www.ramada.com**
The Shelton Ramada has won numerous awards from its parent company, including Ramada of the Year, Ramada Food Service of the Year, and the second-place award for Outstanding Food Service. The on-site restaurant serves breakfast, lunch, and dinner. Other features include a lounge, an indoor heated swimming pool, business services, a fitness room and sauna, wake-up service, and 10 meeting rooms. The hotel's 155 guest rooms and suites have such extras as alarm clocks, coffeemakers, free newspapers, hair dryers, cable television, irons, and ironing boards. Refrigerators and microwaves are also available in some rooms. Pets are welcome guests with prior approval.

**Residence Inn by Marriott
Shelton                  $$-$$$
1001 Bridgeport Avenue
(203) 926-9000
www.marriott.com**
Designed for long-term stays, the Residence Inn offers studios and one- and two-bedroom suites. Each suite has a separate sitting and sleeping area and a full kitchen, as well as a work desk, satellite television, high-speed Internet access, voice mail, a hair dryer, an iron and ironing board, and a coffeemaker. Some rooms also have fireplaces. When it's time to wind down, guests can relax in the outdoor swimming pool and hot tub, take advantage of valet laundry services, flip through the complimentary daily newspaper, or enjoy the complimentary continental breakfast. Pets are allowed with additional fees and security deposits.

# RESTAURANTS

F airfield County offers the most interesting, diverse, and tempting selection of restaurants in Connecticut—or at least we county residents like to think so. From Thai to Spanish, French, and Italian, you can find it here. Many of the local establishments, particularly in the southern part of the county, seem to have borrowed a page from their nearby Manhattan neighbors, satisfying a demand for trendy interior design and cosmopolitan menus. That said, you can still find family-oriented, red-and-white-checkered-tablecloth spots where the tomato sauce is hearty and the kids can make as much noise as they want.

In general, pizza restaurants, delis, and Chinese take-out spots are plentiful in most towns and are not mentioned specifically here. Chain restaurants such as Bertucci's, Applebee's, Ruby Tuesday, Chili's, and Bennigan's are numerous in the more populated urban areas but somewhat hard to find in the inner suburbs. The same can be said for fast-food outlets.

This chapter highlights some of the better known and most popular eateries in the region: A few have been around for what seems like forever, while others are relative newcomers. Prices are as variable as the cuisine. In some areas it's easy to drop $200 on a dinner for two. But frugal diners shouldn't panic, because it's also easy to find a wonderful spot where you and three friends can enjoy a hearty meal for well under $50. Fairfield County restaurants have attitude, history, and a huge variety of offerings from border to border. Gourmands or other adventurous eaters won't want to limit themselves to their own town or even their own end of the county. You may have to travel a bit to find that great barbecue joint or an authentic French bistro, but your taste buds will thank you in the end.

## PRICE CODE

Hungry newcomers should note that few things change more rapidly in Fairfield County than the dining scene: Although the information in these listings was current at the time of this writing, restaurants tend to come and go (or simply change names and locations) with surprising speed. Prices and menu items change frequently as well. The following scale reflects the average cost of a dinner for two, not including appetizers, drinks, or desserts. Lunchtime meals are usually (but not always) significantly less expensive.

| | |
|---|---|
| $ | less than $20 |
| $$ | $20 to $40 |
| $$$ | $41 to $60 |
| $$$$ | $61 and higher |

## SOUTHERN FAIRFIELD COUNTY

## Bridgeport

**Black Rock Castle**        $-$$
**2895 Fairfield Avenue**
**(203) 336-9990**
Located in the hip Black Rock section of town, "the Castle" is an Irish-themed eatery that was built as a replica of a real castle of the same name on the River Less in Ireland. The menu offers traditional favorites like shepherd's pie, bangers and mash, and corned beef and cabbage, along with salads, soups, appetizers, and a variety of chicken, seafood, and steak dishes. You can also reserve rooms for private events, including baby showers and birthday parties. This place is hopping on the weekends. (For more information, see the listing in the Nightlife chapter.)

## Bloodroot $-$$
### 85 Ferris Street
### (203) 576-9168

For more than 25 years, this "feminist restaurant and bookstore" has been serving up homemade vegetarian fare to an appreciative clientele. On any given day, the blackboard lists a handful of main courses, salads, soups, and sandwiches—the list changes almost every day. Lunch choices often include omelettes, almond-butter-and-jelly sandwiches, marinated tofu, quiche, and house-made breads. At dinnertime you're likely to find gazpacho, Greek salads, enchiladas, and many dairy-free dessert choices. Enjoy your meal at the outdoor tables or in the indoor dining room, or place your order to go.

## Captain's Cove Seaport Restaurant $
### 1 Bostwick Avenue, Black Rock Harbor
### (203) 368-3710

The keyword is "casual" at this fun, kid-friendly spot located in the up-and-coming Captain's Cove Seaport. Open March through October, the restaurant can accommodate up to 400 people and offers a large, varied menu with burgers, hot dogs, sandwiches, seafood plates, soups, and daily specials. On a nice day, take your meal outdoors to linger in the deck seating area or on one of the boardwalk's benches. You can also make reservations for large parties, reserve the space for special events, and order anything on the menu as takeout.

## King & I $$
### 545 Broadbridge Road
### (203) 374-2081

Dig into hot and spicy Thai food at this cozy family restaurant located near the Trumbull line. The eatery serves both traditional and unusual Asian dishes, including *pad preow whan,* a sautéed shrimp dish with sweet-and-sour sauce, chicken, pork, pineapple, and ginger, and *tod mun,* a fish cake with curry paste, cucumber sauce, and beans. Certain dishes can be cooked either extra spicy or extra mild, depending on your level of bravery.

## Parc 1070 $-$$
### 1070 Main Street
### (203) 334-1234

Located within the Bridgeport Holiday Inn, Parc 1070 is a casual restaurant serving breakfast, lunch, and dinner. Diners will also find a "deli buffet" on the lunch menu on Monday, complete with hot pastrami, turkey, corned beef, ham, roast beef, and a variety of cheeses. At dinnertime expect a good selection of seafood, steak, and chicken dishes. The most popular meal here is breakfast (not so easy to find in Fairfield County), where the choices include omelettes, pancakes, sausage, bacon, fruit, toast, and other favorites.

## Vazzy's $$
### 513 Broadbridge Avenue
### (203) 371-8046

Specializing in "pan pasta" and brick-oven pizza, Vazzy's serves its pasta in the same sizzling pan it was cooked in. Concoctions include spaghetti with white clam sauce, cavatelli with broccoli and garlic, tortellini with chicken and pesto sauce, and the Vazzy's Special with penne, veggies, garlic, cheese, and either chicken or shrimp. The restaurant's 10-inch gourmet pizzas have topping like shrimp, clams, ricotta cheese, ham, onions, and even bacon and eggs. Steak, chicken, ravioli, and seafood dishes are also available, as is take-out service.

## Ye Olde Tollgate $$-$$$
### 360 Fairfield Avenue
### (203) 337-9944

Steak is the guest of honor at Ye Old Tollgate, a Fairfield Avenue restaurant that opened in 2000. Expect a sedate, mahogany, men's club–style atmosphere with a full bar. Dry-aged prime T-bones, porterhouses, and sirloin strips accompany such menu items as Caesar salad, grilled lobster tail, hash browns, roasted chicken, crabmeat cocktail, cheesecake with strawberries, pecan pie, and chocolate mousse. Lunch is served Monday through Friday; dinner is served every night of the week.

# Darien

**Centro Ristorante & Bar**      **$$**
**319 Post Road**
**(203) 655-4772**

Centro's claim to fame is its gourmet thin-crust pizza; some call it the best around. But there are also plenty of other northern Italian dishes on the menu, including capaccio, Shrimp Splendido, penne sabilla, seafood risotto, rigatoni alla vodka, lemon chicken, and linguine with clams. Salads, burgers, and soups also are plentiful. If you're short on time, the restaurant has preprepared meals to go: Just heat them up at home. You'll also find regular happy hours, a lunch menu, daily specials, and a wine and beer list. The restaurant also has two other locations in Greenwich and Fairfield.

**Chuck's Steak House**      **$$-$$$**
**1340 Post Road**
**(203) 655-2254**

The a la carte menu at Chuck's lists many of the beefy steaks you might expect, including filet mignon, prime rib, teriyaki or Cajun top sirloin, and barbecue ribs. But you'll also find pork chops, teriyaki and lemon-pepper chicken breast, swordfish, broiled scallops, king crab legs, and surf-and-turf combinations. All main courses come with unlimited trips to the soup-and-salad bar. The atmosphere at Chuck's is rowdy and fun; expect a considerable wait during peak hours, especially on Saturday night. The steak house also has another popular location in Danbury, near the Danbury Fair Mall.

**Coromandel Cuisine**      **$$**
**25 Old Kings Highway North**
**(203) 662-1213**

Located within the Goodwives Shopping Center, this Indian restaurant has sleek black furnishings and a cosmopolitan feel. Busy weekday workers can pick up a "lunch box" to go, packed complete with an entree, a vegetable, and rice. Sit-down diners will find a menu filled with choices like *nellure chapla koora* (fish curry with chili peppers and poppy seeds), *uppu kari* (lamb with shallots and garlic), *bhagara baingan* (spicy eggplant), *mirapakaya mamsam koora* (lamb with gravy and chili peppers), and more *kozhumbu* (okra and lentil dumplings).

**Giovanni's II**      **$$$-$$$$**
**2748 Post Road**
**(203) 325-9979**

Like its sister location in Stamford, Giovanni's II offers a plethora of steaks and seafood, served a la carte or as part of a "complete dinner." Those who opt for a dinner can choose an appetizer from a list that includes oysters, clams, fried mozzarella, French onion soup, and fried calamari. The lunch menu offers these as well as several salad specials, including calamari salad, spinach salad, and Caesar salad. Diners will also find specially designed menus on Valentine's Day, Mother's Day, New Year's Eve, and other holidays.

# Fairfield

**Antonio's**      **$$**
**284 Black Rock Turnpike**
**(203) 335-2329**

New Haven is famous for its coal-fired brick-oven pizza: thin and crispy with a slightly charred crust. Antonio's has brought that taste to Fairfield County, offering its own version of the much-loved pies along with fresh-baked breads and a wine bar. Other specialties of the house include littleneck clams over linguine, citrus salmon, pork chop pizziola, stuffed shells Florentine, and cavatelle Antonio. For starters try the Black Rock hot antipasto, bruschetta, clams casino, pasta fagioli soup, or insalata Tuscany.

**Archie Moore's**      **$-$$**
**48 Sanford Street**
**(203) 256-9295**

A favorite hangout for locals, Archie Moore's is open late and offers happy hours with a full menu throughout the week. If you're looking for something light, try a chef's salad, a sesame chicken salad, or the soup of the day served in a bread bowl. Or buckle down with Archie's nachos and buffalo wings, always a favorite. Sandwich selections include BLTs, the "pulled pig" sandwich, beer-battered chicken, grilled cheese, and the foot-long hot dog platter. This is a casual spot, so roll up your sleeves and enjoy.

### Centro Ristorante & Bar          $$
**1435 Post Road**
**(203) 255-1210**
This Centro location offers outdoor patio seating, a great location in bustling downtown Fairfield, and "to go" Italian meals that you can cook at home. For more information about the restaurant, see the Darien listing.

### Firehouse Deli          $
**22 Reef Road**
**(203) 255-5527**
The Firehouse Deli has the distinction of being a landmark as well as a great restaurant. It's located on the site of Fairfield's first firehouse, where the Hook and Ladder Company served the town until 1955. Today you can stop by to pick up breakfast or lunch, choosing from bagels, muffins, soups, quiche, salad plates, macaroni salad, coleslaw, desserts, and of course sandwiches. Some of the best-selling combinations are roast beef with Swiss cheese and Russian dressing, corned-beef and pastrami on rye, the veggie pita with sprouts and honey mustard, and roast beef with red peppers.

### La Colline Verte          $$$
**75 Hillside Road**
**(203) 256-9242**
Located in the Greenfield Hills district, La Colline Verte serves French specialties in a formal atmosphere. Dinner selections range from hors d'oeuvres like lobster bisque and puffed pastry with snails to such main courses as red snapper in a caramelized mango sauce, monkfish medallions with coconut milk and curry, beef tenderloin with béarnaise sauce, and braised pheasant in red wine. A lunch menu offers poached salmon fillet, sautéed sea scallops, beef tenderloin tips, and other midday options. And who can forget the desserts? Choices include praline-buttercream cake, soufflés, and chestnut mousse.

### Liana's Trattoria          $$-$$$
**591 Tunxis Hill Road**
**(203) 368-1235**
With fresh ingredients and a limited menu, Liana's serves up high-quality Italian favorites. Homemade gnocchi, ravioli, fettucine, and other pastas topped with a variety of sauces and vegetables are offered alongside soups, lasagna, eggplant parmigiana, and other meat, seafood, and chicken dishes. Some diners make a special trip here just for the decadent desserts and extensive wine list. The restaurant recently received a "face-lift" award from the local chamber of commerce.

### Paci          $$$
**96 Station Street**
**(203) 259-9600**
Housed in a restored railroad station terminal, Paci's atmosphere is as central to the dining experience as the food itself. The two-story Italian restaurant has a cathedral ceiling, curved wood beams, and a tucked-away location in the quaint Southport district. The menu changes seasonally, although you can expect to find dishes like pan-seared chicken with red and yellow peppers, pappardelle with broccoli rabe, ravioli di asparagi, sliced steak salad, Long Island breast of duck, and linguini with shrimp. Homemade desserts run the gamut from biscotti to cannoli, lemon tart, and pistachio ice cream.

### Pearl of Budapest          $$
**57 Unquowa Road**
**(203) 259-4777**
There aren't too many restaurants in Fairfield County (or in Connecticut, for that matter) where you can dine on Hungarian specialties while listening to live violin music. This is a unique spot serving authen-

tic, hard-to-find dishes like *hortobagyi palacsinta* (meat-filled pancakes), *lecso kolbasszal* (ratatouille with sausage, peppers, and onion), *cigany pecsenye* (pork with sausage and bacon), and *gundel tokany* (sautéed steak with beans, asparagus, and mushrooms). Cherry strudel, dessert pancakes, or Neapolitan ice cream make a nice ending to your meal.

### Rooster's                    $$
**1418 Post Road**
**(203) 254-2439**

Rise and shine for breakfast favorites at Rooster's, or sleep in and enjoy lunch or dinner. The restaurant specializes in "classic comfort foods," including New England pot roast, chicken potpie, New York sirloin, grilled tuna, chili casserole, meat loaf, and baked scrod. In keeping with the "comfort" theme, most dishes are served with either potatoes or vegetables. For larger groups, a banquet area known as "the Loft" is also available.

### Saint Tropez Bistro Francais    $$$
**52 Sanford Street**
**(203) 254-8209**
**www.saint-tropez-bistro.com**

Serving French-Mediterranean cuisine, Saint Tropez features the creation of chef Etienne Menozzi. The authentic dishes range from *magret de canard à l'orange* (duck served with orange sauce) to *lasagne aux fruits de mer sauce homardine* (pasta with seafood and lobster sauce) and *entrecôte au Roquefort* (grilled steak with blue cheese). Finish your meal with a crème brûlée, a sorbet, an espresso, or a cappuccino. The bistro is open for lunch Monday through Saturday and open for dinner nightly. The dining room can also be reserved for private celebrations and business gatherings.

### Sarabande              $$-$$$
**12 Unquowa Place**
**(203) 259-8084**

Although seafood is emphasized at this cozy restaurant, the menu also features a host of "land-based" staples. Try the omelettes, gourmet pizzas, soups, pastas, and meats on the lunch menu. Or sample such dinner entrees as sesame-crusted tuna, filet of sole, linguini with lobster, penne with chicken, New York strip steak, and pan-seared halibut. Linger over your meal in the indoor dining room or out on the patio seating area. If you'd like a glass of wine with dinner, the wine list has more than 65 options. Daily lunch and dinner specials are also available.

### Villa del Sol               $$
**1229 Post Road**
**(203) 254-0123**

What Mexican meal would be complete without Sloppy Nachos? Or maybe you'd rather start with the Mexican wings or the stuffed jalapeños. However you warm up your taste buds, you're sure to find something to keep the fire going when the main dishes arrive at Villa del Sol. Choices include vegetable burritos, pepitos steak sandwiches, chimichangas, fajitas, wraps, huevos rancheros, tacos, enchiladas, and other traditional dishes made with pork, beef, chicken, seafood, rice, and vegetables. The eatery also has a sister location in downtown Westport.

# Greenwich

### Abis                        $$
**381 Greenwich Avenue**
**(203) 862-9100**

Serving traditional Japanese cuisine, this restaurant is the heart of the action on Greenwich Avenue. Choose from soups, noodle dishes, sushi, sashimi, and seafood, including specialties such as *tako-su* (sliced octopus with vinegar sauce) and *hijiki* (cooked black seaweed), along with tamer selections like *hotategai yaki* (grilled scallops with teriyaki sauce) and chicken *katsu* (chicken cutlet with vegetables). Some dishes are designed to be big enough to share. Brunch is served on Sunday.

**Boxcar Cantina** $
**44 Old Field Point Road**
**(203) 661-4774**
**www.boxcarcantina.com**
This lighthearted Mexican eatery has lots to please both kids and adults, from the fun cowboy paraphernalia to the strong margaritas. At lunchtime feast on Tee Pee Nachos, Gringo Chile, Jack Cheddar Enchiladas, and the Boxcar Green Chile Cheeseburger Burrito, to name a few. The dinner menu features similar specialties, including Quatro Tacos, San Antonio Fajitas, Red Chili Onion Rings, Mexican Pizza, the Southwestern Chopped Salad, and "cowboy quenchers" like the Boxcar Sangria.

**Centro at the Mill** $$
**328 Pemberwick Road**
**(203) 531-5514**
The Greenwich Centro location offers the eatery's famous thin-crust pizzas, seasoned breadsticks, big salads, and hearty Italian dishes. But this popular spot also provides views of a waterfall and an outdoor patio for alfresco dining. For more information about Centro, see the Darien listing.

**Chola** $$-$$$
**107-109 Greenwich Avenue**
**(203) 869-0700**
Monday through Friday, busy executives can pick up a quick meal-to-go with one of Chola's popular "lunch boxes." On Sunday, however, diners can take it slow at the weekly Maharaja Buffet, where they'll find a tandoori stand, a chaat stand, udipi dishes, and Madras coffees. Some of Chola's specialty plates are *mirapakai kodi* (chicken with coconut, onions, and chili peppers), *paneer khurchan* (paneer cheese with onions, peppers, and tomato sauce), and *chingri malai* (shrimp with cumin seeds, ginger, and raisins).

**Figaro** $$-$$$
**372 Greenwich Avenue**
**(203) 622-0018**
This "everyday bistro" offers separate brunch, lunch, dinner, and children's menus with traditional favorites and unique creations. Dinner options range from pastas, salads, and pizzas to heartier entrees like steak, fish, and lamb. At lunchtime take your pick of sandwiches, burgers, pasta meals, grilled fish, and even filet mignon. The brunch menu, meanwhile, offers wonderful weekend fare like eggs Benedict and the Greenwich Breakfast. Larger parties of 20 to 90 people can reserve the patio, a separate dining area, or the whole restaurant for special events such as wedding showers or birthday parties.

**Hunan Gourmet** $$
**68 East Putnam Avenue**
**(203) 869-1940**
Asian cuisine is the specialty of Hunan Gourmet, where the menu changes every so often with new Thai, Szechuan, and Chinese specialties. Starters include satay beef, shiitake vegetable soup, steamed dumplings, and noodles with sesame hot sauce. Then move on to meat and seafood dishes such as Grand Marnier prawns, roast duck with baby bok choy, tangerine beef, Thai curry, and grilled sea bass with ginger. You'll also find a bar and lounge serving Asian beers, island-style drinks, and even green-tea ice cream.

**L'escale** $$$
**500 Steamboat Road**
**(203) 661-4600**
**www.lescalerestaurant.com**
Located on the water next to the new Delamar hotel, L'escale offers a menu and an ambience inspired by Provence. The Mediterranean flavors come through in the dinner, lunch, breakfast, and brunch menus, which feature such creations as traditional pisto soup, squid a la pancha, penne arrabiata, tarragon-crusted rack of lamb, pulled duck sandwich, garlic-cream linguini, banana pancakes, and brioche French toast. In the lounge, diners can enjoy unique drinks, a bar menu, and even full dinners, all while looking out over Long Island Sound.

# Down-home Diners

When you're craving pancakes, hash browns, and high-polished chrome, nothing will satisfy like a diner. Stamford alone is home to three: Curley's Diner (62 West Park Place, 203-348-2020); the Pinstripes Diner (954 East Main Street, 203-323-3176); and the Parkway Diner (1066 High Ridge Road, 203-329-9511). In other areas of the county, try one of these: the Westporter Diner in Norwalk (469 Westport Avenue, 203-847-4656); the New Englander Diner in Danbury (Ives Street, 203-744-1837); the recently renovated Orem's Diner in Wilton (209 Danbury Road, 203-762-7370); the '50s-style Blue Colony Diner in Newtown (Church Hill Road, 203-426-0745); and the Fairfield Diner in Fairfield (90 Kings Highway Cutoff, 203-335-4090).

## Luca's                          $$$-$$$$
### 35 Church Street
### (203) 869-4403

This hearty steak house will satisfy carnivores with generous portions of rib eye, sirloin, T-bone, filet mignon, and chateaubriand. But Luca's also provides plenty of menu variety for diners who aren't on the hunt, offering selections such as penne alla vodka, Caesar salad, clams casino, filet of sole, and chicken Francese. Parents will especially appreciate the children's menu, which offers dishes like the Tid Bit Plate, chicken fingers, and chopped sirloin.

## Mediterraneo                    $$$
### 366 Greenwich Avenue
### (203) 629-4747

Chefs Robert Bognar and Albert DeAngelis change their menu each season, always including a variety of appetizers, pasta dishes, meat and seafood entrees, and fresh sides like garlic mashed potatoes and grilled baby vegetables. You can almost always find a few gourmet pizzas, along with main courses such as wood-roasted halibut with orzo pasta, Maryland crab cakes with a sweet onion salad, and marinated lamb kabob with mint yogurt. Salads, oysters, mussels, and lobster bisque are likely appetizer offerings.

## Pasta Vera                      $-$$
### 48 Greenwich Avenue
### (203) 661-9705

Expecting guests? Pasta Vera specializes in creating complete Italian meals for takeout: Just stop by, browse the choices, and heat up your selections at home. And we're not talking about spaghetti and meatballs here: The huge variety of options includes antipasti, salads, gourmet pizzas, panini, and such dishes as *capellini al bosco, lasagna di verdure, pollo alla portobello, linguini con scampi, ravioli con spinachi,* and *cavitelli Bolognese.* No one will ever suspect you didn't slave away in the kitchen all day.

## Restaurant Jean-Louis           $$$$
### 61 Lewis Street
### (203) 622-8450
### www.restaurantjean-louis.com

This Greenwich staple has been serving fine French cuisine to locals and visitors for more than 18 years. The self-described "never pretentious" restaurant is run by Jean-Louis Gerin, a chef born in the French Alps who has apprenticed for some of the best-known chefs in his home country. The Monday-through-Friday lunch menu includes goujeonnette of cod and green apple sorbet. At dinnertime you'll find the menu filled with options such as seared sea scallops, Montauk striped bass, stuffed boneless quail, and filet mignon. Reservations are recommended.

**Terra**                            $$$
**156 Greenwich Avenue**
**(203) 629-5222**
Executive chef Albert DeAngelis (who also lends his talents to Mediterraneo, above) continues to please regulars at Terra with creative antipasti, salads, and main courses. For a lighter touch, choose one of the gourmet pizzas made with such toppings as asparagus, goat cheese, grilled eggplant, hot sausage, yellow tomatoes, and of course fresh mozzarella. Carnivores can opt instead for oven-roasted chicken, lobster, charred steak, striped bass, duck, salmon, and tuna.

**Thataway Cafe**                    $$
**409 Greenwich Avenue**
**(203) 622-0947**
**www.thatawaycafe.com**
This casual restaurant is a great lunch spot, serving plain-and-simple sandwiches, starters, and burgers, along with jazzed-up dinner entrees for later in the day. Choose from fun starters like nachos, fried calamari, buffalo wings, soups, and salads; then try the Whichaway Burger, the Sorry Charlie sandwich, the Avenue Sandwich, the Thataway Mixed Grill, and four varieties of fajitas. Dessert options include tempters like banana cream pie and Oreo tiramisu. Everything on the menu is available for takeout.

**Thomas Henkelmann**                $$$$
**420 Field Point Road**
**(203) 869-7500**
**www.thomashenkelmann.com**
Located within the Homestead Inn, Thomas Henkelmann is a gourmet restaurant named for its executive chef and proprietor. Hors d'oeuvres selections include mushroom ravioli with sweetbreads, sautéed shrimp with artichoke hearts, and

Hudson Valley duck foie gras. For an entree you might choose lamb wrapped in spinach and watercress, grilled salmon filet, filet mignon, or fricassee of Maine lobster. A sommelier can help you choose a wine from the extensive list available. For more information about the Homestead Inn, see the Accommodations chapter.

# New Canaan

**Bistro Bonne Nuit**                $$$
**12-14 Forest Street**
**(203) 966-5303**
Serving French and Italian dishes, this homey bistro was designed to mimic the warm eateries of Provence. Appetizers include French onion soup, escargot with mushrooms, and roast beef Napolean. For a main course you might choose chicken curry Le Cirque, steak frites, lamb shank, Provençale fish soup, grilled salmon St. Tropez, or lemon sole. But save room for dessert, including decadent options like bananas Foster, crème brûlée, and mousse au chocolat. The bistro is open for dinner Tuesday through Sunday nights; daily specials, a wine list, and takeout are also available.

**Ching's Table**                    $$-$$$
**64 Main Street**
**(203) 972-2830**
**www.chingsrestaurant.com**
Asian food aficionados throughout the area know about Ching's, a New Canaan eatery serving delicious Pan-Asian cuisine. At lunchtime, local businesspeople take a midday break to enjoy Thai spring rolls, lemongrass grilled shrimp salads, wok sesame chicken, glazed ginger beef, and sautéed mixed vegetables. At dinnertime, families and couples flock here for specialties like glazed ginger duck, pan-seared sesame tuna, grilled filet mignon with shrimp, pan-pan noodles, pan-seared scallops, grilled lemongrass shrimp, and Singapore rice noodles.

**Gates Restaurant & Bar**  $$
10 Forest Street
(203) 966-8666

With tile floors, leafy plants, and terra-cotta touches, Gates Restaurant & Bar has a distinctly Mediterranean feel. Dine inside or on the outdoor patio, or hang out at the bar while listening to live jazz on Friday and Saturday nights. The lunch and dinner menus include soups, omelettes, burgers, salads, sandwiches, sweet potato fries, and such entrees as shrimp stir-fry, glazed salmon, calamari fra diavolo, sesame-crusted mahimahi, sirloin steak, Maryland crab cakes, penne Toscana, St. Tropez chicken, and roasted chicken risotto. Reservations are recommended.

**Plum Tree**  $$
70 Main Street
(203) 966-8050

Located across from the New Canaan Town Hall, this longtime favorite brings the taste of Japan to Fairfield County. Hibachi pork, sirloin, sea scallops, and chicken are always popular, as is the restaurant's cooked and raw sushi, which is sold by the piece. Or take the road less traveled and choose sashimi, baby octopus, whole steamed soybeans, deep-fried tofu, broiled eel, chicken in chili sauce, Japanese pickles, a "Bento box," or wheat noodles sautéed with vegetables and pork.

**Roger Sherman Inn**  $$$$
195 Oenoke Ridge
(203) 966-4541
www.rogershermaninn.com

In addition to providing overnight lodging, the Roger Sherman Inn is also home to an elegant restaurant. Lunch, dinner, and Sunday brunch are all available, offering eggs Benedict with smoked salmon, grilled Black Angus steak, roasted rack of lamb, chateaubriand, vegetarian plates, mesclun and radiccio salad, lobster bisque, rosettes of smoked salmon, filet of trout, casserole of Maine mussels, and rainbow trout with green grapes. For more information about the Roger Sherman Inn, see the Accommodations chapter.

**Running Fish**  $$
62 Main Street
(203) 966-0101

As you might guess from the name, Running Fish provides local diners with a menu full of fresh seafood selections. Appetizers (or "Trawlers," as they're called here) include samplings of lobster crepe, crab cakes, and steamed mussels. When it's time for dinner, you can choose from imaginatively designed dishes filled with ingredients like shrimp, scallops, lobster, Chilean sea bass, asparagus, calamari, chicken, tuna, halibut, sirloin steak, pea pods, and spicy and sweet sauces. Lunch is served Monday through Friday; dinner is available Monday through Saturday.

**Sole Ristorante**  $$-$$$
105 Elm Street
(203) 972-8887

The imaginatively designed interior of Sole complements the fun menu: Diners can chose from gourmet pizzas, antipasti, and pasta dishes such as *mezzirigatoni* (half-rigatoni with red-pepper cream), *pappardelle al ragu* (portobello mushroom with ricotta and Bolognese sauce), and *capellini mare e monte* (angel hair pasta with lobster and vegetables). Meat- and seafood-eaters will also appreciate the *secondi piatti* dishes like stuffed shrimp, strip steak, roasted chicken, swordfish, soft-shell crab, salmon, and yellowfin tuna.

**Sushi 25**  $$
25 Elm Street
(203) 966-2338

Sushi 25 serves up a wide variety of a la carte sushi and sashimi rolls made with tuna, mackerel, eel, shrimp, striped bass, fluke, and many other seafaring species. Specialties of the house include the Lobster Tango Roll, the Sushi 25 Roll (shrimp tempura and mango), the Boston Roll (shrimp, cucumber, and spicy mayo), the Fujiamama Roll (pepper tuna and avocado), and the Tempura King Crab Roll. At lunchtime you can also choose from plates like broccoli with soy ginger sauce, miso soup, Hunan-style scallops and shrimp, and ginger duck.

## Tequila Mockingbird $$
### 6 Forest Street
### (203) 966-2222
This is a fun place for amigos to relax and enjoy authentic Mexican food all the way up here in New Canaan. Colorful murals, tablecloths, and wall hangings set the stage for the food, which includes favorites like tacos, enchiladas, fajitas, nachos, quesadillas, chimichangas, burritos, and combination plates that let you sample a few of each. And then, of course, there are the tequilas: Choose from Don Eduardo, Cabo Wabo, Casta, Cuervo, El Tesoro, Don Julio, Del Dueno, and numerous others.

## Thali Regional Cuisine of India $$-$$$
### 87 Main Street
### (203) 972-8332
### www.thali.com
You may want to start with the bread bar and a signature martini at Thali, an Indian restaurant with dramatic interior touches like a waterfall, colorful grain displays within the tabletops, ceiling speakers shaped like beehives, a copper bar, and custom-designed lighting. Appetizer favorites include ragda patties, kabab platters for two, and tawa crab; when it's time for dinner, choose from *gongura mamsam* (leg of lamb with chilis), *kori gassi* (Manglorian chicken curry in coconut), *tandoori phool* (cauliflower in marinade), *chingri malai korma* (shrimp in cream sauce flavored with cardamom), and other house dishes.

# Norwalk

## Adams Rib at the Norwalk Inn
## & Conference Center $$$
### 99 East Avenue
### (203) 838-5531
### www.norwalkinn.com
The Norwalk Inn & Conference Center is known for welcoming overnight guests (see

Accommodations for more information) as well as for filling their bellies at the down-home Adam's Rib restaurant. Sit-down lunch and dinner menus include poached salmon, filet mignon, shrimp brochette, filet of sole almondine, grilled chicken, and grilled swordfish. Or guests can choose the buffet, available for both lunch and dinner and featuring chicken scampi, honey-glazed ham, potatoes au gratin, zucchini Milan, baked lasagna, chicken Cordon Bleu, twice-baked potatoes, and other selections.

## Brewhouse Restaurant
## and Tasting Room $$
### 13 Marshall Street
### (203) 853-9110
Located in the heart of the action in SoNo, the Brewhouse is a laid-back spot with burgers, daily specials, a children's menu, and of course a great selection of beers. For more information about the Brewhouse's drinks and menu selections, see the Nightlife chapter.

## Dry Dock Cafe $
### 215 Main Street
### (203) 847-1333
### www.drydockcafe.com
Affordable and laid-back, the Dry Dock Cafe serves a wide variety of meals designed to please every member of the family. You might want to start with chili, fried potato skins, garlic bread, or French onion soup, and then share a thin-crust pizza topped with prosciutto, broccoli rabe, sausage, onions, or roasted peppers. Or sample a triple-decker cheeseburger club, a Tex Mex burger, a Cajun chicken sandwich, a BLT, a stromboli steak wedge, or a Philly cheesesteak sandwich. Dry Docks's homemade dessert offering include cheese cake with strawberries, apple crisp, and Mississippi mud pie.

## El Acapulco $-$$
### 84 Washington Street
### (203) 853-6217
This SoNo Mexican restaurant has a fairly large and casual dining room serving lots of combination plates with tamales, enchi-

ladas, burritos, tacos, flautas, fajitas, and other hot-and-spicy favorites. You'll also find lunch specials and a children's menu with chicken tenders, hot dogs, hamburgers, tacos, and enchiladas. El Acapulco is closed on Monday.

## Harbor Lights $$–$$$
### 82 Seaview Avenue
### (203) 866-3364

This casual waterfront restaurant has an understandable emphasis on seafood. Even during winter, diners can experience the beauty of Long Island Sound with enclosed "outdoor" seating that becomes truly alfresco in the summer months. You can also eat in the indoor dining areas, choosing from appetizers and entrees like escargot casserole, the Harbor Lights Fish Sandwich, swordfish picante, grilled shrimp kebab, baked phyllo Brie, Mediterranean sea bass, filet mignon, and tricolor fettucine. The eatery also offers a raw bar with clams, oysters, and shrimp.

## Lime Restaurant $
### 168 Main Avenue
### (203) 846-9240

This mecca for vegetarians is a low-key spot with outdoor seating, takeout, and catering services available. Open seven days a week, the Lime provides nonmeat specialties such as black-bean chili, veggie loaf, soy and veggie burgers, pita sandwiches, a variety of burritos, breads, hot and cold drinks, desserts, and plenty of salad selections. Many of the sandwiches, salads, and hot meals use organic ingredients, and all are made fresh on-site. A few nonvegetarian options are offered as well, including chicken and fish.

## Match $$–$$$
### 98 Washington Street
### (203) 852-1088

Best known for its thin-crust, wood-fired-oven pizzas, Match has a busy lunchtime scene as well as lively crowds in the evening. For more information about Match, see the Nightlife chapter.

## Meigas Restaurant $$$
### 10 Wall Street
### (203) 866-8800
### www.meigasrestaurant.com

Chef Ignacio Blanco opened this Spanish eatery (formerly the site of Meson Galicia) in 2002. Diners can expect a formal atmosphere, complete with a bow-tied waitstaff, white tablecloths, and an extensive wine list. First courses include *ensalata de pato* (duck confit salad), *pulpo* (grilled octopus), and *mojama* (cured tuna). For the second course, choose from such plates as *vieras* (sautéed sea scallops), *pato* (grilled duck breast), *codorniz* (stuffed quail), *pollo* (stuffed free-range chicken), and *fletan* (baked halibut).

## Milano Restaurant $$
### 58-60 North Main Street
### (203) 852-7089
### www.milanosono.com

There are few better places for date night than Milano, which is located steps away from the local movie theater in downtown SoNo. You and your sweetheart can choose from authentic Italian specialties like *penne trussardi* (sautéed pasta with sausage and shallots), *bistecca trevisana* (marinated steak with herbs and olive oil), *antipasto Milano* (prosciutto, mushrooms, eggplant, and cheese), and *tortelloni zegna* (meat-filled tortelloni in cream sauce). If you still have room, linger over a sweet ending like *torta di ricotta* (cheesecake), *caramello della casa* (crème caramel), *tiramisu,* or *tartufo.*

## Papaya Thai $$
### 24 Marshall Street
### (203) 866-THAI

Papaya, a Thai and Asian barbecue restaurant, is bringing a bit of spice to SoNo. Not for the faint of taste buds, the eatery spares no seasoning in creative dishes like ginger lamb, panang curry chicken, fire-fried rice, Thai spicy beef, daredevil barbecue, and Bangkok basil boar. A variety of sushi rolls are also offered, along with a la carte barbecue tidbits such as squid, eggplant, gingko nut, and quail eggs. Can't decide? The sampler plates do all the hard work for you.

## Pasta Nostra $$-$$$
**116 Washington Street**
**(203) 854-9700**
The wine list changes monthly at this Italian eatery, which has been featured on the *Martha Stewart Living* television show. The main attraction here for gourmands is the wide selection of homemade pastas, topped with a variety of sauces, meats, and vegetables. Antipasti, salads, and chicken and meat entrees are also available. The restaurant is open Wednesday, Thursday, Friday, and Saturday nights only. Reservations are recommended.

## Porterhouse $$$-$$$$
**124 Washington Street**
**(203) 855-0441**
**www.porterhouserestaurant.com**
Of course the key item on this restaurant's menu is the porterhouse steak, served with potato, vegetable, and your choice of sauces. But you can also enjoy filet mignon, T-bone, and rib-eye steaks cooked to your liking. Not in a red-meat mood? Try the oven-roasted salmon, sesame-crusted seared tuna, or even a pineapple-crusted rack of wild boar. The SoNo eatery also offers a "raw and claw" bar and a good selection of appetizers, salads, and desserts. The wine list provides more than 175 choices.

## Rattlesnake Venom and Grub $-$$
**2 South Main Street**
**(203) 852-1716**
The Rattlesnake recently moved about a block away from its former Washington Street location to its new digs on South Main Street; luckily, the fun atmosphere and spicy food are still the same. Choose from such crowd-pleasing favorites as buffalo wings, red-hot chili poppers, chicken sandwiches, grilled skewers, tostada salsa, burritos, and Key lime pie. A children's menu and a wide selection of beers are also available.

## Restaurant at Rowayton Seafood $$
**89 Rowayton Avenue**
**(203) 866-4488**
Tucked away in the quaint district of Rowayton, this bustling eatery is located next to the equally busy seafood market of the same name. Drive in or float in; the waterfront location makes it easy for landlubbers and boaters alike. The prime seating is located out on the deck, but you can also enjoy your meal in the cozy interior dining room. The menu offers catch-of-the-day selections like Atlantic salmon, lobster, grilled mahimahi, fried calamari, New England clam chowder, Maine steamers, and linguini with clams. This place is popular, especially in summer: Reservations are recommended.

## Silvermine Tavern $$$
**194 Perry Avenue**
**(203) 847-4558**
Located in the charming Silvermine district on the Norwalk–New Canaan line, the Silvermine Tavern leads the pack when it comes to ambience. Whether you eat in the historic dining room or out on the patio overlooking the waterfall, you're sure to have a memorable meal. Try an appetizer like mushroom ravioli, roasted-walnut salad, or skewered sea scallops, and then move on to main courses such as seafood capellini, filet mignon, New England chicken potpie, or cheese-stuffed chicken breast. The photogenic restaurant is also a popular site for weddings and other special occasions. (See the Accommodations chapter for more information on the tavern's lodging facilities.)

## SoNo Seaport Seafood $$
**100 Water Street**
**(203) 854-9483**
Located right on the water, SoNo Seaport has some of the best views in town, a fish market, a bar, and a full menu of appetizers, soups, and seafood specialties. Try the bay scallops, king crab legs, Maine lobster, grilled swordfish, tuna salad, fisherman's platter, calamari, or clam strips. "Landlubber" choices include chili dogs,

barbecued chicken, cheeseburger platters, and fried-chicken sandwiches. Daily specials, a raw bar, desserts, and a children's menu are also available.

### Sunset Grille     $$
### 52 Calf Pasture Beach Road
### (203) 866-4177

The food at this East Norwalk grille, located in the Cove Marina, doesn't fit easily into any one category: Expect to find a bit of Italian, Asian, Spanish, and even American Southwestern tastes in the dishes. The dinner menu provides such choices as scallops *pomodoro,* lobster sauté, baby-back ribs, fried shrimp, and *zuppa di pesce* for two. Lunch offerings include burgers, fried clams, vegetable sandwiches, tortilla wraps, salads, and steamers. There's even a separate bar menu with smaller portions and appetizers.

### Tuscan Oven     $$$
### 544 Main Avenue
### (203) 846-4600
### www.tuscanoven.com

Choose from brunch, lunch, and dinner menus at this Norwalk trattoria offering a taste of Italy. In addition to antipasti and salads, dinner selections also include gourmet pizzas, *linguini alle vongole* (pasta with clams and olive oil), *filetto di Manzo all agro* (beef tenderloin in port wine sauce), and *spaghetti ai frutti di mare* (pasta with seafood). At lunch you'll find similar salads and hearty dishes, as well as panini sandwiches made with such ingredients as chicken, peppers, mozzarella, tomato, and basil pesto. The restaurant has another location in nearby Mount Kisco, New York.

# Stamford

### Brock's Restaurant     $$
### 1209 High Ridge Road
### (203) 357-1679

Brock's is best known for its huge salad bar, which includes more than 100 fixings for green salads, pasta salads, fruit salads, and tacos. A Sunday brunch buffet continues the tradition with countless pastries, eggs, waffles, bacon, seafood, ham, potatoes, pancakes, and other midday favorites. The regular lunch and dinner menus feature items such as chowder, onion rings, barbecued chicken, baked sea scallops, sandwiches, burgers, baby-back ribs, beef stew, corned beef and cabbage, and sweets on a dessert tray. Wines by the glass and beers on tap are also available.

### Cafe Tango     $
### 105 Broad Street
### (203) 967-0089
### www.cafetango.net

The emphasis at Cafe Tango is on gourmet coffee and loose teas; visitors can also munch on quiche, salads, soups, and house-baked pastries and other desserts. All coffees served at the environmentally friendly cafe are certified as fair trade, bird friendly, organic, or shade-grown. In addition, a portion of the company's profits will benefit impoverished people in coffee-producing countries.

### Giovanni's     $$$-$$$$
### 1297 Long Ridge Road
### (203) 322-8870
### www.giovannis.com

This self-proclaimed "serious steakhouse" offers lunch and catering menus in addition to its standard dinner menus. If you're stopping by at dinnertime, expect to find an a la carte selection of steaks, chops, seafood, and chicken courses, along with side dishes, salads, and appetizers. Or choose the "complete dinner" option—select one of 10 appetizers, one entree (such as surf-and-turf, lamb chops, or lobster tail), and a dessert. Kids have their own menu at Giovanni's.

### Grand     $$-$$$$
### 15 Bank Street
### (203) 323-3232
### www.stamfordgrand.com

Brooding, contemporary, and sleek, Grand puts a spin on traditional favorites and gives them attitude. Macaroni and cheese becomes Mac and Cheese with Truffles and Gruyere. Fettucine becomes Lobster Fettucine with Pancetta and Petite Peas. Pizza becomes Tuna Pizza with Miso and Wasabi Cream. Diners choose from "Little Plates," "Big Plates," and "Bar Plates" in a bilevel space with unisex bathrooms, steel and fiberglass walls, and a lounge with couches that overlooks the downtown area. After dinner, sip a cappuccino or espresso while you enjoy fruit salad, chocolate fondue, or apple tarte tatin.

## Il Falco Ristorante $$$
### Broad Street
### (203) 327-0002
### www.ilfalco.com

The wine list at Il Falco offers more than 1,700 choices. The menu selection is not quite that extensive, but it does offer antipasti, soups, salads, and dishes like *tortellini alla Bolognese,* fettucine Alfredo, risotto with mushrooms, *pollo vigneto* (chicken with champagne), red snapper alla Siciliana, *filetto di centro ai ferri* (broiled filet mignon), and *medaglioni al Barolo* (beef with wine and mushrooms). The lunch menu includes lighter portions of similar beef, pasta, and seafood dishes, along with salads and soups.

## Kotobuki $$
### 457 Summer Street
### (203) 359-4747

Have a yen for Japanese cuisine? Kotobuki can scratch that itch with lunch and dinner menus filled with specialties from the island nation. Perhaps you're in the mood to pick and choose items from the a la carte sushi bar. Or maybe you're looking for something along the lines of steamed salmon, pork in ginger sauce, a vegetable sauté, barbecued eel, shrimp tempura, or swordfish teriyaki. For an appetizer, try a bowl of miso asari soup or seaweed salad.

## Long Ridge Tavern $$$
### 2635 Long Ridge Road
### (203) 329-7818

The menu changes seasonally at the Long Ridge Tavern, a restaurant with a bar, a terrace, and four dining rooms: the Palmer, the Tavern, the Hunt, and the Nutmeg. Each room can seat 40 to 80 people and can be reserved for special occasions such as baby showers, rehearsal dinners, and bar/bat mitzvahs. Menu options run the gamut from quiche and burgers to pot roast, pan-roasted salmon, chicken potpie, grilled veggie wraps, filet mignon, sea scallops, and mesquite-smoked duck.

## Luna Rossa $$
### 2107 Summer Street
### (203) 358-9590

On any given night, there are eight or so varieties of antipasti available at this Summer Street restaurant and pizzeria: That should give you an idea of the wide selection of main courses available. Carnivores can sink their teeth into garlic-crusted filet mignon or aged rib-eye steak. Other entree options include chicken piccata, zuppa di pesce, fettucine Alfredo, salmon, and swordfish piccata. Or try one of the brick-oven pizzas, including Neapolitan, Baby Eggplant, Funghi, and Puttanesca.

## Morton's of Chicago $$$-$$$$
### 377 North State Street
### (203) 324-3939

Founded in the Windy City, the Morton's steak house empire is known for its "men's club" atmosphere and carnivore-pleasing menu choices. The Stamford location (the only one in Connecticut) is no exception: The "boardrooms" and main dining areas are furnished with Oriental rugs, mahogany woodwork, leather booths, glass partitions, and white tablecloths. The waitstaff presents menu items at your table to help you decide among filet Oskar, Cajun rib-eye steak, porterhouse, veal chops, New York strip steak au poivre, crab cakes, lobster, broiled salmon, prime rib, and lamb chops.

## Myrna's Mediterranean Bistro $-$$
### 866 East Main Street
### (203) 325-8736

Eat in, take out, or enjoy free delivery at Myrna's, a pizzeria and bistro on U.S.

Route 1. For the lighter appetite, the restaurant offers tuna salad, pita sandwiches, the "chicken delight" baguette, falafel, and shrimp salad, among others. Entrees range from a three-skewer mixed grill to whole- and half-rotisserie chicken, oven-baked kibbe, and stewed chicken with rice. Pizza toppings include veggies, ricotta cheese, roasted peppers, sun-dried tomatoes, and bacon.

**Quattro Pazzi**                    $$-$$$
**245 Hope Street**
**(203) 964-1801**
Pasta is the unapologetic focus at this popular Italian restaurant, where starters, entrees, and desserts are all generously proportioned. You can order whole or half portions of appetizers like *antipasto caldo misto* (with shrimp, mushrooms and clams), *portobello grigliato* (with mushrooms, cheese, and prosciutto), and *capellini poverino* (with goat cheese, olives, and capers). Moving on to main courses, options include *linguini con broccolini,* grilled lamb chops with vegetables and sausage, and other meat, pasta, and seafood dishes. Diners can eat indoors or out on the patio.

**Sandwich Maestro**                    $
**90 Atlantic Street**
**(203) 325-0802**
**www.sandwichmaestro.com**
Billing itself as "a true gourmet sandwich shop," the Sandwich Maestro specializes in delivering trays and platters to local businesses during the week. Breakfast items, salads, chili, quiche, and individual sandwiches are also available. Some favorites include the Mostly Mozart-rella (cheese with eggplant, peppers, and alfalfa sprouts), Ozawa's Surprise (a "meatless meat loaf" sandwich), Chicken Litton (chicken, cheddar, and peppers), Levi's Lox (smoked salmon on a bagel with cream cheese and eggs), and Le Boulez (eggplant, zucchini, squash, and Brie on a baguette).

**Telluride**                    $$-$$$$
**245 Bedford Street**
**(203) 357-7679**
**www.telluriderestaurant.com**
As the name implies, Telluride is designed to give diners a rustic lodgelike experience with rough-hewn furniture, candles, and eclectic wall hangings. But the food is anything but backcountry: Artistic dishes blend ingredients like eggplant chutney, calamari, ahi tuna, bok choy, and seviche to form colorful, unique appetizers and main courses. At lunchtime a variety of seafood, beef, and vegetable sandwiches are available, along with gourmet pizzas. At dinner choose from pasta, pork, steak, salad, and beef creations, including the Four Corners Burger, Ravioli Canyon de Chelly, and Cowboy Empanadas.

# Stratford

**Allen's East**                    $$
**60 Beach Drive**
**(203) 378-0556**
Casseroles are a specialty at Allen's, where diners can choose from lobster Newburg, shrimp and broccoli, shrimp Creole, seafood fra diavolo with pasta, and other casserole combinations. The seafood restaurant also offers broiled swordfish, fried clam strips, soft-shell crabs, New York sirloin steak, surf-and-turf plates, and fried seafood platters. Lobsters and king crab legs are also available. A good selection of salads, soups, and hot and cold appetizers round out the menu.

**Augustyn's Blue Goose**
**Restaurant**                    $$-$$$
**326 Ferry Boulevard**
**(203) 375-9130**
The Blue Goose welcomes large parties (up to 100 people) for special occasions like rehearsal dinners, baby showers, and even small weddings. Or just come with a few friends to enjoy American and Italian specialties. The dining room menu offers soups, appetizers, and several pasta

dishes, along with such entrees as filet of salmon, the broiled seafood platter, rack of lamb, pork chops, and Boston scrod. A children's menu lets the kids dig into chicken fingers, burgers, and other treats.

### Marbella Restaurant and Tapas Bar   $$
### 1479 Barnum Avenue
### (203) 378-6702

This bright and sunny eatery serves Spanish dishes in an airy dining room with sconces, wood furniture, and a pastel-toned decor. You and your friends can order several plates of tapas to share, including *gambas al ajillo* (shrimp with garlic sauce), *calamares fritos* (fried calamari), and *samburinas con pochas* (scallops with beans). Or dig into Mediterranean specialties on the lunch and dinner menus, such as pork medallion with spinach, pan-seared chicken breast, fettucini with spinach, saffron crepes, roasted pork loin, paella, shrimp with scallops and squid, and grilled rib-eye steak.

### Plouf! Le Bistro de la Mer   $$-$$$
### 14 Beach Drive
### (203) 386-1477

Funky and fun, this bistro has multicolored walls, a checkerboard floor, and great views of Long Island Sound. The cuisine is French, with special attention to seafood. Oysters, mesclun salad, sea scallops, or fish soup might start your meal. Entree choices include *moules frites a la Bruxelloise* (steamed mussel casserole), *onglet Marchand de vin* (steak with red wine sauce), *soufflé au fromage* (cheese soufflé), and *fillet de saunon en croute* (filet of salmon in puff pastry). Sorbets, vanilla ice cream with pear, crème caramel, and peach melba make for nice endings.

### Seascape Restaurant   $$
### 14 Beach Drive
### (203) 375-2149

Locals love this cozy restaurant with water views from nearly every table. The menu includes selections for vegetarians as well as meat- and seafood-eaters. You might want to start with Seascape's Gorgonzola

bread, red pepper Parmesan toast, or shrimp cocktail. The main courses range from sautéed sole to chicken Marsala, pan-fried striped bass, pistachio-crusted red snapper, and marinated pork chops. Pasta options abound as well, including angel hair pescatore and lobster ravioli. On Sunday diners can also enjoy brunch with live jazz music.

# Trumbull

### Gratzi   $$
### 180 Hawley Lane
### (203) 378-1400

Located inside the Marriott Merritt Parkway, this restaurant caters to business travelers and local families with upscale pasta and seafood dishes. Along with standbys like chicken parmigiana and New York sirloin, you'll also find more unusual selections, such as cinnamon-chili-rubbed chicken, *penne ambrosianna,* sesame-soy tuna, and *calamari fritti.* Diners can also opt to start their meal with chowder, Caesar salad, or onion soup.

### Marisa's Ristorante & Lounge   $$
### 6540 Main Street
### (203) 459-4225

Recently renovated, Marisa's offers an indoor dining room with a grand piano, an outdoor patio seating area, a bar, and a menu full of Italian specialties. Start with an antipasto, a tomato and mozzarella salad, or hot slices of garlic bread, and then move on to favorites like filet mignon, oysters on the half shell, linguini primavera, shrimp Napoletano, lasagna, *zuppa di pesce,* chicken provolone, grilled calamari, or a 32-ounce porterhouse steak. Desserts run the gamut from tiramisu to cheesecake.

### Olde Towne Restaurant   $$
### 60 Quality Street
### (203) 261-9436

Old Towne's extensive menu is sure to make even the pickiest diner happy, whether you're looking for a simple roast beef grinder, a hot plate of chicken

Marsala, a burger, or even a seafood supper like shrimp fra diavolo. The chef's soup changes daily; you can also order traditional or specialty pizzas along with calzones, club sandwiches, salads, and antipasto. The restaurant is located in the large Stop & Shop Plaza across the street from the Trumbull Public Library.

# Weston

### Cobb's Mill Inn                                    $$$
**12 Old Mill Road**
**(203) 227-7221**
One of Fairfield County's most scenic spots, Cobb's Mill Inn sits beside a waterfall in a restored, pre–Revolutionary War mill building. The restaurant in its present form has been serving hungry diners for more than 80 years. Each of the nine dining rooms is awash with history and ambience, offering hardwood floors, antique furnishings, open-beam ceilings, white tablecloths, and lace curtains. Lunch, dinner, and Sunday brunch are all available, complete with dishes like crackling calamari salad, baked-onion soup, Chilean sea bass, roasted Amish chicken, steak frites, duck a l'orange, shiitake mushroom omelettes, filet mignon, oysters Rockefeller, Belgian waffles, and seafood crepes.

# Westport

### Acqua                                    $$-$$$
**43 Main Street**
**(203) 222-8899**
The menu at this chic eatery changes with every season, but you can expect to find dishes made with fresh produce, hearty fishes and meats, and colorful garnish. Main courses might include fish salad, seafood ravioli, veal chops, pasta tossed with chicken and tomatoes, Black Angus steak, and seared salmon. Gourmet pizzas made with ingredients like arugula, yellow tomato sauce, fresh basil, and green peppers are another specialty of the house.

### Black Duck Cafe                                    $
**605 Riverside Avenue**
**(203) 227-7978**
An affordable, family-friendly spot, the Black Duck offers fun meals like the Triple "Ducker" Sandwich, Doctor Proctor's Bleu Cheeseburger, Southern Fried "Duck" Fingers, and a meat platter known as Here's the Beef. The kids will love the special children's menu and hot dog cart; adults will appreciate the daily specials, New England clam chowder, Cajun popcorn shrimp, clams on the half shell, and French onion soup. The restaurant also serves up more than 12 kinds of burgers.

### Bombay                                    $$
**616 Post Road East**
**(203) 226-0211**
Bombay has a full bar, daily specials, a banquet room, smoking and nonsmoking areas, live sitar music every Tuesday night, and of course plenty of tasty Indian food on lunch and dinner menus. Choose from a wide selection of dishes made with *murg* (chicken), *gosht* (lamb), *samunder* (seafood), *sabzi ke bagh se* (vegetables), *chawal* (rice), and *thokri* (Indian breads). During the week you can also pick up a lunch box prepacked with tandoori chicken, chicken curry, lamb curry, or a vegetarian selection.

### Bridge Cafe                                    $$$
**5 Riverside Avenue**
**(203) 226-4800**
This downtown eatery is located directly on the river, providing great views of the water and the bridge. Some portions of the menu change seasonally, while other specialties of the house remain constant throughout the year. Salads, including the Bridge Salad with arugula, avocado, and endive, are popular at lunchtime. Entrees are heavily seafood based, with options such as grilled halibut with fava bean puree, sea scallops with potato puree, pan-seared tuna with cucumber salad, miso barbecued salmon with eggplant relish, organic chicken breast with roasted potatoes, and pistachio-crusted rack of lamb.

# The Scoop on Ice Cream

Few local ice-cream shops are better known or better loved than Dr. Mike's in downtown Bethel (158 Greenwood Avenue, 203-792-4388) and Monroe (444 Main Street, 203-452-0499). Suffice to say, you'll want to leave your diet at home. Marcus Dairy Bar in Danbury (5 Sugar Hollow Road, 203-748-5611) is another local favorite: In addition to providing home-delivery of its milk products, the dairy draws crowds with its ice-cream flavors like black raspberry, coconut-almond bar, cookie dough, and butter pecan. Motorcycle enthusiasts have also made Marcus a popular site for rallies and other gatherings. Timothy's Ice Cream in Bridgeport (2974 Fairfield Avenue, 203-366-7496), serving up generous cones and sundaes, is yet another spot that's sure to be lively on hot summer evenings.

### Chef's Table $
**44 Church Lane**
**(203) 226-3663**
A favorite stop for lunch, the Chef's Table offers a huge variety of freshly made soups. The soups (including vegetarian, beef, and chicken varieties) change each day, so just wander up to the self-serve containers and spoon out your favorite. The eatery also serves up hot daily entrees, side dishes, burritos, gourmet wraps, and sandwiches on a variety of breads. Choose a premade version, or order your own unique concoction at the deli counter. Chips, sweets, and cold drinks are also available. After you enjoy your meal, walk a block to window-shop downtown.

### Conte's Fish Market and Grill $$$
**540 Riverside Avenue**
**(203) 226-3474**
Even though Fairfield County is located along Long Island Sound, the seashore too often feels far away. Conte's captures the maritime essence of its locale with a bustling fish market and seafood restaurant serving delicacies primarily found in the water. The lunch menu features light fare like popcorn shrimp, seafood salads, crab sandwiches, and lobster rolls. At dinnertime start with a lobster bisque and move on to steamed mussels, clams casino, teriyaki-style pork chops, lemon chicken, steamed Nova Scotia lobster, red snapper filet, and other dishes.

### Mario's Place $$
**36 Railroad Place**
**(203) 226-0308**
The service is fast, and the food is hearty. At Mario's you won't find anything fancy, but you will find old-fashioned Italian-American dishes that keep the regulars coming back for more. Pasta options include baked ziti, spinach tortellini, fetuccini Alfredo, and plain-and-simple spaghetti and meatballs. Or choose prime rib, baked haddock, broiled lamb chops, or shrimp scampi. Garlic bread can start your meal; a dish of caramel custard or spumoni can add the finishing touches.

### Peppermill $$-$$$
**1700 Post Road East**
**(203) 259-8155**
This local favorite has been filling hungry bellies in Westport for more than 30 years. An "all you can eat" soup and salad bar accompanies burgers, cobb salads,

fish-and-chips, steak sandwiches, and onion rings at lunchtime. When dinner rolls around, choose from menu items like prime rib, New York strip, seafood bisque, lobster, and such kid-friendly options as chicken fingers and ground sirloin. The Sunday brunch buffet offers fish, pasta, chicken, eggs Benedict, home fries, rice, beef, seafood, and other choices. Diners can eat inside or outside (seasonally) and enjoy a wine list and take-out services.

### Red Barn Restaurant $$–$$$
### 292 Wilton Road
### (203) 222-9549
### www.redbarnrestaurant.com

This historic Westport eatery has six dining rooms, four working fireplaces, outdoor seating on the patio, and lunch and dinner offerings like pork, chicken, swordfish, lobster tails, pasta, lamb chops, sandwiches, potpie, soups, and salads. Friday night diners will also find a seafood buffet with desserts, salads, and more than 20 dishes from the sea. Sunday brunch, served during two seatings at 11:30 A.M. and 1:30 P.M., includes roast beef, bagels with lox and cream cheese, shrimp cocktail, Belgian waffles, fruit, salad, baked ham, and home fries. A children's menu is also available.

### Sakura $$
### 680 Post Road East
### (203) 222-0802

One of Westport's most popular restaurants, Sakura offers an a la carte menu with tuna, sea urchin, salmon, mackerel, tofu, and yellowtail sushi and sashimi. If you'd prefer to order a whole dinner, try the mix-and-match sushi bar dinners that include three to nine pieces each. Teriyaki, katsu, and tempura bento dinners are also available, as are hot and cold appetizers. You can have your meal prepared at your table, hibachi style, and choose from the main dining room, private tatami rooms, or the outdoor dining patio.

### Seminara's Ristorante Italiano $$–$$$
### 256 Post Road East
### (203) 222-0188

Seminara's follows the Italian tradition of "primo" and "secondo" courses, each more filling and hearty than the last. Antipasto choices include pan-roasted sea scallops and Sicilian-style rice balls stuffed with cheese. Then move on to main dishes: clams with sausage and white wine; fusilli pasta with chicken, mushrooms, and garlic; roasted breast of duck; gourmet pizza; penne with spinach and mozzarella; sesame-and-almond-crusted tuna; or rib-eye steak with garlic and olives, to name a few. Lunch and pretheater menus are also available, as is an extensive wine and beer selection.

### Splash Pacific Rim Grill $$–$$$
### 260 Compo Road South
### (203) 226-3316
### www.innatlongshore.com

Offering one of the best locations in town, this fun restaurant and bar is located directly on the water and beside the golf course at the Inn at Longshore. The best seat in the house is on the patio deck, where locals gather for alfresco dining at lunch and dinner. The family-style entrees include sushi, chicken with mushrooms and chili peppers, gazpacho, ahi tuna, Peking duck, and spicy coconut shrimp. A full bar is also available, as are towering desserts. (For more information about the inn, see Accommodations.)

### Taipan $$
### 376 Post Road East
### (203) 227-7400

Tucked away in an anonymous strip plaza, this Pan-Asian restaurant seems unassuming enough. But step inside and you'll be transported to a carefully designed dining experience complete with crinkled-tin divider walls, recessed colored lighting, and a seating area that sits atop a huge koi pond. Outdoor seating is also available during the warmer seasons. The menu includes spicy, colorful dishes that complement the tropical design, as well as milder favorites like lo mein and fried rice.

**Tavern on Main** $$-$$$
**146 Main Street**
**(203) 221-7222**
**www.tavernonmain.com**
Tavern on Main, located in the heart of downtown, is one of Westport's anchor restaurants. A place to see and be seen, the tavern resides in an early 1800s-era colonial home and boasts three fireplaces, beamed ceilings, and a large outdoor terrace with plenty of seating. At lunchtime you might find dishes such as eggs Benedict, Connecticut cobb salad, wild mushroom ravioli, and a smoked barbecue-beef sandwich. For dinner try potato-wrapped sea bass, vegetable-and-polenta lasagna, and the "simply grilled" fish of the day. Drink selections include champagne, whites, reds, and Chardonnay.

**Tengda Asian Bistro** $$
**1330 Post Road East**
**(203) 255-6115**
If you want something light, Tengda can satisfy with curried coconut shrimp soup, calamari salad, spring rolls, satay tofu, and edamame. Or choose a Japanese "lunch box" with ingredients like shrimp, salmon, chicken, and eel. Sushi and sashimi—including sea urchin, salmon roe, octopus, squid, white tuna, and striped bass—are also available by the piece. Those with heartier appetites can choose from such main dishes as Tengda curried hot pot, Thai red snapper, Asian spiced breast of duck, horseradish-encrusted pork tenderloin, and spicy mango chicken.

**Three Bears Restaurant** $$-$$$
**Route 33**
**(203) 227-7219**
Some sections of the Three Bears' historic building are more than 200 years old; it is Westport's oldest eatery. Today you'll find cozy dining areas such as Goldilock's Room, the Old Dining Room, and the Den, filled with the murmur of happy diners as

well as antique furniture, lamps, and windows. At lunchtime choose from such items as burrito roll-ups, chicken Caesar salad, penne pasta, and grilled clam pizza. At dinnertime you'll find seafood popovers, potato-and-cheese tarts, barbecue-glazed salmon, tortilla soup, filet mignon, and vegetarian pasta.

**Villa del Sol** $$
**36 Elm Street**
**(203) 226-7912**
Like its sister location (see the Fairfield listing), this Mexican eatery also serves up hot-and-spicy dishes for lunch and dinner. The Westport location also offers an outdoor seating area and a location that's close to downtown shops.

# Wilton

**Hunan Cafe** $-$$
**228 Town Green**
**(203) 761-8991**
This Asian restaurant is draped in earth tones, right down to the chairs that look as though they've been dipped in green tea. Daily lunch specials provide fast, inexpensive choices like General Tso's chicken, chicken with cashew nuts, pork with garlic sauce, orange beef, shrimp with mixed vegetables, and eggplant with bean curd. Dinnertime selections include mango chicken, crispy spring rolls, moo shu chicken, black-bean beef, mango pork, scallops with string beans, ginger shrimp, beef with snow peas, and tofu vegetable soup.

**Old Schoolhouse Grill** $
**34 Cannon Road, Cannondale Village**
**(203) 762-8810**
If you're looking for old-fashioned New England ambience, it doesn't get much more quaint than this. Tucked inside a genuine one-room schoolhouse (well, a former one-room schoolhouse) and surrounded by antiques shops and a babbling brook, this casual grill restaurant offers indoor as well as outdoor seating.

RESTAURANTS

## Quick Bites

Looking for road food? Fairfield County has some of the best greasy, delicious, quick eats anywhere in the state. It's also the home turf of two of the industry's best-known "casual food" writers: Jane and Michael Stern, authors of *Roadfood* (2002), *Blue Plate Specials and Blue Ribbon Chefs* (2001), *Eat Your Way Across the U.S.A.* (1999), and other titles. For the best local hot dogs, burgers, cheesesteaks, and other treats, try these popular spots: Swanky Franks in Norwalk (182 Connecticut Avenue, 203-838-8969); the Roadside Chili House in Bethel (44 Stony Hill Road, 203-790-5064); Super Duper Weenie in Fairfield (306 Black Rock Turnpike, 203-334-3647); Danny's Drive-In in Stratford (90 Ferry Boulevard, 203-378-6728); the Botsford Drive-In in Newtown (282 South Main Street, 203-426-4279); Fisherman's Net in Darien (11 Old Kings Highway, 203-655-0561); the Shelton Dog House in Shelton (480 Howe Avenue, 203-924-7594); and the Sycamore Drive-In Restaurant in Bethel (282 Greenwood Avenue, 203-748-2716).

Fun menu items play up the theme, including the Teachers Pet (grilled chicken breast sandwich), the Principal (steak sandwich), and the Schoolhouse Deli Dog. And in a spot like this, the children's menu takes priority: The kids can choose from burgers, chicken fingers, and more.

### Tom E Toes                                    $$
**5 River Road**
**(203) 834-0733**
**www.tometoes.com**
This popular restaurant and pizzeria has been serving up hot pizzas and other Italian dishes to locals for more than 12 years. Art exhibits, French doors, live music, a patio seating area, a "slice bar," a children's menu, and take-out service add to the homey appeal, as do tortellini carbonara, cannelloni Corleone, and Atlantic salmon piccata. Lunchtime diners can choose from a variety of salads, pasta dishes, and hot and cold sandwiches. The restaurant's

owners also support the community by sponsoring Little League baseball, supporting fund-raisers for the Wilton Teen Center and other groups, and showcasing the work of local artists.

### Tomiko                                        $$
**15 River Road**
**(203) 761-6770**
Japanese cuisine is the focus at Tomiko, a Wilton eatery serving a wide selection of appetizers, main courses, and a la carte sushi and sashimi. The friendly waitstaff wear kimonos and will help you decide between the many options, including broiled, sautéed, and fried chicken, beef, pork, and seafood dishes. All lunch items are served with rice, soup, and salad. Or order your "lunch box" to go and enjoy it back at the office. Sushi rolls are made with salmon, tuna, shrimp, eel, and other fish species. Outdoor dining is also available on the patio.

# NORTHERN FAIRFIELD COUNTY

## Bethel

**Front Street Fish House**    **$$**
**1 Front Street**
**(203) 778-5253**
Formerly known as One Front Street, this downtown restaurant recently changed its name—and its image—with a revamped menu and attitude. For more information about the Front Street Fish House and its pub, the Cranky Fish Saloon, see the Nightlife chapter.

**Greenwoods Restaurant**    **$$**
**186 Greenwood Avenue**
**(203) 748-3900**
Located in the beautiful and historic Opera House building, Greenwoods is one of downtown's anchors and a popular stop for lunch, dinner, and late-night socializing. For more information about Greenwoods' restaurant and pub, see the Nightlife chapter.

**Helga's**    **$$**
**55 Stony Hill Road**
**(203) 797-1860**
When visiting Germans head to your restaurant for an authentic taste of home, you know you're doing something right. Helga's is an unassuming restaurant on U.S. Route 6 with a large stone chimney and a white stucco exterior. Inside, diners will find hardwood floors, exposed beams, a friendly welcome, and hearty meals. The emphasis here is on meat, and lots of it: Choose from dishes like *jager schnitzel* (breaded and fried pork cutlet), *rouladen* (simmered sirloin with bacon and mushrooms), and beef goulash. In summer stop by for a beer on the patio while listening to live accordion music.

**La Fortuna**    **$$$**
**37 Stony Hill Road**
**(203) 797-0909**
This Italian eatery has been serving diners from Bethel and nearby towns for more than 20 years. Recently renovated, La Fortuna continues to cater to families and couples with homemade pasta and other dishes and also offers banquet facilities for parties, executive meetings, and other special events. Entrees include shrimp scampi, gnocchi in Bolognese sauce, chicken cacciatore, grilled sirloin steak, rigatoni pastarella, manicotti with tomato sauce, chicken piccata, and filet mignon. In a departure from the traditional Italian theme, the menu also includes a wide variety of a la carte sushi and sashimi selections.

**La Zingara Ristorante**    **$$**
**P. T. Barnum Square**
**(203) 744-7500**
A newcomer to Bethel, the upscale La Zingara Italian eatery replaced a Mexican restaurant in the downtown area's P. T. Barnum Square. Begin your meal with one of the many antipasti or salads, and then move on to plates like *garganelli all buttera* (pasta with sausage and peas), *paillard D'Angelo* (grilled lamb with olive oil and Parmesan), *spaghetti alle vongole* (spaghetti with clams and wine sauce), and *bistecca alla pizzaiola* (grilled steak with onion and capers). Tiramisu and cheesecake are among the desserts available. On Sunday a hearty brunch offers two courses and a dessert.

**Plain Jane's**    **$$**
**208 Greenwood Avenue**
**(203) 797-1515**
For more than 25 years, Plain Jane's has been serving lunch and dinner to an appreciative Bethel crowd. Despite the name, the restaurant's menu items are anything but plain. You may want to start with hummus tahini, chicken wings, fruit salad, spinach salad, or seafood-stuffed mushrooms. At lunchtime main dish selections include the vegetable pouch sandwich, personal pizzas, a Reuben sandwich, or the quiche of the day. At dinner choose from filet of scrod, linguini Diego, grilled pork chops, sesame chicken salad, shrimp and chicken piccata, New York sirloin, and other entrees.

### Stony Hill Inn $$
**46 Stony Hill Road**
**(203) 743-5533**

The inn is perhaps best known for its landscaped grounds, complete with a pond and swans. The attractive surroundings make it a popular site for weddings, and the restaurant has plenty of banquet rooms available for receptions, meetings, and other events. Local diners can also enjoy the inn's American cuisine on any old night of the week: Friday night stands out with a surf-and-turf buffet; Sunday brings an always packed brunch buffet. The regular menu's wide selection of chicken, beef, pasta, and seafood dishes can please everyone at the table.

# Brookfield

### Antonio's Italian Bistro $$
**270 Federal Road**
**(203) 740-8664**

Antonio's specializes in hosting and catering special events like meetings, anniversary parties, and bridal showers. The restaurant also offers extensive menus for lunch and dinner, including appetizers, soups, salads, and antipasti. Lunchtime offerings feature hot grinders, specialty pasta dishes, mozzarella salads, and other creations made with eggplant, chicken, and seafood. At dinnertime expect to find such entrees as pasta with clam sauce, surf-and-turf combinations, chicken Basilico, filet of sole, eggplant rollitini, pasta puttanesca, chicken Marsala, lasagna, and stuffed lobster tail.

### Pancho's and Gringo's $-$$
**779 Federal Road**
**(203) 775-0096**

Casual and fun, Pancho's and Gringo's serves up Mexican fare in a colorful, mariachi-soaked atmosphere. As with many other Mexican restaurants, the appetizers are often the best part of meal. Here the choices include super quesadillas, stuffed jalapeños, sloppy nachos, shrimp Veracruz, and chili con queso. The

taco salad is served in a tortilla shell with beef or chicken; combination platters include samplings of tacos, enchiladas, burritos, and chimichangas made with beef, chicken, or cheese. The eatery has another location in Ridgefield.

### Pasta Garden $$
**174 Federal Road**
**(203) 775-0426**

Located on busy Federal Road near Costco, Pasta Garden is a family-oriented place with an emphasis on Italian food. Few would disagree that the highlight here is the homemade pasta selection: Everything from spaghetti to fusilli, angel hair, and ziti is thick, flavorful, and made fresh daily on the premises. The front area of the restaurant is devoted to takeout, including pizza; the rear dining area provides a homey atmosphere for couples, friends, and families. Separate banquet rooms can also be reserved for birthday parties and other special occasions.

# Danbury

### Bangkok $$
**72 Newtown Road**
**(203) 791-0640**
**www.bangkokrestaurant.com**

Bangkok has the distinction of being the first Thai restaurant in Connecticut. Today it sticks to its original roots with more than 60 authentic Thai dishes, including hot-and-spicy soups, salads, and entrees. Most dishes are made with rice, noodles, seafood, beef, pork, chicken, or some combination of these ingredients. Try the *panang nhua* (steak simmered in coconut milk), *kai phat pak* (chicken with hot green peppers), or *goong pat prik no my* (shrimp with chili and bamboo shoots). The menu uses asterisks to let you know which dishes are particularly spicy.

### Cafe on the Green $$-$$$
**Richter Park Golf Course**
**100 Aunt Hack Road**
**(203) 792-2550**

The "Green" of this cafe's name refers not to a park or town center but to the greens at Richter Park Golf Course. A nice spot for special occasions, the eatery serves both lunch and dinner. After starting with crab cakes, steamed mussels, or minestrone soup, move on to such entrees as *fettucine pescara* (spinach pasta with crab sauce), *pollo alla Andrea* (chicken with portobello mushrooms and peas), *cappellini mare monte* (sautéed shrimp with garlic and mushrooms), and spaghetti Siciliano (spaghetti with capers and black olives). Enjoy your meal in the dining room or outside on the romantic veranda.

**Chuck's Steak House          $$-$$$**
**20 Segar Street**
**(203) 792-5555**
The Danbury Chuck's location has a hopping bar scene as well as enough steak and chops to satisfy the hungriest diner. Vegetarians aren't left out, either. They can find fresh bread, salad fixin's, and soups at the all-you-can-eat salad bar. For more information about Chuck's, see the Darien listing.

**Colorado Brewery          $$-$$$**
**6 Delay Street**
**(203) 791-1450**
**www.thecoloradobrewery.com**
Located at the Danbury Green across from the new skating rink, the Colorado Brewery has become one of the city's busiest spots for dining and drinking. Hungry visitors can sit in the dining area with a full meal or mingle at the bar with munchies. For more information about the brewery's food and drink offerings, see the Nightlife chapter.

**Jim Barbarie's Restaurant          $$-$$$**
**47 Padanarum Road**
**(203) 743-3287**
Jim Barbarie's is best known for its steaks, chops, and surf-and-turf meals, including filet mignon, prime ribs, rack of lamb, pork chops, stuffed lobster, Black Angus top sirloin, and crab legs. But the restaurant also serves a wide variety of pasta dishes,

including calamari fra diavolo and penne vodka, and poultry meals like chicken Marsala and grilled breast of duck. The lunch menu also includes hot and cold sandwiches, steaks, seafood, desserts, and specialty coffees.

**Old Sorrento Italian Restaurant          $$**
**32 Newtown Road**
**(203) 748-1322**
**www.oldsorrento.com**
At lunchtime the Old Sorrento serves up light fare such as steamed mussels, pasta fagioli soup, hot grinders, pizza, salads, burgers, and sandwiches, along with heartier Italian dishes. The dinner menu offers a good mix of entrees, including linguini with clam sauce, penne alla vodka, filet of sole, chicken with capers and wine sauce, seafood combination specials, steak Sorrento, surf-and-turf plates, chicken parmigiana, and baked ravioli with cheese. Children's menu items, soups, salads, pizzas, desserts, espresso, and antipasti are also available at dinnertime.

**Ondine          $$$-$$$$**
**69 Pembroke Road**
**(203) 746-4900**
If you think you have to travel to the southern end of the county for gourmet French cuisine, Ondine will come as a pleasant surprise. Tucked away on Route 37 near the Danbury–New Fairfield border, this elegant eatery offers prix fixe and a la

*JK's Restaurant in Danbury (126 South Street, 203-743-4004) is becoming renowned for its buffalo-wing hot sauce and Texas Hot Wieners. RV owners, motorcycle riders, and other long-distance travelers frequently mention the restaurant in their newsletters and recommend it to others who might be passing through the area. Locals seem to favor the spicy concoctions, too, as witnessed by the crowds on weekdays and weekend nights.*

carte menus with hors d'oeuvres, *potage,* and *les plats* dishes served with artistic flair. Choose from selections such as *terrine de faisan au foie de canard* (pâté of pheasant with duck liver), *gigot de lotte aux graines de moutarde* (monkfish with mustard seeds and cabbage), *caneton calvados* (roast duck with apples), and a chocolate torte with cherries.

### Sesame Seed                          $-$$
**68 West Wooster Street**
**(203) 743-9850**

A bit harder to find than most other Danbury eateries, Sesame Seed is worth the effort. The restaurant serves sandwiches, wraps, huge salads, lasagna, spinach pie, many vegetarian options, and Middle Eastern specialties like baklava, hummus, shish kebab, and falafel. The fun, laid-back ambience includes a cozy dining room decorated with baskets, antiques, and other eclectic knickknacks. Sesame Seed is especially popular with local businesspeople, who order the tasty meals and sandwiches as takeout.

### Two Steps Downtown Grill            $$
**5 Ives Street**
**(203) 794-0032**

Two Steps, located at the city's downtown green, is a big part of the dining and bar scene in Danbury. Visitors come to eat, drink, socialize, or just gawk at the wild cowboy-boot "sculptures" (created with every theme imaginable) hanging from the ceiling. For more information about Two Steps, see the Nightlife chapter.

# Monroe

### Panino's                            $$
**179 Main Street**
**(203) 452-5557**

This small, casual eatery provides hot, fresh Italian food in a laid-back environment. Calzone choices include the Protein Packer, the Tony Bennet, and the Marco Pollo (with chicken, of course). Or select a seafood dish like clams over linguine,

Mama's Calamari, or Seafood Panino. The "Pastabilities" section of the menu offers all the usual favorites, along with some unique creations, such as Boogie Woogie Bolognese, Spaghetti Light My Fire, and Panino's Carbonara. The restaurant's gourmet pizzas, available in small, medium, and large sizes, are available in-house or as takeout.

### Roberto's                          $$-$$$
**505 Main Street**
**(203) 268-5723**

Located on a hill overlooking Main Street (Route 25), Roberto's specializes in hosting groups for weddings, birthdays, business get-togethers, and showers. But families and couples will also enjoy a bit of individual attention in the dining room, where the restaurant serves up generous portions of chicken Marsala, *zuppa di pesce,* lasagna, rigatoni with meatballs, clams *posillipo,* fettucini Alfredo, and other Italian dishes. Take your time with the menu while you munch on the complimentary broccoli-cheese bread.

### Sennen                             $$
**435 Main Street**
**(203) 452-8221**

This Japanese restaurant is a relative newcomer to the Fairfield County dining scene, offering a welcome taste of distinction to the heavily pizza-populated Monroe. Some of the more adventurous appetizers include *tako su* (sliced octopus with vinegar dressing), *hijiki* (cooked seaweed), and *oshinko* (pickled vegetables). For dinner choose from teriyaki, tempura, katsu, and fried dishes, or sample one of the complete sushi bar dinners. Bento boxes, complete with miso soup, shrimp and vegetable tempura, salmon or chicken teriyaki, and sushi, are available at lunchtime.

### 707 on Main                        $$-$$$
**707 Main Street**
**(203) 261-2652**

A newly built addition to Monroe, 707 on Main offers several dining rooms and a somewhat casual/somewhat buttoned-up atmosphere. The menu includes appetizers like empanada, oysters on the half shell, and porcini ravioli and entrees such as filet mignon, penne vodka, High Octane Ribs, lobster diavolo, chicken and risotto, and jambalaya. Pizza and a children's menu provide even more selections. The restaurant also hosts private events, including wedding receptions. For more information about the 707 on Main lounge, see the Nightlife chapter.

**Trattoria Carl Anthony**          $$–$$$
**477 Main Street**
**(203) 268-8486**
The exterior of Carl Anthony's, located in the ordinary-looking Clock Tower Square Plaza, doesn't give a hint about the trendy atmosphere waiting inside. Flickering candles, orange martinis, and the steady murmur of conversation make this the hippest place in town—expect a crowd, especially on Saturday night. Chef Sam DeVellis cooks up impressive-looking dishes that complement their surroundings, from towering free-range chicken on mashed potatoes to Chilean sea bass pantelleria and scaloppini piccata. Diners will also find individual gourmet pizzas made with chunky mozzarella and plum tomatoes.

# New Fairfield

**New Fairfield Luncheonette**          $
**Route 37**
**(203) 746-7011**
Hang out and meet the locals at the New Fairfield Luncheonette, a casual, friendly eatery serving lunch specials. Whether you're looking for something hot and grilled or cold and crispy, the luncheonette can satisfy your midday cravings with sandwiches on a variety of breads, soups, potato chips and French fries, baked goods and snacks, coffee, and cold fountain drinks. Most meals cost less than $7.00 or $8.00.

**Portofino Restaurant**          $–$$
**88 Route 37**
**(203) 746-3604**
Some diners at Portofino opt for shareable thin-crust pizzas, covered with toppings like pepperoni, onions, mushrooms, peppers, or just lots and lots of cheese. If you'd rather have a dish all to yourself, the menu offers a range of Italian options, including a variety of chicken, seafood, and pasta entrees with red and cream sauces. The restaurant is open for lunch and dinner. Takeout is also available, and reservations are accepted (but not necessary).

# Newtown

**Inn at Newtown**          $$–$$$
**19 Main Street**
**(203) 270-1876**
**www.theinnatnewtown.com**
Formerly known as the Mary Hawley Inn, this 1857 home-turned-inn has long played a central role in Newtown's history. Ms. Hawley was an early resident and benefactor who paid for the construction of a local school, a bridge, Edmond Town Hall, and other structures in town. Today diners can visit her former home on Main Street for bistro-style fare, including dishes like shallots and duck with pasta, salmon with mango and jicama, filet mignon with mashed potatoes, crab cakes with corn salad, and a BLT salad with smoked bacon. For more information about the inn's bar, Proud Mary's, see the Nightlife chapter. For more information about overnight lodging, see Accommodations.

**Mexicali Rose**          $
**71 South Main Street**
**(203) 270-7003**
It's easy to miss this tiny restaurant, but don't. Tucked away in a shopping center along Route 25, Mexicali Rose features home cooking, big portions, mix-and-match eclectic furnishings, a mural painted on the floor, and handmade chips

and salsa that outmatch any in Fairfield County. Served with plastic flatware and sometimes paper plates, the dishes include vegetarian burritos, beef and chicken fajitas, cheese quesadillas, nachos with everything, Mexi-cheesesteak on a tortilla, black-bean soup, Yucatan salad, and more. The take-out service is always busting; a few tables are also available.

**Mona Lisa** $$
**160 South Main Street**
**(203) 426-6685**
Mona Lisa recently moved down the street into a new, spiffed-up location (the site of the former Old Newtown Tavern) but still serves Italian meals such as lasagna, eggplant parmigiana, sirloin steak, lamb brochette, filet of sole, chicken cacciatore, calamari, clams casino, and angel hair pasta with meatballs. The atmosphere is elegant and historic; plenty of outdoor patio seating is also available during the warmer months. You'll also find a decent wine list and desserts like cheesecake, tiramisu, and caramel custard.

**My Place Restaurant** $$
**8 Queen Street**
**(203) 270-7061**
Located out in front of the Big Y shopping center, My Place is a family-oriented restaurant with a diverse menu, a wine list, and a full bar. Lighter appetites can go for potato skins, buffalo wings, or spinach bread. Those looking for something heartier can peruse items like pasta fagioli, chicken Rocco, butternut squash ravioli, grilled shrimp, fajitas, Caribbean duck, penne with chicken and broccoli, specialty pizzas, and grinders. Delivery and take-out services are also available. For more information about the restaurant's bar area, see the Mark's Tap Room listing in the Nightlife chapter.

**New Wok** $$
**228 South Main Street**
**(203) 270-3878**
The word is spreading about New Wok, a small Asian eatery tucked into the Sand Hill shopping center on Route 25. Although take-out service is available (along with traditional favorites like sweet-and-sour chicken, pork lo mein, and Hunan-style beef), the food here goes beyond your typical Chinese take-out offerings. The Chef's Selections include Dragon and Phoenix (chicken and shrimp in spicy sauce), ginger scallion duck, Szechuan peppercorn duo, Four Seasons (chicken, beef, pork, and shrimp with vegetables), crispy walnut shrimp and chicken, and crispy orange beef.

**Sunderban** $$
**316 South Main Street**
**(203) 426-7143**
This tucked-away restaurant is located near a busy intersection in the Botsford section of town, across from the new Post Office. Diners who love Indian food don't seem to mind traveling here from northern spots like New Milford, New Fairfield, and Bethel, especially considering how difficult it is to find the cuisine in this region of the county. The menu includes a full range of vegetarian dishes, breads, seafood, chicken, lamb, *biryani*, and tandoori, including *aloo gobi,* shrimp *saag,* lamb *biryani,* tandoori salmon, traditional Indian salad, and mushroom curry.

# Redding

**Spinning Wheel Inn** $$
**Route 58**
**(203) 938-9815**
Former Redding resident Mark Twain was once a regular at this historic inn, which has been renovated over the years but still maintains a distinctly "old New England" feel. Diners can reflect on the past while feasting on roast leg of lamb, sautéed shrimp and scallops, Maine lobster linguini, mixed-grill pasta, seared filet of beef, or the chef's potpie of the day. The Sunday brunch menu features apple pancakes, omelettes, the French Toast Tower, old-fashioned oatmeal, and eggs Benedict. Later in the day, the Family Sunday Dinner

is a four-course meal that is sure to fill hungry bellies.

### Squire's Redding Roadhouse $$-$$$
### 406 Redding Roadhouse
### (203) 938-3388
Located at the intersection of Routes 53 and 107, the Redding Roadhouse packs 'em in with lunch and dinner items like baby spinach salad, cider-glazed chicken, hunter's stew, prime rib, barbecued baby-back ribs, lobster fettucine, thin-crust pizza, squash ravioli, and stuffed shrimp. The restaurant's "World Famous Sunday Brunch" offers Belgian waffles, home fries, muffins, shrimp cocktail, assorted cheeses, bacon, scrambled eggs, and an omelette station. The Roadhouse is also a hot spot in the evenings; see the listing under Nightlife for more information.

# Ridgefield

### Bailey's Backyard $$-$$$
### 23 Bailey Avenue
### (203) 431-0796
Serving New American cuisine, Bailey's Backyard has comparatively sized indoor and outdoor seating areas, a wine list, and even take-out and delivery service. At lunch expect to find warm goat-cheese spinach salad, grilled salmon wraps, breaded-eggplant sandwiches, Bailey's Burgers, and other light fare. The hearty dinner dishes include filet mignon, macadamia-crusted tuna, rigatoni with sausage, pecan-crusted tuna, stuffed pork loin, and classic cioppino. The kid's menu provides such child-friendly choices as hot dogs, pasta, burgers, and chicken fingers.

### Bernard's Inn at Ridgefield $$$$
### 20 West Lane
### (203) 438-8282
### www.bernardsridgefield.com
Enjoy a taste of France at Bernard's, a four-room eatery run by chefs Bernard and Sarah Boissou. The menu changes regularly, but you can expect to find authentic French delicacies such as foie gras, duck confit, haricots verts, petits fours, fondant au chocolate, and of course crème brûlée. Sunday diners will find a prix fixe brunch menu. Bernard's also specializes in hosting special events, especially weddings. The inn's formal gardens, upscale menus, banquet packages, and large indoor space on the upper level make it popular locale for parties of up to 120 guests.

### Elms Restaurant and Tavern $$-$$$
### 500 Main Street
### (203) 438-2541
### www.elmsinn.com
The Elms Restaurant offers two types of menus: The casual "tavern fare" version includes such items as bangers and mash, grilled chicken sandwiches, clam chowder, and burgers. In the main dining rooms, choose from starter items such as bitter-sweet salad, grilled duck breast, and goat-cheese ravioli, and then move on to entrees like seafood stew, grilled venison, pan-roasted monkfish, lobster shepherd pie, apple-smoked magret duck, roasted chicken breast, and grilled lamb. For more information about the Elms Inn, see the Accommodations chapter.

### Pancho's and Gringo's $-$$
### U.S. Route 7 South
### (203) 438-2696
The Ridgefield location of Pancho's and Gringo's offers hot and cheesy renditions of Mexican favorites, including entrees, combination plates, soups, salads, and appetizers. For more information see the Brookfield listing.

### Sangeet Fine Indian Cuisine $$
### 296 Ethan Allen Highway (U.S. Route 7)
### (203) 894-1080
Located on the premises of the Ridgefield Motor Inn, this family-owned restaurant cooks up Indian breads, soups, and full-size dinner like *pudina paratha* (whole wheat bread stuffed with mint), *murg kadai* (chicken cooked in a wok with peppers and onions), *gosht sheikh kabab* (lamb, onions, and herbs cooked on a

skewer), and *dal maharani* (kidney beans flavored with ginger). During the week, prepacked lunch bags are available for the busy business crowd and harried parents-on-the-run.

**Southwest Cafe**                    $$
**109 Danbury Road**
**(203) 431-3398**
This tiny cafe is small in size but big in taste. Avocado, cilantro, garlic, and green and red chili peppers spice up dishes on the lunch and dinner menus, including enchiladas, rellenos, taco salad, nachos, Tex-Mex chili, flautas, chalupas, tostadas, Mexican pizzas, and fajitas. The restaurant's "skinny" entrees, such as the warm cilantro chicken salad and vegetable burritos, are low-cal and low-fat. Combination plates allow diners to sample a few different offerings at once; the kids' menu offers great choices for little ones.

**Spagone Ristorante**                $$
**113 Danbury Road**
**(203) 438-5518**
The red, black, and gold decor at Spagone is sleek and dramatic. This Italian restaurant offers daily lunch and dinner specials, catering services, a wine list, and private-event hosting for special occasions. Lunch items include grilled salmon, chicken piccata, and maccoroncelli. At dinnertime choose from such entrees as *piccata di pollo al limone* (chicken with white wine and lemon), shrimp scampi over linguini, and *salmon all grigli con vegetali* (grilled salmon with vegetables). All the desserts, including white chocolate cheesecake and tiramisu, are made in-house.

**Stonehenge Inn and Restaurant**    $$$
**U.S. Route 7**
**P.O. Box 667, Ridgefield 06877**
**(203) 438-6511**
**www.stonehengeinn-ct.com**
Diners can enjoy continental-French cuisine at the Stonehenge Inn and Restaurant, where dinner is served Monday

through Saturday nights. Fresh, in-season ingredients are used to create such dishes as eggplant and goat cheese gâteau, Maryland crab cakes, wild mushrooms in puff pastry, sautéed sea scallops, Alaskan halibut, seared duck breast, and soup du jour. For dessert try the pineapple coconut soufflé, French apple tart, or Tahitian vanilla crème brûlée. For more information about Stonehenge lodging, see the Accommodations chapter.

**Wild Ginger Cafe**              $$-$$$
**461 Main Street**
**(203) 431-4588**
Cosmopolitan and upscale, the Wild Ginger Cafe looks as though it might be more at home in Manhattan than in Ridgefield. Luckily for locals, the owners decided to bring their Asian cuisine here. For an appetizer try the cream-corn egg-drop soup, Thai spring rolls, Japanese seaweed salad, or pan-fried dumplings. When it's time for a main course, you just choose your "base"—pork, chicken, prawns, beef, scallops, tofu, or prawns—and then choose your sauce (spicy black bean, sambal, spicy mango, glazed ginger, red curry, or Szechuan peppercorn). Fried rice, pad Thai, and lo mein are also available.

# Shelton

**Metro Grille & Bar**                 $$
**882 Bridgeport Avenue**
**(203) 929-1000**
The Metro Grille & Bar offers an eclectic decor, lunch and dinner menus with fusion cuisine, and happy hour every weeknight. Onion au gratin soup, Sonoma salad, and chicken wings are just a few of the starters. Main courses include grilled pizzas, black-pepper fettucine, penne pasta with artichoke hearts, Asian wok-seared shrimp, fish mesclun, prime rib, lemon-pepper chicken, porterhouse steak, and filet mignon. The Metro also provides catering and delivery services.

**Ristorante Marini**  $$-$$$
**232 Leavenworth Road**
**(203) 929-5177**

Rustic brick walls, white tablecloths, and romantic lighting accentuate the upscale atmosphere at Marini's. Italian dishes here are made with fresh produce, high-quality meats, and catch-of-day fish: Choose from antipasti and entrees such as shrimp scampi with shallots, spaghetti carbonara, penne alla vodka, penne with broccoli, clams casino, chicken Marsala, New York strip steak with Gorgonzola cheese, filet of sole, and Mediterranean seafood over pasta. When all that flavor makes you thirsty, choose from a full wine and beer selection. Take-out pizza is also available.

**Vincent's Italian Restaurant**  $$
**526 Shelton Avenue**
**(203) 929-9104**

Valley diners will find Vincent's in the Huntington Village Shopping Center and can choose from a variety of traditional Italian meals and hot pizzas. The priciest items on the menu are the seafood dishes, which include clams marinara, shrimp rim-ini, and calamari. Pasta dishes are baked with bubbling cheese on top or served with tomato and Alfredo sauces. Grinders, steaks, and salads are also available, and pizzas run the gamut from plain old cheese to the BLT and "chicken supreme" specialties.

# Sherman

**American Pie Company**  $-$$
**29 Route 37**
**(860) 350-0662**

This place is packed on weekends, hosting Fairfield County families as well as those from across the border in upstate New York. The restaurant is perhaps best known for its hot breakfasts and weekend brunches, although lunch and dinner are also available. If you don't have time for a sit-down meal, stop by for a wide selection of baked goodies, including muffins, cookies, pies, cakes, and breads. Eat indoors or out in the patio seating area. Beer and wine are served in the evening.

# NIGHTLIFE Ⓨ

No one would accuse Fairfield County of being a hot spot for night owls. Being located so close to the "city that never sleeps" creates inevitable comparisons: Southwestern Connecticut definitely sleeps—and often goes to bed early. Despite a few trendy pockets, the overall region remains rooted in a family-friendly atmosphere that favors Strawberry Festivals over techno music—much to the chagrin of local singles and others who like to mix, mingle, and watch the sun come up. Nevertheless, it's not impossible to find hopping brewpubs, live bands, sports bars, and even dance clubs—if you know where to look.

Many of the county's bars fall into the category of "restaurant/lounge." You can enjoy a good meal and then stay late or skip the meal and just show up later for a beer, martini, or scotch on the rocks. A few businesses stand on their own as nightspots *sans* restaurant, but these are few and far between. Some spots are geared toward an upscale, after-work crowd; others attract ready-to-party college students. Live music is surprisingly varied and easy to find, including everything from cover bands to acoustic cafes and heavy metal. In general, those who are craving a night on the town will find the most options in Stamford, South Norwalk (SoNo), Fairfield, and Danbury. Some of the most popular after-hours destinations are sorted below by town. As you might expect, these businesses open, close, change hands, and change names frequently, so be sure to call before making the drive.

## SOUTHERN FAIRFIELD COUNTY

## Bridgeport

### Acoustic Cafe
**2926 Fairfield Avenue**
**(203) 335-3655**
**www.acoustiCafe.com**
Live music is always the focus at the Acoustic Cafe, a five-year-old Black Rock spot where singers and their instruments get to shine. You'll also be able to hang out at poetry readings, open-mic nights, open jam sessions, guest-speaker presentations, and other events. And there's no need to go hungry or thirsty: The cafe also serves munchies, sandwiches, desserts, wine, beer, coffee, and more. Some events are free; some require a ticket for admission. Visit the Web site for upcoming shows and ticket prices.

### Black Rock & Blue
**3488 Fairfield Avenue**
**(203) 384-1167**
Located on the Fairfield-Bridgeport line, this fun spot—"the biggest little bar in town"—serves up live music, dancing, and even karaoke nights (usually Wednesday). Local cover bands are always around on the weekends playing recent hits and classic rock tunes. Drink specials, munchies, and an overall loud and boisterous atmosphere keep the party animals coming.

### Black Rock Castle
**2895 Fairfield Avenue**
**(203) 336-9990**
Irish eyes are always smiling at the Black Rock Castle, a restaurant and pub that was designed to resemble a real-life castle in Ireland. Family crests hang on the walls, live Irish music is playing on Sunday afternoon, and Guinness—along with 20 other

beers—is always on tap. On weekends (Thursday through Saturday nights) expect to find happy hours, DJs, live bands, and dancing. Three dining rooms also serve up Emerald Isle and American favorites. For more information see the listing in the Restaurants chapter.

## Picasso's
**3074 Fairfield Avenue**
**(203) 335-2500**

The site of the former Nauti Dolphin restaurant, Picasso's still serves the gourmet pizzas and Italian meals of its predecessor. But the addition of a cool, full bar has turned the site into a popular destination for the later-night crowd as well. Don't be surprised to find live music on weekends, including jazz and swing.

# Fairfield

## Archie Moore's
**48 Sanford Street**
**(203) 256-9295**

This is a casual, "neighborhood" kind of place to sidle up to the bar and enjoy a few drinks and appetizers with friends. For more information, see the listing in the Restaurants chapter.

## Ash Creek Saloon
**93 Post Road**
**(203) 255-5131**

On a Saturday night, you'll have a long wait for a table at this popular barbecue spot. Luckily the packed bar area provides plenty of diversions while you look forward to baby-back ribs, steaks, burgers, and other messy meals. Live bands playing blues and other types of music are often around on weekends, and the cowboy-crazy atmosphere (complete with a wagon-wheel chandelier) is fun for regulars and newcomers alike.

## Barcelona Restaurant & Wine Bar
**4180 Black Rock Turnpike**
**(203) 255-0800**
**www.barcelonawinebar.com**

Upscale and elegant, Barcelona appeals to those seeking a more refined night on the town. The full bar serves up cocktails, specialty beers, and a huge selection of wines by the glass. Visitors can enjoy a full Mediterranean meal or a la carte tapas to go along with their drinks. The menu offers everything from potato tortillas to stuffed piquillo peppers, oysters, cod croquettes, marinated eggplant, and lobster risotto. The restaurant offers two other locations in Greenwich and SoNo. The Greenwich location also serves lunch; the SoNo location stays open until 2:00 A.M. on weekends.

## Boston Billiard Club
**111 Black Rock Turnpike**
**(203) 335-2255**

As you might guess from the name, this spot (actually part of a larger chain) specializes in loud music, cold beer, and plenty of pool. Rack 'em up and hang out awhile; the bartenders will keep the pitchers coming, and the mini-tournaments are always raging. Local leagues also play regular competitions here and at the Danbury location. Order your drink at the bar or from a member of the wandering waitstaff; the club caters strictly to an over-21 crowd.

## O Bar
**52 Sanford Street**
**(203) 254-8094**

Located within the Saint Tropez Bistro Francais restaurant, the O Bar tends to attract more gourmands than students. The eatery offers such French specialties as sautéed foie gras, Brie and vegetable tarts, and crème brûlée, while the full-service bar provides satellite television, drink specials, beers, and wines by the glass. The atmosphere is casual but not *too* casual: You'll probably want to iron and tuck in your shirt.

## Sky Box
**1494 Post Road**
**(203) 259-7535**

College students, young professionals, and a variety of other night owls flock to Sky

Box for a casual environment and plenty of opportunities to mingle. Live music keeps 'em dancing three nights a week; billiards, dart games, and television sports broadcasts keep the rest of the visitors happy as well. After-work and weekend crowds seem equally appreciative of Sky Box's brews, music, and entertainment.

### Southport Brewing Company
### 2600 Post Road
### (203) 256-BEER
### www.southportbrewing.com

The Southport Brewing Company (and its sister location, SBC Downtown in Stamford) boasts happy hours, family nights, Sunday brunches, Octoberfest parties, and even late-night happy hours with mixed-drink and beer specials. Both locations brew their own beers on-site and offer on-tap selections like Black Rock Stout, Big Head Brewnette, Connecticut Pale Ale, Olde Blue Eyes Blueberry Ale, the Southporter, Southtoberfest, and Fairfield Red. Can't decide? Try a beer sampler. You can also choose Maryland crab cakes, calamari, burgers, pizza, sandwiches, steak, and pasta from the lunch and dinner menus.

# Greenwich

### Barcelona Restaurant & Wine Bar
### 18 West Putnam Avenue
### (203) 983-6400
### www.barcelonawinebar.com

Choose from extensive wine lists and tapas menus at Barcelona, a Greenwich bar and restaurant with a distinctly Mediterranean feel. For more information see the Fairfield listing.

### Bleu
### 339 Greenwich Avenue
### (203) 661-9377

This French bistro serves up full meals, smaller starters, and plenty of drinks in its upscale dining room and bar area. Despite its other many fine features, however, the buzz about Bleu remains focused on its . . .

restrooms. (The stall doors are clear and turn opaque only when you lock them.) The Travel Channel even rated them among the world's top-10 restrooms on a recent show.

### Boxing Cat Grill
### 1392 East Putnam Avenue
### (203) 698-1995

Catch a meal or your favorite local band at the Boxing Cat, where acts like the Avengers, Funkestra, and Tor & the Newcomers often perform dance music and classic rock. Looking for a light bite? The grill serves shrimp cocktail, vegetable dumplings, salads, black bean soup, and buffalo wings, along with heartier fare like shellfish fra diavolo, Chilean sea bass, marinated lamb, burgers, black-pepper fettucine, and grilled salmon.

### Sundown Saloon
### 403 Greenwich Avenue
### (203) 629-8212
### www.thatawaycafe.com

Billed as "a taste of the old west in Greenwich," the Sundown Saloon offers drafts like Bass Ale, Anchor Steam, Sam Adams, and Red Dog; Rolling Rock, Becks, and Amstel Light by the bottle; white and red wines; plenty of tequilas; and a daily happy hour with $2.00 drafts. The bartender will also be happy to mix you up specialties like Hard Rum Punch, Mexican Coffee, and Hot Rum Cider. Enjoy your drinks with a sandwich, appetizer, dessert, or other items from the saloon's menu.

### Tavola
### 99 Railroad Avenue
### (203) 422-0563

This trattoria and wine bar offers an extensive selection of reds and whites, along with draft beers like Bass Ale, Guinness, Spaten Oktoberfest, Pilsner Urquell, and Blue Moon Belgian White Ale. Enjoy your drink at the bar, or sit down in the dining room for Italian specialties like *rigatoni alla buttera, penne alla Bolognese, grigliata mista,* and the restaurant's well-known brick-oven pizzas.

# Norwalk

**Amberjacks: A Coastal Grill**
**99 Washington Street**
**(203) 853–4332**
**www.amberjacks.net**
The live-band action starts around 10:00 P.M. at Amberjacks, a restaurant and bar in SoNo with a lively atmosphere and good food. The annual Luau party in May—complete with grass skirts and a pig roast—is always a crowd pleaser. Weekend crowds often enjoy their drinks and music with such menu items as fried calamari, quesadillas, oysters, skewered Thai beef, and shrimp cocktail. Amberjacks has a sister location at 35 New Haven Avenue in Milford, Connecticut.

**Bar 11**
**11 Washington Street**
**(203) 831–8472**
The crowds are young and energetic at Bar 11, a large nightclub billed as "a visual and sound experience" with extra-loud music and extra-strong drinks. The club is strictly over-21, with DJs playing dance and pop music from 8:00 P.M. to 2:00 A.M. on weekends. Bring your best flirty smile and an open attitude.

**Barcelona Restaurant & Wine Bar**
**63–65 North Main Street**
**(203) 854–9088**
**www.barcelonawinebar.com**
Like its two other locations in Fairfield and Greenwich, this Barcelona offers special events, catering, tapas, and expansive wine lists that cover regions of Spain like Rueda, Priorat, Valdeorras, and Cava. For more information see the Fairfield listing.

**Brewhouse Restaurant and Tasting Room**
**13 Marshall Street**
**(203) 853–9110**
**www.sonobrewhouse.com**
The beer selection is extensive at the Brewhouse, including such bottled varieties as Sierra Nevada and Paulaner Hefeweisen and drafts like Stalla Artois, Brooklyn Brown Ale, and Pilsner Urquell.

Happy hours provide drink and munchies specials. After work or on weekends, you'll also find live bands playing Afro-Cuban, funk, rock 'n' roll, and more. If you're hungry, start with a bowl of clam chowder or black-bean chili, and then move on to a veggie burger, Maine crab cake salad, lobster roll sandwich, wiener schnitzel, or lobster ravioli. Ten-inch pizzas have toppings such as eggplant, goat cheese, shrimp, sausage, and classic "three cheese."

**Ego**
**18 South Main Street**
**(203) 854–9116**
Hip-hop, techno, and even oldies stress the speakers at Ego, a lively bar and lounge that often imports visiting DJs from New York City. Most visitors are dressed to impress (the dress code is strictly enforced) and looking to hang out, dance, drink, and meet new people. The atmosphere is slick, modern, and shiny.

**Jeremiah Donovan's**
**138 Washington Street**
**(203) 838–3430**
Donovan's has a little something for every laid-back, late-night reveler, including live bands on Wednesday night, a sports bar, televisions, generous wine and beer lists, and closing hours at 2:00 A.M. on Friday and Saturday. Established in 1889, the bar served as a supermarket temporarily during the Prohibition era, though rumor has it that you could still find a few libations in the back room. Today the beer flows freely, along with the music, conversation, and food. A full menu offers starters, burgers, and sandwiches.

**Liquid**
**112 Washington Street**
**(203) 866–0800**
With two floors of action, Liquid has a true dance-club atmosphere with pounding bass, flashing lights, and cold drinks. Each floor has its own bar and different type of music. Leave your coat at the door and boogy all night. This is a great

place for singles to find one another, and the plethora of nearby restaurants makes it a nice after-dinner destination. The club even offers a nonalcoholic teen dance party on Sunday night.

## The Loft
### 97 Washington Street
### (203) 838-6555

This martini lounge is an ultrahip spot for young professionals and singles, who sip their drinks at the bar, in the upstairs lounging area, or beside the dance floor. The live music helps visitors get their groove on, and many come back time and again to hear the "regulars" perform. Television buffs might also find it interesting to note that the Loft's original Chocolate Martini was recently featured as one of the country's "Best Chocolate Indulgences" on the Food Network's *Top 5* show.

## Match
### 98 Washington Street
### (203) 852-1088

In polls, locals often rank this bar and restaurant among the best in the county. Young professionals sidle up to the bar for cocktails and mingling after work and on weekends. The place is also packed during mealtimes, when couples, singles, and families dine on Match's signature thin-crust pizzas, hearty entrees, salads, and appetizers like fried calamari, Asian-inspired tuna tartare, crab cakes, and sushi rolls.

## O'Neill's Pub & Restaurant
### 77 North Main Street
### (203) 838-0222

You won't do too much dancing at O'Neill's, but you will do plenty of tasting of genuine Irish brews and food. After you enjoy a plate of bangers and glass or two of Guinness, work off all you nervous energy with a game of pool or perhaps darts. This casual bar is popular among those looking for a laid-back atmosphere, friendly faces, and plenty of food and drink options.

## Rib-Eye Bar & Grill
### 430 Main Avenue
### (203) 840-1865

The happy-hour specials at Rib-Eye include 20-cent wings on Tuesday, half-price drinks on Monday, and $2.00 shooters on Friday. Whether you're there for lunch, dinner, happy hour, or late-night carousing, the bar provides plenty of other diversions as well, including a big-screen television, dartboards, and pool tables. The menu includes burgers, sandwiches, salads, stuffed potatoes, nachos, chicken tenders, and of course rib-eye steaks. Alcoholic and nonalcoholic specialty drinks are also plentiful.

## Shenanigans Nite Club
### 80 Washington Street
### (203) 853-0142
### www.shenaniganssono.com

Local and visiting bands like INK, Big Boned, and the Buggernuts play to the crowd at Shenanigans, where you'll also find DJs playing dance and hip-hop. (Shenanigans' "DJ Juan" has been voted the county's best disc jockey in local polls.) Every Wednesday tune in for an acoustic jam with $2.50 Bud and Bud Light and $1.00 shots. Live bands are on stage every Thursday, Friday, and Saturday night. The bar is also available for private party rentals. For upcoming band line-ups and special events, check out the club's Web site.

## SoNo Caffeine
### 133 Washington Street
### (203) 857-4224
### www.caffeinecoffee.com

You won't find booze at this SoNo nightspot (and day spot), but you will find plenty of hot java, food, and live music. Relax on one of the comfy couches and listen to acoustic jam sessions, cabaret singers, and smooth tunes of every variety. (Guitar players and singer-songwriters are the most frequent performers.) Espresso, lattes, cappuccino, and good ol' coffee are available in "pepped," "buzzed," and "wired" varieties. You can also munch on salads, shrimp, cheeses, sandwiches, and lots of sweets.

# Stamford

### Bobby Valentine's
### 225 Main Street
### (203) 348-0010
Called a "sports gallery cafe," this shrine to all things Mets is co-owned by Bobby Valentine, former manager of the Mets and the Rangers. Memorabilia and collectibles line the walls, including jerseys, bats, baseball cards, and signed prints. Visitors can enjoy drinks at the bar or sit in the dining room to taste "Legendary Leadoffs" like Mookie's Fried Mozzarella and Dykstra's Buffalo Wings, or Keith "Mex" Hernandez Nachos. "The Champions" (entrees) include the 1969 Champs Filet Mignon and the 2000 Champs Salmon Filet.

### Bourbon Street
### 20 Summer Street
### (203) 324-5071
Clams, salmon, crab, and oysters are all available at Bourbon Street's raw bar; you can wash down your selections with cold beers and cocktails at the lively bar. You'll also find seafood, beef, and pasta entrees—all with a bit of a kick of course—at this nod to New Orleans cuisine and nightlife.

### Coach's
### 200 Atlantic Street
### (203) 969-2622
Is *this* where everybody knows your name? Regulars at Coach's, a sports bar with attitude, would say so. Whether you're into golf, rugby, baseball, football, or any sport in between, you'll probably find it playing on one of the bar's gazillion televisions. You can also play pool or foosball while you sip your drinks, or choose from an assortment of hot and cold appetizers. Coach's offers a good variety of domestic and imported beers, wines, and liquors.

### Crab Shell
### 46 Southfield Avenue
### (203) 967-7229
### www.crabshell-seafood.com
This seafood restaurant has a great location—right on the water—along with function rooms, lunch and dinner menus, and a marina. But the place really perks up at night, when the bar is crowded with jovial boaters and locals and live bands play in the summer. The bar even offers a special "night menu" with items like steamers, popcorn shrimp, lobster rolls, buffalo wings, curly fries, and quesadillas. Or sip on a beer, a glass of wine, or one of many varieties of frozen cocktails.

### Hula Hank's Island Grille & Bar
### 261 Main Street
### (203) 316-0278
### www.hulahanks.com
Break out your grass skirt and head over to Hula Hanks, where the warm reception and tropical atmosphere are especially appreciated in, say, January. Beers and colorful frozen drinks go well with fun menu items like Pacific Rim skewers, shrimp cocktail, grilled mahimahi, the Hula Burger, and the Hula Combo with banana shrimp, calamari, and chicken fingers. The bar is open until 2:00 A.M. on weekends, so there's no need to hurry outside into that winter wind.

### Lava Lounge
### 184 Summer Street
### (203) 602-0722
### www.lavalounge-stamford.com
A martini lounge and dance club, the Lava Lounge is a local hot spot with sultry red lighting, cool drinks, and a trendy atmosphere. DJs play everything from techno to jazz, pop, and Latin music Thursday through Sunday. Specialty drinks include the Godiva Chocolate Kiss, the Blue Moon, the French Martini, the Opal, the Lava Punch, the Magma Martini, and the Raspberrytini. Wine, champagne, and beer are also available.

## Northern Lights at the Stamford Marriott
**2 Stamford Forum**
**(203) 357-9555**
**www.marriott.com**

Grilled tuna satay, the "fork and knife" burger, oyster shooters with lemon vodka, polenta fries, Thai chicken, and "adult" macaroni and cheese with lobster are just some of the "pass-around" tasty snacks available throughout the day at Northern Lights, a relatively new lounge and restaurant located within the Stamford Marriott. The bar is also known for its live jazz, wines and champagnes by the glass, single-malt scotch list, and specialty drinks like the Northern Lights Martini, the Chocolate Martini, and the Patron Margarita. (For more information about the Marriott, see the Accommodations chapter.)

## Rack 'n' Roll
**268 Atlantic Street**
**(203) 327-9911**
**www.racknrollbilliards.com**

This billiards club and bar features pool tournaments every Thursday, traveling tournaments, dartboards and dart leagues, tons of tables, a bar, and wandering waitresses ready to take your order. Bass Ale, Bud Light, Red Hook Blonde Ale, and Guinness are all on tap. If all that playing and drinking makes you hungry, choose from menu items like pizza, chicken fingers, burgers, french fries, and daily specials. Visit the Web site to learn about upcoming tournaments and current league openings.

## SBC Downtown
**131 Summer Street**
**(203) 327-BEER**
**www.southportbrewing.com**

Why sip an import when you can enjoy brews made right here in Fairfield County? SBC's homebrewed specialties include Pequot IPA, the StamPorter, and Mill Hill Pilsner. For more information about drinks, special events, and menu offerings, see the listing for SBC Downtown's sister location, the Southport Brewing Company, in Fairfield.

## Temple Bar
**120 Bedford Street**
**(203) 708-9000**
**www.thetemplebar.com**

Located in the downtown area, the Temple Bar attracts locals and visitors looking for hearty fare, a cold beer, and a no-hassle atmosphere. But this is no simple neighborhood hangout: The spot offers 10,000 square feet for eating, drinking, and even dancing to jazz, folk, and traditional Irish music. Many of the interior's decorative details, including the bars and decorative arches, were imported directly from Europe. Enjoy a full meal or just choose from appetizers like onion rings, popcorn shrimp, buffalo wings, and nachos.

## Terrace Club
**1938 West Main Street**
**(203) 961-9770**
**www.terraceclub.com**

Ballroom dancing, country-western nights, R&B parties, buffet dinners, DJ dance parties, and Friday-night happy hours are just a few of the scheduled events you can join at the Terrace Club. The site boasts an 1,800-square-foot dance floor, flashing lights, bars, and a 2:00 A.M. closing time. But the biggest draw at the Terrace Club is Latin Night, which attracts people from around Connecticut and New York with merengue bands, DJs, and group salsa lessons. Some events have a cover charge; check the Web site for upcoming schedules and admission prices.

## Thirsty Turtle
**84 West Park Place**
**(203) 973-0300**

Screaming Broccoli, Dog Voices, Monster, and the Zoo are just a few of the local bands that regularly make an on-stage ruckus at the Thirsty Turtle. And you won't get thirsty while you rock 'n' roll: Specialty drinks here include the Turtle Shell, the Red-Eared Slider, the Hard Shell, the Purple Turtle, the Twisted Tortoise, and the Shell Shocker. Come for a visit any night of the week, or stop in for a special event like the Halloween Party, the Proud to be an American Party, or the '70s Theme Party.

# Westport

### Splash
### 260 Compo Road
### (203) 454-7798

The curving bar, translucent tiles, and flickering lights at Splash all call to mind an underwater atmosphere—which makes sense, considering the bar's location next to Long Island Sound. The wine list includes more than 130 selections, and beers and mixed drinks are always at the ready. Relax inside or outside, and enjoy your drinks with appetizers like steamed mussels, crab cakes with corn salsa, and spareribs with honey soy sauce. Splash is located at the Inn at Longshore.

### V Restaurant & Wine Bar
### 1460 Post Road
### (203) 259-1160

Although it does offers happy hours, singles nights, a huge wine list, cognacs, beers, and ports, V seems more focused on its food than its bar scene. That's not such a bad thing, especially when you consider the menu. Specialties include sesame-crusted mahimahi, crab quesadillas, portobello pizza, penne diavolo, charred adobo steak, and macadamia nut–crusted chicken. A caveat for night owls: V closes at 11:00 P.M. on weekends, but this might be a good place to start your night before ending up somewhere else.

### Viva Zapata
### 530 Riverside Avenue
### (203) 227-8226

Viva Zapata provides the backdrop for a variety of occasions, whether you want to knock back a tequila with friends, peruse the wine list with your date, or simply chow down on Mexican munchies in a laid-back atmosphere. House drinks include banana daiquiris, the Brave Bull, the Tequila Sunrise, and of course piña coladas. You'll also find plenty of beers to choose from, including Corona, Tecate, Rolling Rock, Becks, Negra Modelo, and Amstel.

# NORTHERN FAIRFIELD COUNTY

# Bethel

### Front Street Fish House
### and Cranky Fish Saloon
### 1 Front Street
### (203) 778-5253

Once known as One Front Street, the new bar and eatery has a fishy focus but the same upbeat atmosphere. Before the party gets started, fill your belly with chowders, soups, and entrees like grilled swordfish steak, lobster ravioli, Caesar salad, and seafood and pasta combinations. (For the little ones, the kids' menu includes coconut shrimp, grilled-cheese sandwiches, and fish-and-chips.) In the evening enjoy live music; beers on tap and in bottles; white, blush, and red wines; and specialties of the house like the Cranky White Citrus Sangria. And don't worry if you're not feeling cheerful: The motto at this place is "Eat, Drink, and be Cranky."

### Greenwoods Restaurant and Pub
### 186 Greenwood Avenue
### (203) 748-3900

The late-night pub at Greenwoods is open seven days a week, offering a special pub menu (look for burgers and lots of munchies) along with Bass Ale, Guinness Stout, New Castle Brown, and more than 100 other domestic and imported beers. As popular as it is, the nightlife isn't the only attraction at this historic site. Diners can also choose their favorites from lunch and dinner menu items such as grilled ahi tuna, seafood marinara, roast duck, chicken sandwiches, Picadilly shrimp cakes, and shareable platters known as "pass arounds." Capuccino, espresso, and desserts are also available. You can eat in one of the three dining rooms, in the pub, or out on the patio in warm weather.

### Sycamore Diner
### 282 Greenwood Avenue
### (203) 748-2716

Why, you might ask, is a diner included in

the Nightlife chapter? Because the Sycamore is simply one of the best spots in Bethel for evening fun, especially when the classic-car rallies set up shop here on the weekends with '50s music, contests, and plenty of opportunities to check under the hood of some really cool cars. Inside, the diner serves up food and drinks designed to evoke simpler times, including milk shakes, root-beer floats, malts, and Dagwood burgers with fries. Open since the 1940s, the Sycamore still offers traditional carhop service.

# Brookfield

### Down the Hatch
### 292 Candlewood Lake
### (203) 775-6635
Located directly on Candlewood Lake, this scenic restaurant and bar offers lunch, dinner, and late-night lounging. Local radio stations broadcast from the huge outdoor deck as weekend patrons hang out with music, drinks, and good company. If you're hungry, try the peel-and-eat shrimp, burgers, and other eats served in an ultracasual style with paper towels and plastic tableware. Parking can be tricky, so try to carpool if possible. Down the Hatch is closed in winter.

# Danbury

### Boston Billiards Club
### 20 Backus Avenue
### (203) 798-7665
Well-maintained and lively, the Boston Billiards Club chain keeps regulars coming with its munchies, drinks, pool tournaments, casual games, and laid-back environment. For more information see the Fairfield listing.

### Classic Rock Brew Pub
### 1 Wibling Road
### (203) 792-4430
Overlooking the airport runways, the Classic Rock Brew Pub serves a few home-

made beers, including Wheat and Honey Maple, along with bottled standbys. As you might expect from the name, the music selection is primarily good ol' rock 'n' roll with a little blues and folk mixed in from time to time. Upstairs in the dining room, you can order burgers, seafood, pasta, sandwiches, buffalo wings, salads, and even sweets.

### Colorado Brewery
### 6 Delay Street
### (203) 791-1450
### www.thecoloradobrewery.com
This is one of the newer bars to hit the Danbury scene. The towering ceiling hovers over the Colorado Brewery's two distinct gathering areas: one for dining and one for the bar. Lounge patrons can flirt and dance to live bands while sipping homemade brews like Old Hand Ale, Hat Trick IPA, Gorgeous Blonde, Wheat Me, and Red Rocks Amber Ale. If it's dinner you want, the surprisingly upscale menu offers pan-seared diver sea scallops, Long Island duckling, herb-roasted chicken, and starters like calamari, quesadillas, and chicken wings.

### Molly Darcy's
### 39-A Mill Plain Road
### (203) 794-0449
"If you are drinking to forget, please pay in advance." So say the barkeeps at this Irish-themed hangout where you'll find a not-so-serious attitude and plenty of camaraderie. In addition to providing authentic Emerald Isle meals and munchies, Molly Darcy's also prides itself on filling your mug with the best foamy lagers, ales, and stouts. The bar has started an annual golf tournament to benefit the local volunteer fire department; call or stop by to learn more or to get involved.

### Teddy's Night Club
### 80 Newtown Road
### (203) 792-4000
### www.danburyct.holiday-inn.com
Located within the Holiday Inn, Teddy's is

one of the busiest places around for white- and blue-collar mingling singles. The after-work happy hours feature buffets and drink specials from 4:00 to 8:00 P.M. Monday through Friday. Other popular events include Oldies' Nights, Karaoke Nights, and Sunday Night Singles Parties. Teddy's DJs play danceable music every night of the week. For more information about the Holiday Inn, see the Accommodations chapter.

### TK's American Cafe
### 255 White Street
### (203) 730-1776

This sports bar caters to the college crowd—not surprising, considering that West Conn is located within walking distance. But you'll also find visitors in search of TK's famous buffalo wings (in 26 flavors) drenched in extra-spicy sauce. The bar has 12 beers on tap, more than 30 varieties in bottles, video games, 4 satellite dishes, and 30 televisions broadcasting every imaginable type of game or contest. Happy hours offer 25-cent wings and $2.00 Bud bottles. Monday Night Football and live acoustic jams are also popular.

### Tuxedo Junction
### 2 Ives Street
### (203) 748-2561
### www.tuxedojunction.net

This down-and-dirty rock 'n' roll bar often hosts good local cover bands as well as comedy acts, all-female and all-male dance revues, and even classic acts like Blue Oyster Cult and Whitesnake. Two bars straddle the dance floor and stage, while pool tables sit in the background to keep nondancers busy. The club sits next to the downtown green, located close to the parking garage and several restaurants. The Web site lists all upcoming shows and events.

### Two Steps Downtown Grille
### 5 Ives Street
### (203) 794-0032

West Conn students and local professionals favor Two Steps for its lively bar, on-the-green location, and casual but tasty food. But the bar and restaurant's most prominent feature is its cowboy boots: seemingly hundreds of them, decorated in whimsical guises and hanging from the ceiling. The Tex-Mex choices here include nachos, fajitas, rotisserie chicken, pasta, lots of sandwiches, burgers, vegetarian options, Jamaican jerk sandwiches, buffalo wings, chicken fingers, fried seafood, and chips and salsa.

# Monroe

### Buffalo Bill's Steakhouse
### 650 Main Street
### (203) 445-9672

Located unobtrusively in a shopping plaza along Route 25, Buffalo Bill's is one of the only places in town to let your hair down with music, pool tables, beers, and TV sporting events. The lounge area offers $1.00 domestic drafts during Sunday NASCAR events, 25-cent hot dogs on Tuesday night, and 10-cent buffalo wings on Wednesday night. In total, the bar has 22 televisions—3 of them big-screen. In the restaurant area you'll also find a family-friendly atmosphere where barbecued ribs, seafood, steaks, and pasta dishes are served.

### 707 on Main
### 707 Main Street
### (203) 261-2662

This fairly new restaurant offers a bar area that's growing popular with those hoping to meet friends and relax in a low-key atmosphere. Live acoustic performers entertain lounge patrons on Thursday, Friday, and Saturday nights. Appetizer options include vegetable tempura, empanada, oysters, and buffalo wings. In the main dining areas you can also sample dishes like barbecued ribs, filet mignon, shrimp piccata, and lobster fra diavolo.

# Newtown

### Fireside Inn
### 123 South Main Street
### (203) 426-7001

Although the Fireside Inn also serves as a site for weddings and other special events, singles and dancers flock to the place on Wednesday night for ballroom dance gatherings. Patrons pay a $12 cover fee and enjoy dinner, drinks, a dance lesson, and plenty of downtime to practice their moves to Latin, swing, and other tunes played by a DJ. And don't be intimidated if you've never tried this kind of dancing before: You'll find novices as well as experts in the friendly crowd.

### Hot Shots Sports Pub & Cafe
### 71 South Main Street
### (203) 270-0391
### www.hotshotssportspub.nv.switch
### board.com

A bit smaller than its sister location on U.S. Route 6 (see listing below), Hot Shots is a casual, neighborhood kind of place with Monday-through-Friday happy hours, two pool tables, a shuffleboard table, a satellite dish, and a big-screen television. Choose from 12 different drafts while you listen to the jukebox, shoot a few darts, play video games, or try your hand at karaoke on Thursday night. The bar stays open until 2:00 A.M. on weekends.

### Hot Shots II Grille
### 130 Mount Pleasant Road
### (203) 270-3373

This relatively new sports bar, located right off exit 9 on I-84, has pool tables, big-screen televisions, dartboards, an outdoor deck seating area, and sports memorabilia displayed on the walls. Visitors can expect to find karaoke nights on Tuesday and Saturday, a DJ on Friday, and live solo acoustic performances on Thursday. The bar serves up more than 10 beers on tap, including Sam Adams, Guinness, and Bass Ale. The pub is owned by the managers of Hot Shots on Main Street (see listing above).

### Mark's Tap Room
### 8 Queen Street
### (203) 270-7061

Located within My Place Restaurant, this cozy bar area offers plenty of munchies—choose from fried ravioli, Louisiana crab dip, fried calamari, buffalo wings, potato skins, and more—as well as a full selection of beer, wine, and mixed drinks. Try a "draft sampler": one four-ounce taste of each of the drafts, including Sierra Nevada Pale Ale and Guinness. There is also a selection of wheat beers, porters, and stouts. But the choices don't stop there: You'll also find Belgian specialties, pilsners, barley wines, scotch ales, and domestic favorites. For more information about My Place, see the Restaurants chapter.

### Proud Mary's
### 19 Main Street
### (203) 270-1876

One of Newtown's best-kept secrets, Proud Mary's is a contemporary lounge located in the lower level of the Inn at Newtown (formerly known as the Mary Hawley Inn). Try one of the bar's signature martinis, including the Black Forest, the Jolly Rancher, and the White Chocolate Martini. Or perhaps you'll want to sip a white wine, champagne, or beer while listening to live music on Friday night. For more information about the Inn at Newtown, see the Accommodations chapter.

# Redding

### Georgetown Saloon
### 8 Main Street
### (203) 544-8003
### www.georgetownsaloon.com

There's always something going on at the Georgetown Saloon, from pig roasts and open-mic nights to "7 Card Stud" lunch contests and live music. The Web site lists all upcoming band schedules, featuring jazz nights, electric blues, rock 'n' roll, country, and cover tunes. Pilsners, ales, coffees, and wines by the glass and bottle are always plentiful, as are snacks like potato skins, buffalo wings, crab cakes, and chili. But the saloon is perhaps best known for its barbecue: While you're listening to the band, sink your teeth into ribs, beef brisket, chicken, or shrimp coated in the bar's spicy sauce.

### Squire's Redding Roadhouse
### 406 Redding Road
### (203) 938-3388

You might not expect to find such a fun joint in such a sleepy section of the county, but here it is. The Redding Roadhouse has burgers, sandwiches, salads, seafood, steaks, chicken wings, and other food favorites, along with plenty of beers, live music, dancing, and a down-home, friendly atmosphere. Fireplaces are everywhere, and outdoor seating is available on the patio in the summertime. You can eat in the dining area or right at the bar.

## Shelton

### Metro Grille & Bar
### 882 Bridgeport Avenue
### (203) 929-1000

An eclectic decor, good food, and a laid-back attitude make the Metro Grille & Bar popular with the hungry after-work and weekend crowds. Metro happy hours feature drink and food specials, including hand-carved roast beef on Friday. You can wash it down with microbrews, martinis, single-malt scotch, or other choices from the well-stocked bar. If you're coming for dinner, try the quesadillas, personal pizzas, burgers, Maryland crab cakes, or porterhouse steaks.

# SHOPPING

In Fairfield County, shopping bags are as common a sight as SUVs and golden retrievers. The area could fairly be called a shopper's paradise, particularly in Westport, Greenwich, and New Canaan, where boutiques are plentiful and selections are fun, varied, and almost invariably upscale.

That's not to say that discount and chain stores are unavailable. For the most part you'll have to visit the larger urban areas of Bridgeport, Stamford, Danbury, and Fairfield to find big-box stores like Bob's; Home Depot; Linens 'n Things; Toys R Us; Borders Books and Music; Bed, Bath & Beyond; Barnes & Noble; Marshall's; and WalMart. Fairly recent big-brand additions to the area include Target and Kohl's stores. We also have our share of mammoth malls (see Shopping Malls) filled with the country's best-known clothing, jewelry, and department stores.

The following is a sampling of the more interesting and unique shops and boutiques in the area, with a concentration on independently owned and operated businesses. Most of the stores listed are located in the southern region of the county. That's not because the northern region has no shopping opportunities; rather, many of the businesses in the Greater Danbury area tend to be chain stores.

*If you want to park your car once and enjoy boutiques, brick sidewalks, coffee shops, restaurants, and galleries all in one spot, head to one of Fairfield County's shopping districts. Greenwich Avenue is the most famous, but other great spots include Downtown Bethel, Downtown New Canaan, Downtown Ridgefield, Downtown Westport, Downtown Stamford, and SoNo.*

## ANTIQUES

**English Heritage Antiques**
**13 South Avenue, New Canaan**
**(203) 966-2979**
English period furniture is the focus at English Heritage, where the antiques selection includes fine wood tables and chairs, china, candlesticks, chandeliers, Oriental rugs, oil paintings, porcelain, upholstered chairs, armoires, writing desks, engravings, dressers, mirrors, coffee tables, and chiffoniers. All the items in the two-story showroom are imported directly from England.

**Greenwood Antiques and Consignments**
**153 Greenwood Avenue, Bethel**
**(203) 798-6984**
You'll walk by this small and charming shop, a great spot for browsing, while you're in the downtown area. The stock includes plenty of children's items, including books, toys, and collectibles. You'll also find headboards, end tables, lamps, mirrors, rugs, hanging light fixtures, china, kitchen gadgets, decorative knickknacks, and other household goods. The items usually spill out onto the sidewalk.

**Ivy Urn**
**115 Mason Street, Greenwich**
**(203) 661-5287**
**www.ivyurn.com**
The Ivy Urn specializes in antique items such as Wedgewood, iron plant stands and other iron accessories, clocks, 19th-century furniture, and porcelain. The store also stocks a wide selection of silk flowers, eclectic birdhouses, topiaries, decoupage, clocks, miniature and occasional chairs, planters, garden statuary, silk embroidery, jewelry cases, and French cutlery.

**Patricia Funt Antiques**
**110 Main Street, New Canaan**
**(203) 966-6139**
**www.patriciafuntantiques.com**

Formerly located in Manhattan, this cozy antiques shop stocks an array of unusual items, including napkin rings, corkscrews, wood carvings, pottery, miniatures, snuff boxes, and royalty-themed collectibles. Shoppers can also browse shelves full of model boats, animal sculptures, oil paintings, cups and saucers, wall hangings, and picture frames.

### Stratford Antique Center
**400 Honeyspot Road, Stratford**
**(203) 378-7754**
Located just off I-95, this large, easy-to-find emporium is a great spot for rainy-day browsing. More than 200 antiques dealers rent display space in the warehouselike building and exhibit everything from inexpensive trinkets to hefty pieces of furniture. The stock changes fairly regularly, but you can usually find sports and political collectibles, tables and chairs, wooden chests, kitchen accessories, wall hangings, books, garden statuary, rugs, and jewelry from days past.

### United House Wrecking
**535 Hope Street, Stamford**
**(203) 348-5371**
**www.unitedhousewrecking.com**
Billed as "Connecticut's largest antiques emporium," United House Wrecking is truly a huge and diverse place. Shoppers looking for unique furniture will find period reproductions, estate pieces, and even retro-'50s styles. Browse a bit further and you'll stumble across stained-glass windows, chandeliers, spindles, table lamps, wall hangings, and more. Outdoor statuary, benches, and terra-cotta pieces are also in abundance.

## BOOKS

### Books on the Common
**109 Danbury Road, Ridgefield**
**(203) 431-9100**
This is one of the busiest independent bookstores in Fairfield County, offering an expansive selection of fiction, nonfiction,

local-interest, travel, literature, and lifestyle titles. (And what they don't have in stock, they can order.) Magazines and smaller gift items like bookmarks and writing journals are also available. The shop is perhaps best known for its credo of personalized service; the staff is dedicated to helping you track down what you need.

### Diane's Books
**8A Grigg Street, Greenwich**
**(203) 869-1515**
**www.dianesbooks.com**
A local favorite among bibliophiles, Diane's specializes in family-oriented books for kids and adults; the shop claims to have the largest selection in the country. Classics and the latest travel, cooking, mysteries, local-interest, and nonfiction titles are also available. Authors often stop by for signings and readings. During the holiday season, Diane's has "angel trees" with opportunities for customers to purchase books for children in need. Gift wrapping is always free.

### Elm Street Books
**175 Elm Street, New Canaan**
**(203) 966-4545**
**www.elmstreetbooks.com**
This relatively new community bookstore stocks all the national best-sellers in hard cover and paperback, as well as local best-sellers, summer reading favorites, and staff-recommended titles. Special events are held in the store and at local libraries and include book signings, readings, and even cooking demonstrations by local and nationally known authors. The Web site lets customers browse titles and subjects, read descriptions, and order books online.

### Friends of Ferguson Library Bookstores
**115 Vine Road and 1 Public Library Plaza, Stamford**
**(203) 964-1000**
These nonprofit stores, located at the Ferguson Library main branch and Henry Bennett Branch, are staffed entirely by volunteers. All sale proceeds benefit the Ferguson Library. The shops offer "gently

used" books, CDs, and videos, all of which have been donated. The Friends also supply other nonprofit agencies with books and supplies when needed.

## Just Books
**11 East Putnam Avenue, Greenwich**
**(203) 869-5023**
**www.justbooks.org**

Stop into Just Books for whodunits, classic literature, cookbooks, and just about any other published works you could hope to find. Local-interest books like *Walking Trails of Greenwich and Surrounding Areas* (Greenwich Audubon Society), *Anderson Guide to Enjoying Greenwich* (Anderson Associates), and *The Cos Cob Art Colony* (Susan Larkin) are always available, as are best-sellers, mysteries, reference titles, and nonfiction books in a variety of categories. Customers are also treated to regular book signings by authors, a monthly newsletter, book club gatherings, and special events for children.

## Just Books, Too
**28 Arcadia Road, Greenwich**
**(203) 637-0760**
**www.justbooks.org**

Located in the Old Greenwich section of town, this shop is the sister site of Just Books on East Putnam Avenue. See the listing above for more information.

# CHILDREN'S CLOTHING, FURNITURE, TOYS, AND ACCESSORIES

## Baby and Toy Superstore
**11 Forest Street, Stamford**
**(203) 327-1333**
**www.babyandtoy.com**

Children's bunk beds, rugs, lamps, desks, and dressers for toddlers through teens are all available at this giant two-floor showroom. Expecting a baby? The Baby and Toy Superstore also has a registry for parents-to-be and stocks everything you might need, including strollers, car seats, bottles, bibs, swings, bassinets, cradles, changing tables, playpens, bathing supplies, gliders, squeaky toys, and teething rings.

## Blessings
**1864 Post Road East, Westport**
**(203) 255-1122**

Blessings is a popular spot for parents-to-be who want to start compiling a baby registry. The shop carries tiny T-shirts, blankets, dungarees, booties, stuffed animals, and other cute items for infants. Blessings also offers a selection of picture frames, jewelry and other gift items, clothing for older children, and free gift-wrapping services.

## Giggles
**300 Heights Road, Darien**
**(203) 656-2212**

This store has a fun name and an equally fun selection. Whether your child is a newborn, a toddler, or older, you'll find something to satisfy. Onesies, jumpers, tights, dresses, jackets, shoes, jeans, shorts, T-shirts, hair accessories, toys, and more items are in stock in bright colors, peaceful pastels, and gender-specific designs.

## Kid's Supply Co.
**14 Railroad Avenue, Greenwich**
**(203) 422-2100**

**24 Taylor Place, Westport**
**(203) 454-4888**

Young ones' bedroom furniture and accessory needs are all taken care of Kid's Supply Co., a local company that also has a location in New York City. Expect to find practical and fun items, including giant model airplanes, bedding, dressers, bunk beds, changing tables, cribs, area rugs, lamps, linens, daybeds, desks, armoires, fabrics, waste baskets, pillows, and bookshelves.

## Petit Patapon
**271 Greenwich Avenue, Greenwich**
**(203) 861-2037**

**1107 High Ridge Road, Stamford**
**(203) 329-1035**

**66 Post Road East, Westport**
**(203) 227–8987**
Fashion-minded tykes can look their best
in Petit Patapon's styles for newborns,
toddlers, and elementary-age boys and
girls. These three locations are among the
store's only locations in the United States;
the others are located in France, Spain,
Italy, Taiwan, Sweden, and other locales.
The high-end clothing collection includes
jumpers, jackets, layette sets, knit caps,
dresses, booties, rain gear, tights, blue
jeans, and swimwear.

**Precious Cargo**
**17 Sanford Street, Fairfield**
**(203) 254–6686**
This cute shop has the same eclectic
atmosphere as its sister "adult" store,
Cargo Bay (see listing below) but with an
emphasis on kids' accessories and clothing. Parents will find a play area with toys,
a rocking chair, and a baby-changing station, along with such brands as Deux par
Deux, Cakewalk, Sweet Potatoes, Mulber-
ribush, and Catmini.

**SoNo Kids**
**117 Washington Street, Norwalk**
**(203) 853–3665**
Small and eclectic, SoNo Kids stocks an
array of trendy children's clothing, toys,
and accessories. Choose from purses,
sneakers, sweaters, pins, dresses, dolls,
hats, dungarees, earrings, party hats,
coordinating outfits, play sets, and more
for boys and girls. Hip and fashion-
conscious kids and parents will find the
very latest styles.

**Toy Chest**
**441 Main Street, Ridgefield**
**(203) 431–9227**
Zany, trendy, educational, and entertaining
are all words you could use to describe this
kids' toy store. Your children will find all
their favorite characters here, from Bob the
Builder to Barbie, as well as playhouses,
construction sets, costume jewelry, trucks,
stuffed animals, talking and dancing dolls,
science-exploration kits, and model cars.

## CLOTHING AND ACCESSORIES

**Anne Fontaine**
**234 Greenwich Avenue, Greenwich**
**(203) 422–2433**
This is one of the few American boutique
locations for the Paris-based clothing
designer. (Others are in Beverly Hills, New
York City, and Boston.) Collections change
each season, with offerings such as
pantsuits, blouses, silk accessories,
sweaters, skirts, and eveningwear. Ruffles,
frills, and embroidery are evident in many
pieces, as are sleek, simpler styles.

**Botticelli**
**22 Greenwich Avenue, Greenwich**
**(203) 622–0330**
**www.botticellishoes.com**
Botticelli is a luxury footwear designer
with three shops in New York City and
one here in Greenwich. The styles change
with every season, so check in often for
the latest offerings in slides, pumps, high
heels, sandals, moccasins, loafers, and
men's dress shoes. Accessories and outerwear made with leather and thermal fabrics are also offered.

**Cargo Bay**
**1561 Post Road, Fairfield**
**(203) 254–8387**
In addition to gift items such as picture
frames and jewelry, Cargo Bay stocks this
season's trendiest casualwear and accessories for women. In-stock brands include
Work Order, Hard Tail, Kiko, Shoshanna,
Robin Jordan, Blue Cult, Liquid, and Free
People. Seat-belt bags are among the
most popular items. The atmosphere is
fun and laid-back, with wicker chairs and
magazines.

**Edward Tunick, Men's Clothier**
**340 Heights Road, Darien**
**(203) 655–1688**
**www.edwardtunick.com**
For more than 26 years, Edward Tunick
has been a mainstay in southern Fairfield
County with Newport Blue sportswear,

Palm Beach suits, Cross Creek dress shirts, Alynn ties and belts, and Rainforest outerwear. Another popular item is the line of Leather Man sandals, which are handmade in Connecticut. Locals can even find T-shirts, hats, and other items emblazoned with DARIEN and CONNECTICUT embroidery. The store also sells and rents tuxedos.

**Family Britches**
**39 Elm Street, New Canaan**
**(203) 966-0518**
**www.familybritches.com**
Family Britches provides high-end clothing and accessories for men, women, and boys, including jackets, ties, sweaters, blouses, and slacks. Staffers even offer an "invisible valet" service that includes a consultation, a listing of all the items in your wardrobe (with suggested accompanying accessories), seasonal updates, shoe shines, alterations, fittings, and custom-designed clothing. The store has another location in nearby Chappaqua, New York.

**Helen Ainson**
**1078 Post Road, Darien**
**(203) 655-9841**
**www.helenainson.com**
This elegant shop provides special-occasion clothing and accessories for women, with more than 150 manufacturers and designers represented in the store at any one time. Helen Ainson is the place local women and girls go when it's time to pick out a mother-of-the-bride dress, prom dress, fund-raiser gala dress, or cocktail dress. Businesswear separates and sportswear are also available.

**Mitchells of Westport**
**670 Post Road East, Westport**
**(203) 227-5165**
**www.mitchellsonline.com**
Perhaps best known for its collections of upscale men's clothing, Mitchells of Westport offers tailored garments for men by Burberry, Joseph Abboud, Ballin, Prada, Dolce & Gabbana, Hugo Boos, and others. Shoemakers Salvatore Ferragamo, Ecco, and Cole Haan are also represented, as

are selections of sportswear, outerwear, and a variety of leather goods. Women's clothing, jewelry, and accessories are abundant. The store has long been a staple of the Westport shopping scene.

**Plaza Too**
**68 Greenwich Avenue, Greenwich**
**(203) 618-1023**
**www.plazatoo.com**
Plaza Too specializes in shoes and accessories. Visitors will find the latest trends and styles represented in the shopping selection. Browse shoe-designer brands such as Miu Miu, Cole Haan, Vera Wang, Via Spoga, Lilly Pulitzer, Kenneth Cole, Casadei, and Giuseppe Zanotti, to name a few. Kate Spade, Isabella Fiore, and Herve Chapelier handbags are also in stock, as are Donna Karan hosiery, Grace Chuang scarves, Eric Javits hats, and DKNY belts.

**Richards of Greenwich**
**359 Greenwich Avenue, Greenwich**
**(203) 622-0551**
**www.mitchellsonline.com**
Run by the same people who own Mitchells of Westport (see above), Richards sells items for men and women that, in many cases, have just made their way off catwalks. Women's designer collections include Oscar de la Renta, Hermès, Jean Paul Gaultier, Escada, Loro Piana, and Marc Jacobs. When it's time to choose eveningwear, you'll browse silk and satin dresses by Heidi Weisel, Carmen Marc Volvo, and Badgley Mischka. The store also provides accessories, shoes, and jewelry for men and women.

**Tahiti Street**
**113 Greenwich Avenue, Greenwich**
**(203) 622-1878**
**www.tahitistreet.com**
"Sun and funwear" are the focus at Tahiti Street, which specializes in swimwear, cover-ups, sandals, sarongs, pareos, and other items tailor-made for lounging on the beach or by the pool. Customers will find designer items from Calvin Klein, Nautica, Ralph Lauren, Vix, La Blanca,

DKNY, Anne Cole, Manuel Canovas, and others, as well as imported suits from sun-drenched locales like Brazil and Spain. The shop also offers another location in Scarsdale, New York.

**Vineyard Vines**
**16 Division Street, Greenwich**
**(800) 892-4982**
**www.vineyardvines.com**
Ties, ties, and more ties. Vineyard Vines specializes in men's neckware with designs influenced by the scenery and lifestyle of Martha's Vineyard. Pastels, primary colors, and hundreds of bold and subtle designs are all available in double-lined imported silk. Holiday ties featuring Santa, snowmen, and candy canes are especially popular gift items. The company also sells belts, boxer shorts, scarves, and cummerbund sets.

## CRAFT AND NEEDLEPOINT SUPPLIES

**Craft Basket**
**117 Old State Road, Brookfield**
**(203) 740-2999**
This two-story craft-supply store is worth a drive from just about anywhere in the county, especially if you're on the lookout for hard-to-find items. Upstairs on the main level, shoppers will find unfinished wood products, kids' craft sets, figurines, dried flowers, yarns, party supplies, paints and brushes, and holiday-themed craft supplies. Downstairs, the selection includes numerous cross-stitch patterns, small and extra-large picture frames, rubber stamping supplies, calligraphy sets, posterboard, and more.

**Great American Stamp Store**
**1015 Post Road East, Westport**
**(203) 221-1229**
If you can imagine a shape or an object, the Great American Stamp Store probably offers it in rubber-stamp form. From animals and letters to buildings, sports themes, and botanicals, this shop carries big and small stamps with a wide variety of ink colors. Scrapbook-makers will also like the selection of papers, scissors, ribbons, stencils, and other necessities.

**Knitting Niche**
**115 Mason Street, Greenwich**
**(203) 869-6205**
**www.knittingniche.com**
Knitting hobbyists will find a mind-numbing array of yarns at this shop, including brands such as Noro, Jaeger, Karabella, Mission Falls, Lang, Austermann, and Fiesta. They'll also find patterns, buttons, needles, instructional books, knitting bags, and other relevant accessories. Regularly scheduled classes like "Knitting 101" and "Finishing with Finesse" will help newcomers and even experienced knitters pick up some tips.

**Next Station Needlepoint**
**72 Grove Street, New Canaan**
**(203) 966-5613**
Specializing strictly in needlepoint, this full-service shop stocks hand-painted canvases for wall hangings, rugs, pillows, belts, backgammon boards, Christmas stockings, eyeglass cases, and other keepsakes. The holiday and special-events selection includes designs for Christmas, Chanukah, Halloween, Thanksgiving, Easter, weddings, and more. Staff members take pride in providing quality framing and matting for finished works.

**Village Ewe**
**224 Sound Beach Avenue, Greenwich**
**(203) 637-3953**
**www.the-village-ewe.com**
The Village Ewe is a full-service needlepoint studio with designs for Christmas stockings, eyeglass cases, picture frames, rugs, seat covers, wall hangings, belts, checkers and tic-tac-toe boards, and handbags. You'll also find scissors, books, needle cases, stretch frames, thimbles, totebags, and anything else you might need to finish your masterpieces. Regular classes and finishing services are also available.

# FINE ART AND FRAMING

**Fairfield Gallery & Frame**
**1630 Post Road, Fairfield**
**(203) 255-1277**
**www.fairfieldgallery.com**
The original paintings, prints, and sculptures exhibited at Fairfield Gallery depict a variety of subject matter, from wildlife to still life. The gallery also specializes in custom and conservation-quality framing with mats, dry-mounting, and more than 3,000 mouldings to choose from. Restoration services are also available for older or damaged works of art.

**Geary Gallery**
**576 Boston Post Road, Darien**
**(203) 655-6633**
**www.gearygallery.com**
Collectors and others who appreciate fine art visit the Geary Gallery regularly to view the rotating exhibits filled with works by local and regional artists. Such artists as A. N. Wyeth, Eric Holch, Gene Sparkman, Michael Aiezza, Robert Waltsak, Ben Jones, Sandra Aldrich, Ray Ellis, and Dana Goodfellow have all exhibited and sold works through the gallery. The Geary Gallery's on-site companion business is Accent Picture Framing and Restoration, where conservators repair and clean older and damaged pieces.

**Greenwich Workshop Gallery**
**1657 Post Road, Fairfield**
**(203) 255-4613**
**www.greenwichfinearts.com**
Despite the name, this gallery is located in Fairfield, offering hundreds of original watercolors, oil paintings, prints, sculptures, and other works for collectors and other fine-art enthusiasts. Featured artists have included Charles Wysocki, Daniel Dos Santos, Mo Dafeng, Bev Doolittle, and Paul Landry. Books and other art-related objects and gift items are also for sale.

**Handwright Gallery and Framing**
**95 Main Street, New Canaan**
**(203) 966-7660**
**www.handwrightgallery.com**
Using only museum-quality mats and frames, the Handwright Gallery provides custom framing to suit every taste. Antique, modern, hand-carved, and even 22k gold-leaf designs are available. In the gallery, oil paintings, antique maps, vintage posters, sculptures, botanical drawings, and other works of fine art are exhibited in rotating displays. Recent featured artists have included Jim Rodgers, Hunter Mallory, and Claire Conant.

**Image Arts of Greenwich**
**134 East Putnam Avenue, Greenwich**
**(203) 625-5509**
**www.imageartsgreenwich.com**
Image Arts can restore your old photographs or take new portraits of your family, pets, favorite objects, and home. The on-site gallery exhibits limited-edition prints, frames, and images on canvas, many of which are for sale. Image Arts' custom-framing service, using conservation- and museum-quality materials, can put the finishing touches on your prized works of art.

**Labriola Frame and Art Gallery**
**1061 High Ridge Road, Stamford**
**(203) 322-8756**
Artist Sandy Labriola established her frame and art gallery in 2000 as a way of showcasing local artists and providing a selection of gifts, frames, and works of art in various mediums. Members of the Loft Artists Association and the Silvermine Guild of Art are frequent contributors to the rotating exhibits. Custom framing, matting, and personalized decor services are all available. The shop also hosts lectures and special events throughout the year.

**Lois Richards Galleries**
**54 Greenwich Avenue, Greenwich**
**(203) 661-4441**
**www.loisrichards.com**
Lois Richards Galleries exhibits artists who have also displayed their work in museum and private collections around the world. Oil painting, watercolor, and sculpture are some of the media presented by such

artists as Jean Francois Bourgeat, Bunny Adelman, Moshe Rosenthalis, Nicole Blanchard, Yi Kai, and Michel-Henry. The gallery also hosts regular cocktail receptions, brunches, and previews for new exhibits, which often double as fundraisers for local charities.

### Picture That
### 84 Courtland Avenue, Stamford
### (203) 977-8203
This minority-owned company specializes in providing culturally diverse products, works of art, and art-education seminars for individual collectors, corporations, nonprofit organizations, and schools. Available videos, posters, paintings, and books explore a variety of cultures and orientations, including African American, Latino, Asian, Native American, persons with disabilities, gay and lesbian, Judaism, Christianity, and Buddhism. On-site facilities include an art gallery, a cultural center, and a gift shop.

### Street & O'Neill Galleries
### 152 Danbury Road, Wilton
### (203) 762-3474
### www.vintagemaps.com
Concentrating on antique maps and prints, Street & O'Neill offers the restored work of cartographers from countries around the world and all periods of history. Maps of all regions of the United States are a specialty. Custom framing services are also available, as is a search service to help you find just the map you're looking for.

## GARDENING AND LANDSCAPING SUPPLIES

### Hollandia Nurseries
### 103 Old Hawleyville Road, Bethel
### (203) 743-0267
Expect a crowd at Hollandia starting around Mother's Day. This large full-service landscaping and gardening center has several greenhouses, acres of young trees and shrubs, mulch, stone for walkways, a wide variety of perennials and annuals, and a gift shop stocked with statuary, topiaries, holiday items, welcome signs, and other decorative pieces. The helpful staff is happy to answer your gardening and plant-related questions.

### Nielsen's
### 1405 Post Road, Darien
### (203) 655-2541
### www.nielsensflorist.com
Nielsen's has been a Fairfield County gardening and landscaping staple for more than 60 years. The florist and garden center has an on-site greenhouse with tropical plants, orchids, and indoor flowering plants, as well as an outdoor area with shrubs, trees, perennials, and springtime annuals. Customers can preview the plants they might like to try by browsing through the display garden out back. Delivery service is also available.

### Sam Bridge Nursery & Greenhouses
### 437 North Street, Greenwich
### (203) 869-3418
### www.sambridge.com
From planters and fertilizers to evergreens, roses, and perennials, Sam Bridge stocks whatever you might need to make your garden grow. Visitors will find more than 50,000 plants (in more than 1,200 varieties) available during spring, summer, and fall. During the holiday season you'll also find Christmas trees, tree stands, wreaths, twinkling lights, and several different varieties of poinsettias.

*Shopping for fresh produce, flowers, jams, and cheese is a treat at local farmers' markets, which take place throughout the week in Stratford, Weston, Bridgeport, Rowayton, Bethel, and other county locales. For a complete listing of farmers' market locations and schedules, visit the Connecticut Department of Agriculture's Web site at www.state.ct.us/doag or call (860) 713-2500.*

**Smith & Hawken**
**30 East Avenue, New Canaan**
**(203) 972-0820**
A haven for gardeners, Smith & Hawken carries a wide variety of outdoor furniture and accessories for exterior living spaces. Choose from planters, window boxes, pottery, spades and other tools, composters, sprinklers, greenhouses, barbecue grills, storage chests, boccie sets, benches, hammocks, and a variety of outdoor lighting options. At the time of this writing, the store was planning to open another location in Westport.

**Twombly Nursery**
**163 Barn Hill Road, Monroe**
**(203) 261-2133**
**www.twomblynursery.com**
Located in a quiet, residential section of town, this tucked-away nursery hides a treasure trove of perennials, annuals, trees, shrubs, planters, mulch, and other landscaping essentials. The nursery is particularly well known for its unique "winter garden" displays, large selections of unusual or distinct plants, and comprehensive landscape-design services. Some customers come all the way from upstate New York and other locales.

# GIFTS

**A Country Touch**
**126 Greenwood Avenue, Bethel**
**(203) 791-8877**
This down-home shop is filled with colonial colors and New England–inspired country gifts. Browse a selection of hand-painted pots, baskets, and trays, dried floral arrangements, plant stands, welcome signs and mats, framed prints, candles, lamps, and salt-and-pepper shakers. The store's full-service florist shop creates individual arrangements as well as larger order for weddings, parties, and other special events.

**Adirondack Store**
**90 Main Street, New Canaan**
**(203) 972-0221**
**www.adirondacks.com**
With locations in Saranac Lake, New York, and New Canaan, the Adirondack Store offers a fun collection of books, framed prints, rustic Great Camp–style furniture, birch-bark picture frames and candle holders, welcome mats, antler chandeliers, model canoes, and other gift and home items inspired by the Great North Woods of New York. The store also stocks books and toys for kids and holiday-themed items.

**Agabhumi**
**22 Magee Avenue, Stamford**
**(203) 325-2274**
Showcasing "the best of Bali," this fun shop calls to mind tropical breezes and sand between your toes. Pottery, earrings, straw handbags and beach bags, teapots and cups, necklaces, pins, and writing journals are all part of the inventory, as are clothing items like flip-flop sandals, sarongs, hats, and visors. All of Agabhumi's merchandise is imported directly from Bali.

**Bethel Religious Store**
**162 Greenwood Avenue, Bethel**
**(203) 730-9893**
Need a gift for a christening, wedding, first communion, bar mitzvah, or other religious celebration? You'll find what you need at this well-stocked and cheery shop selling everything from bookmarks and mugs to wall hangings, jewelry, figurines, lapel pins, Chanukah candles, greeting cards, inspirational books, and children's clothing.

**Blue Moon Gifts**
**178 Greenwood Avenue, Bethel**
**(203) 798-6717**
A relative newcomer on the local shopping scene, Blue Moon Gifts is located in the heart of downtown and offers an

artistic touch with numerous hand-painted and handcrafted items. The selection includes colorful jewelry, hanging ornaments, name-brand and one-of-a-kind figurines, writing journals, wreaths, planters and pots, candle holders, and silk scarves.

### Emily's Gourmet Food & Gifts
### 170 Greenwood Avenue, Bethel
### (203) 743-3513

Emily's will help you stock up your own cabinets or find that unique something to bring to a housewarming party, wedding shower, or dinner at a friend's house. The cold deli cases house a vast array of hard-to-find cheeses, sauces, dips, and meats; the nearby shelves are stocked with a variety of pasta, teas, coffees, candies, and crackers. At the other end of the store, shoppers will find cloth tablecloths with matching napkins and table runners, picnic baskets, pottery and glass kitchen items, pot holders, and premade gift baskets filled with nonperishable foods and kitchen gadgets.

### Gift Cottage
### 154 Greenwood Avenue, Bethel
### (203) 730-1000

The Gift Cottage celebrated its 10th anniversary in 2003, a longevity that can likely be attributed to a unique selection and fair prices. The store is located in a historic house, with browsers moving from room to room in search of greeting cards, stationery sets, jewelry, Yankee candles, wedding and christening items, Crabtree and Evelyn bath items, Hauser chocolates, and ribbons and bows. The store also offers a wedding registry service for brides and grooms.

### Knobel Brothers
### Locust Hill Road and Settlers Trail, Darien
### (203) 655-0156
### www.knobelbrothers.com

This off-the-beaten-trail retailer has been providing gifts to local residents for more than 75 years. One of the shop's most popular lines is its large selection of model train sets. Other items for sale

include pottery, handcrafted furniture, glassware, rugs, jewelry, ties and scarves, decorative lamps, bags, and ornaments and other holiday items. The store also stocks tools and hardware essentials.

### Objects of Envy
### 600 West Putnam Avenue, Greenwich
### (866) 866-ENVY (3689)
### www.objectsofenvy.com

This gift gallery contains glass, pottery, crystal, and painted items made by craftspeople from around the region, the country, and the world. Some are limited editions; others are one-of-a-kind. The selection of art glass pieces includes bowls, paperweights, sculpture, vases, and goblets. Pottery items include functional bowls, vases, candlesticks, and trays, as well as other purely decorative items.

### Sassafrass
### 132 Washington Street, Norwalk
### (203) 838-2499

If you're looking for fun seasonal items, Sassafrass is the place to go. The shop is renowned for its selection of spooky Halloween decor, December holiday ornaments and furnishings, and springtime pastel knickknacks. Shoppers can also browse embroidered pillows, WELCOME signs, dried flower arrangements, candle holders, soaps, clocks, greeting cards, picture frames, and other rotating items.

### Save the Children Gift Shop
### 54 Wilton Road, Westport
### (203) 221-4030
### www.savethechildren.org

Colorful and diverse, this well-stocked store is located at the Westport headquarters of the nonprofit Save the Children. The most popular items here are the multicolored ties with child-inspired designs, but shoppers will also find jewelry, books, games, toys, greeting cards, calendars, baskets, clothing, and mugs imported from around the world. All proceeds benefit Save the Children's national and international programs.

# Think Globally, Eat Locally

Recent immigrants and adventurous gourmands can get a taste of faraway cultures at the county's ethnic food-and-gift stores. One of these is sure to please: Scandia Food & Gifts in Norwalk (30 High Street, 203-838-2087); the India Spice & Gift Shop in Bridgeport (3295 Fairfield Avenue, 203-384-0666 ); Fuji Mart in Old Greenwich (1212 East Putnam Avenue, 203-628-2107); the Pot O' Gold Irish Gift Shop in Danbury (39B Mill Plain Road, 203-744-6012); Mediterranean Specialties in Brookfield (106 Federal Road, 203-740-7177); and A Taste of Holland in South Norwalk (83 Washington Street, 203-838-6161).

Most of these locations offer pre-packaged gift baskets, freshly made desserts, and even clothing emblazoned with appropriate country flags and symbols.

**Where in the World**
**29 Unquowa Road, Fairfield**
**(203) 254-2627**
**www.gowhereintheworld.com**
No matter where in the world you're going, this well-stocked store can provide you with all the travel gear you might need. Guidebooks, maps, suitcases, and gift sets are all available, as are kids' games and activities designed to keep them busy on the plane or in the car. The shop even helps adoptive parents-to-be with information about adopting abroad and multicultural baby gifts.

## GOURMET AND SPECIALTY FOODS

**Nature's Way Health Foods**
**922 Barnum Avenue, Stratford**
**(203) 377-3652**
Nature's Way shoppers can explore the store's frozen food, dairy, personal care, vitamin, grocery, bulk, and produce departments, all stocked with organic and natural foods and other products. Among the 32-or-so staff members are a clinical nutritionist, an herbalist, and a dietician. The store also offers about four lectures per month, covering a variety of health- and nutrition-related topics.

**Stew Leonard's**
**99 Federal Road, Danbury**
**(203) 790-8030**

**100 Westport Avenue, Norwalk**
**(203) 847-7214**
Although Stew's is billed as "the world's largest dairy store," each Fairfield County location actually carries a big selection of other grocery items as well. Look for sushi, fresh fruits and veggies, prepackaged meals, pizza-to-order, cereal, candy, gourmet cheeses, juices, milk, a salad bar, fish, baked goods, and coffees. Many of the items are available in bulk. A variety of motorized dancing cows, chickens, and other characters make this a fun stop for kids.

**Trader Joe's**
**113 Mill Plain Road, Danbury**
**(203) 739-0098**

**436 Boston Post Road, Darien**
**(203) 656-1414**

**2258 Black Rock Turnpike, Fairfield**
**(203) 330-8301**

**400 Post Road East, Westport**
**(203) 226-8966**
This California import has made a big splash in our neck of the woods with its large, grocery-storelike selection of pro-

duce, breads, coffees, meats and cheeses, prepackaged vegetarian meals, pet foods, frozen foods, soups, yogurt, juices, candy, gourmet hors d'ouvres, and cookies. The emphasis here is on all-natural and organic foods, and you'll find few better selections in the region.

### Wilton Organic Gourmet
### 33 Danbury Road, Wilton
### (203) 762-9711
Providing all-natural foods and body-care products, the Wilton Organic Gourmet stocks organic fruits and vegetables, free-range poultry and meat products, organic dairy items, a variety of all-natural and sugar-free desserts, books, magazines, nutritional supplements, and soaps and shampoos made with all-natural ingredients. At lunchtime, shoppers can also pick up sandwiches, salads, and soups to go.

## HOME FURNISHINGS

### And Company, Inc.
### 108 Washington Street, Norwalk
### (203) 831-8855
This upscale home and garden store stocks an interesting mix of clothing, watches, shoes, cosmetics, briefcases, pillows, fabric swatches, rugs, pottery, bedding, and handbags. The store also specializes in hard-to-find Kiehl's products and is located in the midst of the downtown shopping and dining district.

### Belgian Huis
### 409 Main Street, Ridgefield
### (203) 438-5599
As the proprietors of Belgian Huis will tell you, chocolates aren't the only high-quality items made in Belgium. This store sells reproduction Flemish tapestries, Brussels lace, Libeco-Lagae table and bed linens, Val Saint-Lambert crystal stemware, V. Pierre lamps, tapestry pillow covers, and imported terry bath towels. Owner Hans Bulteryst is a native of Belgian.

*If you go grocery shopping at Stew Leonard's (100 Westport Avenue in Norwalk or 99 Federal Road in Danbury), be sure to show up with an empty stomach. The well-known local chain, billed as "the world's largest dairy store," often tempts shoppers with free samples, including apple pie, broken cookies, orange juice, chopped-up blueberry muffins, and cheese wedges. The stores also offer salad bars, frozen-yogurt counters, fresh-coffee vendors, and cook-out meals.*

### Casa Bella
### 101 Wilton Town Green, Wilton
### (203) 834-1490
Located on the town green, this home-furnishing and gift store offers a selection of tables, chairs, stationery, candles, glassware, fine fabrics, centerpieces, serving pieces, lamps, and elegant gifts ranging in price from $20 to $1,000. Casa Bella staff members also provide accessory design and interior-space planning services upon request.

### Country Living Imports
### 226 Mill Street, Greenwich
### (203) 531-9460
The emphasis here is on rustic wood furniture, all handcrafted and imported from Brazil. Corner tables, hutches and cabinets, coffee tables, kitchen tables, benches, and end tables are all on display, as are a variety of custom-jewelry pieces. Some wood pieces are unadorned; others feature detailed painting or inlay designs.

### Design Solutions
### 146 Elm Street, New Canaan
### (203) 966-3116
### www.designsolutions.com
Design Solutions offers furniture and accessories for the home, including a fun selection for children's and teenagers' bedrooms. Choose from wood and uphol-stered furniture, area rugs, lamps, mirrors,

pottery, linens, and other basics, along with whimsical extras designed to showcase individual style. In-house design services are also available.

### European's Furniture and Gifts
**213 Main Street, Danbury**
**(203) 797-0761**
European's has been providing mattresses, bed frames, headboards, tables, chairs, lamps, armoires, dressers, mirrors, coffee tables, end tables, and other furniture essentials in Danbury for more than 20 years. The store also offers decorative extras such as crystal, ceramics, flatware, draperies, table linens, and gift items. Serta, Sealy, Lane, Kimball, and Stanley are some of the brands carried.

### F&M Lighting Showroom
**29 Federal Road, Danbury**
**(203) 744-7445**
F&M, a lighting showroom and electrical supply store, stocks parts, bulbs, wires, and other repair essentials, as well as a huge array of indoor and outdoor light fixtures for home and landscaping design. Shoppers can browse wrought-iron, brass, wood-trimmed, glass, and metal designs for lampposts, chandeliers, floor lamps, table lamps, recessed lighting, track lighting, and exterior lighting for walkways and patios.

### Fairfield Lighting and Design
**356 Black Rock Turnpike, Fairfield**
**(203) 384-2209**
**www.fairfieldlighting.com**
Hanging lights and chandeliers of every conceivable design hang from the ceiling at Fairfield Lighting and Design, a full-service lighting showroom. Choose from sconces, track lighting, recessed lighting, ceiling fans, floor lamps, table lamps, chandeliers, and other types of lighting. The store also provides lighting-design services for residential and commercial remodels and new construction.

### Kitchen Corner
**2359 Black Rock Turnpike, Fairfield**
**(203) 374-1118**
This store stocks everything you might need for the kitchen, including bakeware, pots and pans, small appliances, placemats, dish towels, cake-decorating supplies, aprons, cutlery, and a variety of gadgets and gizmos. Popular in-stock brands include KitchenAid, Calphalon, J. A. Henckels, Pimpernel, All-Clad, Oxo, Picnic Time, Krups, Braun, and Regal.

### Klaff's
**28 Washington Street, Norwalk**
**(203) 866-1603**
**www.klaffs.com**
Homeowners will have ball wandering through Klaff's vast collections of decorative and functional hardware, furniture, and accessories, including bathtubs, vanities, indoor and outdoor light fixtures, tile and stone, countertops, flooring, cabinetry, and decorative hardware. The store also offers smaller satellite locations in Danbury (11 Newtown Road) and Westport (14 Post Road East).

### Lynnens
**278 Greenwich Avenue, Greenwich**
**(203) 629-3659**
**www.lynnens.com**
At Lynnens, shoppers will find sheets ranging from 200 to 1,020 thread count, including solids, patterns, and embroidered styles. Luxurious quilts, pillows, blankets, dust ruffles, and comforters finish off the bedroom looks. The store also carries a line of sleepwear, as well as bath linens and accessories, handkerchiefs, table coverings, and baby-room items like bumpers, crib sheets, blankets, and tissue-box covers.

### Newtown Curtains
**Newtown**
**(203) 270-8643**
**www.newtowncurtains.com**
This home-based business offers ultrapersonalized service with home consultations, fabrication, and installation. Customers

can choose from a wide selection of custom drapery, window toppers, table linens, curtain rods, fringe, tassels, window blinds, and fabrics from makers such as Waverly and Robert Allen. At the time of this writing, the owner was hoping to open a storefront in the near future.

## Safavieh
**230 Atlantic Street, Stamford**
**(203) 327-4800**
The furniture collections offered at Safavieh include Coach Leather, La Barge, Hancock & Moore, Hickory Chair, Ralph Lauren, Bevan Funnell Limited, and Maitland-Smith, as well as imported French and English pieces. In addition to its Atlantic Street showroom, the company also has a 100,000-square-foot warehouse filled with furniture and coordinating accessories.

## Tile Shop
**34 Church Hill Road, Newtown**
**(203) 270-9784**

**427 Main Street, Ridgefield**
**(203) 438-9338**
**www.tiletiletile.com**
The Tile Shop's two showroom locations each stock marble, granite, handmade ceramics, and limestone inspired by rustic and historic locales in Italy. In addition, shoppers will find French terra-cotta tiles, slate, onyx, glass, metal, and other materials. Stone finishing styles include pillowed, brushed, cobbled, polished, and tumbled; in-house craftspeople are also available to install the materials in your chosen pattern or design.

## Waterworks
**29 Park Avenue, Danbury**
**(203) 792-9979**

**23 West Putnam Avenue, Greenwich**
**(203) 869-7766**

**181 Main Street, Westport**
**(203) 227-5008**
Although Waterworks is now a national chain, the high-end bath products store was started here in Danbury by the family that still oversees operations today. The three local showrooms offer a selection of bathtubs, faucets, lighting, tile and stone, mirrors, hardware, towel racks, toilets, bidets, soaps, cups and toothbrush holders, robes, personal-care sets, and shelving, cabinets, and other furniture for the bath.

# JEWELRY

## Addessi of Ridgefield
**387 Main Street, Ridgefield**
**(888) ADDESSI**
**www.addessi.com**
Addessi's jewelry collections include sparkling creations made with white and colored diamonds, gold, silver, Tahitian pearls, golden pearls, emeralds, platinum, sapphires, and other precious gems and metals—all displayed in a 2,200-square-foot showroom. The company also offers watch repair, engraving, pearl restringing, custom jewelry design, and jewelry repair services.

## Betteridge
**117 Greenwich Avenue, Greenwich**
**(203) 869-0124**
**www.betteridge.com**
Betteridge jewelers have been selling top-of-the-line estate pieces on "the Ave" since 1897. These antique and unique pieces represent two centuries of jewelry design, incorporating precious stones, necklaces, key chains, earrings, brooches, belt buckles, money clips, bracelets, rings, and others. Watch selections range from Swiss Army and Ebel to Cartier, Breitling, and Patek Philippe. Corporate gift items, gift coins, and a gift-consulting service are also available.

## Brinsmaids
**35 Elm Street, New Canaan**
**(203) 966-8654**
**www.brinsmaids.com**
Brinsmaids offers classic, contemporary, and eclectic jewelry designs with dia-

monds, black pearls, gold, silver, precious and semiprecious stones, and more. The store's designer jewelry includes collections from Robert Lee Morris, Lisa Jenks, Lalique, Michael Bondanza, Baume & Mercier, and Henry Dunay.

### Carolee
**19 East Elm Street, Greenwich**
**(203) 629-1515, (800) CAROLEE**
**www.carolee.com**
You'll find plenty of pearl necklaces at Carolee, a "lifestyle boutique" that also displays silver hoop earrings, CZ studs, chokers, interchangeable charms, leather handbags, enamel picture frames with colorful designs, a collection of sterling silver bracelets and necklaces, and watches with leather, fabric, and metallic bands. A Carolee bridal boutique offers diamond earrings, jeweled pictured frames, and even tiaras.

### Leslie's Jewelry Connection
**265 Federal Road, Brookfield**
**(203) 740-0800**
**www.lesliesjewelryconnection.com**
Those planning for a prom, wedding, cocktail party, or other special occasion will find a good selection of costume jewelry and other accessories at Leslie's. Choose from such items as silver chains, jeweled purses, faux-pearl necklaces, scarves, sunglasses, charms, broaches, crystal tiaras and necklaces, bracelets, earrings, and custom-designed pieces.

### Lux Bond & Green
**169 Greenwich Avenue, Greenwich**
**(203) 629-0900**

**139 Main Street, Westport**
**(203) 227-1300**
**www.lbgreen.com**
The Westport and Greenwich locations of Lux Bond & Green offer a large selection of not only jewelry but also a variety of decorative home items like stemware, dishes, and clocks. Diamond jewelry is a specialty: Look for engagement rings, bracelets, pendants, pins, and loose diamonds. Cus-

tomers can also browse cultured pearls, sterling, silver, gold, and precious stones.

### Manfredi
**121 Greenwich Avenue, Greenwich**
**(203) 843-7655**
**www.manfredijewels.com**
This upscale jeweler offers estate pieces, repair and restoration of family heirlooms, and a corporate gift-giving program that includes such items as Mont Blanc pens, Swarovski crystal, and cuff links. The store also stocks sparkling new jewelry pieces of every variety, including diamonds, pearls, precious and semiprecious stones, rings, watches, watchbands, earrings, necklaces, bracelets, and charms.

### Nagi Jewelers
**828 High Ridge Road, Stamford**
**(203) 964-0551**
**www.nagis.net**
For nearly 25 years Nagi has been providing the greater Stamford community with jewelry design, cleaning, and repair. For men the store offers cuff links, sports watches, designer watches, money clips, and rings. Women can choose from bracelets, rings, necklaces, and earrings made with colored stones, pearls, diamonds, platinum, and gold.

### Quality Gem
**180 Old Hawleyville Road, Bethel**
**(203) 748-4239**
This longtime local favorite offers custom-designed jewelry encrusted with cultured pearls, rubies, emeralds, diamonds, amethysts, sapphires, and other precious and semiprecious stones. Engagement rings, necklaces, bracelets, anklets, and charms can be made from gold, silver, and platinum; look for your birthstone as well.

### World Diamond Store
**56 Mill Plain Road, Danbury**
**(203) 778-6644**
**www.worlddiamondstore.com**
There's no divided focus here: The World Diamond Store expends all its

time and energy on finding, cutting, and designing diamond jewelry. As you might imagine, engagement rings are a specialty, but you'll also find earrings, bracelets, necklaces, and more. The staff includes salespeople, casters, wax carvers, diamond setters, engravers, polishers, and goldsmiths.

## PET SUPPLIES AND SERVICES

**Bone Jour**
**383 Main Street, Ridgefield**
**(203) 438-1616**
This "pet spa" and supply store is as fun as a roll in the mud for pooches, who can enjoy sniffing a selection of doggie biscuits, cookies, rawhides, treats, leashes, collars, bowls, and animal-related gifts. Bone Jour's main business is its grooming facility, which offers baths, cuts, brush-outs, nail clips, and other squeaky-clean services.

**Choice Pet Supply**
**1947 Black Rock Turnpike, Fairfield**
**(203) 334-4242**

**44 Amogene Expressway, Greenwich**
**(203) 869-4999**

**535 Monroe Turnpike, Monroe**
**(203) 261-1222**

**360 Connecticut Avenue, Norwalk**
**(203) 853-2777**

**949 High Ridge Road, Stamford**
**(203) 968-2600**
Choice Pet is a local chain that has expanded since opening its first store in 1979. Shoppers at all the locations will find a complete selection of foods, including such brands as Iams, Eukanuba, Natura, and Science Diet. The shelves are also filled with toys, treats, books, and supplies for dogs, cats, birds, gerbils, fish, ferrets, and rabbits. Delivery service is available at some locations.

*Downtown Westport's shops, restaurants, and boutiques will keep you busy. But if you're visiting in spring, the parking area beside the river can offer surprises. Swans often nest in the marshy area next to the lot by trampling the tall reeds to build huge (but cozy-looking) beds. The birds seem undisturbed by nearby joggers and walkers on the sidewalk.*

**Earth Animal**
**606 Post Road East, Westport**
**(203) 227-8094**
**www.earthanimal.com**
With a focus on holistic care and organic ingredients, Earth Animal stocks a variety of herbal remedies, nutritional supplements, homeopathic remedies, and whole foods from makers such as Dr. Harvey's, Halo Spot, and Felidae. Pet lovers will also find books, travel gear, bandanas, handmade collars and leashes, bowls, birdseed, Kitty Kaviar, breath fresheners, and a variety of biscuits and treats at "Aunt Tillie's Gourmet Bakery."

## SHOPPING MALLS

**Danbury Fair Mall**
**7 Backus Avenue, Danbury**
**(203) 830-4380**
This is one of New England's largest shopping malls and provides Fairfield County's most extensive shopping selection. The mall got its name because it is located on the site of the former Danbury Fair, a yearly event that offered circus performers, agricultural shows, rides, and games. Today the Ferris wheels and livestock have been replaced by hundred of stores on two levels, including Sears, Filene's, Macy's, JCPenney, Lord & Taylor, Godiva Chocolates, Brookstone, Ann Taylor, Yankee Candle, Old Navy, Casual Corner, Victoria's Secret, J. Crew, and Pottery Barn. If

all that shopping makes you hungry, stop by the large food court—located next to the carousel on the second level—or sit down at Ruby Tuesday or Pizzaria Uno restaurants. The mall also hosts special events throughout the year like arts-and-crafts shows, home and lifestyle shows, sports cards and memorabilia shows, and visits with Santa and the Easter Bunny. Within a five-minute drive, you'll also find smaller shopping centers and restaurants like Red Lobster, Olive Garden, and Chuck's Steak House.

### Stamford Town Center
### 100 Greyrock Place, Stamford
### (203) 324-0935

Opened in 1982, the Stamford Town Center mall is home to more than 130 stores and restaurants. You'll find the biggies here, including Saks Fifth Avenue, Macy's, and Filene's. Visitors can also expect to browse independent and chain retailers such as Mimi Maternity, Rainbow Toys, Abercrombie & Fitch, Seventh Sense, Casual Corner, Bath & Body Works, Nature's Renaissance, the Children's Place, Express, Gap, Kay Jewelers, and Lindt Chocolates. Fast-food dining options include Master Wok, TCBY, Mrs. Field's Original Cookie Company, Green Leaf, Wetzel's Pretzels, Sbarro, A&W All American Food, and the Coffee Beanery.

### Westfield Shoppingtown Trumbull
### 5065 Main Street, Trumbull
### (203) 372-4500

Located just off the Merritt Parkway near the Bridgeport city border, Westfield Shoppingtown Trumbull (better known to locals as "the Trumbull mall") has anchor stores like JCPenney, Macy's, and Filene's, as well as a host of smaller chain stores like Eddie Bauer, CVS, Zales Jewelers, Footlocker, Waldenbooks, Fashion Bug, Lenscrafters, Naturalizer, Ritz Camera, Talbots, Aeropostale, and Things Remembered. The food court, located on the lower lever, offers a seating area and quick-serve eateries like Bain's Deli, McDonald's, Taco Bell, Sbarro, and Pretzel

Time. At the time of this writing, the mall also had one sit-down restaurant, Ruby Tuesday, and was planning to open a Bennigan's Restaurant in the near future.

## SPA SERVICES AND PRODUCTS

### A New Beginning
### 68 Stony Hill Road, Bethel
### (203) 743-9795
### www.anbsalonspa.com

Body treatments at A New Beginning include aromatic body wraps, essential back treatments, and lymphatic drainage therapy. Visitors can also indulge in Swedish massage, prenatal massage, hot-stone massage, facials, manicures, pedicures, and waxing services. Salon and spa packages, including bridal treatments, are also available.

### Adam Broderick Salon and Spa
### 89 Danbury Road, Ridgefield
### (203) 431-4156
### www.adambroderick.com

Cross off all the names on your holiday list with Adam Broderick gift certificates, including such options as "Gentleman's Spa," "Stress Eliminator," "Sunless Renewal," and "Celebration." Clients can also purchase cosmetics and hair and body products or pamper themselves with deep-tissue massage, mother-to-be massage, hydrotherapy, botanical facials, seaweed wraps, Sedona mud wraps, and bridal hair styling.

### Derma Clinic
### 299 Post Road East, Westport
### (203) 227-0771
### www.dermaclinicspa.com

Unwind at the Derma's Clinic's Retreat Rooms, designed to ease your mind and body with thick towels, soft slippers, fresh-cut flowers, and relaxing music. Spa services include hydrotherapy, facials, waxing, massage, mineral wraps, and hair and nail treatments. The men's clinic provides back scrubs, manicures, sports massage, and other services created with male clients in mind. Gift certificates are available.

## Lanphier Day Spa
**25-52 Old Kings Highway North, Darien**
**(203) 656-4444**
**www.lanphierdayspa.com**
Full body massage, herbal steam showers, facials, salt-glow body treatments, body bronzer treatments, stone massage, waxing, makeup application, sports massage, sea-mud body masks, and manicures are just a few of the services available at Lanphier Day Spa. A full-service hair salon offers cuts, color treatments, and styling for men, women, and children. Visitors can also purchase a variety of shampoos, lotions, and other beauty products.

## Stonewater Spa and Boutique
**151 Greenwich Avenue, Greenwich**
**(203) 622-7424**
**www.stonewater.com**
Visitors at Stonewater can browse body-care products by such makers as Aveda, Cali, Nailtiques, Essie, Pacifica, Elizabeth W, and OPI, along with robes, neck wraps, slippers, and relaxation CDs. The spa also offers full-body massage, facials, makeup application, hair care, manicures and pedicures, body treatments, and microdermabrasion services.

## Take Time Relaxation Center
**130 Greenwood Avenue, Bethel**
**(203) 792-2456**
Feeling stressed? Go to downtown Bethel and stop into Take Time for a bit of quick relief. The spa and relaxation center offers Swedish massage, acupressure, reflexology, Reiki, facials, and hot-stone massage, along with yoga classes, presentations, and workshops in subjects like feng shui, dream interpretation, and kinesiology. Class schedules and topics change every season; call for the latest times and offerings.

# SPORTS AND RECREATION

## Bethel Cycle & Fitness
**120 Greenwood Avenue, Bethel**
**(203) 792-4640**
**www.bethelcycle.com**
Bethel Cycle carries every type of two-wheeled transport, from your child's first bike to high-end, professional racing bicycles. Brands include Cannondale, Colnago, Pinarello, and Look. You'll also find a full line of biking accessories and clothing. The company has been in its downtown location for more than 28 years, and cyclists come from near and far to take advantage of the shop's professional bike fitting and repair services. Contact the staff for more information about group rides and the local cycling club.

## Beval Saddlery
**50 Pine Street, New Canaan**
**(203) 966-7828**
**www.beval.com**
Equestrians need look no farther for equipment, clothing, accessories, and other items necessary to their sport. Bats, crops, saddles, bits, boots, leg wraps, polo wraps, halters, leads, bridles, spurs, training equipment, and travel bags are all on hand, featuring a variety of brands and designers. Clothing for people and horses is also available, including chaps, breeches, jodhpurs, helmets, dress sheets, stable blankets, and fly sheets.

## Darien Sport Shop
**1127 Post Road, Darien**
**(203) 655-2575**
**www.dariensport.com**
You'll find a variety of sportswear for men, women, and children at the Darien Sport Shop, along with hockey pucks, ski wax, thermal underwear, snowboards, camping equipment, cross-country skis, fishing rods, wet suits, basketballs, tennis racquets, and anything else you might need to pursue your favorite sport. The store is also home to the popular Cafe DCA, a nonprofit eatery where volunteers cook

## CLOSE-UP

# Retail and Corporate Giants

More than a few well-known companies are headquartered right here in Fairfield County, boasting brands that are household names in America and around the world. Couch potatoes might be surprised to learn that the Ethan Allen furniture company has a mammoth showroom, an inn, and a restaurant to anchor its headquarters in Danbury. Right down the road in Bethel, the Cannondale bike company makes racing and recreational cycles that are among the top sellers for biking enthusiasts everywhere. In Trumbull, Pilot Pen's corporate headquarters oversees the sale of more than two million writing implements each day around the globe.

Shelton can stake claim to not one but two mythic giants in the world of retail. Swiss Army Brands, a company best known for its oh-so-cool gadgets, watches, and knives, is a local resident. And kids-at-heart will appreciate the town's other big name, the Wiffle Ball Company. The company's signature light-weight white balls and yellow bats were invented in Shelton, and the company has continued their manufacture here for more than 50 years.

The greater Stamford area houses the largest number of bigwig corporations, including the somewhat infamous WWE (World Wrestling Entertainment), which hosts wrestling competitions like RAW and TNA. If all that wrestling action makes you thirsty, the area also has two beverage companies that make plenty of concoctions to refresh your parched lips: SoBe Beverages, makers of sweet drinks like Lizard Lightning, Long John Lizard's Grape Grog, and SoBe Zen Tea, is located in Norwalk; Mott's, best known for its apple juice and juice blends, is headquartered in Stamford. Two up-and-coming cable channels, OLN (Outdoor Life Network) and Speedvision, also manage their operations in Stamford. And let's not forget two of America's largest corporations: General Electric and Xerox both call Stamford home.

and serve lunch to raise scholarship money for students in need.

**Gotta Dance**
**130 Federal Road, Danbury**
**(203) 791–9905**
**www.shopgottadance.com**
Get your dancing feet in motion at this dance-supply store, where you'll find kids' and adults' shoes for pointe, jazz, Latin, ballroom, Irish step, tap, and other favorites. In-stock shoe brands include Capezio, Sansha, Antonio Pacelli, and Coast. In addition, Gotta Dance provides body wear and accessories for cheerleading, gymnastics, twirling, skating, aerobics, and even team sports.

**Greenwich Bicycles**
**40 West Putnam Avenue, Greenwich**
**(203) 869–4141**
**www.greenwichbikes.com**
Greenwich Bicycles offers sales as well as service for kids, adults, professional racers,

and other enthusiasts. Rain gear, helmets, car racks, bike shorts, hydration systems, and shoes are all here, as well as bicycle brands like Santa Cruz, Trek, Cannondale, Baby Jogger, Diamondback, and Merlin. Customers can also stop in for free estimates, tune-ups, and repairs. The store's sister location is Westport Bicycles (see listing later in this chapter).

## Greenwich Golf
### 222 Mill Street, Greenwich
### (203) 532-4810
### www.greenwichgolf.com

This shop is devoted to one of Fairfield County's favorite pastimes: Custom fittings, alterations, and repair of golf equipment are the specialty of the house. Customers will also find head designs by Snake Eyes, Golfsmith, and Toski; shafts by True Temper, Innovative, and Apache; and grips by Royal Grip, Golf Pride, and Winn, among others. In-stock putters include Ralph Maltby, Parente Golf, and MCS.

## Gut Reaction
### 356 Heights Road, Darien
### (203) 656-9590
### www.gut-reaction.com

This cleverly titled store specializes in racquet sports, including tennis, racquetball, badminton, and squash. For more than 20 years, the store has been providing local sports enthusiasts with sneakers, tennis skirts and shorts, grips, headbands, sunglasses, water bottles, hand exercisers, wristbands, visors, and of course lots of racquets of every type and style. Private and semiprivate lessons are also offered.

## Outdoor Sports Center
### 80 Danbury Road, Wilton
### (203) 762-8797
### www.outdoorsports.com

With a giant showroom space, the Outdoor Sports Center aims to please just about every type of sportsman and -woman. Visitors can browse canoes, kayaks, skis, skates, snowboards, bicycles, tents, car

racks, hiking boots, mountain-climbing equipment, gloves, coats, and other apparel and gear. Ski and snowboard rentals are also available for kids and adults.

## Pedigree Ski Shop
### 350 Bedford Street, Stamford
### (203) 324-2200

Skis, snowboards, bindings, boots, gloves, hats, poles, and even thermal underwear are in stock at Pedigree, just waiting for your next trip to the slopes. But winter isn't the only season the store is ready for: The wide selection of sporting equipment also includes in-line skates, tennis racquets, running sneakers, bathing suits, sunglasses, two-way radios, and more. The store has two other nearby locations over the state line in White Plains and Bedford Hills, New York.

## RER Motor City
### 126 Main Street, Monroe
### (203) 459-1299

Kawasaki, Honda, Seadoo, Polaris, and Yamaha are some of the brands carried at this motor-sports superstore. The company sells everything from personal watercraft (popular with the Candlewood Lake set) to all-terrain vehicles, jet boats, go-karts, motorcycles, mopeds, snowmobiles, trailers, and even generators. Customers also have access to spare parts, motor-sports accessories, and a complete service department.

## Westport Bicycles
### 1560 Post Road East, Westport
### (203) 254-0451
### www.greenwichbikes.com

Cyclists can stock up on clothing and equipment at Westport Bicycles, which offers a full line of bikes and related gear, as well as a complete repair service. For more information see the Greenwich Bicycles listing (above).

# STATIONERY AND ENGRAVING

### Kate's Paperie
**125 Greenwich Avenue, Greenwich**
**(203) 861-0025**
Kate's has four locations in Manhattan and one here on Greenwich Avenue. In addition to providing custom printing, gift-wrap accessories, and corporate gift-giving services, the shop also offers signature collections of colorful papers, stationery, ribbons, and diaries. For those planning a special occasion, Kate's stocks wedding albums, wedding invitations, and even a variety of personalized favors for bridal and baby showers.

### Papers of Note
**Westport**
**(203) 341-8788**
Located in a private home, this stationery store offers one-on-one, personalized service for all of its clients. Children can play with toys or watch a video while Mom or Dad sip tea and browse the samples of wedding invitations, birth announcements, bar mitzvah invitations, personal stationery, greeting cards, and notecards. The shop is open by appointment; call for details.

### The Papery of Greenwich
**268 Greenwich Avenue, Greenwich**
**(203) 869-1888**
**www.thepapery.com**
With brands like Crane's, Carlson Craft, Julie Holcomb, and Birchcraft Studios, The Papery can create elegant invitations, announcements, personalized stationery, and business cards. The store will also emboss graphics and letters onto napkins, towels, memo pads, calendars, coasters, and other items. A full line of holiday cards incorporates patriotic, religious, and individualized themes.

### Therese Saint Clair
**23 Lewis Street, Greenwich**
**(203) 661-3909**
**www.theresesaintclair.com**
Therese Saint Clair has been providing personal stationery, invitations, frames, and photo albums to the greater Greenwich area for more than 26 years. Calligraphy, in-house printing, and a variety of papers are also available, as are engraving and gold-stamping. In recent years the shop has expanded its storefront selection to include gift items for "everyday" and special occasions.

### Truly Yours LLC
**Newtown**
**(203) 426-2331**
**www.trulyyoursllc.com**
A home-based business, Truly Yours provides northern Fairfield County residents with a selection of fine papers and engraving services for personalized stationery. Brides and grooms can choose from invitations, announcements, programs, and thank-you cards, as well as wedding and shower favors, napkins, matchbooks, and other extras. Birth announcements, adoption announcements, and christening invitations are also available. Call for an appointment.

# ATTRACTIONS

From aquariums to zoos, this relatively small region offers a surprising number of attractions for local residents and visitors. Some are focused on fun, offering seaside shopping, wine tastings, and scenic lighthouse tours. Others place an emphasis on entertainment as well as education with wildlife programs, train rides, botany exhibits, firefighting memorabilia, and scientific explorations. Working farms offer a chance to pick your own produce and Christmas trees. The county's many historic homes and museums offer an enticing glimpse into the past; most are run by tireless volunteers at local historical societies. The rotating exhibits, costumed house tours, dioramas, and special events preserve the culture and artifacts of each town's history; extensive research libraries allow amateur genealogists to explore their roots.

The sites listed here have plenty to offer adults and families. If you're looking for attractions that would appeal mainly to children, however, check out the varied listings in the Kidstuff chapter. Both sections detail plenty of locales designed to make the most of rainy *and* sunny days.

## PRICE CODE

Hours and admission price codes are included in each listing, although some details might have changed slightly from the time of this writing. The following scale indicates admission prices per person. At attractions offering free admission, donations are always gratefully welcomed.

| | |
|---|---|
| $ | up to $5.00 |
| $$ | $5.01 to $10.00 |
| $$$ | $10.01 to $20.00 |
| $$$$ | more than $20.00 |

## GENERAL ATTRACTIONS

### Arena at Harbor Yard
**600 Main Street, Bridgeport**
**(203) 382-9600**
**www.arenaatharboryard.com**
Perhaps best known as the home of the Bridgeport Sound Tigers hockey team (see the Spectator Sports chapter), the newly constructed Arena at Harbor Yard also hosts a variety of other large shows, concerts, and expositions throughout the year. Recent events have included professional figure-skating shows; acts like Cher, Fleetwood Mac, and Matchbox Twenty; preseason NBA and NHL games; Boston Pops Holiday Concerts; the Lipizzaner Stallions; gymnastics competitions; and a wide variety of consumer expos and other special events. Ticket prices vary by the seat and event; call or visit the Web site for the latest show listings. For more information about children's activities at the Arena, see the Kidstuff chapter.

### Boothe Memorial Park
### and Museum                                   Free
**Main Street, Stratford**
**(203) 378-0630**
Boothe Memorial, listed on the National Register of Historic Places, is one of the county's most unusual attractions. The 32-acre park was once occupied by the Boothe family, who were among the first European settlers of Stratford. In the early 20th century, two Boothe brothers used their family wealth to amass historical artifacts and build (or buy) unusual buildings for the property. In addition to the main homestead building, visitors can tour a carriage house, the Americana Museum, a miniature lighthouse, the Clock Tower Museum, a trolley station, and a black-

smith shop. In June the park's elaborate formal rose garden is overflowing with scent and color. The grounds at Boothe Memorial are open from dawn to dusk June through September; the museum is open Tuesday through Friday 11:00 A.M. to 1:00 P.M. and Saturday and Sunday 1:00 to 2:00 P.M. The park is also home to the Big Eye telescope and the Boothe Memorial Astronomical Society (203-377-9933; www.bmas.org), which meets on the first and third Fridays of each month.

## Captain's Cove Seaport
**1 Bostwick Avenue, Bridgeport**
**(203) 335-1433**
**www.captainscoveseaport.com**
This seasonal Black Rock Harbor attraction brings people to the Bridgeport waterfront with harbor cruises, Sunday afternoon concerts, tours of the Revolutionary War–era frigate HMS *Rose,* charter fishing trips, dive boats, and a boardwalk along the water. A variety of gift shops, including The WigWam, Touch of Crafts, From Stem to Stem, Toy Shop, and Candy Land, are housed in charming buildings designed to resemble seaside cottages. The seaport also has a casual restaurant, a nightclub, a heliport, and a host of special events throughout the summer.

## Connecticut's Beardsley Zoo          $$
**1875 Noble Avenue, Bridgeport**
**(203) 394-6565**
**www.beardsleyzoo.org**
The Beardsley just celebrated its 80th anniversary as one of the most popular attractions in the state. A lot has changed in those 80 years, including a shift in focus from merely displaying animals to playing an essential role in education and conservation of endangered and threatened species. Today, on-site and outreach educational programs reach more than 50,000 students each year. The zoo also participates in the Species Survival Program, the Zoo Conservation Outreach Group, university research, and various

workshops and lectures. Some of the endangered species on exhibit include ocelot, maned wolf, golden lion tamarin, Andean condor, and Amur (Siberian) tiger.

But the zoo also makes plenty of room for fun, offering birthday parties, group tours, two gift shops, a picnic grove, a restaurant, and a snack bar. During your visit, you won't want to miss the prairie dog exhibit with "pop-up" viewing areas; the farmyard with pigs, sheep, goats, and even owls; the indoor South American rain forest exhibit with a free-flight aviary and lots of aquatic animals; a steamy greenhouse filled with lush exotic and native plants; and the walking trail that runs alongside the pronghorn, deer, and bison habitats. Zoo special events for kids and adults, including picnics, concerts, and theater presentations, take place throughout the year to celebrate Valentine's Day, St. Patrick's Day, Earth Day, Pet Awareness Day, Mother's Day, Father's Day, Thanksgiving, and numerous other occasions. General admission is free for Zoo Society members and children under age three. The Beardsley is open 9:00 A.M. to 4:00 P.M. daily except Thanksgiving Day, Christmas Day, and New Year's Day.

## IMAX Theater at the Maritime
## Aquarium at Norwalk          $$
**10 North Water Street, Norwalk**
**(203) 852-0700**
**www.maritimeaquarium.org**
This is Connecticut's only IMAX theater, where visitors can move one step beyond the regular moviegoing experience and feel as though they've literally jumped inside the film. The seats seem to sit more on top of than behind one another, allowing for completely unobstructed views. But the key to an IMAX film is the special filming techniques and the screen itself, which is six stories high and eight stories wide. Most of the movies shown at IMAX theaters aim to be both educational and entertaining. The films change seasonally; recent offerings have included *Everest,*

*Galapagos, Space Station, Titanica, The Living Sea, Alaska: Spirit of the Wild,* and *Shackleton's Antarctic Adventure.* Call or visit the Web site for the latest schedules and listings. Seniors and children receive slightly discounted rates.

**Maritime Aquarium at Norwalk**    **$$**
**10 North Water Street, Norwalk**
**(203) 852-0700**
**www.maritimeaquarium.org**
The Maritime Aquarium has become a center of activity in SoNo, offering an ever-expanding array of programs, exhibits, classes, and more good reasons to visit. Traveling exhibits change seasonally. Regular exhibits and features include touch tanks, Communities Beneath the Sound, the Maritime Hall, the Ocean Playspace, Travelers from the Tropics, Jellyfish Encounter, boat-building classes, guest speakers, interactive nautical displays, and lively habitats filled with seals, coral, sting rays, loggerhead sea turtles, horseshoe crabs, starfish, sharks, and more than 1,000 other species. The recent $9.5 million expansion added an environmental education center, the Olin Technology Lab, a marine science lab, a multipurpose room/auditorium, and the Perkins-Elmer Instruments Lab. Another popular feature of the aquarium is its research vessel, which offers study cruises for children and adults.

If all that learning makes you hungry, the Cascade Cafe provides burgers, salads, chowder, sandwiches, and other treats, as well as a view of the seal pool. The gift shop is full of stuffed animals, books, toys, hats, T-shirts, jewelry, figurines, activity sets, learning tools, and collectibles—all with a by-the-sea theme. Hours of operation are 10:00 A.M. to 5:00 P.M. daily from September through June (except Christmas Day and Thanksgiving Day) and 10:00 A.M. to 6:00 P.M. in July and August. The aquarium is also home to the IMAX Theater (see earlier listing for more theater information).

**Sheffield Island and the**
**Sheffield Island Lighthouse**
**Norwalk Seaport Association**
**132 Water Street, Norwalk**
**(203) 838-9444**
**www.seaport.org**
The distinctive and beautiful Sheffield Island Lighthouse is one of Fairfield County's favorite treasures. Activated in 1868, the light sits off the coast of Norwalk on scenic Sheffield Island and is maintained by the Norwalk Seaport Association's volunteers and staff members. For a fee, the association's ferry service transports thousands of visitors each year to the island, where you can explore nature trails, have a picnic, climb the light tower, and view displays of furniture and other artifacts that give an accurate picture of day-to-day life for light-keepers in the 19th century. Bird-watchers will want to bring their binoculars—the island serves as temporary or permanent home to variety of local and migratory birds. A variety of school programs, birthday party events, and summer vacation programs get kids involved as well. The ferry is also used for sightseeing tours of the harbor and the Norwalk Islands. Call or visit the Seaport Association's Web site for updated ferry schedules, fees, and the latest information about special events on the island.

# MUSEUMS

**Barnum Museum**    **$**
**820 Main Street, Bridgeport**
**(203) 331-1104**
**www.barnum-museum.org**
Step right up, folks! This eclectic museum is dedicated to the exploits of Bridgeport's most famous (and infamous?) resident, P. T. Barnum. Learn more about Barnum's well-known "finds," including Chang and Eng (the original "Siamese Twins"), Jenny Lind (a singer known as the Swedish Nightingale), Tom Thumb and

Lavinia Warren, and others. Other features include Great Adventure, a permanent exhibit detailing the industrialization of Bridgeport in the 19th century, and traveling shows of black-and-white photography, holiday-themed railroad exhibits, and more. Families also flock to Breakfast at the Barnum, a monthly show and continental breakfast featuring puppets, bubble-art makers, dancers, storytellers, and other kid-themed performances. The museum is open Tuesday through Saturday 10:00 A.M. to 4:30 P.M. and Sunday noon to 4:30 P.M. Admission is free for children under age four. The site can also be reserved for birthday parties and other special events.

*Most of the region's museums and attractions charge admission fees, with discounts usually given to children, groups, and senior citizens. If you happen to be free on a Tuesday, stop by the Bruce Museum in Greenwich: The usual $5.00 entrance fee is waived on that day.*

### Bethel Historical Firefighters Museum                                    Free
### 38 South Street, Bethel
### (203) 794-8523

Located within the operational Bethel firehouse, this museum is maintained by the town's volunteer fire department. The collection includes tools, clothing, and memorabilia that detail the department's heroes and history. Highlights include "Old Fogotten," the department's first hand-drawn water pump, helmets, fire marks, and coats. It's a great place for scout troops, school group field trips, and anyone else who is interested in learning more about the town's firefighting history. The museum is open by appointment; call to schedule a tour or learn about upcoming special events.

### Bruce Museum of Arts and Science    $
### 1 Museum Drive, Greenwich
### (203) 869-0376

This state-of-the-art museum sits on the property of former Greenwich resident Robert M. Bruce, who left his land and stone mansion to the town under the stipulation that it be used to create a public museum. In 1993 a new building was constructed to replace the older one, complete with galleries, temperature-controlled storage facilities for more than 15,000 artifacts and works of art, meeting and activity rooms, and a gift shop. Permanent exhibits include a natural history collection of North American flora, fauna, geology, and fossils and an anthropology collection featuring Native American artifacts. Rotating exhibitions change regularly and feature black-and-white photography, paintings, jewelry, maps, sculpture, sketches, and a wide variety of other mediums. Past shows have included Contacting Pablo Picasso, Copper Through the Ages, Robert Bateman: A Retrospective, The Great American Nude, The Art of M. C. Escher, and Posters from the United Nations. The Bruce is open Tuesday through Saturday 10:00 A.M. to 5:00 P.M. and Sunday 1:00 to 5:00 P.M. The museum is closed on Monday and major holidays. Admission is free for museum members and children under age five.

### Danbury Railway Museum                $
### 120 White Street, Danbury
### (203) 778-8337
### www.danbury.org/drm

Created and run entirely by volunteers, the Danbury Railway Museum is located in the historic downtown railway station. The site pays homage to the region's railroading past with exhibits of rail-industry artifacts and operating model train displays. The museum also hosts special events for kids and adults throughout the year, including railyard train rides, family picnics, "haunted" train rides at Halloween, Santa rides during the holiday season, the annual Train Show and Rail Fair, and local and long-distance rail excursions. A well-stocked research library helps aficionados delve deeper with books, maps, old timetables, pictures, and other reference materials. The museum's hours of operation are 10:00 A.M. to 5:00 P.M. Tuesday through Saturday and noon to 5:00 P.M. on Sunday. Admission is free for children under age four.

**Discovery Museum** $$
**4450 Park Avenue, Bridgeport**
**(203) 372-3521**
**www.discoverymuseum.org**
Bridgeport's Discovery Museum is located about a half mile from Merritt Parkway exit 47. Devoted exclusively to the exploration of science and technology, the museum hosts traveling exhibitions as well as in-house exhibits, a high-definition theater, a planetarium, school vacation programs, and one-day classes and programs. The museum is closed on Monday. For more information about the museum, including a sampling of exhibits, presentations, and unique programs, see the Kidstuff chapter.

**Garbage Museum** Free
**1410 Honeyspot Road Extension, Stratford**
**(203) 381-9571**
Sound unpalatable? Don't be fooled. The Garbage Museum is a fun spot dedicated to teaching the public about the three R's of conservation: Reduce, Reuse, and Recycle. Although the attraction is open to visitors of all ages, the programs, activities, displays, and events primarily cater to children. For more information about the Garbage Museum, see the listing in the Kidstuff chapter.

**Military Museum of Southern**
**New England** $
**125 Park Avenue, Danbury**
**(203) 790-9277**
**www.usmilitarymuseum.org**
The Military Museum is a modern, bright facility dedicated to preserving the legacy of local soldiers and pivotal battles in our

nation's and region's history. Six galleries display life-size dioramas, vehicles, weapons, and artifacts pertaining to the 10th Mountain Division, World War I, World War II, and others. Visitors can even use the "Vietnam Wall" computer to quickly locate a friend or loved one's name on Vietnam Memorial in Washington, D.C. Regularly scheduled Open Turret Days allow kids and adults to climb inside the tanks and armored vehicles parked outside the museum's entrance. A gift shop provides a selection of military-themed books and collectibles. The museum is open Tuesday through Saturday 10:00 A.M. to 5:00 P.M. (except nonpatriotic holidays) and Sunday noon to 5:00 P.M. Group tours are available by appointment during normal operating hours.

**National Helicopter Museum** Free
**2480 Main Street, Stratford**
**(203) 375-5766**
Aviation fans will love this small but informative museum located within the former Stratford Railroad Station. It's perhaps no surprise that the site devotes considerable energies and exhibit space to Igor Sikorsky, the Russian immigrant who founded Stratford's Sikorsky Aircraft. Other rotating exhibits include drawings and paintings, engine parts, cockpits, prototypes, models, photographs, war-era crafts, and other displays devoted to all things helicopter. The museum is open seasonally from Memorial Day to Columbus Day 1:00 to 4:00 P.M., Wednesday through Saturday. Donations are welcomed.

**Norwalk Museum** Free
**41 North Main Street, Norwalk**
**(203) 866-0202**
The volunteers and staffers at this SoNo site have catalogued, recorded, and preserved the history of Norwalk for the benefit of today's residents and future generations. Visitors to the museum will find exhibits dedicated to the city's oystering industry, manufacturing heyday, effects of the Great Depression, and lifestyle developments in clothing, toys, jewelry,

household items, pottery, and photography. Those hoping to research family and city history can explore the vast collection of books, postcards, newspapers, maps, and other reference materials in the research library. Other features include a gift shop, a conference room, the Lockwood Gallery, and three rotating exhibits. The museum is open Wednesday through Sunday 1:00 to 5:00 P.M., except major holidays. The research archives are open by appointment.

## NATURE CENTERS

### Audubon Center in Greenwich $
**613 Riversville Road, Greenwich**
**(203) 869-5272**
**www.audubon.org**
This National Audubon Center is also affiliated with Connecticut Audubon; both organizations are dedicated to preserving wildlife habitat locally and globally. The 686-acre Greenwich site offers 15 miles of trails, an art gallery, wetlands, meadows, a nature-themed gift shop, a summer day camp for children, and numerous festival and fund-raisers throughout the year. Educational programs vary from month to month but often include such offerings as the Owl Prowl, the Autumn Foliage Walk, Migrating Monarchs, the Greenwich Point Bird Walk, and Green Architecture for the Thoughtful Homeowner. School groups often visit the sanctuary for field trips, and staff naturalists are also available to visit schools, scout troop meetings, and other locales to provide fun workshops about birds, trees, changing seasons, rocks and minerals, insects, and other topics. Admission is free for National Audubon Society members. The center is open 9:00 A.M. to 5:00 P.M. daily.

### Bartlett Arboretum Free
**151 Brookdale Road, Stamford**
**(203) 322-6971**
Bartlett Arboretum is home to an impressive variety of plant and wildlife species, as well as a visitor center, a greenhouse, an

education building, art exhibits, and numerous gardens. Unpaved walking trails wind past a pond, meadows, forested areas, wildflower fields, and wetlands: The "Swamp Walk" even has a raised boardwalk above the water. Complete trail guides are available at the visitor center. The arboretum is open year-round from 8:30 A.M. to sunset. Admission is free, although donations are gratefully accepted. Annual membership is also available.

### Connecticut Audubon Birdcraft Museum $
**314 Unquowa Road, Fairfield**
**(203) 259-0416**
**www.ctaudubon.org**
This property was the very first songbird sanctuary in the United States. Today's volunteers and staff members aim to continue the tradition of wildlife conservation with a natural history museum, walking trails, and a nature sanctuary that is home to more than 100 species of birds, bird-banding demonstrations, guided tours, children's activities, and a variety of educational programs. Classes change with the seasons, although some popular programs include bird-carving, Awesome Owls, Kinderscience, Birdcraft ABC's, and others designed for adults, families, and young children. Admission is free to all Connecticut Audubon Society members. The center is open Tuesday through Friday 10:00 A.M. to 5:00 P.M. and Saturday and Sunday noon to 4:00 P.M.

### Connecticut Audubon Society at Fairfield Free
**2325 Burr Street, Fairfield**
**(203) 259-6305**
**www.ctaudubon.org**
Visitors to this Connecticut Audubon site will find 7 miles of nature trails (including one wheelchair-accessible trail), a birds of prey compound, boardwalks, a solar greenhouse, a research library, rotating exhibits, a replica of an Algonquin wigwam, an observation platform, bridges, a gift shop, and a variety of species of flora and fauna. Popular children's programs

include Nature Nursery, Migration Madness, Changing Colors, Talkin' Turkey, and Going Batty. Adults and families can also attend special events like Enchanted Forest, Reptile Education Days, Fall Festival, and the Meet the Birds live animal show. The center is open Tuesday through Saturday 9:00 A.M. to 4:30 P.M. throughout the year. In spring and fall it's also open on Sunday noon to 4:30 P.M.

**Darien Nature Center**      **Free**
**120 Brookside Road, Darien**
**(203) 655-7459**
**http://dnc.darien.org**
Outdoorsmen and -women will appreciate this nature center located in Darien's Cherry Lawn Park. Popular features of the center include nature trails, a pond, rotating exhibits, a children's garden, and a variety of educational programs for adults, children, and families. In addition, live-animal habitats house such species as prairie dogs, snakes, turtles, screech owls, an iguana, and ferrets. Donations for animal acre are welcomed. The center is open Monday through Friday 9:00 A.M. to 4:00 P.M. and Saturday 10:00 A.M. to 2:00 P.M. For more information about children's programs at the Darien Nature Center, see the Kidstuff chapter.

**Discovery Center at Ridgefield**
**P.O. Box 926, Ridgefield 06877**
**(203) 438-1063**
**www.ridgefielddiscovery.org**
Appealing to local residents of all ages, the Discovery Center of Ridgefield is a nonprofit organization dedicated to the appreciation of the natural world. Each month brings new classes, programs, presentations, hikes, camp sessions, and astronomy get-togethers; most of the programs take place in Ridgefield locations, although some are held in Redding and other nearby towns. Participants can choose from canoe trips, garden tours, birdhouse-building, live-animal presentations, cross-country ski trips, hikes in Connecticut and nearby states, Ridgefield-area nature walks, local history programs,

symposiums on deer management and other topics, book discussions, astronomy classes, and many more gatherings. Fees for individual programs vary for nonmembers. Discovery Center members attend most programs for free or pay a reduced fee. Membership fees vary from $30 to $500 per year, depending on how much you would like to donate. The center also provides a selection of classes and programs aimed specifically at children. For more information see the Kidstuff chapter.

*You shouldn't have trouble accessing your favorite Fairfield County parks and museums on weekends, although many are closed to the public on Monday. Local historical societies' museums and research libraries tend to have more limited hours than other attractions, so be sure to call ahead before making the journey.*

**Earthplace: The Nature Discovery Center**
**10 Woodside Lane, Westport**
**(203) 227-7253**
**www.earthplace.org**
Art exhibits, walking trails, gardens, special events, and children's programs are all part of the scene at Earthplace, a 50-acre Westport museum and nature center. If you're looking to stretch your legs, try the High Woods Trail, Swamp Loop Trail, Newman-Woodward Trail, or Wadsworth Trail, which wind past wetlands, streams, beech forests, stone walls, open fields, and wildflowers. Indoors, you'll find photo galleries, a state-licensed nursery school, a natural history museum with rotating exhibits, a wildlife rehabilitation program, and activity rooms. Summer programs include Tots Summer Fun, Ecology Adventures, and Nature Trekkers. Adults can take part in the Fall Hawk Watch, Mushroom Hunter classes, and "Yuck Day" family programs. For more information about the center's children's programs, see the Kidstuff chapter. Membership fees range from

$25 to $1,000 per year, or you can pay for individual programs as you participate. The Earthplace building is open Monday through Saturday 9:00 A.M. to 5:00 P.M. and Sunday 1:00 to 4:00 P.M. The grounds are open daily from 7:00 A.M. to dusk.

**Highstead Arboretum**   Free
**127 Lonetown Road (Route 107), Redding**
**(203) 938-8809**
**www.pages.prodigy.net/highstead arboretum**
The 36 acres of woodlands at Highstead Arboretum form an interesting blend of habitats (some man-made) designed to preserve and protect native plant species. Self-guided tours take visitors on trails and boardwalks that wind past wetlands, meadows, a three-acre pond, woods, the Laurel Collection, and the Azalea Collection. On-site flora species include witch hazel, ash, American beech, and seven species of oak. A restored-barn visitor center offers maps, a reference library, a herbarium, lectures, and classes. Dogs, bicycles, food, and smoking are not allowed. Memberships are available.

**New Canaan Nature Center**   Free
**144 Oenoke Ridge, New Canaan**
**(203) 966-6536**
**www.newcanaannature.org**
Apple-cider making, maple syruping, canoe trips, field studies, live-animal presentations, and botany classes are all popular programs at the New Canaan Nature Center. Adults can also take advantage of Early Morning Bird Walks, the Annual Fall Fair, and educational classes in subjects like wildflower identification, landscape design, gardening, flower arranging, birdsong identification, ecology, rain forests, owls, and more. The staff leads trips and tours to nearby locations, including Nantucket and Block Island, as well as distant locales like Belize, Yellowstone, and Peru. The 40-acre center has two ponds, forests, a marsh, meadows, an observation tower, a visitor center, a gift shop, a greenhouse, gardens, and 2 miles of walking trails. The New Canaan Nature Cen-

ter's buildings are open Monday through Saturday 9:00 A.M. to 4:00 P.M. The grounds are open daily from dawn to dusk. Donations are welcomed. For more information about children's programs at the center, see the Kidstuff chapter.

**SoundWaters**   Free
**1281 Cove Road, Stamford**
**(203) 323-1978**
**www.soundwaters.org**
Located within Stamford's beloved Cove Island Park, SoundWaters is a waterfront museum and education center devoted to teaching kids and adults about the natural history and ecosystems of Long Island Sound. Programs exploring wildlife, river systems, marshes, history, culture, conservation, and music are held on-site for individuals, families, school groups, corporations, and other interested parties. The programs can also be held off-site with one of the organization's outreach efforts. Rotating exhibits at the Cove Island facility, known as the SoundWaters Community Center for Environmental Education, are displayed in the History/Community Room and the Environmental Business Room. The group also operates the schooner *SoundWaters,* which offers educational ecology sails and sunset sails for the public. All trips leave from the Brewer's Yacht Haven Marina in Stamford. The SoundWater Community Center for Environmental Education is open Tuesday through Saturday 10:00 A.M. to 5:00 P.M. and Sunday noon to 5:00 P.M.

**Stamford Museum**
**& Nature Center**   $-$$
**39 Scofieldtown Road, Stamford**
**(203) 322-1646**
**www.stamfordmuseum.org**
It's hard to figure out what to do first at the Stamford Museum & Nature Center: Maybe visit the Overbrook Natural Science Center, where you'll find Nature's Playground for kids; a 300-foot boardwalk; a pond with turtles, frogs, and fish; and a nature trail. Or perhaps you'll want to head directly to Heckscher Farm, a

working farm that's home to sheep, pigs, goats, ducks, chickens, llamas, cows, alpacas, and horses. (If you want to see feeding time, arrive at 9:30 A.M.) The museum is also home to permanent and traveling exhibits that encompass a variety of topics. Exhibits change regularly but have included baseball-card collections, quilts, a history of children's cars, fine art, astronomy, and Native American culture. Seasonal, family-oriented events are held throughout the year, including Winterfest in January, Maple Sugaring in March, Harvest Day in September, and Apple Cidering in October. The center's Country Store and Museum Store stock natural history books, farm-themed gifts and collectibles, food, gardening manuals, and other items; all sales benefit the center. The main building and Overbrook Natural Science Center are open Monday through Saturday 9:00 A.M. to 5:00 P.M. and Sunday 11:00 A.M. to 5:00 P.M. Heckscher Farm is open every day 9:00 A.M. to 4:00 P.M.; Nature's Playground is open every day 9:00 A.M. to 5:00 P.M.

**Woodcock Nature Center          Free**
**56 Deer Run Road, Wilton**
**(203) 762-7280**
**www.woodcocknaturecenter.org**
Hiking trails, stone walls, a boardwalk, wetlands, and mature stands of trees are all part of the scenery at the Woodcock Nature Center. The 146 acres are protected with wildlife in mind, although local residents are welcome to explore the trails and participate in the center's many environmental education programs. The program offerings include field trips, the NatureKids enrichment program, after-school programs, a summer camp, and holiday-themed events. A trail map is available on the center's Web site or at the trailheads. Restrooms and picnic areas are also available. The trails are open from dawn to dusk daily; the visitor center is open from 9:30 A.M. to 4:30 P.M. Monday through Friday.

# HISTORICAL ATTRACTIONS

**Bates-Scofield House Museum     Free**
**45 Old Kings Highway North, Darien**
**(203) 655-9233**
This 1736 saltbox is maintained by the Darien Historical Society, which offers guided tours, a research library, exhibition galleries, and a collection of books and artifacts detailing the town's history. Visitors are also welcome to browse the museum's herb garden, kept beautiful by the Garden Club of Darien. The society hosts regular and special events throughout the year, including Heritage and Holiday Happenings, Christmas in Connecticut, Hands-on History Days, Vintage Valentines, and Antiques Alfresco. Rotating exhibits of clothing, art, and artifacts are also offered. Tours of the Bates-Scofield House are available Wednesday and Thursday from 2:00 to 4:00 P.M. for a small fee. The research library is open Tuesday and Friday 9:00 A.M. to 2:00 P.M. and Wednesday and Thursday 9:00 A.M. to 4:00 P.M.

**Bush-Holley Historic Site   Free; tours $$**
**39 Strickland Road, Greenwich**
**(203) 869-6899**
This 1730 homestead, located in the Cos Cob section of town, is a museum as well as the headquarters of the Historical Society of the Town of Greenwich. Rotating exhibitions and a permanent collection pay homage to the area's distinction as the first art colony in Connecticut, displaying items like furniture, clothing, textiles, jewelry, toys, tools, and paintings that document earlier times. Visitors to the property will find a restored 19th-century barn and artist's studio, a visitor center located within the old village post office, and flower gardens. The society's workshops, lectures, and presentations help residents take a more hands-on approach to history; archives, deeds, maps, and other reference materials can help those who are interested in research and genealogy. The visitor center and

Museum Shop are open Tuesday through Sunday noon to 4:00 P.M., except on major holidays. There is no charge to visit the grounds, visitor center, and archives. Tours of the Bush-Holley House are available by appointment and are free for members and children under age 12.

---

ℹ️ *Looking for a good read and a bit of history? The Mark Twain Library in Redding was founded by the author himself in memory of his daughter, Jean. The library's facilities were recently expanded and updated—we think he'd be pleased. The building is located at the intersection of Route 53 and Diamond Hill Road. Call (203) 938-2545.*

---

**David Northrup House Museum        Free**
**10 Route 37, Sherman**
**(860) 354-3083**
**www.shermanhistorical.org**
This restored 1829 homestead is maintained by the Sherman Historical Society on the northern border of the county. It is named for the family who lived in the house during the 1800s, including David Northrup, Sherman's first town clerk; David Northrup Jr., who served as a state representative; and David Ward Northrup, who served as secretary of state. Visitors will find a walking trail, a restored barn, a pasture, and preserved furniture and artifacts inside the house. Special events, including lectures, fund-raisers, and Holiday Open Houses, are held here throughout the year. The society also operates a nearby attraction known as The Old Store (3 Route 37), where volunteers sell antiques, collectibles, and other gift items. The Northrup House is open for tours by appointment. The Old Store is open to the public Wednesday through Saturday noon to 4:00 P.M. and Sunday 11:00 A.M. to 3:00 P.M.

**Fairfield Historical Society        Free**
**636 Old Post Road, Fairfield**
**(203) 259-1598**
**www.fairfieldhistoricalsociety.org**

Appropriately located within the Historic District, the Fairfield Historical Society manages a museum and library at 636 Old Post Road as well as the 18th-century Ogden House at 1520 Bronson Road. This former farmhouse is surrounded by gardens and filled with antiques and period pieces. The museum houses more than 15,000 artifacts, some dating from prehistoric times. The society presents two different exhibits each year to highlight certain aspects of the collection, touching on everything from clothing to weapons, agriculture, and notable residents. The group's other activities include walking tours of local historic areas, archaeological digs, storytelling hours for preschoolers, a summer history camp, and tours for school groups. Those interested in learning more about genealogy or the town's history should make a special effort to visit the society's vast research library, where the shelves are stocked with more than 10,000 books pertaining to Fairfield and the many families who have played a role in its legacy. The museum and library are open Tuesday through Saturday 10:00 A.M. to 4:30 P.M. and Sunday 1:00 to 4:30 P.M. From May to October the Ogden House is open Saturday and Sunday 1:00 to 4:30 P.M. Donations are welcomed.

**Keeler Tavern Museum        $**
**132 Main Street, Ridgefield**
**(203) 438-5485**
**www.keelertavernmuseum.org**
Although it is best known as a former tavern, this circa 1713 picturesque museum has actually served many purposes for past Ridgefield residents, including stints as a stagecoach stop, a hotel, a post office, and a farmhouse. Today you'll find costumed docents leading tours around the historic property, showing visitors the Costume Display Room, hosting afternoon teas, providing garden lectures and tours, and exhibiting rotating displays of art, textiles, furniture, tools, household objects, wall hangings, and more. An on-site museum shop provides historic-themed books, pottery, gifts, and collectibles for

# Holiday Houses

If you're dying to get a peek inside some of the area's private historic homes, you might want to bide your time until December. This is the month when many local homes become part of "Holiday House Tours," festooned with lights, holly berries, poinsettias, and other decorations. In Westport the homes are decorated by professional floral designers, with all house tour proceeds benefiting the Westport Historical Society. The Historical Society of the Town of Greenwich holds a similar event. And in Newtown the house tours are accompanied by a Holiday Festival, complete with a "town crier," tea parties, and revelers who dress up in period costumes and parade up and down Main Street's historic district. For information call the Westport Historical Society at (203) 222-1424, the Historical Society of the Town of Greenwich at (203) 869-6899, or the Newtown Historical Society at (203) 426-5937.

sale. The museum's Garden House is a popular setting for wedding receptions, anniversary parties, and even business meetings. Tours are available Wednesday, Saturday, and Sunday from 1:00 to 4:00 P.M., with the last tour beginning at 3:30 P.M. The museum office is open Monday through Friday 9:00 A.M. to 5:00 P.M.

### Lockwood-Mathews Mansion
### Museum                               $$
### 295 West Avenue, Norwalk
### (203) 838-9799
### www.lockwoodmathews.org
Even in an area known for its big houses, this impressive 52-room museum and mansion stands out from the crowd. It was built by banker and railroad tycoon LeGrand Lockwood from 1864 to 1868. Today it is recognized as a National Historic Landmark and one of the earliest examples of Second Empire–style homes built in America. Such a dramatic setting lends itself well to weddings, retreats, and other special occasions, and the museum is indeed available for rent. Lockwood-Mathews also houses a permanent collection of artifacts and hosts a variety of workshops, programs, and events, including picnics, classes, guided tours, kid-oriented tours and activities, and ongoing preservation projects. Admission is free for museum members and children under age 12. The Lockwood-Mathews property and house are open to the public Wednesday through Sunday noon to 5:00 P.M.

### Matthew Curtiss House            Free
### 44 Main Street, Newtown
### (203) 426-5937
The Newtown Historical Society maintains this 18th-century house museum, a well-preserved structure that details 1700s Newtown life with period furniture, beehive oven, tall windows, austere saltbox construction, and numerous household items and artifacts—many of which were made or used by past Newtown residents. Costumed tour guides help visitors piece together the day-to-day rituals of this earlier time in the town's history, and special programs like candle-dipping, cooking, folk-art painting, and blacksmithing provide a more hands-on approach to learning about history. The Matthew Curtiss House is located in Main Street's historic district, within walking distance of the well-known flagpole, Inn at Newtown, Ram Pasture, and Edmond Town Hall. The museum is open for tours and programs on designated dates throughout the year; call for the latest schedules.

# Boo! Fairfield County's "Haunted" Places

Many New England locales are rumored to be haunted by the ghosts of past residents, and Fairfield County is no exception. Spooky cemeteries and historic homes throughout the area enjoy a reputation for late-night creakings, transparent apparitions, and unexplained phenomena. But a few spots in particular stand out from the pack when it comes to scary stories.

Near the top of the list has to be the Boothe Homestead, located at Boothe Memorial Park in Stratford. Now a museum, the homestead is part of a collection of buildings—including a clanging clock tower—built on the site by a pair of eccentric brothers. The house has windows of red glass that create an eerie red-glow effect in the front hallway and elaborate "puzzle floors" assembled with tile and other materials. Many people have claimed to see spirits here, particularly in the upstairs sunporch that has served as a military-memorabilia room and a nursery. Some visitors have even fainted on the porch, including those who claimed to have no prior knowledge of the museum's creepy reputation.

Another supposedly cursed Stratford home was the Phelps Mansion on Elm Street. Although it has since been torn down, the magnificent estate was once the talk of the town—first for its extravagant beauty and then for its unfortunate "hauntings" that cursed the resident family. A local reverend named Dr. Eliakim Phelps lived in the home with his family in 1850, when the alleged happenings began to occur. It all began when the Phelps family came home from church to find grotesque stuffed dummies assembled in the living room and hanging from the ceiling. Although the reverend dismantled them in anger, the family awoke to find the dummies mysteriously reassembled the next morning. In the following weeks, the Phelps family and other witnesses were bothered by constant banging sounds in the home that came to be known as the "Stratford knockings." Several pieces of furniture also seemed to move around on their own and then break into pieces. The curious events were even chronicled in the local newspaper of the time, the *Bridgeport Standard*.

More than 120 years later, a nearby haunting got more than local media coverage—this time the spooky story made national-news headlines and attracted onlookers from around the United States. The "Lindley Street Hauntings," as they came to be called, began on November 24, 1974, in a tiny house on Lindley Street in Bridgeport. The police responded to a terrified call from the homeowners and arrived to find furniture and appliances—including the television, the refrigerator, and a table—shifting, moving, and toppling over without any apparent human help. Numerous police and fire officials claimed to have witnessed the strange happenings, and some even said they heard the family's cat talking to them in an angry voice and then singing Christmas carols. Some blamed the events on the family's adopted daughter, Marcia, who lived a fairly isolated existence in the home with her parents. As thousands of onlookers began to converge on the street, the police superintendent called the hauntings a hoax, closed the case, and ordered the crowds to disperse. Years later, locals are still wondering: Was it really a hoax? Or did the police simply close the case to get rid of the unruly crowds? The house is still standing on Lindley Street today.

A bit farther north in Newtown, one local ghost seems more intent on merry-making and mischief than arousing fear. The Hillbrow House on historic Main Street is one of the town's most popular Halloween stops. During the Revolutionary War, French troops reportedly marched through Newtown and stopped at the house when they smelled fresh bread baking inside. The owners of the home, who were British supporters, refused to share the bread with the troops. The angry soldiers forced the man of the house, a sick senior citizen, to march up and down the local streets. The man returned to Hillbrow House after the ordeal and died in his bed. The current residents of the home say the man is still around and likes to hide pipes, silverware, kitchen utensils, and other objects around the house. The people in the home don't seem to mind, but resident dogs have long been bothered by a mischievous presence that pulls their tails and makes them whine and bark at seemingly empty space.

Haunted houses aside, a ghost story wouldn't be a ghost story without a cemetery. The old Union Cemetery in Easton obliges with tipping headstones, faded engravings, and even a resident ghost. She's usually called the White Lady: Witnesses to the apparition say she seems to be wearing a white nightgown and bonnet and wanders among the gravestones and along the side of the road. Some late-night drivers in the area have even stopped when they saw the ghost, thinking she was a stranded woman who needed help. (In some cases, the witnesses say she was holding up her hand in a "please stop" gesture.) Other ghosts have reportedly been spotted here as well. Some blame the cemetery's location; the busy intersection of Routes 59 and 136 has been the site of several fatal accidents.

And as if all those spooky graveyards and haunted houses weren't enough, Fairfield County is also home to two of America's most famous "ghost hunters," Ed and Lorraine Warren. The married couple, who live in Monroe, travel around the world to investigate the paranormal and became known for their work on cases that later became the basis for the movies *The Amityville Horror* and *The Haunted.* Ed also published a book in 1993 called *Graveyard,* based on his experiences at the Union Cemetery in Easton. So the next time you're huddled around a campfire and want to raise a few goose bumps, keep these local tales in mind. Truth or fiction? Only the ghosts know for sure.

## New Canaan Historical Society    Free
### 13 Oenoke Ridge, New Canaan
### (203) 966-1776
www.nchistory.org

The New Canaan Historical Society maintains four of the town's most distinctive historical buildings: the Hanford-Silliman House (1764); the Rock School (1799); the Town House, New Canaan's first Town Hall (1825); and the Rogers Studio (1878). The group also operates a tool museum and print shop, the Cody Drug Store, and exhibits of antique dolls, Connecticut clocks, costumes, and textiles. The on-site Jane Watson Irwin Memorial Library is the home of extensive town records, genealogical records, historic photographs, and a collection of book by New Canaan authors. The society extends its reach by hosting or supporting School Days programs, children's workshops about colonial life, and internships for high-school and college students. Guided tours are available for adults, families, and school groups. Annual events include the Open House and Victorian Tea (held on the first Saturday in December) and the Ice Cream Social (held on the second Sunday in June). Hours for the museums, traveling exhibits, historic homes, and research library vary by season; call for details. Donations are welcomed.

## Stamford Historical Society    Free
### 1508 High Ridge Road, Stamford
### (203) 329-1183
www.stamfordhistory.org

Established in 1901, the Stamford Historical Society has a mission to safeguard the city's history of families, architecture, heroes, and inevitable development through the years. Special events include book discussions, history lectures, and even trips to historical sites in Connecticut and nearby states. The Book Corner offers *Stamford, Our Pride* (Julian Padowicz, 1999); *Stamford in the Gilded Age* (Ronald Marcus, The Globe Pequot Press, 1969); *Stamford: An Illustrated History* (Estelle F.

Feinstein, Joyce S. Pendery, and Robert Lockwood Mills, 2002); and other titles. The Shop Downstairs stocks gently used furniture, knickknacks, jewelry, collectibles, and other household items; all profits benefit the society. Local residents are welcome to explore the library for information about the town's history and genealogy research. The gallery, research library, and bookstore are open Tuesday through Saturday noon to 4:00 P.M. The gift shop is open Thursday, Friday, and Saturday noon to 3:00 P.M.

## Weir Farm National Historic Site    Free
### 735 Nod Hill Road, Wilton
### (203) 834-2421

J. Alden Weir, one of America's most influential Impressionist painters, lived and worked at this 60-acre property for more than 40 years. Today Weir Farm hosts visiting artists for residency programs and also welcomes amateur painters, photographers, sculptors, and other artists to set up shop for an hour or day, take in the scenery, and get inspired. Easels and cameras are everywhere here, as are hikers, children, families, couples, and others who want to enjoy rock walls, walking trails, and a bit of history. The farm is maintained by the National Park Service, and rangers often give guided tours of the property's grounds, artist studios, barns, and Weir's original homestead. The visitor center is open Wednesday through Sunday 8:30 A.M. to 5:00 P.M. The grounds are open to public from dawn to dusk every day.

## Westport Historical Society    Free
### 25 Avery Place, Westport
### (203) 222-1424
www.westporthistory.org

The Westport Historical Society is headquartered at the 1795 Wheeler House on the edge of the downtown shopping district. Founded in 1889, the society is dedicated to preserving local artifacts, folklore, and Westport's historic buildings. Wheeler

House, which is listed on the National Register of Historic Places, is an Italianate-style Victorian with three exhibit rooms and a gift shop. An octagonal-roof barn on the property was recently restored and now houses the Museum of Westport History. The society not only houses books in its research library but also publishes them: Some titles include *Westport, Connecticut: The Story of a New England Town's Rise to Prominence* by Woody Klein and *Stories from Westport's Past* by Joanna Foster. The society's exhibits change regularly. Past shows include Flags and Quilts from the Westport Historical Society, The Bridge Not Taken: Benedict Arnold Outwitted, and Celebrity Cartoonist Holiday Cards. Donations are welcomed. The society's Wheeler House headquarters is open Tuesday through Friday 10:00 A.M. to 4:00 P.M. and Saturday noon to 3:00 P.M.

### Wilton Heritage Museum                    Free
### 224 Danbury Road, Wilton
### (203) 762–7257

Visitors at the Wilton Heritage Museum can wander through the rooms of two 18th-century local homes to get a feel for Wilton life in the late 1700s. The Sloan-Raymond-Fitch House and the Betts-Sturges-Blackmar House have been meticulously restored with authentic period furniture, flooring, toys, tools, wall hangings, art, and ordinary household objects. The on-site gift shop provides a selection of books, maps, and other items pertaining to Wilton's history. The property's Burt Barn, built in the 19th century, houses a variety of rotating exhibits. Other attractions include a blacksmith shop and the restored Abbott Barn. The Wilton Heritage Museum is open Monday through Thursday 9:00 A.M. to 4:00 P.M. and Sunday 1:00 to 4:00 P.M. Donations are welcomed.

## FARMS

Agriculture was once the primary profession in Connecticut. Today burgeoning populations and development have crowded but not eliminated local farms. You can still buy freshly grown cucumbers, recently gathered eggs, or brightly blooming flowers in Fairfield County during the warm months. Cut-your-own Christmas tree farms bulge at the seams in December, and pumpkin patches attract crowds in October. No matter what type of fruit, bouquet, or holiday accoutrement you're looking for, the county's beautiful farms have all the ingredients for an afternoon of fresh air and fresh produce.

All the farms listed below are free and open to the public, with occasional small fees charged for special attractions. Some offer farm stands, pick-your-own days, gift shops, special events, hayrides, and more; others stick to simpler procedures. Most of the farms are located in the less-populated, northern regions of the county.

### Beardsley Organic Farm
### 276 Leavenworth Road, Shelton
### (203) 929–3080

All the fruits, vegetables, herbs, and flowers available at Beardsley's farm stand are certified organic. Shoppers can also browse baked goods, floral arrangements, jellies and jams, gift baskets, and cookbooks in the farm's gift shop.

### Blue Jay Orchards
### 125 Plumtrees Road, Bethel
### (203) 748–0119
### www.bluejayorchards.com

Like most orchards, this one really comes to life in fall. Blue Jay offers plenty of pick-your-own apple action (including 30 apple varieties), as well as pumpkin patches, hayrides, pies, cider doughnuts, cookbooks, and gift baskets.

## Hubbell Farm at French's Corner
**61 East Village Road, Shelton**
**(203) 929-2052**
Established in the early 1800s, Hubbell Farm still grows herbs in a greenhouse and sells them at an on-site farm shop and herb barn. The farm's sheep provide wool for the blankets, scarves, and hats sold in the shop, where dried flowers, holiday wreaths, and other gifts are also available.

## Jones Family Farm
**Israel Hill Road, Shelton**
**(203) 929-8425**
This 400-acre farm offers something for nearly every season, including pick-your-own strawberries, blueberries, and sunflowers in warm weather and a cut-your-own Christmas tree farm in winter. Jones also has an annual pumpkin festival, a craft cottage, and free hayrides to its fields.

## Larson's Farm Market
**401 Federal Road (U.S. Route 7)**
**Brookfield**
**(203) 740-2790**
**www.larsonsfarmmarket.com**
Larson's Farm Market offers sweet corn, apples, blueberries, grapes, lemons, peaches, pears, melons, and other produce at various times throughout the year. In the fall season, visitors come from far and wide to get lost in Larson's seven-acre Amazing Corn Maze. An admission fee is charged. The design changes every year, so don't expect to go once and have it all figured out.

## Plasko's Farm and Green Thumb Gardens
**670 Daniels Farm Road, Trumbull**
**(203) 268-2716**
**www.plaskosfarm.com**
The biggest draw at this Trumbull farm is its wonderfully confusing corn maze, which is open to the public from early September to early November. An admission fee is charged. The farm also offers piles of pumpkins, a bakery, three flower greenhouses, gift items, jams and jellies, and more.

## Silverman's Farm
**451 Sport Hill Road, Easton**
**(203) 261-3306**
**www.silvermansfarm.com**
Silverman's promises "the total farm experience," with everything from a cider mill and a florist to pumpkin patches; pick-your-own peaches, nectarines, and apples; and a large farm market with jellies, jams, honey, and baked goods. Visitors will also find sunflower fields, holiday items, and even a petting zoo on-site. There is a small admission fee for the petting zoo.

## Taylor Family Farm
**57 Great Plain Road, Danbury**
**(203) 744-1798**
Stop by the Taylor Family Farm for hayrides, produce in summer, pick-your-own pumpkins in fall, a farm stand, cider, Indian corn, gourds, corn stalks, and other decorative and gift items.

## Warrups Farm
**51 John Read Road, West Redding**
**(203) 938-9403**
This all-organic farm stands out with pick-your-own pumpkins, vegetables, fruits, and even flowers. Visitors can also enjoy hayrides and a farm stand, which is open from July to October with herbs, flowers, produce, pumpkins, and more.

## Wells Hollow Farm
**656 Bridgeport Avenue, Shelton**
**(203) 926-0524**
Pick up some hanging flower baskets, pick your own pumpkins and apples, or choose a Christmas tree at Wells Hollow Farm. The site caters to kindergarten and nursery school groups with guided tours that include hayrides and feeding the cows.

## White Silo Farm and Winery
**32 Route 37 East, Sherman**
**(860) 355-0271**
**www.whitesilowinery.com**
Visitors to White Silo Farm can pick their own rhubarb, raspberries, and blackberries in September and October. Another

favorite activity here is touring the winery, where rhubarb, blackberry, and raspberry wines are made from farm-grown fruit.

# CHRISTMAS TREES

When December rolls around, a seemingly endless parade of cars can be seen leaving Easton with trees strapped to the roof. This bucolic town is the mecca for those seeking an authentic walk-around-until-you-find-just-the-right-one, cut-your-own Christmas tree experience, although plenty of other tree farms can be found in spots like Newtown, Shelton, and Redding. Most of the farms will provide you with a saw, a hayride out to the fields, and even a mesh bundling and rope for your car. All you need to bring is a warm hat and an eye for that perfect conical shape.

**Caesar's Nursery and Christmas Tree Farm**
883 Federal Road, Brookfield
(203) 775-9198

**Everett's Corner Tree Farm**
136 Sherwood Road, Easton
(203) 268-2508

**Fairview Tree Farm**
486 Walnut Tree Hill Road, Shelton
(203) 944-9090

**Four Corners Farms**
55 Hattertown Road, Newtown
(203) 426-5532

**Four Maples Farm**
49 Walnut Tree Hill Road, Newtown
(203) 426-0163

**Foxview Farm**
25 Hundred Acres Road, Newtown
(203) 426-5675

**Ganim's Christmas Tree Farm**
130 Center Road, Easton
(203) 459-9581

**Gordon's Tree Farm**
488 Sport Hill Road, Easton
(203) 261-TREE

**Jones Family Farms**
266 Israel Hill Road, Shelton
(203) 929-8425

**Maple Row Tree Farm**
538 North Park Avenue, Easton
(203) 261-9577

**Medridge Farm**
113 Walnut Tree Hill Road, Newtown
(203) 426-9178

**Paproski's Tree Farm**
5 Hattertown Road, Newtown
(203) 426-4017

**Paradise Tree Farm**
224 Lonetown Road, Redding
(203) 938-2490

**Richardson Tree Farm of the Connecticut Audubon Society**
Sasco Creek Road, Westport
(203) 932-5430

**Staib Tree Farm**
49 Walnut Hill Road, Bethel
(203) 748-1610

**Waidelich's Tree Farm**
35 Silvermine Road, Brookfield
(203) 775-9198

**Zinser's Brookfield Christmas Tree Farm**
49 Obtuse Road, Brookfield
(203) 775-4567

# VINEYARDS

**DiGrazia Vineyards**     Free
131 Tower Road, Brookfield
(203) 775-1616
www.digrazia.com
Part of Connecticut's "Wine Trail," DiGrazia Vineyards welcomes visitors to its winery

to learn more about winemaking, sample some vintages, and perhaps enjoy a picnic on the grounds. DiGrazia's unique offerings include Blacksmith, Winterberry, and Yankee Frost dessert wines; White Magnolia port; Autumn Spice and Vintage Festival whites; Berrywood and Fieldstone Reserve reds; and a variety of other sacramental, new, and no-sulfite wines. The property is also available for rent for wedding, showers, and other special occasions. The tasting room and winery are open to the public Wednesday through Sunday 11:00 A.M. to 5:00 P.M. Ongoing tours are available throughout the day on Saturday and Sunday.

**McLaughlin Vineyards**     **Free**
**Albert's Hill Road, Newtown**
**(203) 426–1533**

Tucked into the quiet Sandy Hook district of Newtown, McLaughlin Vineyards is a 160-acre property that's known not only for wine but also for its maple syrup production and perennial flower gardens. The third-generation vineyard produces a variety of vintages, including Chardonnay, Riesling, Merlot, Cabernet Sauvignon, and numerous white, red, and blush wines. McLaughlin's wines are also available for purchase through a mail-order catalog. The winery offers a summer jazz series, hiking trails, and property rentals for parties and meetings. From January to May the tasting room is open Saturday and Sunday 11:00 A.M. to 5:00 P.M. June through December the hours of operation are 11:00 A.M. to 5:00 P.M. daily. Winery tours are available by appointment.

# KIDSTUFF 👥

No matter what the weather or season, Fairfield County packs a punch for children. Science and nature museums provide hands-on learning (with a dose of fun, of course), out-of-the-ordinary adventures, and unique opportunities for exploration. Ice rinks, sports centers, and sailing clubs help to develop healthy young minds and bodies. Bear-stuffing workshops, jewelry-making centers, and pottery studios let kids be kids in child-friendly, supportive environments.

The region's attractions also help children focus on their favorite passions. Young animal lovers will find plenty of furry, feathered, and scaled friends in Fairfield County—from barnyard pigs in Stamford to seals in Norwalk and ocelots in Bridgeport. Or maybe your little one is happiest with a paintbrush in her hands. No problem; art classes and programs abound from Westport to Danbury. Aspiring Cal Ripkens can get specialized baseball training in Monroe or watch Atlantic League teams battle it out in the Arena at Harbor Yard. Inquisitive young minds will find more than a few logs to turn over at nature centers in Ridgefield, New Canaan, Fairfield, and Darien.

When that all-important birthday rolls around, keep these organizations and facilities in mind: Most offer party packages complete with food, decorations, and themed entertainment. In addition to the attractions and centers listed here, many of the local private racquet clubs and country clubs also offer child-oriented classes and programs. If you're a member, ask management what they can offer the youngest members of your family.

## PRICE CODE

The following scale indicates admission prices per person.

| | |
|---|---|
| $ | up to $5.00 |
| $$ | $5.01 to $10.00 |
| $$$ | $10.01 to $20.00 |
| $$$$ | more than $20.00 |

## ATTRACTIONS

**Arena at Harbor Yard**
**600 Main Street, Bridgeport**
**(203) 382-9600**
**www.arenaatharboryard.com**
**www.soundtigers.com**
Bridgeport's brand-new arena and ice rink has been a big draw for hockey fans around the region, and kids are no exception. The Sound Tigers hockey team (see the Spectator Sports chapter) even offers a Kids Club membership for ages 2 to 12 that includes newsletters, discounts, and other special benefits and events for fans in the 2-to-12 age group. Birthday parties at the arena are also popular: Super Celebrations and On-the-Glass Spectacular Celebrations ($179 to $249) are both available, offering seats in the alcohol-free section of the arena, a Sound Tigers T-shirt for the birthday child, a "Happy Birthday" announcement over the loudspeakers, Sound Tiger invitations, and a visit from Storm, the team's blue-tiger mascot. Storm also hosts his own child-oriented Web site and encourages hugs and high-fives from young fans as he makes his rounds during the games.

**Ballpark at Harbor Yard** $$$
**500 Main Street, Bridgeport**
**(203) 345-4800**
**www.bridgeportbluefish.com**
Everyone's favorite local baseball team, the Atlantic League Bridgeport Bluefish, offers a special welcome for young fans. The team's Small Fry Club welcomes local

children (ages 4 to 12) to join the $20 club, which includes an ID card, free admission to all Bluefish games, raffle tickets for the chance at prizes, a discount on gift shop merchandise, and admission to members-only clinics and events with Bluefish players. The clubhouse also provides B.B.'s Birthday Blowout packages ($225): Ten children and two adults can take in a game, hang out in the Kids' Cove play area, enjoy hot dogs and dessert, hear a birthday message over the PA system during the game, and take advantage of a pregame autograph session. For more information about the Ballpark and the Bridgeport Bluefish, see the Spectator Sports chapter.

### Connecticut's Beardsley Zoo     $$-$$$
**1875 Noble Avenue, Bridgeport**
**(203) 394-6565**
**www.beardsleyzoo.org**
Connecticut's Beardsley Zoo caters to kids, offering discounted rates for school groups; birthday parties with themes, crafts, storytelling, and food; and even Just for Kids animal-related activities on its Web page. Special events throughout the year are also designed with little ones in mind: At the "U and Me" educational program, three- and four-year-olds can enjoy animal encounters, crafts, and stories. Backyard Beasts, a school vacation program, is designed for kindergarteners and elementary-schoolers. The weekday Animal Tales storytelling program exposes kids to live animals and fun, educational tales about wildlife. The Teddy Bear Picnic offers those activities as well as a "Teddy Bear Clinic." The basic birthday-party package costs $14 per child. For complete information about the zoo, see the Attractions chapter.

### Larson's Amazing Corn Maze     $$
**401 Federal Road, Brookfield**
**(203) 740-2790**
**www.larsonsfarmmarket.com**
Larson's Farm Market provides local residents with fresh fruits and vegetables, jams, jellies, salad dressings, and olive oils.

But your kids are more likely to appreciate Larson's other big attraction: a massive, seven-acre corn maze where the fun is all about getting lost. The theme and maze design changes every year, so don't even bother trying to memorize your way out. The farm also has hayrides, adults' and children's "quiz trails," smaller "six-minute mazes" for the youngest visitors, and a gift shop. Admission to the maze is free for children under age three. Larson's typically opens in August and closes in November, with operating hours between 10:00 A.M. and 6:00 P.M. on weekends in August through October. In October and November the farm also has Moonlight Maze hours from 3:00 to 10:00 P.M.

### Maritime Aquarium at Norwalk     $$
**10 North Water Street, Norwalk**
**(203) 852-0700**
**www.maritimeaquarium.org**
The Maritime Aquarium is one of the most popular sites for field trips in Fairfield County, and with good reason: Parents and teachers can choose from age-specific programs held at the exhibits, in the IMAX theater, on board a study cruise, or out in the woods or at the shoreline. The aquarium also hosts educational, fun programs for children and families outside school, in which kids and adults learn about seals, sea turtles, coral reefs, jellyfish, otters, and other species of marine life. For more information about the Maritime Aquarium, including hours, see the listing in the Attractions chapter.

## MUSEUMS AND NATURE CENTERS

### Darien Nature Center     Free
**120 Brookside Road, Darien**
**(203) 655-7459**
**http://dnc.darien.org**
The Darien Nature Center works hard to promote an appreciation of animals and the natural world, and kids are a big part of that focus. Weekday, weekend, and summer programs aim to expose children

to plants, geology, mammals, insects, and other features of the outdoors. Some of the most popular programs include Nature's Playroom, a preschooler-focused 10-week session; Small Wonders, a nature discovery program held on Saturday morning; summer vacation programs like Our Living Planet and Environmental Explorers; Science in Action for children in grades 4 through 6; a book club known as Reading Ravens; after-school programs like Nature Detectives and Trail Trekkers; and animal- and nature-themed birthday parties. For more information about the center, see the Attractions chapter.

**Discovery Center at Ridgefield**
**P.O. Box 926, Ridgefield 06877**
**(203) 438-1063**
**www.ridgefielddiscovery.org**
Although the Discovery Center at Ridgefield has plenty of programs aimed at adults (see the Attractions chapter), the nature-appreciation organization also devotes much of its programming to children. Some of the more popular programs include preamble walks for preschoolers, campouts with campfire "tinfoil meals," storytelling sessions, the Little Red Schoolhouse program in a one-room schoolhouse, live-animal presentations, the Toddler Turtle Walk, stargazing programs, winter wildlife classes, and a summer camp workshop where kids learn about insects, mammals, plants, and geology. Individuals, families, scout groups, and others are all welcome. Fees for individual programs vary for nonmembers. Members can attend most programs for free or receive a discount on the rates. Membership fees vary from $30 to $500 per year, depending on how much you would like to donate.

**Discovery Museum**                      **$$**
**4450 Park Avenue, Bridgeport**
**(203) 372-3521**
**www.discoverymuseum.org**
Visitors of all ages are welcome at this science and technology museum, although most programs are specifically designed

*The Barnum Museum's Breakfast at the Barnum series is catching on with local families: Located within an art gallery at the Bridgeport museum, the monthly program includes a continental breakfast followed by a live musical performance, puppet show, or theatrical presentation. All shows are designed to be kid-friendly.*

to entertain and enlighten children. Some of the Discovery Museum's best-known attractions are the Challenger Learning Center, where visitors can take part in a simulated mission-control operation for the space shuttle; Cinemuse, a high-definition theater with shows for kids and adults; and the Henry B. duPont Planetarium with Dolby Surround Sound and child-specific programs. Permanent exhibits include Discoverytown for preschoolers, Humpty Dumpty's Puzzle Playland, the Psychedelic Light Theater, and Hoop Smarts, where children learn about the math and science of basketball. Some recent exhibits have included Grossology: The (impolite) Science of the Human Body and Sherlock Holmes and the Clocktower Mystery. School vacation camps at the museum focus on fun activities and learning in the areas of literature, history, cooking, science, art, technology, and culture. Families, school groups, and scout troops are frequent visitors, as are adults with an interest in technology. Admission is free for museum members and children under age five. Hours are 10:00 A.M. to 5:00 P.M. Tuesday through Saturday and noon to 5:00 P.M. on Sunday. The museum is closed on Monday.

**Earthplace: The Nature Discovery Center**
**10 Woodside Lane, Westport**
**(203) 227-7253**
**www.earthplace.org**
This museum and nature center offers walking trails, exhibits, and a plethora of children's programs. The state-licensed nursery school helps young ones develop

an appreciation for the natural world, while school programs bring groups of kids to the center to learn about the plants, animals, and geography of the area. Popular children's programs at the center include Saturday Story Time, Leaf Peepers, Fun Junk (about recycling), "Yuck Days," and a summer camp for children in preschool through grade 9. Membership fees range from $25 to $1,000 per year, or you can pay for individual programs as you participate. The Earthplace building is open Monday through Saturday 9:00 A.M. to 5:00 P.M. and Sunday 1:00 to 4:00 P.M. The grounds are open daily from 7:00 A.M. to dusk. For more information about Earthplace, see the Attractions chapter.

*Places not normally associated with kid-focused activities sometimes include programs for the young. The Bush-Holley Historic Site in Greenwich offers occasional "Family Fun" days that expose children and accompanying adults to local history. The Lockwood-Mathews Mansion Museum in Norwalk schedules parent-with-child programs focused on music, history, and art. The Aldrich Museum of Contemporary Art in Ridgefield allows kids to get their hands dirty in experimental art-creation workshops.*

**Garbage Museum                Free**
**1410 Honeyspot Road Extension, Stratford**
**(203) 381-9571**
Children are so busy climbing, touching, watching, and playing at the Garbage Museum that they might not even realize they're learning key conservation concepts about waste management and recycling. Everyone's favorite mascot, the towering Trash-o-saurus sculpture, is made from (you guessed it) recycled garbage. Visitors can also get a bird's-eye view of the on-site recycling center by

walking through clear glass walkways that wind above the dumping and sorting areas. A giant simulated compost pile helps kids understand how that complex system works, and a variety of exhibits show how changing small daily habits can make a big difference in reducing waste. Individuals and families of all ages are welcome, although school groups are the most common visitors here. Donations are welcomed. September to June the museum is open noon to 4:00 P.M. Wednesday through Friday. July and August operating hours are 10:00 A.M. to 4:00 P.M. Tuesday through Friday.

**New Canaan Nature Center        Free**
**144 Oenoke Ridge, New Canaan**
**(203) 966-6536**
**www.newcanaannature.org**
Kids and animals make a natural pair, and the New Canaan Nature Center brings them together with live-animal demonstrations, Birds of Prey Days, bird-watching outings, and other special events. The center also offers seasonal programs designed especially for children, including Nurturing Nature for toddlers, Junior Animal Keepers for kids in grades 6 through 8, Fall Follies for ages three through five, the Beginner's Nature Program preschool, the Nature Detectives Program, and birthday parties. The center has plenty to offer adults as well. For more information see the Attractions chapter.

**Stamford Museum**
**& Nature Center              $-$$**
**39 Scofieldtown Road, Stamford**
**(203) 322-1646**
**www.stamfordmuseum.org**
Kids love the farm animals at the Stamford Museum & Nature Center, not to mention the frog pond, lake picnics, wagon rides, maple sugaring programs, school-group and scout-troop tours, the huge playground, and other activities and programs aimed at children and families. For complete information about the museum, see the Attractions chapter.

**Stepping Stones Museum
for Children** **$$**
303 West Avenue, Norwalk
(203) 899-0530
www.steppingstonesmuseum.org

Few three-year-olds can contain themselves at Toddler Terrain, the section of the Stepping Stones Museum for Children that's dedicated to this energetic age group. And what seven-year-old couldn't expand his imagination at Waterscape, a wet and wild exhibit where kids wear raincoats and explore waterfalls, streambeds, a fog machine, and other tools for learning about the nature of water. Other museum exhibits include Express Yourself, where children experiment with different modes of communication; I Spy Connecticut, where visitors can climb inside trains, submarines, and other vessels; and In the Works, where kids can learn about gravity and velocity by testing machines and building race cars. The museum also has a cafe and gift shop and hosts school classrooms, scout troops, birthday party celebrations, and other groups. Self-guided tours and projects include Connie Servation's River Ramble, Chlora and Phil Green's Plant Project, Weather Wise, and the Discovery Tour. Stepping Stones is open to the public Tuesday through Sunday 10:00 A.M. to 5:00 P.M.

# RAINY-DAY ACTIVITIES

**All Fired Up** **$$-$$$**
113 Danbury Road, Ridgefield
(203) 431-8845

Located within Copps Hill Commons on Route 35, All Fired Up is a paint-it-yourself pottery studio specializing in kids' birthday parties—three party packages are available that vary in scope and price. In addition, the studio offers a summer day camp for children, "Mommy and Me" classes, private individualized lessons, and after-school programs. Prices vary according to the program and pottery pieces chosen. Classes and special events are available for adults as well. All Fired Up is open 10:00 A.M. to 6:00 P.M. on Wednesday, Thursday, Saturday, and Sunday and noon to 10:00 P.M. on Friday.

**Art & Soul/The Bead Bar** **$$-$$$**
80 Main Street, New Canaan
(203) 972-1610

Jewelry and art connoisseurs of all ages will enjoy a visit to this dual-purpose activity center offering jewelry-making and pottery-painting workshops. At the Bead Bar visitors can choose from hundreds of semiprecious stones, beads, and glass from around the world in every imaginable color. The beads are strung in one-of-a-kind combinations to make necklaces, anklets, bracelets, key chains, and more. Or sidle on up to the pottery-painting counter, where you'll pick out an unfinished ceramic cookie jar, platter, picture frame, teapot, mug, or bowl and decorate it in as wild—or mild—a style as you want. A week later, the kiln-fired piece is ready to be picked up. In addition to hosting children's birthday parties, kids-days-out, and summer-camp art programs, Art & Soul/The Bead Bar is also a popular spot for baby showers, book club gatherings, and monthly Ladies' Nights. The price of your finished piece will depend on which beads or pottery pieces you choose. The studio's hours of operation are Tuesday through Saturday 11:00 A.M. to 6:00 P.M. and Sunday noon to 5:00 P.M. The shop is closed on Sunday in summer.

**Enchanted Garden** **$$$-$$$$**
165 Danbury Road, Ridgefield
(203) 431-3350
www.enchantedgardenkids.com

This child-development center and performing arts studio offers classes and programs for six-month-olds, toddlers, elementary-schoolers, middle-schoolers, high-schoolers, and adults. For babies offerings include Music in Motion and Happy Feet. Kindergarteners can enjoy Off-Broadway Kids, tap dancing, and other programs. For elementary-age children the center offers its School of Dance, Center Stage, and Stagecraft programs. For everyone else, Jazz Repertory, Yoga,

Ballet, and Repertory Theater are some of the available classes. The center's birthday parties are renowned in the area and offer more than 20 themes, including Rock 'n' Roll, Outer Space, Cowboys, Science, Baking, Pirates, Mermaids, Teddy Bears, and more. Prices and class times vary; call or visit the Web site to see this season's schedule.

*Most of the local libraries present regular story hours, free of charge, for children of all ages. Schedules usually change by the month; call your local branch for the latest offerings.*

**Lakeside Pottery**                $$$-$$$$
**543 Newfield Avenue, Stamford**
**(203) 323-2222**
**www.lakesidepottery.com**
Adults and children can both hone their artistic skills at Lakeside, a pottery school, gallery, and studio where visitors learn throwing, firing, and glazing techniques. In addition to beginner's and advanced classes for all ages, the studio offers an eight-week instructional program for children ages 8 to 12, a summer camp program for children ages 8 to 15, birthday party packages, workshops, private lessons, and Open Studio hours. Registration prices and class dates vary according to type of program. Call for details about availability and pricing for upcoming classes and programs. Birthday party packages cost $18 per hour, plus firing fees and food costs. The minimum recommended age is seven years old.

**Linda's Loveable Bears**        $$$-$$$$
**158 Greenwood Avenue, Bethel**
**(203) 778-BEAR**
This cuddly shop is becoming very popular for birthday parties and other children's gatherings. Participants stuff their bears by hand; give them names, birth certificates, and ID bracelets; and then hand them over for stitching. The partygoers also design a bag to carry their

newest family member home in, wrap their finished bear in a receiving blanket, and take them home (no car seat required). Adults also appreciate Linda's wide selection of stuffed bears and collectibles. In addition, the shop offers a personalizing service. For example, your "graduation bear" can include the name of your favorite grad's school, and new parents can receive a bear personalized with their child's name, birth weight, and other pertinent information.

**Mother Earth Mining Gallery**        $$$$
**806 Federal Road, Brookfield**
**(203) 775-6272**
**www.motherearthcrystals.com**
Some visitors to Mother Earth just come to browse the big selection of stuffed animals, dinosaur fossil–dig kits, kaleidoscopes, stickers, puzzles, and other fun stuff. But most come for the gallery's main attraction: a "mine" where groups of eight or fewer children can muck around with helmets and search for real gemstones. Party packages include a mining video and a globe cake with buttercream icing. While the kids are busy, adults can explore the gallery of fine jewelry and crystal giftware. Mother Earth's group mining packages cost $22 per child, with a suggested age of five and older. The gallery is open Monday and Wednesday through Saturday (closed Tuesday) from 10:00 A.M. to 6:00 P.M. and Sunday from noon to 5:00 P.M.

# THE ARTS

**Creative Castle**                $$$-$$$$
**1200 Post Road East, Westport**
**(203) 226-5090**
**www.creativecastle.net**
The Creative Castle (located in the New Learning Center on Post Road) is a hands-on, relaxed art studio designed especially for toddlers and other young children. Classes are age-specific in their focus and serve kids from 18 months old all the way up to 7 years old. The pupils will take courses such as Color Sampler and Musi-

cal Paints and learn all about mixed media, colors, basic geometry, music, movement, painting, and drawing. The children also enjoy playtimes with books, toys, puzzles, games, and stories. Class fees, times, and dates vary. Call or visit the Web site for updated schedules.

## Downtown Cabaret Theater  $$$$
**263 Golden Hill Street, Bridgeport**
**(203) 576-1636**
**www.dtcab.com**
The Cabaret Theater's Children's Company stages several new shows for kids each season. Some recent performances have included *Rudolph, Cinderella, Three Billy Goats Gruff, Pinocchio,* and *Frankenstein and the Three Bears.* Kids enjoy bringing snacks and drinks to the shows. Field trip packages and birthday parties (complete with a "Happy Birthday" song from the theater performers) are also available. Showtimes are Saturday and Sunday at noon and 2:30 P.M. Selected shows are also performed on schoolday afternoons. Call or visit the Web site for this season's shows and times. For more information about the Downtown Cabaret Theater, see The Arts chapter.

## Playhouse on the Green  $$$
**177 State Street, Bridgeport**
**(203) 345-4800**
**www.playhouseonthegreen.org**
The Polka Dot Kids program at this beautiful downtown theater (formerly known as the Polka Dot Playhouse) provides plenty of ways for kids to fall in love with the world of theater. Live productions, musical concerts, puppet shows, storytelling, juggling acts, and clown performances are just some of the program's offerings. Some recent shows have included *Rumplestiltskin, The Elephant Child, Bubblemania,* and *Mike Mulligan and his Steam Shovel.* Birthday party packages are also available. All shows start at either 10:00 A.M. or noon on show day. Call or visit the Web site for this season's show schedule. For more information about the Playhouse on the Green, see The Arts chapter.

## Quick Center for the Arts at Fairfield University  $$$
**1073 North Benson Road, Fairfield**
**(203) 254-4010**
**www.quickcenter.com**
With two theaters and one art gallery, this performing- and visual-arts center has offered live theater, concerts, and art exhibits since 1990. (See The Arts chapter for more information.) Many of the performances are tailored especially for children, including the popular Young Audience Sunday Series. Recent shows have included *Amelia Bedelia for Mayor and other Stories, Under the Sea with Silly Jellyfish, Peter and the Wolf, Corduroy, Beatrix Potter's Tailor of Gloucester,* and *Shel Silverstein's The Giving Tree and Other Stories.* The center also offers birthday party setups if you purchase 10 or more tickets: They provide the tables and chairs, while you get $2.00 off each ticket and provide the food, decorations, and cake. Times and dates vary with each show. Call or visit the Web site for updated listings.

## Silvermine Guild Arts Center  $$$-$$$$
**1037 Silvermine Road, New Canaan**
**(203) 966-9700**
**www.silvermineart.org**
The mission of the Silvermine Guild is to foster artists, showcase their works, and promote the cultural enrichment of the community. (For more information about the center, see The Arts chapter.) Kids aren't left out of that effort: The guild offers a variety of art classes and workshops for the younger set as well as for adults. Youth and Junior courses include Youth Ceramics, Youth Acrylic and Oil Painting, Portfolio Development, Youth Exploring the Visual Arts, and Journey through Art (ages 4 and 5); Junior Cartooning (ages 7 through 11); Arts for Two (ages 2 and 3 plus a parent); Junior Art from Nature (ages 4 through 9); and Junior Sculpture (ages 7 through 12). Class fees and meeting times vary. Call or visit the Web site for the latest schedules.

**Wooster Community**
**Art Center**                    **$$–$$$$**
**73 Miry Brook Road, Danbury**
**(203) 744-4825**
**www.wcaonline.net**

Fine art isn't just for grown-ups anymore: Kids can get into the act at Wooster Art Center by participating in classes designed to sharpen their fine-motor skills and increase their appreciation for all things artistic. Classes and programs vary from year to year and season to season but typically include offerings such as Fundamentals of Clay (ages 9 to 12); Young People's Photography (ages 10 to 14); Painting (ages 5 to 8); Stone Carving (ages 9 to 12); Drawing and Painting (ages 10 to 14); and Exploring Three Dimension (ages 8 to 12). Making Art Together is designed for toddlers and adults to enjoy together. Prices and class schedules vary; call or visit the Web site for the latest listings. For more information about adult programs at the center, see The Arts chapter.

# SPORTS AND FITNESS

**Danbury Ice Arena**
**1 Independence Way, Danbury**
**(203) 794-1704**
**www.danburyice.com**

Maybe you're hoping your toddler can learn to skate as soon as she learns to walk. Or perhaps your high-schooler is just itching to hit the ice with a local hockey team. Whatever your needs, the new Danbury Ice Arena probably has a child- or teen-focused class or program to suit them. A variety of summer camps, learn-to-skate programs, and even birthday party packages ($11 to $18 per person) are tailored for kids from preschool through high school. And for those just looking for a fun day's activity, public skating hours are available on weekdays as well as weekends. There is a small admission charge for public skating. For more information about the arena, see the Beaches, Parks, and Recreation chapter.

**Darien YMCA**
**2420 Post Road, Darien**
**(203) 655-8228**
**www.darien-ymca.org**

Like many other local YMCAs, the Darien branch has a special emphasis on children's programs. In addition to its Summer Day Camp, the Y also provides youth offerings such as karate (ages 5 to 8), fencing for high-school students, girls' field hockey (grades 3 to 8), parent-and-child swim classes (6 months to 5 years old), Tumble Bee gymnastics classes (ages 1 to 5), and Pee Wee Basketball (grades 1 and 2). A host of adult and family programs are also available. Membership fees are $109 per month for a family and $63 per month for adults. Nonmembers can sign up for classes, but they pay higher fees. The building is open Monday through Friday 6:30 A.M. to 9:45 P.M., Saturday 8:00 A.M. to 6:45 P.M., and Sunday noon to 5:45 P.M.

**Fairfield YMCA**
**841 Old Post Road, Fairfield**
**(203) 255-2834**

YMCA members can take advantage of adult, family, and youth programs at this Fairfield YMCA. Available programs and classes include soccer (ages 4 to 7); youth basketball (ages 6 to 8); T-ball (ages 5 to 7); Tumbling Tots gymnastics (ages 2 to 3); dance (ages 3 to 5); middle school roller-hockey league (grades 6 to 8); and preschool swim lessons (ages 3 to 5). The facility is open Monday through Friday 5:30 A.M. to 10:00 P.M., Saturday 8:00 A.M. to 4:00 P.M., and Sunday 9:00 A.M. to 5:00 P.M. Program membership rates are $30 per year for individuals and $50 per year for families. Full facility membership rates are $114 per year for youths, $696 per year for families, and $458 per year for adults. Nonmembers can sign up for classes but will pay a higher fee.

**Golf Quest**
**Family Sports Center**                    **$$–$$$$**
**1 Sand Cut Road, Brookfield**
**(203) 775-3556**

The Golf Quest Family Sports Center has an activity for every age and skill level; young ones will have fun at the 18-hole miniature golf course, complete with a waterfall and castle. Or let your little slugger take a few swings in one of the seven on-site batting cages and enjoy an ice cream at the snack bar. The new Frozen Ropes Field at Golf Quest also provides a baseball-friendly spot for pitching, hitting, and fielding instruction; after-school programs; and summer camps. The center's birthday party packages include games, contests, time at the driving range, and rounds of minigolf. For more information about Golf Quest, see the Beaches, Parks, and Recreation chapter.

### Graham Dickinson S.P.I.R.I.T.
### Skate Park                    $$-$$$$
### 30 Prospect Street, Ridgefield
### (203) 431-2368

Dedicated to the memory of a 16-year-old Ridgefield resident and skateboard enthusiast, the Graham Dickinson S.P.I.R.I.T. Skate Park provides a safe, fun spot for kids to trick skate, in-line skate, and socialize with friends. The park is located in the town center, just behind the Yanity Gym. Skaters are required to wear helmets, knee pads, and elbow pads. Annual membership costs $125 for Ridgefield residents and $195 for nonresidents. Visitors can also purchase 10-day punch cards ($45 for residents and $75 for nonresidents) and one-day passes ($6.00 for residents and $10.00 for nonresidents). The skate park is open March through December from 2:30 P.M. to dusk on weekdays and noon to dusk on weekends and holidays.

### Greenwich Community
### Sailing                       $$$-$$$$
### Greenwich Point Park
### P.O. Box 195, Greenwich 06870
### (203) 698-0599
### www.longshoresailingschool.com

Like its "sister" site, the Longshore Sailing School (see below), this Old Greenwich sailing education facility offers a Junior Sailing Program with basic and advanced lessons for children ages 9 to 16. Courses are taken in order of difficulty: Intermediate Sailing, for example, follows Basic Sailing, which follows Safe Boating. Prices and schedules vary by session. Families with at least once experienced sailor can also rent keelboats, laser sailboats, Picos, ocean kayaks, and other craft for $16 to $40 per hour. For more information about Greenwich Community Sailing, see the Beaches, Parks, and Recreation chapter.

*Children's art classes, sports programs, and summer camps tend to fill up very quickly—so quickly, in fact, that some facilities are resorting to lottery systems rather than first-come, first-served registration. Always sign up as far in advance as possible. Most summer camps begin the registration process in March. If you wait until the weather warms up, you might be too late.*

### Greenwich Family YMCA
### 50 East Putnam Avenue, Greenwich
### (203) 869-1630
### www.gwymca.org

Members are welcome to take advantage of the Y's varied facilities and kids' programs for infants, elementary-age children, middle-schoolers, and high schoolers. Shrimp and Perch are two of the infant swimming classes; Polliwog, Guppy, Minnow, Starfish, and Eel, and others teach basic swim skills for ages 3 to 12. Toddler Gym, Baby Power, Beginner Gymnastics, Youth Tennis, Little Campers, Adventure Campers, and Yoga Kids are just a few of the other programs available for the Y's youngest visitors. Special events like the Halloween Bash, birthday parties, teen movie nights, Self-Defense for Mothers and Daughters, and summer camps make kids feel welcome. The YMCA is open Monday through Friday 5:00 A.M. to 10:00 P.M., Saturday 6:30 A.M. to 7:00 P.M., and Sunday 8:00 A.M. to 5:00

P.M. A family membership costs $58 per month plus a $100 join fee.

## Longshore Sailing School $$$$
### 260 Compo Road South, Westport
### (203) 226-4646
### www.longshoresailingschool.com

Located at the Westport Longshore Club, this sailing school has plenty to offer adults (see the Beaches, Parks, and Recreation chapter) as well as an extensive Junior Program for kids. Choose from junior courses like Safe Boating and Sailing, Basic Sailing, Intermediate Sailing, Maritime Explorers, Catamarans, Kayak Adventures, and Racing Techniques. All courses teach children about safety on the water, rules and regulations, good sportsmanship, and basic aerodynamics. Boat rentals ($14 to $44 per hour) are also available to experienced sailors.

## Regional YMCA of Western Connecticut
### Bethel, Brookfield, and Danbury
### www.regionalymcawestct.org

The Regional YMCA of Western Connecticut has three locations in northern Fairfield County. Each site offers its own selection of classes and programs for kids and adults. The Grassy Plain Children's Center (57 Grassy Plain Street, Bethel; 203-744-4890) emphasizes learning, fitness, and fun for the youngest members of the community. Toddlers and two-year-olds can take part in music programs, arts and crafts, and swim lessons. As children get older they can attend school vacation camps, advanced swim lessons, cooking classes, field trips, art classes, and even woodworking classes. The Greenknoll Branch (2 Huckleberry Road, Brookfield; 203-775-4444) offers lots of strength training and fitness programs, the Greenknoll Day Camp, and Escape to the Arts classes. The Boughton Street Branch (12 Boughton Street, Danbury; 203-744-1000) has a lap pool, basketball courts, and a Wellness Program devoted to promoting healthy children and adults in the community. Membership fees are $990 per year for families and $699 per year for adults. Hours vary from location to location; call each site for details.

## Stamford Twin Rinks
### 1063 Hope Street, Stamford
### (203) 968-9000
### www.icecenter.com

Open year-round, the Stamford Twin Rinks has a summer hockey camp, "Dynamites" Tot Hockey, parent-and-toddler skating classes, figure-skating lessons, public skate hours, and lots of other features that appeal to kids and parents. Fees vary for public skating, classes, and camps. Active birthday boys and girls will find few better spots for a party: The site offers Bronze-, Silver-, and Gold-level celebrations ($199 to $249) with features like skate rentals, a private party rooms, arcade tokens, cake and ice cream, prizes, and decorations. For more information about the rink, see the Beaches, Parks, and Recreation chapter.

## Westport/Weston YMCA
### 59 Post Road East, Westport
### (203) 226-8981
### www.westportymca.org

This downtown fitness and health facility offers birthday pool parties, a summer day camp, a preschool music program, Youth Fun Nights, the Wooley Bugger Fishing Club, and a variety of other programs designed to appeal to youngsters. Camp Mahackeno allows kids to let loose with swim lessons, crafts, song and dance, canoeing, and nature explorations. Children from 6 months old to 10 years old can get their feet wet at age-appropriate swim lessons with names like Polliwog, Porpoise Club, Seahorse, and Shark. Gymnastics for Cheerleaders classes help high school girls stay physically active. Membership fees are $510 per year for families, $310 per year for adults, and $175 per year for youth. Members also pay a one-time "joining" fee of $50. For most of the year the facility is open Monday through Friday 5:30 A.M. to 10:00 P.M.,

Saturday 8:00 A.M. to 7:30 P.M., and Sunday 9:00 A.M. to 5:00 P.M. Hours vary slightly during summer.

**Wilton YMCA**
**404 Danbury Road, Wilton**
**(203) 762-8384**
**www.wiltonymca.org**
Conveniently located across the street from Wilton High School, this YMCA location shares the organization's commitment to healthy minds and bodies. Available kids' classes include a nursery school, the Creative Two's Program, Movement and Music (ages 1 to 4), Fun and Fitness (ages 3 to 4), Soccer Tots (ages 4 to 5), Bitty Basketball (ages 3 to 5), youth swim lessons, Family Fun Nights, Girl Power strength training for teens, Kinderjocks, and martial arts for all ages. The facility is open Monday through Friday 5:30 A.M. to 10:00 P.M., Saturday 7:30 A.M. to 8:00 P.M., and Sunday 10:00 A.M. to 6:00 P.M. Annual membership fees are $795 per family, $525 per adult, or $175 per child.

**Winter Garden Arena**
**111 Prospect Ridge, Ridgefield**
**(203) 438-4423**
**www.wintergardenarena.com**
The Winter Garden Arena's "Ice Mice" program was designed with toddlers in mind: Children ages 3 to 5 can sign up for fall or winter terms and learn to stand and gently maneuver on skates. Once the children can advance along the entire length of the rink, they graduate to the "Advanced Ice Mice" program, and then . . . the Olympics? The sky's the limit at this ice rink, where other children's programs include Learn to Skate (ages 5 and up); Hockey Development (ages 5 and up); figure skating beginner's classes; and birthday party packages ($279 to $339). Public skating hours and skate rentals are also available. Fees vary for public skating, programs, and classes. For more information see the Beaches, Parks, and Recreation chapter.

# THE ARTS

F ew counties in America can stake claim to eight symphonies, an opera company, four chorales, numerous artists' guilds, and even a ballet company. But southwestern Connecticut residents can count their blessings for all these and more, combining to form a thriving cultural scene that rivals that found almost anywhere else. In any given theater season, locals can sit in on professional productions of musicals, classics, and modern dramas. Community theaters serve up an equally charming collection of shows. Music fans, meanwhile, regularly enjoy world-renowned singers and musicians in concerts on local stages. Art aficionados can browse the works of the masters— along with those of local painters, sculptors, and photographers—at galleries large and small. And with stage and screen stars living in our backyard and next door in New York City, it's perhaps no surprise that many local productions and concerts often feature recognizable and much-loved performers. Sure you can hop on the train and see a Broadway show fairly easily. Increasingly, however, Fairfield County residents are choosing to stay put and appreciate all that the local venues have to offer.

*The Music and Arts Center for Humanity in Bridgeport is a nonprofit school of the arts dedicated to enriching the lives of adults and children with special needs. Originally started as a music school for the blind in 1977, MACH has grown through the years to include programs in dance, theater, visual arts, and other endeavors. Call (203) 366-3300 or visit www.musicandartscenter.org.*

## ARTS CENTERS AND ASSOCIATIONS

**Brookfield Craft Center**
**Route 25**
**P.O. Box 122, Brookfield 06804**
**(203) 775-4526**
Ceramics, woodworking, glassblowing, boat building, decorative arts, pottery, blacksmithing, mural painting, book making, jewelry making, photography, and weaving are just some of the subjects covered at this nonprofit arts education center. Located next to the scenic Still River, the center offers classes, workshops, videos, weekend seminars, a scholarship program, seven teaching studios, and even housing for visiting artists. An on-site gallery showcases members' works and offers items for sale. A quarterly program guide details each season's available classes and programs.

**Charles Ives Center for the Arts**
**Ives Concert Park**
**P.O. Box 2957, Danbury 06813**
**(203) 837-9226**
**www.ivesconcertpark.com**
Named for former Danbury resident Charles Ives (see Close-up), the Charles Ives Center for the Arts has a mission to continue his legacy by promoting the arts in the greater Danbury region. The group accomplishes this aim largely by scheduling and sponsoring music concerts and theatrical productions at the Ives Concert Park, an outdoor amphitheater located on 39 acres at the Westside campus of Western Connecticut University. Willie Nelson, Hall & Oates, Indigo Girls, Trisha Yearwood, Julio Iglesias, and Kenny Loggins are just some of the recent performers at the park. Seats are available on the lawn and in the numbered-seating area next to

the stage. Tickets prices vary by performance and seating choice. You can buy
tickets through Ticketmaster or at the
Ives Concert Park Web site.

## Greenwich Arts Council
### 299 Greenwich Avenue, Greenwich
### (203) 622-3998
### www.greenwicharts.org
The Greenwich Arts Council is involved in
many aspects of arts enrichment in the
town, the most prominent of which is the
council's Greenwich Arts Center. The center hosts a Sunday Salon Series with
singers and musicians, Leisurely
Lunchtime Lectures, and classes in painting, drawing, illustration, music, sculpture,
ballet, photography, and other topics. One
of the council's most popular events is
the springtime Art on the Avenue, when
art of all kinds is displayed in store windows and along the sidewalks on Greenwich Avenue. Breakfast seminars,
children's art programs, and diverse cultural concerts are also offered.

## Levitt Pavilion for the Performing Arts
### Arnold Bernhard Plaza, Westport
### (203) 226-7600
It doesn't get much better than this: Visitors to Levitt Pavilion's annual summer
festival can enjoy dance, theater, music,
and children's shows in an open-air environment—all free of charge. From mid-
June through August, the stage hosts
somewhere between 50 and 55 nights of
performances. Past performers have
included Tony Bennett, Willie Nelson, and
Ray Charles. Attendees can also enjoy
acrobatic dancers, magic shows, comedy
shows, quartet performances, jazz orchestras, country bands, bluegrass musicians,
Caribbean fiestas, closing night galas, and
innumerable other events. The pavilion
itself is located behind the Westport Public Library (the two share a parking lot);
the pavilion's offices are located in the
Westport Parks and Recreation Building
at 260 South Compo Road. The concert
line telephone number is (203) 221-4422.

## Regina A. Quick Center for the Arts
### at Fairfield University
### 1073 North Benson Road, Fairfield
### (203) 254-4010
### www.quickcenter.com
Best known as simply "the Quick Center,"
this vibrant arts center offers locals the
chance to enjoy top-notch chamber music
concerts, theater and dance productions,
young musicians' series, fine art exhibits,
and much more. Many of the performers
come from faraway spots, including Russia,
Ireland, and Africa; others honed their tal-
ents right here in Connecticut. Popular
events include the Young Audience Sunday
Series, Black Box Theater radio dramas, and
Open VISIONS Forum, in which internationally known journalists, CEOs, and performers host discussions on a variety of current
topics. The Quick Center's facilities include
two theaters and an art gallery. Call or visit
the Web site for this season's performance
schedules and ticket prices. At the time of
this writing, the center was planning to offer
online ticket sales.

## Ridgefield Guild of Artists
### 34 Halpin Lane
### P.O. Box 552, Ridgefield 06877
### (203) 438-8863
### www.rgoa.org
This nonprofit, all-volunteer organization
works to promote art appreciation in
Ridgefield and its surrounding communities. The guild offers yearly memberships,
art galleries, lectures and seminars, juried
exhibitions, art classes for adults and children, craft shows, benefit events, a quarterly newsletter, and a gift shop featuring
the works of members. One of the guild's
more popular special events is the annual
Holiday Market, held in November and
December and offering handcrafted artworks for sale.

## Rowayton Arts Center
### 145 Rowayton Avenue, Rowayton
### (Norwalk)
### (203) 866-2744
### www.rowaytonartscenter.org

## CLOSE-UP
# Charles Ives: A Musical Legacy

One of Fairfield County's favorite sons was Charles Ives (1874–1954), the Pulitzer Prize–winning composer known for his innovation, patriotism, and moving hymns. As famous as his name is today among music students, however, Ives was relatively unknown—and often unwelcome—in music circles during much of his lifetime.

Ives's father, George, a band leader, choir director, and cornet player, gave the young Charles his first music lessons. By his teens, Ives was earning a salary by playing the organ at local churches and was considered somewhat of a prodigy by those in the know. He gained inspiration from everyday people and events, often incorporating local Danbury tunes and folklore into his compositions. He refused to follow the musical customs of the day, preferring to create his own unique style. This attitude usually didn't sit well with others in the field. His professors at Yale University, for example, often bristled at his unusual creations. Nevertheless, his works like *The Bells of Yale* and *March No. 6,* with "Here's to Good Old Yale," managed to become popular among other students.

Ives was still in college when his father died unexpectedly of a stroke. Despite his heartache, the young man doggedly pursued his musical career while also working as a clerk with the Mutual Life Insurance Company in New York City. During that time, he used his off hours to compose works such as *The Celestial Country* and the *Violin Sonatas.* Slowly his works became more and more unorthodox as he became more successful in the insurance business. *First Piano Sonata* took eight years to complete; *Tone Roads* and *Scherzo: Over the Pavements* were inspired by New York's street sounds and resembled no other music of the day.

Located within a historic firehouse building, the Rowayton Arts Center offers classes, programs, and workshops in watercolor, still life, collage-making, printing, and other fine-art topics. Numerous children's programs provide an outlet for younger artists. Sculpture, photography, and painting exhibits showcase the works of members. Some of the 700-or-so members are artists; others are volunteers who help out in different ways. Exhibited works are often offered for sale.

**Silvermine Guild Arts Center**
**1037 Silvermine Road, New Canaan**
**(203) 966-9700**
www.silvermineart.org

This bustling organization includes patrons and artists from around the region. The guild's School of Art offers interactive programs and classes in subjects like writing, ceramics, printmaking, jewelry design, drawing, computer graphics, painting, sculpture, art history, and photography. A summer Art Camp is designed with kids in mind. The center's five on-site galleries exhibit members' works throughout the year; a gift shop offers a wide variety of original pieces for sale. Members can also be found in local schools and community centers, providing outreach programs and classes.

In 1908 Ives married nurse Harmony Twichell. That year also marked the beginning of the composer's most fruitful creativity. *Holidays, Second String Quartet, Three Places in New England, Fourth Symphony,* and many other of his greatest works were created in the following decades. But few others heard his music, and those who did hear it did not offer much encouragement. Ives soldiered on. Slowly notable musicians like Aaron Copland began to support and appreciate his efforts, and he earned official recognition with the 1947 Pulitzer Prize for his *Third Symphony.* Charles Ives died in 1954. In the years that followed, his many works began to reach mainstream audiences and placed him in the upper echelons of American music.

Today music aficionados still travel to Danbury to visit some of the places where Ives lived and worked. The Ives Birthplace, located at 5 Mountainville Avenue, contains a desk, a piano, a music stand, and other items that the composer used during his childhood and early-

adult years. The home also houses his death mask.

Ives began his formal music studies by playing the organ at St. James Church, a house of worship that is still located at 25 West Street. (The organ itself is now located down the road at the West Street Congregational Church.) Danbury's Ives Street was named for the composer's prominent family before he himself became renowned. Ives, his wife, and several other relatives are buried at the Wooster Cemetery located on Ellsworth Avenue. For a complete map of these and other Ives-related sites (some of which have been replaced by other buildings), contact the Housatonic Valley Tourism District at 30 Main Street in Danbury (203-790-6124; www.housatonic.org) or the Danbury Museum and Historical Society at 43 Main Street (203-743-5200; www.danburyhistorical.org). Another good source of information is the Charles Ives Society (www.charlesives.org) based at the School of Music, Indiana University in Bloomington.

**Stamford Center for the Arts
(Palace Theatre and Rich Forum)
307 Atlantic Street, Stamford
(203) 358-2313
www.onlyatsca.com**
You name it, you can find it at the Stamford Center for the Arts. The nonprofit organization runs Fairfield County's two busiest performing arts venues: the modern Rich Forum (307 Atlantic Street) and the historic 1,580-seat Palace Theatre (61 Atlantic Street), both of which offer the latest and greatest in music, dance, comedy, and theater. The Rich Forum alone houses two theaters, an art gallery, and a communications center. Local orchestras

and dance companies perform here regularly. Other guest stars have included Lily Tomlin, B. B. King, Lewis Black, Carrot Top, George Winston, Yo-Yo Ma, George Carlin, Ray Romano, Alice Cooper, Tony Bennett, Willie Nelson, and the Alvin Ailey Dance Company. Past and recent guests have also had the chance to enjoy shows like *Smokey Joe's Café, Lord of the Dance, Jesus Christ Superstar, Peter Pan, Death Defying Acts, Tap Dogs,* and *Seussical, The Musical.* Ticket prices vary by performance. For ticket and schedule information, call the Stamford Center for the Arts box office at (203) 325-4466 or visit the organization's Web site.

## Westport Arts Center
### 51 Riverside Avenue, Westport
### (203) 226-1806
### www.westportartscenter.org

The Westport Arts Center aims to satisfy all types of artistic passions with painting exhibits, jazz performances, chamber music, literature discussions, theater productions, children's art workshops, artists' studio tours, film showing, sculpture exhibits, and many more events. All visual arts exhibitions are free to the public; lecture, concert, and theater ticket prices vary by event. The shows and exhibits are held in different auditoriums and galleries around town. Call or visit the Web site for this season's schedules and locations.

## Wooster Community Arts Center
### 73 Miry Brook Road, Danbury
### (203) 744-4825
### www.wcaonline.net

A nonprofit organization, the Wooster Community Arts Center has a mission to enrich the Danbury area with arts education and appreciation. Small class sizes are designed to promote learning in programs about sculpture, painting, photography, pottery, stone carving, and art history, with a separate course catalog for children. The center's faculty includes degreed art professionals from around the country. Classes are open to all interested students; Arts Center members receive a discount on all programs.

*Get a peek behind the proverbial curtain at the Loft Artist Association's annual Open Studios Tour, in which member sculptors, painters, photographers, and others swing open the doors of their workspaces to the general public. The association's studios are located in the old Yale locks factory on 737 Canal Street in Stamford. Call (203) 323-4153 or visit www.loftartists.com for the latest information on this ultra-popular event.*

# FINE ART MUSEUMS AND GALLERIES

## Aldrich Museum of Contemporary Art
### 158 Main Street, Ridgefield
### (203) 438-4519
### www.aldrichart.org

When most people think of historic, family-friendly Ridgefield, the image of controversial, cutting-edge art probably doesn't jump to mind. The founders and staffers at the Aldrich relish the paradox, just as they relish anything that challenges assumptions and turns heads. The museum's collections rival those found in New York City but have the distinct advantage (for us, anyway) of being located right here in Fairfield County. In addition to painting, sculpture, and photography exhibits, the Aldrich also hosts poets, performance artists, musicians, art classes, children's and teens' programs, teachers' programs, and a gift shop. A recent expansion and renovation project was completed in 2004.

## Artists' Market
### 163 Main Street, Norwalk
### (203) 846-2550
### www.artistsmarket.com

Specializing in the work of M. C. Escher, this gallery offers an ongoing Escher exhibit along with original Escher works for sale. Other features of the gallery include a rotating photography exhibit, a customized frame gallery, and a crafts gallery with works by Campbell Studios, Mullanium, Water Wonders, and others.

## Art/Place
### 400 Center Street, Southport (Fairfield)
### (203) 255-9847

Located in a restored southbound train depot in Southport, Art/Place is a gallery space where local sculptors, painters, photographers, and other artists can display and sell their works. Individual and group shows rotate regularly, and new exhibits are usually accompanied by opening receptions. The co-op gallery has about 30 permanent members.

**Bendheim Gallery at the Greenwich Arts Center**
**Greenwich Arts Council**
**299 Greenwich Avenue, Greenwich**
**(203) 622-3998**
**www.greenwicharts.org**
In addition to providing an exhibit space for Greenwich Arts Council members and guests, the Bendheim Gallery also serves as host for many of the council's special events and concerts. Recent shows have included Art in Context: The Art of Expression, Pace Prints—Works on Paper, and Paint the Town: Wet Paint Benefit Auction. Artists can apply to exhibit their works at the gallery by using a form provided on the Greenwich Arts Council's Web site.

**Bruce Museum of Arts and Science**
**1 Museum Drive, Greenwich**
**(203) 869-0376**
**www.brucemuseum.org**
The Bruce is known for its fascinating rotating exhibits that include everything from antique maps to natural history artifacts. Art lovers especially appreciate the Bruce's expansive collections of watercolors, oil paintings, sculptures, photographs, and countless other works. The galleries often display the pieces of masters such as Rodin, Picasso, Weir, Escher, Bateman, and others, along with group shows and exhibits highlighting such topics as war, flowers, dinosaurs, nudes, and the American West. For more information about the Bruce Museum, see the Attractions chapter.

**Charter Oak Gallery**
**1552 Post Road, Fairfield**
**(203) 319-1882**
**www.charteroakgallery.com**
Andrew Wyeth, Jamie Wyeth, Karl Soderland, Jim, Ritchu, Terry Lindsey, and Tom Torak are just some of the artists whose work you'll find for sale at the Charter Oak Gallery. American art of the 19th and 20th centuries is the focus here, with an emphasis on landscapes, still lifes, and other forms of realism. Charter Oak is a relatively new gallery and a member of the Fairfield Gallery Association.

**Housatonic Museum of Art**
**900 Lafayette Boulevard, Bridgeport**
**(203) 332-5052**
**www.hcc.commnet.edu**
Affiliated with Housatonic Community College, this art museum hosts visiting artists, rotating exhibits, educational programs, and a permanent collection that features works by artists such as Picasso, Matisse, Chagall, and Rodin. Because the exhibits change seasonally, even regular visitors can expect find something new around the corner. Past exhibitions have included Ansel Adams: Classic Images, African Art, Forms Derived From a Cube, Amy Bartell and the Mural Project, Lest We Forget: Images of the Civil Rights Movement, and Out of a Clear Blue Sky, which documented the events of September 11, 2001, through photography. Regular lectures, writing programs, and a peer docent program help facilitate learning in the museum and college. The galleries are open Monday through Friday 8:30 A.M. to 5:30 P.M., Saturday 9:00 A.M. to 3:00 P.M., and Sunday noon to 4:00 P.M. On Thursday the hours are extended until 7:00 P.M.

**Norwalk Community College Art Gallery**
**188 Richards Avenue, Norwalk**
**(203) 857-3323**
**www.ncc.commnet.edu**
Located in the East Campus building, this college art gallery features rotating exhibits with works by local and regional artists as well as staff and students. Recent shows have included silver-print photographs by Larry Silver, mixed-media paintings by Susan Sharp, and unique "photoglobes" by James Miller. Artists' works are often on loan from private collectors.

**PMW Gallery**
**530 Roxbury Road, Stamford**
**(203) 968-1699**
**www.pmwgallery.com**
The ever-changing artists on exhibit at PMW have included minimalist Craig Kane, designer Christopher Klumb, painter Suzanne Benton, sketch artist Paul Cad-

mus, photographer Maya Nagel, sculptor Fucigna, and others. An opening reception accompanies most new exhibits. Call or visit the Web site for information on the latest showing.

*Don't confine your search for fine art to galleries and museums: Many local libraries, including those in Westport, Wilton, and Danbury, often feature rotating exhibits by regional artists.*

### Ridgefield Guild of Artists
**34 Halpin Lane**
**P.O. Box 552, Ridgefield 06877**
**(203) 438-8863**
**www.rgoa.org**
Photographers, watercolor painters, sculptors, and other artists can exhibit works at one of the Ridgefield Guild of Artists' three galleries. The guild also hosts an annual juried exhibition in which critics determine winners in categories like Best in Show, The Comstock Drawing Group Award, and general awards for excellence. For more information about the guild, see the listing under Arts Centers and Associations above.

### Silvermine Guild Arts Center
**1037 Silvermine Road, New Canaan**
**(203) 966-9700**
**www.silvermineart.org**
The Silvermine Guild Arts Center is able to present more than 20 shows each year, thanks in part to its extensive gallery facilities that include five separate exhibit spaces. Many solo and group shows feature works by member artists, although well-known visiting painters, sculptors, and photographers also make appearances. See the listing under Arts Centers and Associations above for more information about the Silvermine Guild.

### Southport Harbor Gallery
**656 Harbor Road, Southport (Fairfield)**
**(203) 259-2592**
**www.southportharborgallery.com**
Located in the quaint waterfront area of

Southport Harbor, this gallery showcases the works of a wide variety of contemporary artists. Recent solo shows have included Wanderer's Paradise with J. Geoffrey Leckie, Idyllic Impressions with George Passantino, and Provocative Paintings with Robert Baxter. Group shows, like the recent Summer Delights, are also common.

### Thomas J. Walsh Art Gallery
**Barlow Road, Fairfield**
**(203) 254-4010**
**www.fairfield.edu/quick**
The Walsh Art Gallery, located on the Fairfield University campus at the Quick Center for the Arts, provides a regularly changing spectrum of exhibits. Featured artists include old master, regional professionals, and even students at the university. You can visit during regular hours or even reserve the space for a private function. The gallery is open Tuesday through Saturday 11:00 A.M. to 5:00 P.M. and Sunday noon to 4:00 P.M. For more information about the Quick Center, see the listing under Arts Centers and Associations above.

### Ulla Surland Gallery Eleven
**11 Unquowa Road, Fairfield**
**(203) 259-1572**
The rotating exhibits at Ulla Surland include oil paintings, nudes, abstract landscapes, still lifes, sculptures, paintings on canvas, and other styles. The gallery's downtown location and big windows allow for plenty of warm, natural light and curious passersby. Typically you'll find one artist on display at a time.

### Weir Farm National Historic Site
**735 Nod Hill Road, Wilton**
**(203) 834-2421**
In addition to providing a scenic outdoorsy getaway in Fairfield County, Weir Farm also provides artists and art lovers with a place to appreciate and create works in various mediums. The farm is the former home of Impressionist J. Alden Weir, and today the National Park Service continues his artistic tradition by hosting visiting and resident artists at the site. At

the end of each season, the artists' works go on exhibit in the visitor center galleries. For more information about Weir Farm, see the listing in the Attractions chapter.

### Western Connecticut State University
**181 White Street, Danbury**
**(203) 837-9411**
**www.wcsu.edu**
The midtown campus of WestConn often provides art exhibits at various locales, including the Annual WestConn Alumni Art Show held in Warner Hall; the recent James Joyce Exhibition in the Ruth Haas Library; and various art-related lectures, events, and slide shows held in the Student Center and other campus buildings. The university lists all upcoming exhibits and events, complete with viewing times and locations, on its Web site.

## DANCE

### Connecticut Ballet
**20 Acosta Street, Stamford**
**(203) 964-1211**
The resident dance company of the Stamford Center for the Arts (see listing in Arts Centers and Associations above), the Connecticut Ballet performs locally at the Palace Theatre and the Rich Forum. The group also tours with productions such as *Giselle, Coppelia,* and *The Nutcracker* (featuring George Balanchine's original choreography). The company also brings dance programs to schools in urban areas through its outreach program, which includes the Dance Exposure Assembly Program.

### Klein Memorial Auditorium
**910 Fairfield Avenue, Bridgeport**
**(203) 345-4800**
**www.theklein.org**
The Alvin Ailey Dance Company and other well-known companies have performed on the Klein's stage. Ticket holders also regularly enjoy music and dance productions like *The Nutcracker* and *Saturday Night Fever*. For more information about the

Klein, see the listing under Professional Theater below. A full updated schedule of shows is available at the theater's Web site.

## MUSIC

### American Classical Orchestra
**50 Washington Street, Norwalk**
**(203) 838-6995**
**www.americanclassicalorchestra.org**
This unique company is the only period-instrument orchestra in Connecticut. Musicians play on historic box woodwinds, leather-skinned timpani, valveless horns, and other instruments in an effort to re-create the sounds that the original masters might have heard when they first composed their pieces. The orchestra even sponsors a Classical Music for Kids series with standards like Handel's *Messiah* and fun shows like *Beethoven Lives Upstairs.* All local shows are performed at the Norwalk Concert Hall with ticket prices between $25 and $50. Or choose a subscription for $105 to $200 per season. Tickets and subscriptions are also available for the orchestra's traveling performances in New York City.

### Charles Ives Center for the Arts
**Ives Concert Park**
**P.O. Box 2957, Danbury 06813**
**(203) 837-9226**
**www.ivesconcertpark.com**
The Ives Concert Park presents a full roster of popular musical performers like Sheryl Crow, Julio Iglesias, and Hall & Oates each summer. Choose from a numbered seat, or bring a picnic and enjoy the concert in the lawn seating area. For more information about the Ives Center, see the Charles Ives Center for the Arts listing under Arts Centers and Associations above.

### Command Performance
**36 Tamarack Avenue, Danbury**
**(203) 825-3131**
**www.cperformance.org**
This nonprofit performing-arts organization aims to promote classical music, jazz, and dance throughout the greater

---

*The holiday season is one of the best times to enjoy moving performances by local choir groups and smaller quartets, many of whom perform free shows this time of year in local churches and other venues. Check your local newspaper for listings of last-minute concerts and annual performances.*

---

Danbury area while also reflecting the cultural and ethnic diversity of the region's residents. Concerts and performances typically take place at the Charles Ives Concert Hall at Western Connecticut University in Danbury. Recent shows have featured well-known musicians like Arturo Sandoval and vocalists like Dee Dee Bridgewater. Ticket prices vary by performance but usually range from $25 to $55. Seating charts are available on the group's Web site. Frequent concertgoers will receive discounted tickets.

## Connecticut Grand Opera & Orchestra
### 15 Bank Street, Stamford
### (203) 327-2867
### www.ctgrandopera.org

This nonprofit professional opera company stages full-scale, acclaimed productions throughout the state. Past shows have featured such world-famous performers as Renee Fleming, Peter Smith, Arvin Brown, Sherrill Mines, Mischa Dichter, and Marilyn Horne. Maestro Laurence Golgore conducts the orchestra at performances in Connecticut and around the world. Local productions typically take place at the Palace Theater and the Rich Forum in Stamford. Tickets cost between $32 and $95 per show; subscriptions are available for $84 to $550 per season. A don't-miss event for opera fans is the company's opening night gala, which typically features renowned divas and musicians.

## Connecticut Master Chorale
### P.O. Box 3302, Danbury 06813
### (203) 775-2602
### www.cmchorale.org

In 2002 this group of 55 local singers supplemented its regular local shows with performances at the White House and Carnegie Hall, making for an exciting chapter in the chorale's five-year history. The annual Holiday Prelude Concert is always popular, as are shows that feature works by Handel, Rutter, Mozart, and other greats. The group performs most shows at local churches, and auditions are held regularly in search of new members.

## Danbury Music Centre
### 256 Main Street, Danbury
### (203) 748-1716
### www.danbury.org/musicctr

Few would argue that the Danbury Music Centre is the hub of the classical music scene in the greater Danbury area. The organization aims to enrich local musicians and music appreciators by sponsoring and managing a host of ensembles, including the Danbury Symphony Orchestra, the Danbury Community Orchestra, the Danbury Preparatory String Orchestra, and the Danbury Concert Chorus. In each ensemble, professional directors lead mixed groups of professional and amateur musicians. In a six-week Summer Enrichment Program, the center helps young performers hone their craft. But the group's best-known effort is its annual production of *The Nutcracker* each December, performed by the Danbury Symphony Orchestra. Most shows are free to the public and are held at one of these Danbury locations: the Ives Concert Hall at Western Connecticut State University (181 White Street); the Marian Anderson Recital Hall (256 Main Street); Danbury High School (Route 39); and St. Peter Church (104 Main Street).

## Fairfield County Chorale
### 61 Unquowa Road, Fairfield
### (203) 254-1333
### www.fairfieldcountychorale.org

About 120 voices join together to form the Fairfield County Chorale, a group of dedicated amateur and semiprofessional singers that celebrated its 40th anniversary in 2003. The chorus has performed in Carnegie Hall, the Lincoln Center, the Kennedy Center, Norwalk Concert Hall, and various local and regional venues. The group has also traveled around the world to perform at festivals in Greece, Italy, France, and other locales. Once-a-year auditions, usually held the week after Labor Day, bring new members into the fold. The singers range in age from mid-20s to mid-70s and live in towns and cities throughout the county. Call or visit the Web site for this year's concert schedules.

## Greater Bridgeport Symphony
### 446 University Avenue, Bridgeport
### (203) 576-0263
### www.bridgeportsymphony.org
Maestro Gustav Meier leads his 65-piece (or more) orchestra in performances with guest stars such as the Fairfield University Chamber Singers, the Mendelssohn Choir, Butch Thompson on jazz piano, Jonathan Biss on piano, and Alisa Weilerstein on cello. Concert tickets range in price from $65 to $180. Seasonal subscribers save an average $11 per ticket. In summer the symphony wows crowds with its annual free outdoor pops concert. Other popular events include the Carlson-Horn/Greater Bridgeport Symphony Competition for Young Instrumentalists and Musicians To Go outreach programs and performances.

## Greenwich Symphony Orchestra
### Greenwich High School
### 10 Hillside Road, Greenwich
### (203) 625-8000
### www.greenwichsym.org
For more than 45 seasons, the Greenwich Symphony Orchestra has been bringing classical music to audiences in southwestern Connecticut. Guest soloists and 90 member musicians are led by David Gilbert, who has served as the symphony's music director and conductor since 1975. All performances are held at the Dickerman Hollister Auditorium at Greenwich High School. The group's Young People's Concerts are designed to bring great music to the younger set. The

Chamber Players of the Greenwich Symphony also perform regular concerts featuring first-chair musicians.

## Klein Memorial Auditorium
### 910 Fairfield Avenue, Bridgeport
### (203) 345-4800
### www.theklein.org
In addition to its well-respected theatrical productions, the Klein regularly welcomes guests like Arlo Guthrie, Butch Thompson, Sweet Honey in the Rock, and pianist Adlan Cruz for musical concerts. For more information about the Klein, see the listing under Professional Theater below. Check out the Web site for upcoming concert schedules.

## Mendelssohn Choir of Connecticut
### P.O. Box 150, Fairfield 06824
### (203) 459-8241
### www.mendelssohnchoir.com
Directed by Dr. Carol Ann Maxwell, the Mendelssohn Choir of Connecticut includes about 100 members and performs an average four concerts per year in Fairfield County. Two of the shows, including well-known pieces like *Requiem, Messiah,* and the *Chichester Psalms,* typically take place at the Norwalk Concert Hall in Norwalk City Hall (125 East Avenue); the remaining two are often joint productions with local symphonies or glee clubs. New members are chosen annually through auditions. The choir also runs an outreach program to bring choral music performances, free of charge, to local hospitals, schools, and nursing homes.

## Norwalk Symphony Orchestra
### 1 Park Street, Norwalk
### (203) 847-8844
### www.norwalksymphony.org
Music director and conductor Diane Wittry leads the Norwalk Symphony Orchestra (NSO) at its performances in the Norwalk Concert Hall complex at Norwalk City Hall (125 East Avenue). Although the NSO has been performing in city hall for more than 12 years, the group has been filling the Norwalk air with music at various venues

for more than 64 years. Choose from seats in the orchestra, mezzanine, or balcony for $71 to $129. The symphony also hosts a "(Not) Just for Kids" series of free music education programs in local libraries, as well as regular lectures and miniconcerts with performer David Hollander called "Highlights with Hollander."

## Pro Arte Singers
**P.O. Box 4251, Stamford 06907**
**(203) 322-5970**
**www.ez13.com/proarte**
Choral music is the focus of this 30-year-old singing group based in Stamford. The chorus performs four concerts each season, including the Pro Arte Male Chorus concerts and Traditional Candlelight Christmas. Performances take place at local churches and other venues and typically include pieces by Bach, Mozart, Leonard Bernstein, Johannes Brahms, Frances Poulenc, Franz Schubert, Dave Brubeck, Charles Ives, Felix Mendelssohn, and others. The choir, in whole or in part, is also available for smaller scale performances at private events.

## Ridgefield Playhouse for the Performing Arts
**Governor Street, Ridgefield**
**(203) 438-5795**
**www.ridgefieldplayhouse.org**
José Feliciano was the headliner for the Ridgefield Playhouse's very first opening night performance in December 2000. Since then, the playhouse has been drawing crowds with guests like the Ridgefield Symphony, the Ridgefield Opera Company, Joan Baez, They Might Be Giants, Marcel Marceau, the Bacon Brothers, the Moscow Boys Choir, and more. Family and children's shows like the *Wizard of Oz Sing-a-long* and *Thumbelina* are popular as well.

## Ridgefield Symphony Orchestra
**P.O. Box 289, Ridgefield 06877**
**(203) 438-3889**
**www.ridgefieldsymphony.org**
Maestro Sidney Rothstein leads anywhere from 60 to 90 musicians in each of the Ridgefield Symphony Orchestra's moving regular performances. Five Ridgefield musicians started the orchestra, then called the Ridgefield Symphonette, back in 1965. Today the RSO performs four subscription concerts a year at the Anne S. Richardson Auditorium at Ridgefield High School and two chamber music concerts each year at the Ridgefield Playhouse for the Performing Arts. Annual family concerts, youth competitions, youth concerts, and a youth orchestra serve to bring music and music education to Ridgefield's budding musicians and younger aficionados.

## Stamford Symphony Orchestra
**263 Tresser Boulevard, Stamford**
**(203) 325-1407**
**www.stamfordsymphony.org**
Professional musicians from New York City, Fairfield County, and Westchester County make up the orchestra at the SSO, a symphony that typically performs five classical concerts and three pops concerts each season. Other regular events include a Family Concert Series, Student Concerts for elementary schools, the Annual Benefit Gala, and the Annual Classical Golf Outing. The orchestra is headquartered at the Stamford Center for the Arts and performs most shows at the Palace Theatre. Seasonal subscribers receive discounts on individual ticket prices.

# PROFESSIONAL THEATER

## Downtown Cabaret Theater
**263 Golden Hill Street, Bridgeport**
**(203) 576-1636**
**www.dtcab.com**
This downtown theater offers a fun cabaret experience with tables, a snack bar, bring-your-own food and drinks, and high-quality dramas and musicals. After getting its start at Sacred Heart University, the theater set up shop in its present location in 1975. A recent renovation brought updated lobby, house, and restroom areas. Recent productions have included *Joseph and the Amazing Techni-*

color *Dreamcoat, La Cage Aux Folles, The Sunshine Boys,* and *A Funny Thing Happened on the Way to the Forum.* Subscriptions are available for $124 to $170 per season; single tickets are available for $34.50 to $42.50.

## Klein Memorial Auditorium
**910 Fairfield Avenue, Bridgeport**
**(203) 345-4800**
**www.theklein.org**
Classics, modern dramas, and even full-scale musicals are commonplace at "the Klein," an impressive theater with an ever-changing array of productions. Recent shows have included *Cats, Saturday Night Fever,* and Shakespeare's *Richard III.* The Klein also offers evening theater classes for adults and a children's Saturday Academy with classes in dance and acting. Ticket prices vary according to performance; ticket sales are available at the Klein Box Office or online at the theater's Web site.

## Playhouse on the Green
**177 State Street, Bridgeport**
**(203) 345-4800**
**www.playhouseonthegreen.org**
Formerly known as the Polka Dot Playhouse, this 228-seat theater in downtown Bridgeport offers its guests an up-close-and-personal theatrical experience with productions like *Nunsense, Bus Stop, Noises Off, Sylvia, Forever Plaid, Sleuth, The Fantasticks, Arsenic and Old Lace, Annie Warbucks,* and others. The theater's Polka Dot Kids program provides child-friendly shows on Saturday afternoon ($12 per person). Tickets prices for regularly scheduled shows vary by performance, although they typically cost about $35 each. Subscriptions are available for $80 to $104 per season.

## Square One Theatre Company
**Stratford Theatre**
**2422 Main Street, Stratford**
**(203) 375-8778**
**www.squareonetheatre.com**
This nonprofit professional theater organization (the only full-time company in

Stratford) began in 1990 with a production of *A Walk in the Woods.* Today the group continues to perform a variety of dramatic shows such as *Twelve Angry Men, As It Is in Heaven, The Rainmaker, Absent Friends,* and *Wonderful World.* Three-play subscription packages for Square One are available for $35; single-show tickets cost $16.

## Stamford Theatre Works
**200 Strawberry Hill Avenue, Stamford**
**(203) 359-4414**
**www.stamfordtheatreworks.org**
Located on the campus of Sacred Heart Academy, Stamford Theatre Works is a professional theater company that stages its shows in a historic barn with 150 seats. Some of the company's recent original productions have included *Visiting Mr. Green, The Music of George and Ira Gershwin,* and *Crumbs from the Table of Joy.* Stamford Theatre Works also runs the Purple Cow Children's Theatre and an acting school for children. Tickets cost $8.00 to $29.00 for students, $14.00 to $29.00 for seniors, and $16.00 to $29.00 for adults. Seasonal subscription packages offer ticket discounts.

## Westport Country Playhouse
**25 Powers Court, Westport**
**(203) 227-4177**
**www.westportplayhouse.org**
This is one of Fairfield's County's oldest and best-known theaters, harkening back to the days when Westport was widely recognized as a haven for artists. In 2000 actress Joanne Woodward took over operations and returned the theater to its original glory. Woodward's connections in Hollywood and New York haven't hurt the playhouse's roster of guest stars, either. Paul Newman (Woodward's husband), Gene Wilder, Richard Dreyfuss, Alan Alda, Jill Clayburgh, Richard Thomas, Cicely Tyson, and dozens of other recognizable names from stage and screen have made appearances on the stage. A Kids' Playhouse program brings theater to the younger set as well. Individual ticket prices and subscription prices vary. Call or

visit the playhouse's Web site for updated schedules, ticket prices, and gift certificate information.

# COMMUNITY THEATER

### Acting Company of Greenwich
**P.O. Box 7574, Greenwich 06836**
**(203) 622-0774**
**www.actingcompanyofgreenwich.org**
This community theater group welcomes local actors, musicians, set designers, lighting technicians, fund-raisers, and others to participate in its annual productions, which include comedies, mysteries, and dramas. The most recent season included presentations of *An Enemy of the People, A Murder Is Announced, The Bald Soprano,* and *The Actor's Nightmare.* The group's Web site lists dates and times for all upcoming auditions and performances. Most shows are performed at the First Congregational Church at 108 Sound Beach Avenue.

### Curtain Call
**1349 Newfield Avenue, Stamford**
**(203) 329-8208**
**www.curtaincallinc.com**
Local theater gets serious at Curtain Call, a nonprofit group that presents a rotating selection of shows like *You Can't Take It with You, Who's Afraid of Virginia Woolf?, Jesus Christ Superstar, South Pacific, Play It Again Sam, The Odd Couple, Barefoot in the Park, My Fair Lady,* and *Little Shop of Horrors.* Curtain Call productions are performed at the Sterling Farms Theater Complex on Newfield Avenue. Prices for all shows are $10 for students, $13 for senior citizens, and $20 for adults. A number of different seasonal subscription plans are also available.

### Musicals at Richter
**Richter Park**
**Aunt Hack Road, Danbury**
**(203) 748-6873**
**www.musicalsatrichter.org**
Local musicians, actors, and directors strut their stuff at this outdoor theater:

Past and recent shows include *My Fair Lady, HMS Pinafore, Kiss Me Kate, Guys and Dolls, South Pacific, Fiddler on the Roof, Grease,* and *Joseph and the Amazing Technicolor Dreamcoat.* Memberships and seasonal subscriptions are available. Ticket prices are $15 per show for adults and $12 per show for seniors, students, and children.

### Nutmeg Repertory Theater
**Shelton**
**(203) 944-0080**
**www.geocities.com/nutmegactorsrep**
Better known as "Nutmeg Rep," this theater group is one of Fairfield County's newest. Since 2001 the company has produced *The Glass Menagerie, Art, A Few Good Men, Projections, Sure Thing,* and *Plaza Suite,* always involving local actors and other theater enthusiasts. Auditions are held before each show. Call or visit the Web site for updated schedules and ticket information.

### Perry Players
**307 Atlantic Street, Stamford**
**(203) 358-2305**
**www.perryplayers.com**
This committed company is the resident theater troupe at Stamford Center for the Arts, where the actors perform all their shows in the Rich Forum. The Perry Players was founded in 1986 with its first show, *Wine in the Wilderness,* and went on to perform such plays as *The Knowledge, A Raisin in the Sun, The Piano Lesson, The Boys Next Door,* and even a female version of *The Odd Couple.* Most tickets cost around $25 each. Volunteers are always needed for set design, publicity, directing, fund-raising, and other tasks.

### Ridgefield Theater Barn
**Halpin Lane**
**P.O. Box 59, Ridgefield 06877**
**(203) 431-9850**
**www.theaterbarn.org**
Housed in a renovated dairy barn, this community theater company performs shows in both traditional (rows of seats)

and cabaret (tables with food and drink) styles. All shows have open auditions, and volunteer opportunities are also available for those interested in designing sets, costuming, performing music, and other aspects of production. Recent shows have included *Crimes of the Heart, American Buffalo, Baby, Chapter Two,* and *Angels Over Broadway.* Ticket prices typically range from $12 to $15. Visit the Web site for descriptions and dates for upcoming performances.

## Sherman Playhouse
## Routes 37 and 39
## P.O. Box 471, Sherman 06784
## (860) 354-3622
## www.geocities.com/~shermanplayers

The church at Sherman's town center used to be the site of public whippings. Today, luckily, it hosts a much more pleasant kind of public performance as the stage on which the Sherman Players perform their varied productions. The old church has enjoyed renovations and additions throughout the years and now provides plenty of seating for shows like *West Side Story, As You Like It, Reckless, Weird Romance,* and many others. The company typically performs four shows per season. Ticket prices are $15 to $18; subscriptions cost $60 per season.

## Town Players of New Canaan
## Powerhouse Performing Arts Center
## Waveny Park, New Canaan
## (203) 966-7084
## www.tpnc.org

A nonprofit community theater company, the Town Players of New Canaan regularly holds casting auditions for its family-friendly shows and dramas. All productions are performed in the 120-seat theater at the Powerhouse Performing Arts Center, allowing for a more intimate theatergoing experience. The Players' Stage II productions offer reduced ticket prices and a "theater in the raw" atmosphere with sparse sets and simple lighting.

## Town Players of Newtown
## The Little Theatre
## Orchard Hill Road, Newtown
## (203) 270-9144
## www.danbury.org/townplayers

Established in 1936, the Town Players is one of the longest-running and most respected theater groups around. Performing at the Little Theatre, the players have put on such shows as *Pygmalion, Run for Your Wife, The Murder Room, A Midsummer Night's Dream, Rumors, As You Like It, Six Degrees of Separation, Pack of Lies,* and *Moon Over Buffalo.* Matinee seats are available for $10; tickets for Friday and Saturday night performances are $12. Theatergoers can also buy seasonal ticket packages at a reduced rate.

*Want to see Shakespeare's plays performed the old-fashioned way—outside? Shakespeare on the Sound, a theater troupe made up of local actors, performs classics like* Merchant of Venice *and* As You Like It *each summer on the riverbank of Rowayton's Pinkney Park. For this year's schedule, visit www.shakespeareonthesound.org or call (203) 299-5424.*

## Westport Community Theatre
## 110 Myrtle Avenue, Westport
## (203) 226-5459
## www.westportcommunitytheatre.com

*Trip to Bountiful, Art, A Chorus of Disapproval, Arsenic and Old Lace, Death and the Maiden,* and *Independence* are just some of the productions staged by the Westport Community Theatre company since its inception in 1956. All the tasks—from acting to lighting, set painting, ushering, sound, and props—are accomplished with the help of volunteers. Yearly memberships ($15) are also available. The theater is located at Westport Town Hall.

**Wilton Playshop**
Lovers Lane, Wilton
(203) 762-7629
www.wiltonplayshop.org
Another historic group, the Wilton
Playshop was first established in 1937 and
continues to perform high-quality community theater productions like *Camelot,
Romeo and Juliet, Moon Over Buffalo,* and
*The Butler Did It* (all presented during the
2003–2004 season). Individual and season tickets are available. Auditions are
held regularly for all shows. Even if you
don't want to act, it's easy to get involved:
Volunteers are always needed for the box
office window, set construction, costuming, stage management, lighting, and
other areas of the theater.

## FILM

From two-screen "twins" to gigantic nine-
screen megaplexes, Fairfield County offers
plenty in the way of movie theaters.
Nearly all specialize in showing Hollywood
blockbusters and other popular movies.
One notable exception is the Bethel Cinema, a cozy theater showing mostly
quirky, art house–style films. A call to the
listed phone number at any cinema will
give you a recorded message with today's
shows and times.

# Southern Fairfield County

**Clearview's Greenwich Cinemas**
356 Greenwich Avenue, Greenwich
(203) 869-6030

**Crown Avon Twin**
272 Bedford Street, Stamford
(203) 324-9205

**Crown Landmark**
5 Landmark Square, Stamford
(203) 324-3100

**Crown Majestic 6**
118 Summer Street, Stamford
(203) 323-1690

**Crown Marquis**
100 Quarry Road, Trumbull
(203) 365-6500

**Crown Plaza 3**
2 Railroad Avenue, Greenwich
(203) 869-4030

**Crown Ridgeway Twin**
52 Sixth Street, Stamford
(203) 323-5000

**Crown Royale 6 Cinemas**
542 Westport Avenue, Norwalk
(203) 846-8795

**Crown SoNo Regent**
64 North Main Street, South Norwalk
(203) 899-7979

**Darien Playhouse Twin**
1077 Boston Post Road, Darien
(203) 655-7655

**Fairfield Cinemas at Bullard Square**
Bullard Square Mall, Fairfield
(203) 339-7151

**Garden Cinemas Norwalk**
Isaac Street, Norwalk
(203) 838-4504

**Loews Community Theatre**
1424 Post Road, Fairfield
(203) 255-6555

**New Canaan Playhouse**
89 Elm Street, New Canaan
(203) 966-7908

**Regal Stratford Stadium**
411 Barnum Avenue, Stratford
(203) 381-1000

Showcase Cinemas Bridgeport
286 Canfield Avenue, Bridgeport
(203) 339-7171

SoNo Cinema
15 Washington Street, South Norwalk
(203) 838-1602

State Cinema
990 Hope Street, Stamford
(203) 325-0250

Wilton 4
21 River Road, Wilton
(203) 761-0767

# Northern Fairfield County

Bethel Cinema
269 Greenwood Avenue, Bethel
(203) 778-2100

Edmond Town Hall Theater
45 Main Street, Newtown
(203) 426-2475

Loews Danbury
4-6 International Drive, Danbury
(203) 796-7777

Ridgefield Playhouse
Governor Street, Ridgefield
(203) 438-5795
www.ridgefieldplayhouse.org

# ANNUAL EVENTS

Not surprisingly, winter is the sleepiest time of year in Fairfield County as residents hibernate at home to escape the chilly weather and shorter days. January, February, and March events are infrequent and predominantly indoor—with the notable exception of Winterfest in Stamford. But once those first tulips bloom, look out: The Housatonic Valley and coastal towns come alive with food, frolic, and festivities that last throughout spring, summer, and fall. Two of the region's best-known annual events, the Oyster Festival and the In-Water Boat Show, are both held in Norwalk. Locals can also run road races, watch parades, browse antiques and crafts, sample local cuisines, ride on Ferris wheels, and enjoy a host of other activities in virtually every town and city as the months go by. The best part of these county traditions? If you have to miss this year's event, you'll always get another chance next year.

## JANUARY

**SCAN Annual Art Show**
**Various locations, Newtown**
**(203) 426-6654**
For more than 30 years, the Society of Creative Artists of Newtown (SCAN) has been hosting this annual juried show to spotlight the best creative works by local artists. Some exhibitors are graduates of the Western Connecticut State University's art program; others are self-taught or honed their craft at other institutions. Visitors can expect to see sculptures, paintings, photography, and more. The show has been held at the Cyrenius Booth Library and other sites; call for this year's location and dates.

**Winterfest**
**Stamford Museum and Nature Center**
**39 Scofieldtown Road, Stamford**
**(203) 322-1646**
Started in the 1980s, this celebration of all things winter typically includes ice sculpture displays, hayrides, sled rides, and lots of food and music. In some years the Winterfest also has live reindeer on display. The Stamford Museum and Nature Center's other regular attractions, including a plethora of farm animals and rotating art and history exhibits, are also accessible. Get the kids bundled up and enjoy a day of crisp weather and good fun. Usually held at the end of January.

**Taste of Ridgefield**
**Ridgefield Community Center**
**Main Street, Ridgefield**
**(203) 431-7521**
This tasty annual event raises funds for the Ridgefield Rotary Club and allows local gourmands to sample a wide selection of local specialties in one spot. Chefs from Ridgefield's restaurants gather to prepare and serve creative dishes, with all proceeds benefiting the Rotary Club's Toys for Tots, Adopt-A-Street, Kids Day in the Park, and other programs. Visitors can also enjoy performances by Ridgefield High School musicians and the warm atmosphere of the historic Community Center building. Usually held the last week in January.

## FEBRUARY

**Annual 9-Ball Pool Classic**
**Boston Billiards**
**Kenosia Avenue, Danbury**
**(203) 743-0546**
Walk-ins are welcome to compete at this fun annual competition held in early Feb-

ruary. It often features well-known trick-shot players and other "celebrities" from the 9-ball world. Typically, registration starts on Saturday morning and the competition lasts throughout the weekend. Boston Billiards is located next to the airport and across the street from the Danbury Fair Mall.

### Antiques and Collectibles Show
### Stratford National Guard Armory
### Armory Road, Stratford
### (203) 758-3880

Get out of the cold and browse collectibles from up to 70 dealers at this annual indoor show. Some items rank as valuable antiques; others fall more into the "sentimental keepsake" category. The show is usually held over two weekend days in mid-February, with an admission charge of about $5.00 per person. Visitors can expect to find glassware, postcards, furniture, artwork, jewelry, china, and other items.

### Eastern Scrabble Championship
### Inn at Ethan Allen
### 21 Lake Avenue, Danbury
### (203) 743-0546

Hook, Hot Spot, Double-Double, Parallel Play: These are just some of the terms you'll hear lobbed around at the annual Eastern Scrabble Championship, usually held in mid-February at the Inn at Ethan Allen in Danbury. (The championship celebrated its 10th anniversary in 2004.) Depending on your skill level, you'll compete in Division 1, 2, 3, or 4 play, with an entry fee of between $40 and $75. Advance registration is necessary. If you're not quite ready for the big time, a five-round minitournament is also typically held in February.

### Revolutionary War Mock Battle
### Putnam Cottage
### 243 East Putnam Avenue, Greenwich
### (203) 869-9697

Step back in time to relive old skirmishes at Putnam Cottage, a restored 1690s cot-

*February's Annual Eastern Scrabble Championship is held in Fairfield County to commemorate the first Scrabble manufacturing site: the home of Mr. and Mrs. James Brunot in Newtown.*

tage and tavern where Revolutionary War General Israel Putnam often stayed the night—and once narrowly escaped capture by British soldiers. The cottage is now maintained by the Daughters of the American Revolution. You can also visit throughout the year to view the interior of the building, which is furnished with authentic period pieces.

# MARCH

### Wild Winter Warm-Up
### Danbury Ice Arena
### 1 Independence Way, Danbury
### (203) 797-4511

Gather the family for this end-of-winter celebration offering the "Stew-Off" cooking competition, clowns, ice-skating, music, kids' activities, and more. The event is held in early March at the ice arena as well as at the Colorado Brewery (6 Delay Street), located just across the street. Some of the funds raised are donated to local charities, such as Ann's Place cancer support center.

### St. Patrick's Day Parades
### Greenwich and Danbury
### (203) 531-5223 (Greenwich)

Residents in both the southern and northern regions of the county can celebrate St. Patrick's Day with a bit of wearing-o-the-green and good-natured festivities. In Danbury the parade makes it way down Main Street with pipe bands and other marchers. In Greenwich revelers can catch the parade along Mason Street and Greenwich Avenue. Both events are held in the afternoon, usually around 1:00 or 2:00 P.M.

**Spring Art and Fine Craft Show**
**Bethel Arts Junction**
**5 Depot Place, Bethel**
**(203) 744-7690**
**www.bethelartsjunction.com**
Located within a historic former train depot, the Bethel Arts Junction represents a collection of local artists and hosts special events and shows throughout the year. The spring show spotlights members' works for sale in a variety of mediums, including painting, sculpture, and photography. At other times of the year, visitors can browse the on-site gallery, which offers rotating shows.

*In New England, March is synonymous with maple sugaring, an activity in which trees are tapped to drain the sweet, golden sap that is then transformed into maple syrup. Many of Fairfield County's nature centers have facilities, equipment, and special programs to teach visitors the art and science of this delicious age-old tradition. For a complete listing of all nature centers in the county, see the Attractions chapter.*

**Darien Antiques Show**
**First Congregational Church of Darien**
**14 Brookside Road, Darien**
**(203) 655-0491**
In 2004 the First Congregational Church of Darien hosted its 37th Annual Darien Antiques Show, a popular event designed to benefit the church's outreach efforts. Some of the dealers have been personally displaying their wares at the show for more than 20 years. Visitors can expect to find 17th-, 18th-, and 19th-century antiques such as furniture, jewelry, needlework, and collectibles. Each year in late March the show typically begins with a preview party on Friday night and continues throughout the weekend. Admission fees are $6.00 to $8.00 per person.

**Annual Antiques Show and Open House**
**Edmond Town Hall**
**Main Street, Newtown**
**(203) 426-5937**
The Newtown Historical Society hosts this yearly fund-raiser ($3.00 per person) that gives antiques lovers a chance to browse hundreds of treasures from a multitude of dealers. The gathering usually takes place in late March in the Town Hall gymnasium. After the show, docents are stationed at the historic Matthew Curtis House (also on Main Street) for guided tours of the society's own antiques collections.

**Breath of Spring Craft Show**
**New Fairfield High School**
**54 Gillotti Road, New Fairfield**
**(203) 775-6241**
Year after year, more than 80 crafters and artists from around the Northeast gather at New Fairfield High School to display their wares and entice spring to arrive in full bloom. The event includes a juried show, raffles, children's activities, and bake sales. Admission to the end-of-March event is usually around $4.00 per person.

# APRIL

**Fairfield County Home and Better Living Show**
**Wilton Fieldhouse**
**U.S. Route 7, Wilton**
**(800) 294-7469**
Typically held over two weekend days near the beginning of April, this home show is a popular destination for homeowners throughout the area. Exhibitors display all varieties of products related to home improvement, repair, and decor; others offers up their services for installing siding, windows, and more. The Outdoor Village offers information about decks, sheds, pools, and even tennis courts. Admission fees are generally around $8.00 for adults, with free admission for children.

## Annual Lego Contest
**Discovery Center**
**P.O. Box 926, Ridgefield 06877**
**(203) 438-1063**

Children and parents crowd the room each year when it's time for the annual Lego Contest, usually held in early April. Participants build their most imaginative Lego-inspired structures while judges prowl the displays to decide on the winning sculptures. At the end, certificates and prizes are awarded and the Lego towers come tumbling down. The location varies from year to year. For more information about the Discovery Center, see the Attractions chapter.

## House and Garden Show
**Burr Homestead**
**739 Old Post Road, Fairfield**
**(203) 259-1598**

This popular event is the Fairfield Historical Society's main fund-raiser. In addition to numerous vendors providing home and garden-related goods and services, the show also offers a silent auction with a range of unique items. The event is typically held over two weekend days near the beginning of April. Tickets are also available for a preview party ($100 per person) held the Friday night before the show officially begins.

## Easter Bunny Railyard
**Danbury Railway Museum**
**120 White Street, Danbury**
**(203) 778-8337**

For $6.00 per person, kids and adults can enjoy gift giveaways and a train ride with the Easter Bunny himself at the Danbury Railway Museum. The event is usually held over four weekend days in April. The admission price also covers a visit to the museum, where visitors will find model train displays and other exhibits. For more information about the museum, see the Attractions chapter.

## Annual Easter Egg Hunt
**Mocker Park**
**Route 302, Bethel**
**(203) 794-8531**

Usually held around 1:00 P.M. in Mocker Park, this yearly spring event is sponsored by the Bethel Parks and Recreation Department. Children can hunt for brightly colored eggs in the grass, meet the Easter Bunny up close and personal, guess the number of jelly beans in the jar, and enjoy other activities.

## International Festival
**Arnold Bernard Arts Center**
**University of Bridgeport, Bridgeport**
**(203) 576-4487**

Food is one of the main focuses of this annual festival, which aims to celebrate cultural diversity. Attendees can eat their way from exhibit to exhibit, each filled with specialties from Nepal, India, Japan, Italy, France, Mexico, and a host of other locales—sometimes as many as 26. The festival, held in mid-April, also spotlights the unique dress and traditions of each featured culture and typically attracts more than 1,000 people each year. Tickets for food only cost $8.00 to $12.00 each; tickets for both food and performances cost $10.00 to $15.00 each. Discounts are also available for family groups.

## Earth Day Annual Celebration
**Various locations, Western Connecticut**
**State University, Danbury and Bethel**
**(203) 837-8412**

WestConn students gear up in late April to celebrate Earth Day each year with a host of special events. In past years the festivities have included comedy shows, information kiosks, T-shirt sales, and concerts. The student organization Roots & Shoots is often instrumental in organizing the campus events.

**5K Pancake Breakfast**
**Housatonic Valley Waldorf School**
**40 Dodgingtown Road, Newtown**
**(203) 364-1113**
Participants in this 5K race at the end of April can either run or walk the course. Awards are given to the top three male and female finishers overall and to the top three male and female runners in the under 40, 40 to 60, and over 60 categories. Runners pay $12.00 to $20.00 for entry. (The school's "Kids' Fun Run" for children is held on the same day.) After you burn off all those calories, put them back on the pancake breakfast, which costs $5.00 per adult and $3.00 per child.

**Gracious Home and Garden Show**
**Weston High School**
**115 School Road, Weston**
**(203) 544-8854**
More than 50 designers and collectors are usually on hand at this yearly show, sponsored by the Weston Young Woman's Club at the end of April. Visitors can browse one-of-a-kind furnishings and decorative items while soliciting advice from exhibitors. Displayed items often include rugs, antique furniture, pottery, artwork, baskets, garden accessories, pillows, linens, and more. Admission is $5.00 to $6.00; the proceeds benefit a different charity each year.

**New England Regional Daffodil Show**
**Christ Church Parish Hall**
**254 West Putnam Avenue, Greenwich**
**(203) 661-6142**
Admirers of this varied flower can get their fill of colors and scents at the New England Regional show, hosted by the American Daffodil Society at the end of April. The society's shows are held around the country with an aim to promote scientific research and education about daffodil breeding, diseases, pests, and other topics.

**Antique Auto Show**
**Taylor Farm Park**
**Calf Pasture Beach Road, Norwalk**
**(203) 833-0400**
**www.exchangeclub.com**

Cosponsored by the Norwalk Exchange Club and the Gateway Antique Car Club, this annual show at the end of April lets aficionados get an up-close view of pristine cars and engines from a bygone era. All proceeds benefit the Exchange Club's efforts toward preventing child abuse in Connecticut.

# MAY

**GarlicFest**
**Notre Dame Catholic High School**
**220 Jefferson Street, Fairfield**
**(203) 374-4053**
**www.notredame.org**
Garlic ice cream? You bet. Every possible garlicy concoction is available at the GarlicFest, which was started in 1992 by Father Bill Sangiovanni. Although it began fairly small, the festival has grown to encompass the school's entire football field and attracts thousands of garlic fans. Usually held the first weekend in May. All proceeds benefit the Notre Dame Catholic High School scholarship fund. Hint: Bring breath mints.

**Minute Man Race**
**Compo Beach**
**Compo Beach Road, Westport**
**(203) 222-1388**
**www.wywl.com**
Organized by the Westport Young Women's League, the annual Minute Man Race is a 5K competition that starts at Compo Beach. Runners have been pounding the pavement at this charity fund-raiser since 1980. The record-winning finishers of the past are Tom Harding with 24:30 (1996) and Lisa Knoblich with 28:31 (1995). Think you can beat that? Call or visit the Web site for registration details. The race is usually held the first weekend in May.

**Serendipity: A Fine Art & Craft Show**
**Ballard Park**
**Gilbert and Main Streets, Ridgefield**
**(203) 438-8863**
**www.rgoa.org**

Held outdoors in Ballard Park in early May, this springtime event attracts shoppers and arts admirers looking for one-of-a-kind items. In addition to vendors and exhibits, the show features demonstrations by weavers, jewelry makers, sculptors, painters, and woodworkers, to name just a few. Serendipity is hosted by the Ridgefield Guild of Artists.

### Taste of the Nation
### Various locations
### (203) 323–4185
### www.strength.org

Designed to raise funds for Share Our Strength, an antihunger organization, this yearly event brings chefs, brewers, and bakers together from around the country for one night of food-focused fun. Attendees pay an entry fee and then enjoy unlimited access to samples of culinary creations, including meat and seafood dishes, fine wines, vegetarian entrees, and sinful desserts. The location varies from year to year, but you'll usually find it somewhere in Stamford. Usually held in early May. Be prepared to loosen your belt.

### Springfest
### Paradise Green
### North Main Street, Stratford
### (203) 378–2585

Play games, enjoy cotton candy, try your luck at a raffle, and take a look through the unique items offered for sale and display at this juried arts and crafts fair. Admission for adults is usually around $3.00 per person; kids get in for free. Usually held in early May.

### Annual Juried Spring Art Show
### Cyrenius H. Booth Library
### 25 Main Street, Newtown
### (203) 426–2951

Often held at the library in early May, this yearly show highlights the works of regional artists and gives the art-loving public a chance to enjoy this Newtown spring tradition. Whether you're "just looking" or hoping to start a collection of your own, the show is always a fun place to get a peek at sculptures, drawings, and paintings by a diverse collection of artists.

---

*The Stamford Downtown Special Services District (DSSD) has brought local art to the streets with Art in Public Places. These summertime exhibits have included up Cow Parade Stamford, which featured colorful, life-size statues of cows "grazing" on downtown sidewalks, and the Stamford Safari, which displayed large sculptures of safari animals staring down at passersby. For more information on upcoming exhibits, call (203) 348–5285 or visit www.stamford-downtown.com.*

---

### Annual Book Sale
### New Fairfield Free Public Library
### 2 Brush Hill Road, New Fairfield
### (203) 312–5679

The Friends of the New Fairfield Library invite the public each year to this sale that's sure to please bargain hunters and avid readers. Search though stacks of more than 15,000 used paperbacks and hardcover books, videos, puzzles, and more. All proceeds benefit the library.

### Dogwood Festival
### Greenfield Hill Congregational Church
### Hillside Road, Fairfield
### (203) 259–5596

This is one of the longest-running annual events in Fairfield County; 2005 will mark the 70th anniversary of Fairfield's popular Dogwood Festival. Parishioners of the town's Greenfield Hill Congregational Church organize the festivities each year and attract thousands of visitors with food, music, kids' activities, and vendors. All proceeds benefit charities that help women and children. The event is usually held over Mother's Day weekend, beginning on Friday.

## Housatonic Valley Classic International Pro/Am Bicycle Race

Sparta Cycling, Inc., 920 Broadway
Suite 905, New York, NY
(212) 358-9337
www.housatonicvalleyclassic.com

Filled with professional sponsored teams from around the world, this grueling competition in late May is the real deal in the racing world. It's also fairly new, having first appeared on the local scene in 2001. In a few short years, the qualifying race has made its mark for the racers as well as the local communities, where residents line the streets in full force to cheer for the cyclists trying to break speed records and qualify for other worldwide competitions. The race route winds through Danbury, Ridgefield, Redding, Bethel, Newtown, Brookfield, Bridgewater, New Fairfield, Sherman, and New Milford.

## Bloomin' Metric Bicycle Tour
## Calf Pasture Beach

Calf Pasture Beach Road, Norwalk
(203) 846-8000
www.soundcyclists.com

The Sound Cyclists Bicycle Club hosted its 27th Annual Bloomin' Metric event at the end of May in 2004, offering three rides varying in length from 25 miles to 75 kilometers and 100 kilometers. Riders pay an entry fee that benefits the club as well as Fairfield County Safe Kids, a nonprofit with a mission of reducing the rates of childhood accidents and injuries through prevention.

## Memorial Day Parades

The following towns and cities usually hold Memorial Day celebrations and parades in honor of America's veterans: Bethel (downtown parade); Brookfield (parade along Route 25); Danbury (Rose Street to Rogers Park parade, with memorial services at St. Peter's Church); Ridgefield (parade along Main Street); Weston (5K road race starting at Weston High School); and Sherman (parade along Route 39). Call the local town hall office for this year's dates and times.

## Annual Memorial Day Strawberry Festival
## Brookfield Museum and Historical Society

165 Whisconier Road, Brookfield
(203) 740-8140

Food, music, and fun are the main features of this Memorial Day gathering designed to commemorate the service of military personnel. Attendees can enjoy musical concerts, home-baked treats (including the event specialty: strawberry shortcake), and antique car exhibits.

# JUNE

## Barnum Festival
## Various locations, Bridgeport
(203) 367-8495
www.barnumfestival.com

Started in 1949, this rollicking annual event pays homage to Bridgeport's most famous former resident, P. T. Barnum, while also providing current Bridgeportians with an excuse to celebrate and socialize. Recent festivals have featured antique car shows, golf tournaments, fireworks, dance exhibitions, concerts, the "Barnum Bash," tea parties, luncheons, the Ringmaster's Ball, flea markets, children's activities, road races, polo matches, and the Great Street Parade. Most festival events take place throughout the month of June, although some spill over into May and July as well. The Web site contains up-to-date listings of all festival activities, including dates, times, and locations.

## Stratford Day
## Town Center
## Main Street, Stratford
(203) 377-0771
www.stratfordday.com

For more than 20 years, the town of Stratford has been celebrating its history and residents with an annual downtown festival. Hundreds of crafters, retailers, and food vendors offer ice cream, jewelry, toys, lemonade, art, floral arrangements, cotton candy, and a host of other items, while musicians, singers, and actors entertain the crowds. Nonprofits and other organizations are also usually on hand to provide information and giveaways. Stratford Day is usually held in early June.

## Annual Ridgefield Antiques Market
## 1896 Lounsbury House (Community Center)
## Main Street, Ridgefield
## (203) 438-6962

Dealers from as far away as Florida make the trip to participate in this yearly Ridgefield event, one of the oldest continuously running outdoor antiques markets. Visitors can make close inspections of furnishings, collectibles, and decorative items from more than 150 dealers, each of whom has a unique focus and collecting style. Usually held in early June. There is a small admission fee, usually around $5.00 to $6.00 per person.

## Annual Rocking Rooster Run/Walk 5K
## Starts at Reed Intermediate School
## 3 Trades Lane, Newtown
## (203) 270-4340

The Greystone Electronics Corporation times this race each year and validates the winners, many of whom hail from Newtown, Danbury, Bethel, Monroe, and other neighboring towns and cities. Less speedy contestants can opt for the "Rooster Walk," instead. The race is held in early June.

## Hidden Garden Tour
## Westport Historical Society
## 25 Avery Place, Westport
## (203) 222-1424

Ever wish you could get a peek at the estate gardens hidden behind those tall stone walls? Once a year in early June, the Westport Historical Society gives you that chance by spotlighting up to six gardens in and around Westport. Preregistration admission usually costs $28; $20 for Historical Society members. In addition to the tours, the event includes a raffle and a Garden Market.

## National Trails Day Hike
## Devil's Den Preserve
## Pent Road, Redding/Weston
## (203) 226-4991

Local nature lovers and hiking enthusiasts gather in early June at Devil's Den to celebrate National Trails Day with an invigorating stroll through the Den property. The organized hike, which usually encompasses 5 to 7 miles, is free, but donations to The Nature Conservancy are gratefully accepted. For more information about Devil's Den, see Beaches, Parks, and Recreation.

## CityCenter Grand PRIX
## CityCenter Danbury
## Main Street area, Danbury
## (203) 775-1212
## www.citycenterdanbury.com

This 10K race in early June is the genuine article, featuring regional racers competing for improved standings. Spectators have a great time cheering on the speeding cars as they race through the streets of downtown Danbury. Food vendors, live music, and children's activities are also on hand. CityCenter encompasses one square mile in the heart of the downtown, including the green and the busiest section of Main Street.

## Splash! Festival
## Washington Street and Downtown area
## South Norwalk
## (203) 838-9444

Splash! is yet another great annual festival hosted by the city of Norwalk. Located on the harbor, this event in early June includes Hong Kong Dragon Boat races, a parade, theater productions, music concerts, carnival games, a dunking booth, arts and crafts vendors, food vendors, children's safety demonstrations, a clam chowder cook-off, and more.

## Greenwich Concours D'Elegance
## Roger Sherman Baldwin Park
## 100 Arch Street, Greenwich
## (203) 618-0460
## www.greenwichconcours.com

Typically held near the beginning of the month, the Concours D'Elegance is a celebration of vintage boats, cars, and planes. In addition to the rare vehicles and vessels on display, the gathering also features workshops, demonstrations, art and books for sale, and exhibits by major car companies. Visitors can expect to pay an admission fee of $20 for one day and $30 for two days; children are admitted for free. Proceeds from the event benefit Ameri-Cares, the Stamford-based international aid organization.

## Greek Festival
**Assumption Greek Orthodox Church**
**30 Clapboard Ridge Road, Danbury**
**(203) 748-2992**
This fun annual festival in early June was started in the late 1970s by Father Peter Karloutsos and church parishioners. Since then, the event (sometimes called "The Greek Experience") has steadily grown to include large crowds enjoying Greek-inspired food, music, games, and children's activities. Architectural tours of the church are another popular feature.

## Love in Bloom
**Rose Acres**
**91 Stone Hedge Drive North, Greenwich**
**(203) 531-9471**
What better time than June for a rose garden tour? Love in Bloom is a fundraiser held at the private home and garden of Greenwich resident Gene Bliska—his collection of more than 1,400 plants is the largest private rose garden in Connecticut. In memory of Bliska's wife, Nancy, all proceeds from the annual tour benefit the American Cancer Society. Dates vary, so call ahead.

## Fairfield County Irish Festival
**Seaside Park**
**Barnum Boulevard, Bridgeport**
**(203) 259-4025**
**www.feileinc.org**
Typically held during three days in mid-June, this Irish Festival features plenty of live bands with Irish influences, along with carnival rides, dance demonstrations, and vendors selling all variety of food and gift items. The festival is produced each year by Feile, Inc., a nonprofit dedicated to

promoting Irish culture. Seaside Park is a new location for the festivities, which used to be held at Ludlowe Field in Fairfield.

## Try the Tri! Connecticut Sprint Distance Triathalon
**Lake Candlewood Park**
**Hayestown Road, Danbury**
**(401) 816-0271**
**www.americansportsevents.com**
American Sports Events (ASE) hosts this triathalon event each year in locations around Rhode Island and Connecticut, one of which is in Danbury's Lake Candlewood Park. Triathalons require each contestant to participate in three-part competition, showing their skill in running, swimming, and cycling. Cheering spectators are always welcome. The 2004 event was held in late June. Dates vary, however, so call ahead.

## First Americans' Festival
**Connecticut's Beardsley Zoo**
**1875 Noble Avenue, Bridgeport**
**(203) 877-2811**
**www.beardsleyzoo.org**
A powwow of the White Buffalo Society, this festival includes food vendors, art exhibits, and dance and drumming demonstrations, all focused on Native American culture and history. The festival is usually held over two weekend days in the middle of June. The Sioux, Blackfeet, Cherokee, Creek, Osage, and other tribes are represented.

## Strawberry Festival
**Monroe Congregational Church**
**Church Street, Monroe**
**(203) 268-9327**
Held on the town green across from the Monroe Congregational Church, this outdoor gathering in mid-June features artisans, crafters, bake sales, children's activities, hamburgers and hot dogs, and plenty of smiling faces. Expect to find strawberry cookies, strawberry pie, strawberry ice cream, strawberry jam, and even strawberry-flavored dog biscuits.

## Puerto Rican Day Parade
**Woodward Avenue to Veteran's Park**
**Norwalk**
**(203) 831-0430**

Although the best-known Puerto Rican Parade in the area is in New York City, Norwalk also hosts its own annual celebration of Puerto Rican culture with an annual parade. The event includes closing ceremonies at Veteran's Park and is usually held on a Sunday near the end of the month.

## Fairfield Road Races
**Jennings Beach**
**South Benson Road, Fairfield**
**(203) 481-5933**
**www.fairfieldhalf.org**

This event at the end of June includes two races: the Half Marathon, which winds through 13.1 miles in Fairfield and Westport; and the 5K, a quick, flat course. Both start and end at Jennings Beach, with the Half Marathon starting first. The Half Marathon includes prize money of up to $1,500 for the top overall finishers (men's and women's). Sponsored by numerous local companies, the races also raise funds for charity.

# JULY

## Round Hill Highland Games
**Cranbury Park**
**Cranbury Road, Norwalk**
**(203) 324-1094**
**www.roundhill.org**

Get out the bagpipes and celebrate all things Scottish at this yearly festival in early July that has been entertaining Fairfield County residents for more than 80 years. Activities include numerous races for kids and adults, weight-lifting competitions, dancing demonstrations, fiddling and singing, hammer-throw competitions, pony rides, and an awards ceremony. Admission is usually around $10.00 for adults and $5.00 for children and seniors. No pets are allowed. Kilt-wearing is encouraged but not mandatory. Due to limited parking, a shuttle bus usually transports visitors from a designated nearby parking lot.

## Fourth of July Festivities
**Various locations, Fairfield County**

Celebrate Independence Day in these towns and cities: Bethel (Annual Firecracker 8K Road Race, starting at Barnum Square); Danbury (fireworks at Danbury Town Park and the Danbury Fair Mall); Fairfield (fireworks at Jennings Beach); Greenwich (fireworks at Greenwich High School); New Fairfield (parade along Route 37); Norwalk (fireworks on Calf Pasture Beach); Stamford (fireworks on Cummings Beach); Stratford (fireworks on Short Beach); Weston (fireworks at Weston Middle School); and Westport (fireworks on Compo Beach).

## Friends of the Bethel Library Annual Book Sale
**Bethel Town Hall (Municipal Center)**
**1 School Street, Bethel**
**(203) 794-8756**

Voracious readers can stock up on beach books at this annual sale, which includes thousands of "gently used" CDs, videos, paperbacks, and hardcovers. The sale is usually held the weekend after July 4 in the gymnasium at Town Hall, located just around the corner from the library.

## Puerto Rican Parade of Fairfield County
**Central High School to Seaside Park**
**Bridgeport**
**(203) 366-6462**
**www.prparadeffldcty.org**

In 2003 the Puerto Rican Parade of Fairfield County, Inc. celebrated 10 years with a gala celebration. In addition to its annual parade in early July in downtown Bridgeport, the organization also presents activities such as arts and crafts exhibits and sales, fine art exhibits, school programs, dance and music performances, religious services, and contests. All the group's efforts are aimed at spreading understanding of the Puerto Rican culture.

## Compo Beach Point-to-Point Swim
**Compo Beach**
**Compo Beach Road, Westport**
**(203) 226-8981**

Competitive ocean swimmers come from all over to participate in this 1-mile race hosted by the Westport/Weston YMCA. The swim, which usually attracts about 200 racers, celebrated its 25th anniversary in 2003. Swimmers of all ages (including children and senior citizens) compete in three heats. Prizes are given for the top male and female finishers in each age group. The swim is held in mid-July.

**Rowayton River Ramble**
**Pinkney Park**
**Highland Avenue, Rowayton**
**(203) 857-4217**
**www.rowaytoncurrents.com**
This riverfront festival in mid-July brings Rowayton residents together each year for a day of mingling and fun. Popular activities include pony rides, games, face painting, a dunk tank, a live auction, a parade, canoe and kayak races, refreshments, live music, arts and crafts sales, and fireworks. The event is hosted by the Rowayton Civic Association.

**Christmas in July**
**Norwalk Seaport Association**
**Sheffield Island Lighthouse, Norwalk**
**(203) 838-9444**
**www.seaport.org**
Leave your holiday sweater at home for this one. Scenic Sheffield Island hosts the world's jolliest elf in the heat of the summer at this unusual annual celebration at the end of July. Visitors can tour the lighthouse in its holiday finest while kids get a jump on showing Santa their wish lists. Other activities include art and crafts tables and shopping for such items as nautical-themed Christmas ornaments. For more information about Sheffield Island, see the Attractions chapter.

**Governor's Horse Guard Annual Open House and Horse Show**
**Fairfield Hills, Wildlife Drive, Newtown**
**(203) 426-9046**
**www.thehorseguard.com**
An all-volunteer group, the Governor's Horse Guard is a state militia unit with a

long past dating back to Connecticut's earliest days. At the annual open house, visitors can watch drills, enjoy pony rides, sample refreshments, participate in riding exhibitions, and more. The event is the group's largest fund-raiser, with proceeds benefiting the guard itself as well as local food banks, St. Jude's Children's Cancer Research Hospital, and special-needs riding programs. Date varies from year to year, so call ahead.

**Easton Volunteer Fire Company Carnival**
**One Center Road, Easton**
**(203) 268-2833**
This is Easton's most popular event, attracting residents from in-town and around the county for carnival rides, cotton candy, car shows, live music, games, and a host of other activities. Proceeds from this event at the end of July benefit the fire company's volunteer efforts.

# AUGUST

**Antiques and Treasures Sale**
**Keeler Tavern Museum**
**132 Main Street, Ridgefield**
**(203) 438-5485**
This fund-raiser in early August gives participants the opportunity to shop a wide variety of collectibles, furniture, artworks, jewelry, and other antiques, all donated by local residents and tavern supporters. For more information about the museum, see the Attractions chapter.

**Swim Across the Sound**
**Captain's Cove Seaport, Bridgeport**
**(203) 576-5451**
**www.swimacrossthesound.org**
Sponsored by St. Vincent's Hospital, this yearly athletic competition in early August raises millions of dollars for direct cancer-patient care. Amateur and professional competitors race in individual and relay swims, usually cheered on by thousands of spectators. Related events include Bike Along the Sound, the Cancer Survivor Breakfast, the Sunset Sail to Nowhere, and

the Swim Across the Sound Breast Cancer Luncheon.

## SoNo Arts Celebration
## Downtown South Norwalk
## (203) 866-7916
The streets of downtown SoNo are closed to traffic during this extremely popular annual festival that celebrates artistic expression in all its forms. Attendees can browse exhibits of photography, oil painting, woodworking, glassblowing, drawing, sculpture, and other mediums and also enjoy the craft of performance artists, dancers, musicians, and street performers. There's plenty of food on hand, of course, with vendors selling everything from fresh-squeezed lemonade to baked goods. Usually held in early August. Admission is free.

## Art in the Park
## Ballard Park
## Gilbert and Main Streets, Ridgefield
## (203) 438-8863
Admission is free to this one-day show spotlighting the wares of more than 100 crafters and artisans from around New England. Free children's art classes are also offered. The show, held in late August, is hosted by the Ridgefield Guild of Artists. (This event is very similar to the guild's Serendipity show: See May for more information.)

## St. Jude Italian Festival
## St. Jude Church
## 707 Monroe Turnpike, Monroe
## (203) 261-6404
The excitement builds each year as Monroe residents watch the carnival rides arrive and get assembled at St. Jude's Church on Route 111. Although visitors will find games, rides, and entertainment, this is primarily a food festival. Come with an empty stomach and be prepared to enjoy plenty of Italian specialties. Usually held at the end of August. Parking is available in the field across from the church.

## Cannon Grange Agricultural Fair
## Cannon Grange Hall
## 25 Cannon Road, Wilton
## (203) 846-1840
For more than 70 years, Wilton residents and others have enjoyed the social and entertainment benefits of this fun annual festival, which is always held the Sunday before Labor Day. The old-fashioned celebration includes cooking, gardening, and husbandry contests—complete with blue ribbons—along with bake sales, snack bars, games, watermelon-eating contests, quilt exhibits, auctions, scavenger hunts, and lots more.

# SEPTEMBER

## Annual Labor Day Parade
## Main Street, Newtown
## (203) 426-2695
## www.newtownctlabordayparade.org
American flags, cheering spectators, fire engines, marching bands. This annual parade keeps 'em coming with patriotic and community-centered themes. The event dates back more than 40 years, with participants typically including the Newtown Police Department, the Newtown High School Varsity Cheerleaders, American Legion Post #60, the Newtown Rotary Club, the Newtown Volunteer Ambulance Association, and others.

## Oyster Festival
## Veteran's Park and Seaview Avenue
## Norwalk
## (203) 838-9444
Locals can celebrate the area's rich maritime history—and fill their bellies with seafood—at this annual festival, one of the most popular events in the county. Presented each year in early September by the Norwalk Seaport Association, the celebration usually includes an arts and crafts show, live bands and choral presentations, the Big Boy Toy Show, tall ship tours, harbor cruises, oyster-shucking contests, historical exhibits, and skydiving presentations. Don't worry about leaving hungry. A

food court provides such specialties as lobster, calamari, funnel cakes, clam chowder, bratwurst, shrimp, hamburgers, and of course oysters. Admission is $10.00 per day for adults, $6.00 for seniors, and $3.00 for children. Adult advance tickets are sometimes available at a discount; call for details. Due to parking area limitations, shuttle services are provided to and from six nearby lots. The Web site provides complete directions to each lot.

### Annual Taste of Greater Danbury
### Danbury Green, Danbury
### (203) 791-1711

Presented in early September by CityCenter Danbury, this annual gathering appeals to the eyes, ears, and especially taste buds. Usually presented in and around the green in Downtown, the event features local chefs and restaurants cooking up some of their favorite treats and handing out sample-size portions to passersby. Revelers will also find live bands, magicians, games, clowns, and activities like make-your-own ice cream and pitching-speed contests. Admission is free.

### Sam Elpern Half-Marathon
### Starts at Fox Run Elementary School
### Norwalk
### (203) 838-4984

Cosponsored by the Lightfoot Running Club and the Norwalk Parks and Recreation Department, the Sam Elpern Half-Marathon has been keeping runners on their toes for more than 25 years. Racers can register in advance or on the same day as the event, which is usually held in early September. Awards are given to top finishers, and refreshments are available at the end of the course.

### Puttin' on the Dog
### Roger Sherman Baldwin Park
### Arch Street, Greenwich
### (203) 629-9494
### www.adopt-a-dog.com

Canines and canine lovers are everywhere at this annual fund-raiser for Adopt-A-Dog, Inc., a local nonprofit animal welfare group. The fun includes silly contests ("Best Kisser"), training and agility demonstrations, pet massage, clowns, face painting, a silent auction, pony rides, and refreshments. Held in early September, the event also highlights shelter dogs that need new homes.

### Annual Greater Danbury Irish Festival
### Ives Concert Park
### WestConn Westside Campus, Danbury
### (203) 730-8211

The Ancient Order of Hibernians organizes this Celtic fest each year, offering a children's tent, step-dancing demonstrations, storytellers, pipe bands, harpists, vocalists, and plenty of food and drink. A cultural tent features exhibits on Irish history, genealogy, modern-day culture, and more. Usually held in early September.

### Emmanuel Church Country Fair
### Emmanuel Episcopal Church
### 285 Lyons Plain Road, Weston
### (203) 227-8565
### www.emmanuelweston.org

Fairfield County is home to many long-running fairs, but this one may win the prize for most enduring—and endearing. The year 2004 marked the 98th anniversary of Emmanuel Church's down-home, countrified fair, which often features baking contests, quilt shows, crafts vendors, bake sales, live music, hayrides, a silent auction, and even a candlelit roast beef dinner. The fair is held at the end of September, and most events are free of charge. Leashed dogs are welcome.

### Norwalk International In-Water Boat Show
### Norwalk Cove Marina
### Calf Pasture Beach Road, East Norwalk
### (203) 984-7000

Typically held at the end of the month, this yearly show gives boat enthusiasts and gawkers the chance to step aboard hundreds of in-water yachts, fishing boats, speedboats, personal watercraft, and other vessels. Visitors can browse marine-related gift items, boat accessories, and engines and also enjoy free seminars, food and drink, and children's activities. Admission is $12.00 for adults and $5.00 for children ages 6 to 12; children under age 5 get in free.

## Artisans Alliance Annual Applefest
## Blue Jay Orchards
## Plumtrees Road, Bethel
## (203) 749-0863
This craft show, usually held rain or shine in late September, offers crafters and artisans the chance to display a variety of handmade items for sale. The one-of-a-kind gifts, housewares, and collectibles often include jewelry, quilts, picture frames, pet beds and toys, dolls, Christmas ornaments, wreaths, clothing, and more.

## Fall Festival
## Ogden House and Gardens
## 1520 Bronson Road, Fairfield
## (203) 259-1598
## www.fairfieldhistoricalsociety.org
Actors dressed in colonial garb bring visitors into the past at this annual festival hosted by the Fairfield Historical Society. Other activities for the day include children's games, demonstrations in weaving and other crafts, and Ogden House tours. Vendors are also on hand to make sure festival attendees never get hungry or thirsty. Held at the end of September.

## Harvest Festival
## Paradise Green
## Main Street, Stratford
## (203) 378-1020
This craft fair at the end of September typically includes up to 100 vendors, each selling unique handmade items such as painted clothing, dollhouses, wooden toys, knitted garments, ceramic bowls, greeting cards, calendars, and much more. Plenty of food and drink is also available. The event is hosted by the Unitarian Universalist Church of Greater Bridgeport.

## Greenwich Film Festival
## Various locations, Greenwich
## (203) 454-9604
## www.greenwichfilmfestival.org

Started at the turn of the century (this century, that is), the relatively new Greenwich Film Festival provides opportunities for independent filmmakers to screen their works and for local film buffs to get a sneak peek at the works of up-and-coming directors. Documentaries, feature films, and short films are shown at various venues around Greenwich at the end of September. Kickoff and closing parties round out the event.

## Potato Festival
## St. James Church
## 1 Monument Place, Stratford
## (203) 375-5994
Roasted, fried, baked and topped with sour cream—however you like your potato, you'll probably find something to love at this annual celebration of the most popular tuber around. And when you've had your fill of potatoes, there's always the games, music, art exhibits, and more to enjoy. The festival is usually held in late September or early October.

# OCTOBER

## Annual Juried Art Exhibition
## Ridgefield Guild of Artists
## 34 Halpin Lane, Ridgefield
## (203) 438-8863
This yearly show runs for more than a month, usually starting in early October and lasting through early November. Awards include Best in Show, the Comstock Drawing Group Award, and general Awards for Excellence. The exhibit includes hundreds of paintings, drawings, and mixed-media works from around New England and New York.

## Cystic Fibrosis Bike Tour
## Starts at Sherwood Island State Park
## Sherwood Island Connector, Westport
## (800) 841-2828
Cyclists at this popular fund-raiser (formerly known as the Tony Fenton Bike Tour) can choose one of five routes: 1 mile, 7 miles, 15 miles, 35 miles, or a 62-mile

metric. The competition, held in early October, was started in memory of Tony Fenton, 16-year-old New Canaan resident and cycling enthusiast who died of cystic fibrosis. In addition to the races, participants and spectators can also enjoy auctions, raffles, a picnic lunch, and live music.

### Outdoor Arts Festival
### Bruce Museum of Arts & Science
### 1 Museum Drive, Greenwich
### (203) 869-6786

Usually held over Columbus Day weekend, this juried outdoor arts show includes up to 80 exhibitors. The judging categories include mixed media, watercolor on paper, oil on canvas, sculpture, photography, and drawing. The festival is designed to increase the public's appreciation of fine art and give up-and-coming and established artists a chance to display their works.

### Apple Festival
### North Greenwich Congregational Church
### 606 Riversville Road, Greenwich
### (203) 869-7763

For nearly 20 years the North Greenwich Congregational Church has welcomed visitors to its yearly fall festival featuring children's activities, book sales, arts and crafts vendors, a silent auction, and of course apple pie. (And caramel apples, and apple tarts, and apple muffins . . .) The festival is held in mid-October.

### Family Fall Festival
### Bush-Holley Historic Site
### 39 Strickland Road, Cos Cob (Greenwich)
### (203) 869-6899
### www.hstg.org

Celebrate autumn at this yearly gathering designed with families in mind. Historical demonstrations and exhibits, dance demonstrations, live music, kids' games, and refreshments are all part of the fun. The Bush-Holley Historic Site is the headquarters for the Historical Society of the Town of Greenwich, which hosts the event in mid-October.

### Pumpkin Festival
### Merwin Meadows Town Park
### Lovers Lane, Wilton
### (203) 762-3436

Autumn is a time for celebrating the harvest in New England, and Wilton's Pumpkin Festival is no exception. At this outdoor event held in mid to late October, you can choose the "perfect" pumpkin for carving while also enjoying bake sales, pony rides, face painting, a barbecue lunch, and arts and crafts vendors.

### Annual Redding Antiques Fair
### Lonetown Farm
### 24 Lonetown Road, Redding
### (203) 431-0613

Enjoy the changing leaves as you wander among antique furnishings, silver, dolls, clothing, crafts, and collectibles for sale. The event is usually held near the end of the month, but dates vary, so call ahead. Lonetown Farm is the headquarters of the Redding Historical Society, which sponsors the show.

### Halloween Parade
### Elm Street, New Canaan
### (203) 966-2004

Bring the kids—in costume of course—to this spooky and festive gathering to celebrate All Hallow's Eve. Balloons and goodie bags are provided. The event usually takes place during the day on the Sunday before Halloween; meet up in the Park Street Parking Lot.

### Halloween Costume Contest
### Danbury Green, Downtown Danbury
### (203) 792-1711

Each year the city's youngest ghouls, goblins, and superheroes gather in the Downtown area for a parade, refreshments, face painting, magic acts, and a costume contest. The event usually includes a rain date option in case of inclement weather.

# NOVEMBER

## Veterans Day Ceremonies
**Various locations, Fairfield County**

On November 11, local residents can take a moment to salute the flag and pay homage to veterans past and present with ceremonies at these locations: Bethel (P. T. Barnum Square); Bridgeport (Veteran's Memorial Park); Danbury (War Memorial); Darien (State of Connecticut Veterans' Cemetery); Greenwich (World War I Memorial, outside Post Office); Newtown (Veterans of Foreign Wars Post 308); Norwalk (Norwalk Concert Hall); Ridgefield (Ridgefield Community Center); and Westport (Town Hall Auditorium). Tradition dictates that most Veterans Day ceremonies are scheduled to begin at the 11th hour of the 11th day of the 11th month.

## Balloon Parade Spectacular
**Starts at Summer and Hoyt Streets**
**Downtown Stamford**
**(203) 348-5285**

A Thanksgiving tradition in Fairfield County, the annual Balloon Parade Spectacular usually takes place on the Sunday before the holiday. Marching bands, military personnel, clowns, floats, and fire engines are all part of the fun, but the real highlight of the day is the huge helium-filled balloons: The bobbing and weaving characters include Alvin the Chipmunk, Bullwinkle, SpongeBob SquarePants, Miss Piggy, Bear in the Big Blue House, Kermit the Frog, T-Rex, Elmo, and more of the latest popular creatures (around 30 in all). For die-hards, the day before the parade offers plenty of fun, too, when balloon inflation parties bring enthusiasts out into the streets for more action. The event is billed as one of the nation's largest helium balloon parades. (Note: The name of the parade changes occasionally, depending on which company is sponsoring it. For example, the event used to be known as the Cablevision Balloon Parade Spectacular, but in 2003 it was called the Advocate Parade Spectacular.)

## Enchanted Forest Holiday Stroll
**Various locations, Greenwich**
**(203) 869-9215**

A fund-raiser for the Junior League of Greenwich, this annual event is usually held in locations such as the Greenwich Hyatt Regency or the Greenwich Civic Center at the end of November. Activities for kids and adults include gingerbread house decorating, puppet shows, craftmaking workshops, auctions, magic shows, tea parties, holiday boutique shopping, live music, and an evening gala.

## Holiday Craft Fairs
**Various locations, Fairfield County**

If you're craving unique items to gift wrap this holiday season, November is the best time to find arts and crafts fairs and festivals in the region. For a listing of local shows, see Close-up: Red, Green, and Handmade.

## Holiday Tree Lightings
**Various locations, Fairfield County**

Watch the sparkling lights begin their annual glow at these locations: Bethel (caroling, cider, and carriage rides in P. T. Barnum Square); Danbury (Santa's arrival and refreshments at the Library Plaza); Fairfield (Fairfield Historical Society); New Fairfield (next to Town Hall); Newtown (Ram Pasture); Norwalk (City Hall East Lawn); and Ridgefield (Town Hall on Main Street). The ceremonies usually take place at the end of November or the beginning of December.

# DECEMBER

## Antiquarious Antiques Show
**Greenwich Civic Center**
**Harding Road and Forest Avenue**
**Old Greenwich**
**(203) 869-6899**

Dealers from around the United States vie for a chance to display their antiques at this annual show and sale. In addition to

# Red, Green, and Handmade

Craft fairs are common sights throughout much of the year, with town greens and church lawns often filled with artisans and enthusiastic browsers from April to October. But the arts and crafts scene really heats up when the weather cools down, particularly in preparation for the upcoming holiday season. Come November and December, indoor and outdoor fairs offer gift items, clothing, toys, collectibles, decorative knickknacks, and other items, all made with a one-of-a-kind flair by regional crafters. If you're having trouble checking off all the items on your holiday list, give one of these gatherings a try. Most take place during mid- to late-November, although a few sometimes spill over into early December.

**Annual Christmas Luncheon and Holiday Boutique**
Keeler Tavern Museum
132 Main Street, Ridgefield
(203) 438-5485

**Annual Festival of Crafts Fair**
Whisconier School
17 West Whisconier Road, Brookfield
(203) 740-8140

**Annual Holiday Exhibition and Sale**
Brookfield Craft Center
286 Whisconier Road, Brookfield
(203) 775-4526

**Annual Holiday Renaissance Faire**
O'Neill Center
WCSU Westside Campus, Danbury
(203) 749-0863

**Christmas in Connecticut**
Darien Historical Society
45 Old King's Highway, Darien
(203) 655-9233

**Country Treasures Craft Show**
Masuk High School
1014 Monroe Turnpike, Monroe
(203) 268-0143

**Harvest and Yuletide Fair**
First Congregational Church of Bethel
46 Main Street, Bethel
(203) 748-6112

**Holiday Boutique**
King and Low-Heywood Thomas School
1450 Newfield Avenue, Stamford
(203) 323-0639

the wide selection of furnishings and artwork from the 17th, 18th, and 19th centuries, the event includes gallery tours, lectures, and preview parties. Usually held at the very end of November or in early December.

**Rappelling Santa and Colossal Tree Lighting**
Landmark Square and Latham Park, Stamford
(203) 348-5285
OK, so this isn't your ordinary holiday cel-

Holiday Craft and Gift Fair
Greek Orthodox Church of the
Annunciation
1230 Newfield Avenue, Stamford
(203) 357-8037

Holiday Craft Fair
St. Michael's Episcopal Parish
554 Tunxis Hill Road, Fairfield
(203) 368-3225

Holiday Fair
Christ Episcopal Church
2000 Main Street, Stratford
(203) 375-4447

Holiday Market
New Canaan Nature Center
144 Oenoke Ridge, New Canaan
(203) 966-9577

Holiday Market
Ridgefield Guild of Artists
34 Halpin Lane, Ridgefield
(203) 438-8863

Holly Fair
Turn of River Presbyterian Church
49 Turn of River Road, Stamford
(203) 322-5327

New Canaan Sewing Group
Christmas Sale
St. Mark's Episcopal Church
111 Oenoke Ridge, New Canaan
(203) 966-2947

Sherman Library Holiday Arts &
Crafts Show
Sherman Library
1 Sherman Center, Sherman
(203) 354-2455

Westport Creative Arts Festival
Staples High School
70 North Avenue, Westport
(203) 222-1388

Wilton Historical Society American
Craftsmanship Show
Wilton High School Fieldhouse
395 Danbury Road, Wilton
(203) 762-7257

ebration. Despite its wackiness (or perhaps because of it), this unusual event in early December is an ever-more-popular one in Stamford. To start off the festivities, Santa and a helpful elf rappel down the 22 stories of Stamford's tallest building. When he reaches the bottom, he and throngs of following children march up Bedford Street to light the city's Christmas tree. The nearby First Congregational Church offers free parking and cider to visitors.

## Festival of Lights
**Greenwich Avenue, Greenwich**
**(203) 869-3500**

Greenwich residents gather each year for this parade and celebration that coincides with the start of the holiday lighting displays along Greenwich Avenue. Santa begins the festivities when he arrives on The Ave (in a horse-drawn carriage of course) and then marches up the street to begin the parade. As the marching comes to an end, the town tree is lit in front of the Post Office. The festival usually takes place on a Sunday at the beginning of the month.

## Mark Twain Library Annual Art Show
**Mark Twain Library, Route 53 and Diamond Hill Road, Redding**
**(203) 938-2545**

Usually lasting for two weeks in early December, this juried show features paintings, sculptures, and other works of fine art displayed throughout the library during all its operating hours. The event kicks off with a preview party, complete with live music and refreshments. Each year's show has theme, such as Honoring the Artist.

## Community Holiday Celebration
**Lockwood-Mathews Mansion Museum**
**295 West Avenue, Norwalk**
**(203) 838-9799**

This festive occasion is often centered around a historic theme and includes visits from Santa, caroling, and hot cider and other toasty-warm refreshments. The museum also hosts a Victorian Christmas festival each year with themes such as Five Decades of Christmas Trees.

## First Night Danbury
**Various locations, Downtown Danbury**
**(203) 792-1711**
**www.housatonic.org/1stnight**

Hundreds of volunteers work for months in preparation for this New Year's Eve blowout. First Night festivities include fireworks, ice-skating, rooftop parties, arts and crafts workshops, hypnosis shows, a family parade, karaoke contests, jugglers, puppet shows, a slew of live music concerts, free parking, and a shuttle bus. Attendees can buy a button ($10.00 for adults and $7.00 for seniors and children) that entitles them to admission to most events. The buttons are available at numerous banks and stores around town. Visit the Web site for this year's schedule of performers and events.

## First Night Westport/Weston
**Various locations, Downtown Westport**
**(203) 341-1041**
**www.ci.westport.ct.us**

The fireworks start exploding at midnight over the Saugatuck River during the Westport/Weston First Night celebration, capping off a fun evening of New Year's Eve festivities. The family-friendly, alcohol-free activities include face painting, crafters, comedy shows, dancers, magicians, jazz performances, games, and a Battle of the Bands at the teen center. To attend most events you'll have to buy a button for around $10 per person, available at local shops, banks, and other venues.

## New Year's Eve Labyrinth Walk
**First Presbyterian Church**
**178 Oenoke Ridge Road, New Canaan**
**(203) 966-5459**

Some choose to celebrate New Year's Eve with a party; others opt for a more contemplative event. Visitors can mull over the mysteries of time and space while following the concentric circles in the First Presbyterian Church's replica labyrinth, designed to mimic those found in ancient Europe.

# BEACHES, PARKS, AND RECREATION

## BEACHES

Because we're situated so close to the shore of Long Island Sound, it might seem logical to assume that Fairfield County residents enjoy plenty of access to sandy beaches. That's true in some cases but not in others: While those living in "beach towns" like Westport, Greenwich, Norwalk, and Stamford can readily get parking stickers (read: access) to beaches in their towns, those living a bit farther inland won't find it so easy to enjoy the sand and surf. Until recently, nonresidents were denied beach access altogether—locals paid the taxes to maintain the beaches, and locals enjoyed sole rights to pop open the umbrellas and build sandcastles. But a spate of lawsuits prompted town and city governments to allow access to outsiders, usually by means of purchasing a limited number of nonresident parking passes or paying hefty daily parking fees. This remains a sensitive subject for people on both sides of the issue. Despite the controversy, however, Fairfield County's beaches remain as beguiling as ever. And there's always Sherwood Island State Park, which is open to anyone willing to pay the state-imposed entrance fee.

## Southern Fairfield County

**Burying Hill Beach**
**Burying Hill Road, Westport**
**(203) 341-5090**
This 2.3-acre parcel offers a sandy beach (with some uneven rocky areas), wonderful views, a picnic area, and a wildlife conservation area. Lifeguards are on duty from

Memorial Day through Labor Day. Free parking access is limited to Westport and Weston residents and nonresidents who work full-time in Westport. Parking decals are available at the Parks and Recreation Department for $25 per season for Westport residents and $190 for Weston residents. Nonresidents can apply for one of 230 parking decals which would be eligible the following year at a nonresident rate of $375 per season. Connecticut residents who don't live in Westport can also access the parking lot by paying $6.00 per day on weekdays and $8.00 per day on weekends. The beach opens on the Saturday prior to Memorial Day and closes on Labor Day. Open hours are 5:00 A.M. to 10:00 P.M. Leashed dogs are welcome October to March.

**Calf Pasture Beach**
**Calf Pasture Beach Road, Norwalk**
**(203) 854-7806**
Located in East Norwalk, Calf Pasture Beach is really a combined park/beach on 33 acres with picnic areas, two playgrounds, a softball field, a basketball court, a fishing pier, boat rentals, a snack bar, a boat launch, and a miniature golf course. As you might imagine, the area is at its most crowded during the summer months and on weekends, although early-morning joggers and after-work strollers populate the paths during off-peak hours. Parking at the beach is limited to those with valid parking stickers. Norwalk residents can get the sticker for free. Residents of Redding, New Canaan, Ridgefield, Wilton, and Weston are eligible to purchase "peak" Calf Pasture Beach parking stickers for $160 per year or "off-peak" stickers for $40 per year. The "off-peak" sticker allows access to the

beach Monday through Friday after 5:00 P.M. Daily parking is also available for $15 per day, per car.

## Compo Beach
## Compo Beach Road, Westport
## (203) 341-5090

One of Westport's most popular recreational areas, Compo Beach comprises 29 acres along Long Island Sound with a long, leisurely beach and a massive playground area for the kids. Visitors will also find a snack bar, a boardwalk, restrooms with showers, and lockers. Lifeguards are on duty from Memorial Day through Labor Day. For those who aren't interested in sunbathing, the park offers sand-volleyball courts, a softball field, a marina, and even a skatepark. Westport and Weston residents can purchase parking decals for $25 per season and $190 per season, respectively. Nonresidents can apply now for a parking decal for next year's season, although they will pay a nonresident fee of $375. Nonresidents without a parking decal can also choose to pay a daily parking fee of $15 per day on weekdays and $30 per day on weekends. The beach is open May 1 to September 30 from 4:00 A.M. to midnight. All cars must be out of the parking lot by 1:00 A.M. Leashed dogs are welcome between October and March only.

## Cove Island Park
## Cove Road and Weed Avenue, Stamford
## (203) 977-4688

Cove Island Park juts out into Long Island Sound with 83 acres of sandy and rocky beach, paved trails for walking and biking, a marina, a snack bar, a pavilion, picnic areas, fishing opportunities, playgrounds, tennis courts, restrooms, and softball fields. As with most other area beaches, parking is limited to those with a valid beach sticker. Permanent Stamford residents can purchase a sticker for $20 per season; Stamford summer residents can buy a sticker for $125 per season. Nonresidents have the option of buying a one-day pass for $30, a weekend pass for $40, or a one-week pass for $80. The park is

also the site of SoundWaters environmental education center, which can make things tricky for out-of-towners hoping to visit the center or attend one of its programs. For more information about SoundWaters, see the Attractions chapter. To inquire about parking at the center, call (203) 323-1978.

## Cummings Park and Cummings Park West
## Shippan Avenue, Stamford
## (203) 977-4688

Spread throughout nearly 80 acres, Cumming Park and Cummings Park West provide residents with plenty of opportunities for summer fun. The facilities include a sandy beach, a fishing pier, a marina, tennis courts, basketball courts, restrooms, pavilions, softball and baseball fields, and a boardwalk. A beach pass is required for admission to Cummings Park. The sticker costs $20 per season for permanent Stamford residents, $125 per season for summer residents, and $30 per day for nonresidents. Nonresidents also have the option of purchasing a weekend pass for $40 or a one-week pass for $80.

## Greenwich Point
## End of Shore Road, Greenwich
## (203) 622-7814

Undoubtedly the most impressive of Fairfield County's beaches, Greenwich Point has been the focal point of the recent controversy (and lawsuits) regarding resident/nonresident access to local beaches. You'll forget all that unpleasantness, however, when you catch a glimpse of the 147-acre park's many offerings, including magnificent views of Long Island Sound (and Manhattan in the distance), beach areas, a snack bar, restrooms, flower gardens, lockers, wildlife preservation areas, paved and unpaved paths for walking and biking, a first-aid station, a clambake area (reservations required), the Greenwich Yacht Club, a large picnic area, water fountains, and the Seaside Center of the Bruce Museum. Greenwich residents can access the park for free with a valid parking sticker. For nonresidents a visit will cost $20 per car for parking plus a $10-per-person entry fee. During the off-season there is a parking fee but no entrance fee. The park is open from 6:00 A.M. to sunset. Leashed dogs are welcome only in the off-season, December 1 to March 31.

### Jennings Beach
### South Benson Road, Fairfield
### (203) 256–3010

Visitors at Jennings can splash, sunbathe, relax in the picnic area, grab a snack at the concession stand, launch a boat, or make use of the public restrooms and showers. The water is calm, the crowds include young families and college students, and lifeguards are on duty during busy hours in the high season. The Jennings Beach parking lot is open only to those with valid beach stickers on their cars. For Fairfield residents a beach sticker costs $12 per season. Nonresidents can buy beach stickers for $75 per season. All sticker applications are available by mail or in person at John J. Sullivan Independence Hall during specified hours, typically in early spring. A one-day parking pass is $12 per car. The beach is open from dawn to 11:00 P.M. year-round. Leashed dogs are welcome between October and March, although they are not allowed in the picnic area or playground at any time.

### Long Beach
### Oak Bluff Road, Stratford
### (203) 385–4052

Long Beach has been the subject of recent controversy as local officials decide whether to sell the land to the U.S. Fish and Wildlife Service, sell it to the cottage owners, or keep it as town-maintained property. The barrier beach, a prime nesting site for piping plovers and several other endangered birds, is adjacent to the Stewart B. McKinney National Wildlife Refuge. About 15 acres of the 30-acre site are maintained as a public beach that is currently managed by the town and the Fish and Wildlife Service. Lifeguards are on duty from 10:00 A.M. to 4:30 P.M. June 14 through Labor Day. Stratford residents can access the parking area for free with a valid beach decal. Nonresidents pay $100 per season for parking stickers or $10 per day, per car. Pets and flotation devices are not allowed. The beach is located on the Bridgeport-Stratford line, accessible by driving Oak Bluff Road off Lordship Boulevard. The beach is connected to Bridgeport's Pleasure Beach only during low tide, when you can walk across the McKinney Refuge. There is no way to access Pleasure Beach by car.

### Old Mill Beach
### Old Mill Road, Westport
### (203) 341–5090

This 1.8-acre beach is less crowded than Westport's best-known beach, Compo, but also offers fewer facilities. There is no lifeguard on duty, and parking is extremely limited. All these factors combine to make Old Mill a great spot for quiet relaxation by the shore. Parking access is limited to Westport and Weston residents (or nonresidents who are full-time employees in Westport) displaying a valid parking decal on their cars. Parking decals are available at the Parks and Recreation Department for $25 per year for Westport residents and $190 per year for Weston residents. The beach is open sunrise to sunset from Memorial Day through Labor Day.

### Pear Tree Point Beach
### Pear Tree Point Road, Darien
### (203) 656–7325

Located at the mouth of the Goodwives River, Pear Tree Point Beach encompasses eight acres with picnic tables, wheelchair-accessible areas, a gazebo, restrooms, a snack bar, a boat launch, and two separate beach areas. Darien residents can access the beach with a valid parking permit for $20 per season; Darien summer residents can purchase the permit for $100 per season. Nonresidents must pay $30 for a daily beach pass or $50 for a daily boat-launch pass.

## Penfield Beach
**Fairfield Beach Road, Fairfield**
**(203) 256–3010**
This public beach on Long Island Sound has scenic views, picnic tables, a snack bar, a playground, restrooms, and lockers available for visitors. Fairfield residents can park here for free after purchasing an annual beach sticker for $12. The daily parking fee for nonresidents is $12 per car, or you can purchase a nonresident seasonal sticker for $75. The beach is open throughout the year from dawn to 11:00 P.M. Leashed dogs are welcome during the off-season, October to March. Fairfield's beach stickers include access to both Penfield Beach and Jennings Beach, but residents can also choose to get an annual pass for Penfield Beach only at no charge. The Penfield Pavilion—complete with cabanas, a lounge, a dining room, and changing rooms—is available for rent for groups and special occasions.

*Although summer is the most popular time to visit the beaches, don't discount late fall, winter, and early spring. Nonresidents of beach towns will especially appreciate the free access to beach parking areas (restricted to residents only during the high season), and dog lovers can enjoy romping with Rover along the sand during the chillier months in many areas.*

## Seaside Park
**Barnum Boulevard, Bridgeport**
**(203) 576–7233**
Seaside Park comprises 210 acres with a walking path that extends along a seawall for 2.5 miles. Jutting out into the Sound, the park is also bordered by Black Rock Harbor, Bridgeport Harbor, and Cedar Creek. Lifeguards watch swimmers during peak hours in the high season. The park also offers picnic areas, restrooms, wheel-chair accessibility in some areas, baseball and soccer fields, volleyball and tennis courts, and a snack bar. The park is the access point for walks to the Fayer-weather Lighthouse, a 47-foot tower that stands guard over Long Island Sound. Parking is available at the end of Barnum Boulevard for $5.00 per car, per day.

## Sherwood Island State Park
**Sherwood Island Connector, Westport**
**(203) 226–6983**
The highlight of Sherwood Island—Connecticut's oldest state park—is its 1.5-mile sandy beach, although the site also boasts a snack bar, restrooms, a salt marsh, picnic areas, oak groves, fishing opportunities, and grassy fields. The site is open from Memorial Day through September from 8:00 A.M. to sunset, and parking is plentiful. Connecticut residents pay $5.00 on weekdays and $7.00 on weekends to enter the park; out-of-state residents pay $8.00 on weekdays and $12.00 on weekends. The restrooms, parking area, and picnic shelter are all wheelchair-accessible. Leashed dogs are allowed on the beach October to mid-April. To reach the beach take exit 18 off I-95, and then take the Sherwood Island Connector off U.S. Route 1.

## Short Beach Park
**Short Beach Road, Stratford**
**(203) 385–4052**
Short Beach's 30 acres provide ocean and beach access, a snack bar, a skate park, two Little League fields, a softball field, sand-volleyball courts, tennis courts, basketball courts, a miniature golf course, and a par-3 golf course. Lifeguards are on duty mid-June through Labor Day from 10:00 A.M. to 5:00 P.M. Stratford residents can park at Short Beach for free; nonresidents can purchase a $100 seasonal parking pass or pay $5.00 per day, per car. (The parking fee is waived for customers of the miniature golf course.) The park also offers three wheelchair-accessible picnic pavilions that can accommodate 50 to 100 persons. The pavilions are available

for rent for $40 to $175 for residents and $100 to $400 for nonresidents. Pets are not allowed in the park at any time.

### Weed Beach Park
### Nearwater Lane, Darien
### Exit 10 off I-95
### (203) 656-7325

Despite the somewhat unappealing name, Weed Beach is actually a very picturesque 22-acre spot with six tennis courts (reservations required), five paddle-tennis courts, a picnic area with barbecue grills, a playground, and a snack bar. Family-themed concerts are regularly held at the beach's new staging area. Sailing and windsurfing lessons are also available on-site. The beach is open Memorial Day through Labor Day. Darien residents pay $20 for a seasonal parking pass; out-of-towners pay $30 per day to park at the beach.

# Northern Fairfield County

### Candlewood Town Park
### Hayestown Road, Danbury
### (203) 797-4632

This 11-acre park includes a small sandy beach on Candlewood Lake, as well as picnic tables, a snack bar, and a boat dock. Danbury residents can access the beach for free after purchasing a $15.00 season pass or pay $5.00 per day, per person. Nonresidents are welcome for $10.00 per day, per adult, or $5.00 per day, per child. The park is often the starting point for bike races, swim contests, and even triathlons.

### Squantz Pond State Park
### 178 Shortwoods Road, New Fairfield
### (203) 797-4165

This extremely popular beach has created a bit of frustration for New Fairfield residents, who appreciate the beach's beauty

but not necessarily the crowds that it draws during summer. Parking is limited, and spillover onto nearby streets has caused no small amount of consternation for locals. Nevertheless, Squantz Pond remains one of the town's best-loved jewels. The beach is spacious and scenic, the autumn foliage is unbeatable, and the recreational opportunities are varied. On any given warm day, you'll find visitors swimming, sunbathing, kayaking, canoeing, picnicking, scuba diving, and fishing. The restrooms, fishing pier, and picnic area are all wheelchair-accessible. Leashed dogs are welcome in the park from October through mid-April. For more information about Squantz Pond, see the listing under Parks, below.

### William E. Wolfe Park
### and Great Hollow Lake
### 285 Cutlers Farm Road, Monroe
### (203) 452-5416

The small, sandy Great Hollow Lake beach in Monroe's Wolfe Park is popular with young families. The water on the man-made pond is always calm, and lifeguards stand watch over swimmers during peak hours. Right behind the beach, visitors will find a large playground and a concession stand with plenty of seating (and shade). Monroe residents can purchase a seasonal membership to the park (which includes access to the beach, swimming pool, tennis courts, and playgrounds) for $30 per year. For nonresidents the sticker costs $60 per year. Daily beach passes are also available for $5.00 per person, per day for residents and $10.00 per person, per day for nonresidents. For more information about Wolfe Park, see the listing under Parks, below.

## PARKS

If there's one thing that Fairfield County does well, it's parks. These leafy getaways are everywhere, tucked among city streets and sprawling throughout suburban acres.

## CLOSE-UP

# Candlewood Lake

One of Fairfield County's most scenic and notable natural features, 5,420-acre Candlewood Lake, is not really a "natural" feature at all. The body of water was created by local residents in 1928 to generate power for a growing population. The project was an unparalleled success for the region, both then and now. But for some unlucky residents, that success came with a heavy price.

European settlers first invaded the area just north of Danbury, where the lake now lies, in the 1700s. They pushed out the Schaghticoke tribe and its leader, Chief Squantz (whose name now graces the state park there), through mostly hostile means, eventually paying the Native Americans about $300 for the land. In 1740 the area became known as New Fairfield.

In addition to Squantz Pond, the fertile region was also home to numerous streams, wetlands, springs, and rivers. The Europeans settled in and began farming successfully, producing corn, tobacco, and other crops. The agricultural lifestyle of the region and its residents remained steady for more than 150 years.

In the early 1900s, however, an attorney named J. Henry Roraback began a buying spree: He purchased a large amount of stock in the Housatonic Power Company and then bought up chunks of land along the Connecticut and Housatonic Rivers. His efforts created the Connecticut Light and Power Company, or CL&P. By 1919 the busy company had built the Stevenson Dam and created Lake Zoar.

Some of the larger parks, like Devil's Den, Bear Mountain, Squantz Pond, and Huntington State Park, even provide semichallenging hiking and biking opportunities, although most were created with lounging, strolling, and picnicking in mind. You'll find some of the better known and most popular spots highlighted here. Each town also hosts numerous smaller neighborhood parks and playgrounds, some of which are accessible only by residents. For the most part you'll be welcome to visit the larger parks even as a nonresident, although you might be expected to pay an admission fee. For more information about private nature centers, see the Attractions chapter.

# Southern Fairfield County

**Beardsley Park**
**Noble Avenue, Bridgeport**
**(203) 576-8080**
Located next to Connecticut's Beardsley Zoo (see the Attractions chapter), Beardsley Park provides a bit of much-needed greenery and respite in downtown Bridgeport. The land was originally donated to the city in 1878 by wealthy local resident James Beardsley. Another famous local resident, P. T. Barnum, then used the 100 acres to exercise his fleet of zebras, elephants, and other exotic animals. From

But planners, officials, and power-company executives had bigger plans. To fulfill the electrical-generating capacity needed for future generations, they decided to flood 5,420 acres of northern Fairfield County land and use the reservoir to power an even larger generating station. In the mid-1920s the state gave the power company authority to buy out New Fairfield and Sherman residents living in the area, forcing them from their agricultural lands and homes. Approximately 100 houses, churches, schools, and other buildings were moved, and the contents of local cemeteries were relocated. Because the job was completed in such a hurry, however (less than one year), many of the buildings were left behind.

When it was completed, the flooded reservoir covered more than 8 square miles and created 61 miles of shoreline in New Fairfield, New Milford, Brookfield, Sherman, and Danbury. The lake was named after nearby Candlewood Mountain and quickly became a source of pride for local residents. Today recreational boaters, water-skiers, and anglers crowd the water during the warm months. Summer cottages and year-round homes dot its shores. The lake is especially popular with scuba divers, who come from great distances to glimpse the remnants of the former farming communities—including some intact homes, bridges, and other artifacts—that still linger ghostlike beneath the water's surface. As we power up our laptops, televisions, refrigerators, vacuum cleaners, and light bulbs, few of us realize the debt we owe to those early Fairfield County residents who left so many remnants of their lives submerged in the sparkling lake.

that odd sight came the idea of building a zoo on part of the park's 100 acres. Today you're not likely to stumble across a zebra while strolling through the park, but you will find special events, joggers, kids at play, outdoor concerts, and lunch-break sunbathers.

### Bisceglie-Scribner Pond Park
### Newtown Turnpike, Weston
### (203) 222-2655
This 52-acre park boasts a 2-mile jogging trail, a playground, restrooms, a picnic area with barbecue grills, and its most popular feature: a swimming pond that is fed by underground springs. Bisceglie-Scribner Pond Park is open only to Weston residents with valid annual passes—$100 per family or $50 per individual. There is no charge for residents under the age of 5 or over the age of 60.

### Boothe Memorial Park and Museum
### Main Street, Stratford
### (203) 378-0630
Although Boothe Park is beautiful year-round, you won't find a more fragrant time to visit than late June, when the site's impressive rose garden is in full bloom. In addition to providing a peaceful place to walk, relax, or throw a Frisbee, the park has an eccentric collection of museum buildings—one of which is rumored to be haunted. For more information about Boothe Memorial Park, see the listing in the Attractions chapter.

## Cherry Lawn Park
### 120 Brookside Road, Darien
### (203) 656-7325

The playground at Cherry Lawn, known as "Wee Play," is one of the busiest around. The 27-acre park is also home to a pond, five tennis courts, a softball field, gardens with community plots, restrooms, a gazebo, walking trails, a basketball court, a multiuse sports field, picnic areas, and the Darien Nature Center. Access to the park is available only to Darien residents with a valid parking sticker, available for $20 per year.

*Local bird-watchers are in luck: The Connecticut Ornithological Association is based in Fairfield. The binocular-toting group keeps track of birds in Fairfield County and parks around the state and publishes a quarterly journal. For more information write to the association at 314 Unquowa Road, Fairfield 06824, or visit www.ctbirding.org.*

## Cranbury Park
### Cranbury Road, Norwalk
### (203) 854-7806

This great spot encompasses 190 acres with a pavilion, restrooms, a sculpture garden, a playground, and even an 18-hole "Frisbee golf" course. Hikers and walkers will especially appreciate the nearly 125 acres of forested trails. The park also houses the Gallaher Estate, a stone mansion that can be rented for parties and other special occasions. In summer the Norwalk Recreation and Parks Department hosts free outdoor concerts at Cranbury Park, with musical styles ranging from classical to jazz and bluegrass.

## Devil's Den Preserve
### Pent Road, Redding
### (203) 226-4991

Owned and managed by the Nature Conservancy, this 1,756-acre preserve is the largest area of undeveloped conservation land in Fairfield County. This place is a dream come true for hikers and other outdoors lovers, who flock to the pristine 20 miles of trails in search of escape from nearby congestion. Wildlife watchers can search for the park's elusive coyotes, woodpeckers, red foxes, wood ducks, and ruffed grouse. Amateur botanists seek out the rare pink lady's slipper, cardinal flowers, and mature native trees of all types. In addition, visitors can take part in group hikes and other planned activities for kids and adults. The preserve is open from dawn to dusk every day. Dogs are not allowed. Parking is available at the Pent Road main entrance.

## Devil's Glen Park
### Valley Forge Road, Weston
### (203) 222-2655

Although this might be one of the prettiest parks in Fairfield County, most of us will never see it: The lush glen with waterfalls, hiking trails, and diverse flora and fauna is open only to Weston residents. Resident park passes cost $100 per family or $50 per individual, although children under age 5 and seniors over 60 can get in for free. A small parking area is available on Valley Forge Road.

## Gould Manor Park
### Crestwood Road, Fairfield
### (203) 256-3144

At 13 acres, this public park is one of Fairfield's largest. Parkgoers will find 10 acres of woods and walking trails; a small lake that's popular with anglers, kayakers, canoeists, and other boaters; and an athletic field. In winter Gould Manor attracts scores of ice-skaters. The park is open from sunrise to sunset daily.

## The Green
### East Avenue, Norwalk
### (203) 854-7806

Revolutionary War soldiers once fought skirmishes here. Today local residents and visitors are far more likely to engage in such peaceful activities as picnicking, sunbathing, reading, walking on the paved paths, or relaxing in the gazebo. The green, located within the Historic District, forms a triangle surrounded by East Avenue, St. Paul's Place, and Park Street.

### Indian Ledge Park
### Whitney Avenue, Trumbull
### (203) 452-5075

One of the most popular spots in Trumbull, Indian Ledge comprises 104 acres with walking trails, a softball field, a sledding hill, a playground, a picnic area, restrooms, a "water-spray lot" for hot summer days, an amphitheater, boccie courts, a BMX racing track, and two multipurpose sports fields. Trumbull residents can access the park for free with a valid parking sticker. Nonresidents can inquire with the Trumbull Recreation Department about acquiring one-day passes to the park.

### Lake Mohegan Recreation Area
### Morehouse Highway, Fairfield
### (203) 256-3144

Acquired in 1967, this secluded 170-acre recreation area offers fishing opportunities, picnic areas, wildlife conservation areas, and trails for hiking, biking, and horseback riding. Lake Mohegan is open to Fairfield residents only; a beach pass is required for entry. Seasonal passes for residents cost $30. Parking is available near the intersection of Morehouse Highway and Mohican Hill Road.

### Longshore Club Park
### 260 Compo Road, Westport
### (203) 341-5090

Golfers, tennis players, picnickers, and swimmers will all find something to love about this 169-acre park located along Westport's shoreline. Facilities include three swimming pools, nine tennis courts, one paddle-tennis court, restrooms, lockers, a large playground, a marina, and a snack bar. The park is also the location of the Inn at Longshore, Splash restaurant, and the Longshore Sailing School. The park's 18-hole golf course, driving range, and pro shop are among the town's best-

known attractions. (See the Golf chapter for more information.) In most areas parking is restricted to Westport and Weston residents with valid parking decals, although inn and restaurant guests can park in designated areas. Access to the swimming pools, golf courts, and tennis courts is likewise limited to Westport residents with valid "hand passes" ($30 per year). Golfers will also pay applicable greens fees. The park is open year-round.

### Mead Memorial Park
### Richmond Hill Road, New Canaan
### (203) 966-0502

Tennis courts, baseball fields, picnic areas, a large playground, a pond, and ice-skating are all available at Mead Memorial Park, located off Park Street. Reservations and a resident pass are required for use of the eight regulation tennis courts (two of which are lighted) but not for the one all-weather practice court.

### Mianus River Park and Glen
### Westover Road, Stamford
### (203) 977-4688

The largely undeveloped 185 acres of Mianus River Park and Glen include an expansive network of trails, many of which meander beside the river and interloop with one another. Complete trail maps are available from the Stamford Parks and Recreation Department. The trails are popular with cyclists as well as hikers. Pack a snack and some water; you won't find any on-site.

### Mill River Park
### Washington Boulevard, Stamford
### (203) 977-4688

The 2.4-acre Mill River Park brings a taste of the natural world to downtown Stamford with a walking path, open areas, and benches for relaxing. A new initiative called the Stamford West Side Healthy Communities Project aims to spruce up the "Mill River Corridor" with expansions in and around the park to create a greenway extending from the Merritt Parkway to the waterfront of the South End. Project promoters hope to bring new bike paths, walkways, and plantings to the surrounding Mill River Park area. Volunteers are making the plan a reality by planting shrubs, trees, and other flora in vacant lots along the way.

*Baseball junkies should check out the Jackie Robinson Park of Fame in Stamford, located at the intersection of Richmond Hill and West Main Street. The park has a statue of the baseball great along with, of course, a ball field.*

## Norwalk State Heritage Park
## (Mathews Park)
## West Avenue, Norwalk
## (203) 854-7806

The former site of a private 30-acre estate, Norwalk Heritage Park (better known to some as Mathews Park) is now home to a visitor center, the Pine Island Cemetery, the extravagant Lockwood Mathews Mansion, the Connecticut Graphic Arts Center, Stepping Stones Museum for Children (see the Kidstuff chapter for more information), and Devon's Place, a wheelchair-accessible playground for kids of all abilities. Throughout the year, visitors will also find concerts, art exhibits, and other special events. Parking is available in a lot on Webster Street.

## Old Mine Park
## Old Mine Road, Trumbull
## (203) 452-5075

The 72-acre Old Mine Park is one of Trumbull's largest, featuring a large picnic area, a sports field, two pavilions, a bridge, the Trumbull Counseling Center, restrooms, and myriad hiking trails along a small river. Trumbull residents can enter the park for free but must have a current parks sticker displayed on their cars. Nonresidents can inquire about one-day passes by calling the town's Recreation Department. Old Mine Road is located near the intersection of Routes 25 and 111.

## Roosevelt Forest Park
## Peters Lane, Stratford
## (203) 385-4052

Bikers and hikers enjoy the winding, climbing trails at Roosevelt Forest, a park with lots of wooded areas, a picnic area, wetlands, wildlife-watching opportunities, rustic fences, water views, and plenty of peace and quiet. Limited parking is available.

## Stewart B. McKinney
## National Wildlife Refuge
## Great Meadows Unit, Route 113
## Stratford

## Chimon Island Unit and
## Sheffield Island Unit, Norwalk
## (860) 399-2513

The Stewart B. McKinney National Wildlife Refuge, named for a U.S. congressman who helped create it, is actually spread throughout eight different land parcels in Connecticut. The headquarters is located at the Salt Meadow Unit in Westbook; the three Fairfield County units are in Stratford and Norwalk. Visitation is somewhat limited—at the time of this writing, the Great Meadows Unit was temporarily closed to the public for installation of a new educational trail on the property. In Norwalk you can reach Sheffield Island via ferry from Hope Dock. (See the Attractions chapter for more information about the ferry and Sheffield Island.) All three sites are considered vital habitats for aquatic wildlife species, including endangered roseate terns, common terns, and numerous migrating birds.

## Taylor Farm Park
## Calf Pasture Beach Road, Norwalk
## (203) 854-7806

Taylor Farm is best known as the site of Norwalk's annual Balloon Festival. The 30-acre plot was originally sold to the city by ninth-generation farmers William Marvin Taylor (1921–1973) and Frederick Bradford Taylor (1925–1978). Today visitors can enjoy kite-flying, a playground, an annual auto show, Drums Around the World events, music concerts, YMCA children's camps, and wildlife watching on-site.

### Tilley Pond Park
### Lakeside and West Avenue, Darien
### (203) 656-7325

As you might guess from the name, the highlight of this eight-acre park is Tilley Pond, where visitors can ice-skate or bird-watch. In the colder months you'll even find a warming hut out on the ice to thaw chilly fingers and toes. In warmer weather the easy walking paths provide nice views of the water. Tilley Pond Park is open only to Darien residents, who can buy an annual parking sticker for $20.

### Veteran's Memorial Park (Bridgeport)
### Park Avenue, Bridgeport
### (203) 576-8080

The recently renovated Veteran's Memorial Park aims to honor the military service of Bridgeport veterans with baseball fields, picnic areas, playgrounds, all-purpose playing fields, and green spaces.

### Veteran's Memorial Park (Norwalk)
### Seaview Avenue, Norwalk
### (203) 854-7806

Most local seafood fans know they need to head for Veteran's Memorial Park when the Annual Oyster Festival rolls around each year (see the Annual Events chapter for more information). But the park is also the site of more somber remembrances to the fallen heroes of past American wars. You'll also find views of the harbor, picnic tables, restrooms, and some parking.

### Veteran's Park
### Atlantic Street, Stamford
### (203) 977-4688

This small downtown park provides a respite from Atlantic Street traffic while it honors Stamford's veterans. The memorials include a doughboy statue from the 1920s, a monument depicting the four freedoms, and a granite statue remembering those who served in the Korean and Vietnam conflicts and World War II. Passersby can also enjoy park benches, gardens, and a bulletin board with posts of local interest.

### Waveny Park
### 677 South Avenue, New Canaan
### (203) 966-0502

The New Canaan Recreation Department is headquartered in this massive 250-acre park, which offers 3.5 miles of trails for walking and jogging, a picnic area, tennis courts, a swimming pool, baseball and softball fields, the Lapham Community Center, and the PowerHouse Performing Arts Center. Dogs are welcome on a leash, as long as owners clean up after them. Pool facilities are open to town residents with a membership pass: A family aquatic pass costs $325 per year; an individual pass, $130 per year; and a senior citizen pass, $40 per year. Residents can also bring guests to the pool for $10.00 per visit for adults and $5.00 per visit for children and seniors.

### Weir Farm National Historic Site
### 735 Nod Hill Road, Wilton
### (203) 834-1896

Weir Farm is an ode to J. Alden Weir (1852–1919), one of America's most prominent Impressionist painters, who lived on this 60-acre patch of farmland off and on for 40 years. Today the park is run by the National Park Service, and staff members are always around to answer questions, lead guided tours of the property, and teach educational programs. Most visitors come to walk the trails and enjoy the peaceful scenery, which often include painters at their easels. The park is open year-round. Leashed, well-behaved dogs are welcome. Weir Farm is connected to The Nature Conservancy's Weir Preserve, where you'll find even more hiking trails. For more information see the Attractions chapter.

### Winslow Park
### North Compo Road and Post Road East
### Westport
### (203) 341-1038

With paved walking trails, picnic areas, a bike path, gardens, and open green areas, Winslow Park is popular with seniors, families, and other local residents. But the park is best loved by dog owners, who flock by the dozens to its spacious off-leash play area. Here you'll find canines running, fetching, and chasing one another while their owners socialize and watch the action. Free parking is available near the corner of North Compo Road and Post Road East. Dogs must remain on a leash until they reach the designated dog-run area.

# Northern Fairfield County

### Arthur Harris Linear Park
**100 Pocono Road, Brookfield**
**(203) 775-7310**
Better known simply as Linear Park, this 139-acre space encompasses woods, a gazebo, and portions of the Still River. Two walking trails, Loop A and Loop B, offer more than 3 combined miles of hiking and wildlife-watching. Trail maps are available at the Parks and Recreation Department office on Pocono Road.

### Bear Mountain Reservation
**17 Bear Mountain Road, Danbury**
**(203) 743-0546**
Lovely lookouts and lengthy hikes are all part of the fun at Bear Mountain. This 140-acre park has numerous blazed hiking trails identified by color. Visitors will find posted park rules and hiking trail maps at the entrance gate at the end of the parking lot. Trails wind past sunny meadows, wooded areas, and overlooks of Candlewood Lake. Picnic tables are also available. See the listing in the Hiking section for more information about Bear Mountain.

### Collis P. Huntington State Park
**Sunset Hill Road, Redding/Bethel**
**(203) 938-2285**
This is hands-down one of the very best Fairfield County parks for almost any type of outdoor activity: Bikers gather here to explore the trails; moms flock here with strollers in hand; dog-walkers bring their leashes and best friends; joggers enjoy the paths around the ponds; kayakers splash around in the water; leaf-peepers bring their cameras in autumn; equestrians clop along the paths at a leisurely pace; and friends hunker around the picnic tables for jovial outdoor meals. Despite its many great qualities, however, the park is rarely crowded—a good thing, considering the limited number of parking spots available. Bring comfortable shoes, a camera, and binoculars. You also might want to pack a sandwich and some bottled water, since no facilities (save one pit toilet) are available. Leashed pets are welcome. Huntington is not technically wheelchair-accessible, although a wheelchair could access many areas and trails, provided the ground isn't too wet or muddy. The park straddles Bethel and Redding, although the parking area and main entrance are located in Redding.

### Indian Well State Park
**Howe Avenue (Route 110), Shelton**
**(203) 735-4311**
Somewhat of a hidden gem, Indian Well might surprise you with its challenging hiking trails, waterfalls, scenic streams and pools, picnic areas, and fishing opportunities. There's even a small beach, boat launch, and picnic area beside the Housatonic River. Located on the border of Fairfield and New Haven Counties, the park is open from 8:00 A.M. to sunset year-round. Leashed dogs are welcome on the hiking trails and picnic areas but not on the beach. The picnic area also has a shelter, which is wheelchair-accessible. Limited restroom facilities are available.

### Putnam Memorial State Park
**Route 58, Redding/Bethel**
**(203) 938-2285**
This unusual park combines walking, biking, and hiking opportunities with a history lesson. The property is the site of the Continental Army's 1779 winter encamp-

ment, and you can still see the remnants of the soldiers' day-to-day life like fire pits and cannonballs. For those who want more detail, an on-site museum catalogs and outlines the army's famous (and infamous) escapades at the park. Across the street, an easy-to-walk paved trail winds past a lily pad-filled pond, picnic tables under the towering pines, and graceful wooded areas, making for an enjoyable afternoon stroll. Leashed dogs are welcome. Ice-skating and cross-country skiing are popular winter activities here. Putnam Memorial is open from 8:00 A.M. to sunset every day.

### Seth Low Pierrepont State Park Reserve
### Off Route 116, Ridgefield
### (203) 438-9597

Comprising 305 acres in Ridgefield, Pierrepont State Park attracts locals and visitors hoping to have a picnic, hike the trails, fish, and launch small boats. In winter the grounds are also available for cross-country skiing and ice-skating. Trails take hikers past Lake Naraneka, a marsh, open fields, and thick forested areas with red maple, black birch, shagbark hickory, flowering dogwood, eastern hemlock, and Norway spruce trees.

### Squantz Pond State Park
### 178 Shortwoods Road, New Fairfield
### (203) 797-4165

In addition to providing one of northern Fairfield County's only beaches (see listing under Beaches, above), Squantz Pond also provides reasonably challenging hiking trails for visitors. These aren't just paved paths—the trails require a bit of climbing and maneuvering to reach the most scenic spots on your journey alongside the pond. They are also easy to navigate, so first-timers won't need a map and won't need to worry about getting lost. (The pond is almost always in sight.) Boating is another extremely popular activity here, from sailing to kayaking and canoeing. Bring a picnic lunch and enjoy it on the trails or at one of the park's picnic

areas. Restrooms and a boat launch are also available. And don't abandon Squantz Pond in the cold weather; cross-country skiing, ice-skating, and ice-fishing all make the park fun in winter as well. Parking is somewhat limited, so plan to arrive early in the summer months to compete with the beachgoers. Leashed dogs are welcome from October to mid-April.

### Ram Pasture
### Main Street, Newtown

Located along historic Main Street, this rectangle-shaped green has willow trees, a brook and small pond, wildflowers, and vast grassy areas. It's a great spot for flying a kite, feeding the ducks, tossing a ball, or enjoying a picnic lunch with supplies from one of the nearby delis. As with many other historic New England greens, this one was used by early residents as a pasture for farm animals. Across the street, a lovely garden with walking paths and water fountains sits next to the police station.

### Tarrywile Park and Mansion
### 70 Southern Boulevard, Danbury
### (203) 744-3130

Tarrywile Mansion is a 23-room restored Victorian located within the 650-acre park of the same name. Residents of Danbury and neighboring towns flock to the site for hiking on 7 miles of trails, looking out over the pond, lunching in one of two picnic areas, cross-country skiing, and gardening in adult- and kid-friendly plots. Organized activities at Tarrywile include orienteering, tai chi programs, Winterfest, story hours, footraces, the Boy Scout Klondike and Jamboree, guided hikes, and environmental education classes. If you prefer to go it on your own, choose from one of the park's self-guided tour brochures: the *Tarrywile Nature Tour,* the *Park Tour,* the *Tree Walk,* the *Mansion History Tour,* or the *Historical Gardens at Tarrywile Walk.* You can pick up the brochures during the mansion office's operating hours: Monday through Friday

8:30 A.M. to 4:30 P.M. The mansion can be rented for special events, including meetings and family gatherings. The grounds are open to the public daily from dawn to dusk. Admission is free. Camping is available by permit only

### Webb Mountain Park
### Webb Circle, Monroe
### (203) 452-5416

This out-of-the-way park is a real find for hikers and dog-walkers (leashed pets are welcome). The trails wander through forested areas, over quaint bridges, and up fairly steep hills. A map at the entrance will help you find your way around the color-blazed trails. First-timers won't want to miss the Red Trail, which leads up a hill to an impressive lookout with views of the river and valley. To reach Webb Mountain, take Route 111 to East Village Road, and then turn left onto Webb Circle. The park entrance is a short drive down on the right.

### William E. Wolfe Park
### and Great Hollow Lake
### 285 Cutlers Farm Road, Monroe
### (203) 452-5416

This 309-acre park is actually divided into two sections: The Great Hollow Lake area, located just off of Purdy Hill Road, comprises a 16-acre man-made lake with a 700-foot beach (see listing under Beaches, above), an easy walking trail that wraps around the water, a snack bar, a playground, several picnic areas, and parking. The other side of the park, located off Cutlers Farm Road, is a busy spot with a swimming pool, tennis courts, more playgrounds, athletic fields, and picnic areas. A short hiking trail connects the two major areas, so you can park in one spot and enjoy them both. Seasonal passes are available to residents for $30 per year; nonresidents pay $60 per year. You can also pay a daily fee of $5.00 per person for residents and $10.00 per day for nonresidents. Dogs are not allowed in the park at any time.

# RECREATION
## Biking

### Bradley Park
### Oakledge Lane, Wilton
### (203) 834-6234

Cyclists favor the B-Trail at this 82-acre park, which also offers other biking trails, bridges, and a boardwalk. It will take about 30 minutes for beginning- to intermediate-level mountain bikers to tackle the twists, turns, and drops.

### Collis P. Huntington State Park
### Sunset Hill Road, Redding/Bethel
### (203) 938-2285

This place is a favorite for off-road cyclists as well as hikers; see the listings in the Parks and Hiking sections for more information about Huntington State Park.

### Fairfield County Rambles
### Various locations

Road bikers enjoy hitting the pavement throughout the county, from back roads to busy seaside routes. Local cycling clubs and bike shops (see the Shopping chapter) can give you a rundown on some of their favorites. In the meantime, try one of these: Darien Ramble (14 miles); Greenwich Backcounty (21 miles); Newtown to Weir Farm Ramble (41 miles); Stratford Lordship Ramble (12 miles); Fairfield and Bridgeport "Pizza Loop" (23 miles); Ridgefield Ramble (12 miles); Rowayton Ramble (8.5 miles); and Westport Waterfront Ramble (25 miles).

### Hat City Cyclists
### P.O. Box 1034, Bethel 06801
### www.hatcitycyclists.org

Road and trail bikers unite with a common passion at Hat City Cyclists, a club that offers organized rides, programs, activities, and socialization for biking enthusiasts in the greater Danbury area. The group's largest annual event is CYCLEFEST, a 103-mile ride (shorter lengths are available) through Fairfield and Litchfield County roads. Members also link up with other area cycling clubs for regular or once-in-a-while special events and rides.

### Mianus River Park and Glen
### Westover Road, Stamford
### (203) 977-4688
The 185 acres of Mianus River Park hold some challenging biking trails in the semi-wild interior; local bikers consider it worth the trip to check out the singletrack rides. Complete trail maps are available from the Stamford Parks and Recreation Department. There are no snacks or water on-site, so bring your own.

### Pequonnock River Greenway
### Monroe, Newtown, and Trumbull
This gravel-covered, flat stretch of bike trail—once a railway—is one of New England's wonderful rails-to-trails restored areas. You're more likely to find young families biking here than hard-core off-roaders, primarily because the nice-and-easy path is ideal for the training-wheel set and anyone else who wants to take it slow and look at the scenery. The longest and most popular stretch connects Pepper Street in Monroe with the town's Wolfe Park; parking is available at both ends. In other areas be prepared to spend some time on busy roads that connect different parts of the trail. The Greenway is also one of the best (and one of the only) parklike spots for dog-walkers in Monroe; your pooch is welcome on a leash.

### Pootatuck State Forest
### New Fairfield
### (860) 485-0226
This secluded spot is primarily used by hikers, but bicyclists also benefit from the tucked-away location, challenging trails, and forest views. One complaint from bikers is that recent logging expeditions in the preserve have torn up the trails somewhat; use caution when riding.

### Sound Cyclists Bicycle Club
### P.O. Box 3323, Westport 06880
### (203) 840-1757
### www.soundcyclists.com

The Sound Cyclists Bicycle Club, founded in the late 1970s, promotes cycling in the area and schedules scenic rides nearly every weekend for bikers with a variety of skill levels. On the third Sunday of May, the group hosts a benefit ride known as Bloomin' Metric, the most popular tour in Connecticut, with more than 2,000 participants. Other special events include the spring Bicycle Rodeo, picnics in July and August, and biking field trips outside of Fairfield County.

### Wilton Town Forest
### Patrick Lane, Wilton
### (203) 563-0180
Bikers call the trails at Wilton Town Forest challenging and "technical," with steep drops, bumpy areas, and slippery spots. Parking is available near the intersection of Patrick and Bogus Lanes. Camping is available at the 190-acre preserve; call the Conservation Department for more information.

# Boating

Boating opportunities, whether on a lake, a river, or Long Island Sound, have always provided a major lifestyle advantage for the residents of southwestern Connecticut. In earlier times the coast provided subsistence and important trade routes. Although commercial fishermen and shipping companies still utilize the nearby waters, the ocean, lakes, and rivers of Fairfield County are far more likely to be used for recreational purposes today. Along the coast, private marinas and country clubs provide most of the access for boaters to Long Island Sound, although some public access points, sailing schools, and launches are available. In the northern reaches, Candlewood Lake dominates the boating scene with a little help from Squantz Pond, Lake Lillinonah, and Lake Zoar. During summertime all of these local waterways are overflowing with motorboats, personal watercraft, and paddleboats.

# Recreation Departments

Each town and city in Fairfield County has its own recreation department, usually hosting a wide variety of activities, events, and classes for children and adults. Common recreation programs include summer camps, athletic competitions and leagues, concerts, nature outings, arts and crafts classes, dance programs, swim instruction, holiday-themed events, field trips, and exercise classes. Most programs are open only to residents of that town or city; a participation fee may apply to some classes or activities. For complete schedules and upcoming event listings, contact your own municipality's recreation department office. You can also call these numbers for more information about smaller local parks in each town.

## Southern Fairfield County

Bridgeport Recreation Department and Parks Administration
7 Trumbull Road, Trumbull
(203) 576-7233

Darien Parks and Recreation
Town Hall
2 Renshaw Road, Darien
(203) 656-7325

Easton Parks and Recreation Office
366 Sport Hill Road, Easton
(203) 268-7200

Fairfield Parks and Recreation Department
75 Mill Plain Road, Fairfield
(203) 256-3144

Greenwich Parks and Recreation
Town Hall
101 Field Point Road, Greenwich
(203) 622-6494

New Canaan Parks and Recreation Department
677 South Avenue, New Canaan
(203) 966-2057

Norwalk Recreation and Parks
Norwalk City Hall
125 East Avenue, Norwalk
(203) 899-2778

Stamford Recreation and Leisure Services
Government Center
888 Washington Boulevard, Stamford
(203) 977-4688

Stratford Recreation Department
1 Dome Drive, Stratford
(203) 385-4052

Trumbull Parks and Recreation Department
Trumbull Town Hall Annex
5892 Main Street, Trumbull
(203) 452-5169

## SOUTHERN FAIRFIELD COUNTY

**Below Deck**
**157 Rowayton Avenue, Rowayton (Norwalk)**
**(203) 852-0011**
Located below the Rowayton Market, Below Deck provides access to the Five Mile River with kayak rentals ($30 to $40 per hour, $45 to $65 per half day, $65 to $85 per full day) and the leasing of transient boat slips. Water skis, flip-flops, and other beach and water-sports equipment are available for sale.

Weston Parks and Recreation
56 Norfield Road (temporary address)
Weston
(203) 222-2655

Westport Parks and
Recreation Department
Town Hall
110 Myrtle Avenue, Westport
(203) 341-5090

Wilton Parks and Recreation Department
Comstock Community Center
180 School Road, Wilton
(203) 834-6234

## Northern Fairfield County

Bethel Parks and Recreation Department
1 School Street, Bethel
(203) 794-8531

Brookfield Parks and Recreation
Brookfield Municipal Center
100 Pocono Road, Brookfield
(203) 775-7310

Danbury Parks and
Recreation Department
7 East Hayestown Road, Danbury
(203) 797-4632

Monroe Parks and Recreation Department
Town Hall
7 Fan Hill Road, Monroe
(203) 452-5416

New Fairfield Parks and
Recreation Department
Town Hall
4 Brush Hill Road, New Fairfield
(203) 312-5633

Newtown Parks and
Recreation Department
Police Station Building
3 Main Street, Newtown
(203) 270-4340

Redding Parks and
Recreation Department
Redding Community Center
Lonetown Road, Redding
(203) 938-2551

Ridgefield Parks and
Recreation Department
Recreation Center
195 Danbury Road, Ridgefield
(203) 431-2760

Shelton Parks and Recreation Department
Community Center
41 Church Street, Shelton
(203) 925-8422

Sherman Parks and
Recreation Department
Saw Mill Road (summer) and Route 37
(winter), Sherman
(860) 354-3629

**Darien Windsurfing**
**Weed Beach, Darien**
**(203) 655-6757**
Darien residents can enjoy access to
windsurfing lessons and rentals at this
popular Weed Beach spot. Town residents
can access the beach by purchasing a
parking permit ($20 per season); out-of-

towners can park at Weed Beach (space
permitting) for $30 per day.

**Greenwich Community Sailing**
**Greenwich Point Park**
**P.O. Box 195, Old Greenwich 06870**
**(203) 698-0599**
**www.longshoresailingschool.com**

Adult and junior programs at Greenwich Community Sailing include safe boating courses, basic and intermediate lessons, basic keelboat lessons, and instruction in racing techniques. Visitors can also rent ocean kayaks (doubles and singles) and sailboats at hourly rates. The center even sells used boats at reduced rates.

### Greenwich Rowing Club
**Beacon Point Marina**
**67 River Road, Cos Cob (Greenwich)**
**(203) 422-5258**
**www.greenwichrowing.com**
Open year-round, the Greenwich Rowing Club offers professional-level rowing instruction and programs. Some members are recreational rowers; others compete in local and national competitions. Adult programs, junior programs, and private lessons are all available. Membership is open to all rowing enthusiasts.

### Kayak Adventures
**Norwalk**
**(888) 454-0300**
**www.kayak-adventure.net**
Kayak Adventures provides lessons, rentals, and guided kayak trips in southern Connecticut throughout the year, with trips like the Full Moon Paddle, Offshore Tours, Coastal Tours, Harbor Seal Wildlife Tours, and Two-Hour River Tours.

### Longshore Sailing School
**260 Compo Road South, Westport**
**(203) 226-4646**
**www.longshoresailingschool.com**
Affiliated with Greenwich Community Sailing, the Longshore Sailing School offers rentals of canoes, kayaks, Hobies, Lasers, and other vessels. Boaters can also get their Connecticut Safe Boating Certification here and take classes like Laser Racing, Adult Basic Sailing, Intro to Solo Sailing, and Advanced Catamaran Sailing. The organization also plans winter sailing trips to the Caribbean and other exotic locales.

### Norwalk River Rowing Association
**138 Water Street, Norwalk**
**(203) 299-1546**
**www.norwalkriverrowing.org**
Dedicated to promoting the sport of rowing for all ages, the Norwalk River Rowing Association offers eight-week spring programs with training and races, as well as special events like regattas and galas. Beginner, intermediate, private, and group lessons are all available. Youth rowing opportunities include learn-to-row programs and junior racing teams.

### Norwalk Sailing School
**Calf Pasture Beach, Norwalk**
**(203) 852-1857**
**www.norwalksailingschool.org**
Participants at the Norwalk Sailing School can learn about navigation, safety, knots, and rigging and receive state certification at one of the center's sailing classes for kids and adults. Windsurfing lessons are also available, as are kayak rentals. Children can take part in two-week sailing camps during the summer season.

### Saugatuck River Canoe and Kayak Rentals
**Westport Outfitters**
**44 Calf Pasture Beach Road, Norwalk**
**(203) 831-8036**
Mad River Canoes and Walden Kayaks are some of the brands available at this rental facility. You can put in right at the shop and explore the riverway at your leisure. This site is also the home of Northeast Saltwater Flyfishing, which provides guided fishing services (see Fishing, below).

### Small Boat Shop
**144 Water Street, Norwalk**
**(203) 854-5223**
The Small Boat Shop sells virtually every variety of sailboat, rowboat, and paddleboat on the market. Those not looking to buy might especially appreciate the store's rental selection of kayaks, canoes,

sailboats, and more. Staffers also provide kayaking lessons and winter boat storage.

## Sound Sailing Center
**54 Beach Road, Norwalk**
**(203) 838–1110**
**www.soundsailingcenter.com**
Whether you want to learn to race or simply stay afloat, the Sound Sailing Center has a class or program designed to help you hit the water. Sailboat rentals and charters are also popular, as are junior programs that teach children about water safety and basic sailing skills. Members receive discounts on classes and rentals.

## NORTHERN FAIRFIELD COUNTY

### Candlewood East Marina Club
**204 Candlewood Lake Road, Brookfield**
**(203) 775–2253**
This private facility offers a 240-slip marina, sailing lessons, a playground, a picnic area, a snack bar, a swimming area, boats for sale, parts and service, and dock rental space. Memberships are available on a seasonal basis.

### Clarke Outdoors
**163 U.S. Route 7, West Cornwall**
**(860) 672–6365**
Although Clarke Outdoors is headquartered in Litchfield County, the company's popular canoeing, kayaking, and rafting trips take participants down the Housatonic River into some of northern Fairfield County's most beautiful riverside areas. More adventurous boaters can try the white-water rafting trips.

### Echo Bay Marina
**227 Candlewood Lake Road, Brookfield**
**(203) 775–7077**
In addition to sales, the Echo Bay Marina rents pontoon boats, Bayliner Bowriders, Hurricane deck boats, water skis, and inner tubes. Boat owners can lease dock space at the marina, buy parts and accessories, or relax at the picnic area.

### Indian Well State Park
**Howe Avenue (Route 110), Shelton**
**(203) 735–4311**
Among this park's many charms is its boat launch, which allows small craft to make some waves on Lake Housatonic. See the listing under Parks, above, for more information about Indian Well's facilities.

### Lake Kenosia
**Kenosia Boulevard, Danbury**
**(203) 797–4632**
In addition to providing a picnic area and playground, 25-acre Lake Kenosia Park offers a small beach and canoeing, kayaking, and rowboating opportunities. Bring your own boat.

### Lake Lillinonah
**Hanover Road, Newtown**
**(203) 270–4350**
Lake Lillinonah travels along the border of Fairfield and Litchfield Counties and wraps around Paugussett State Forest, where it meets the Shepaug River. The boat launching area is open from 8:00 A.M. to 8:00 P.M. at the end of Hanover Road. A $40 ramp pass is required and can be purchased at the Newtown Parks and Recreation Department. The launch area has picnic tables and barbecue grills.

### Lake Zoar
**Route 34, Newtown**
**(203) 270–4350**
The Newtown state boat launch on Lake Zoar is a popular starting point for boating adventures on the 33-mile-long lake. Most of the craft are speedy motorboats towing families, water-skiers, and riders on tubes. A launching charge may apply on weekends; call for details. Boaters must comply with the posted 45-mile-per-hour speed limit. Boaters will find another boat ramp for Lake Zoar just outside Fairfield County, on Lakeside Road in Southbury.

**Lattins Cove Boat Launch**
**Lattins Cove, Candlewood Lake**
**Forty Acres Road, Danbury**
Although kayaks, canoes, and other pad-
dleboats are welcome on Candlewood
Lake, the body of water is primarily popu-
lated with motorboats and water-skiers.
This launching site is the primary entrance
to the lake.

**Squantz Pond**
**178 Shortwoods Road, New Fairfield**
**(203) 797-4165**
Visit the state park with your kayak or
canoe to enjoy the peaceful surroundings
and myriad wildlife species. For more
information on Squantz Pond State Park,
see the listing under Beaches, above.

# Charters and Cruises

**Coastal Charter Company**
**Captain's Cove Seaport, Bridgeport**
**(203) 258-8378**
Launching out of Captain's Cove, the
Coastal Charter Company provides yacht
cruises such as the four-to-eight-hour
"Bring Your Own" cruise; the four-hour
Sunset Gourmet Cruise; the three-day Get-
away Cruise; and the three-hour Floating
Lunch Cruise. All trips are aboard the *China
Clipper,* a 53-foot vessel with a full galley,
air-conditioning, and three staterooms.

**Fjord Catering and Charters**
**143 River Road, Cos Cob (Greenwich)**
**(203) 622-4020**
**www.fjordcatering.com**
Fjord's fleet is made up of two 117-foot
luxury yachts, a 74-foot yacht, a 75-foot
double-deck excursion boat, a working
tugboat, and a 65-foot old-fashioned
paddle-wheel boat. Brunch, dinner, and
sightseeing trips take place throughout
the week, as well as on holidays like
Mother's Day, Independence Day, and New
Year's Day. The company also provides
land-based catering for special events.

**Island Cruise Lines**
**Beach Road, Norwalk**
**(203) 852-7241**
**www.islandprincess.com**
Operating out of the Norwalk Cove
Marina, the *Island Princess* is an authentic
side-wheel paddleboat that calls to mind
romantic notions of cruising down the
Mississippi River. The boat can accommodate up to 140 passengers and often plays
host to corporate functions, anniversary
parties, wedding receptions, retirement
parties, and even school field trips.

**Jubilee Yacht Charters**
**Captain's Cove Marina, Bridgeport**
**(203) 270-9992**
This company specializes in planning
crewed and bareboat charter cruises in
destinations around the world, from nearby
Long Island Sound to such faraway locales
as the Caribbean and the Pacific Ocean.
Jubilee represents companies like Horizon,
Florida Yacht Charters, and Virgin Traders.

**Nautical Holidays Yacht Charters**
**7 Spezzano Drive, Riverside (Norwalk)**
**(203) 637-9235**
**www.nauticalholiday.com**
Based in Norwalk and Somerset, England,
Nautical Holidays Yacht Charters provides
luxury crewed yacht charters to pretty
much anywhere you might want to go,
including the Greek Isles, the Bahamas,
Florida, Mexico, and along the Atlantic
seaboard. One-day charters are also available for special occasions in the Connecticut and New York region.

**New England Competitive Sailing Center**
**Brewer Yacht Haven Marina West**
**Stamford**
**(203) 260-1277**
One of the area's most noteworthy boating opportunities can be found at Stamford's New England Competitive Sailing
Center, which was created exclusively to
coach and educate disabled sports enthusiasts in the arena of competitive sailing.
Many of the members are in training for

the Paralympic Games; others compete locally. For more information about memberships and competitions, contact the center at the above number.

### SoundWaters Schooner
**1281 Cove Road, Stamford**
**(203) 323-1978**
**www.soundwaters.org**
One of the most popular educational experiences offered at the SoundWaters environmental center is the ecology sail aboard the center's *SoundWaters* schooner. Departing from the Brewer's Yacht Haven Marina in Stamford, the two-hour cruises feature trawling and close examinations of marine life in the Sound for $25 per adult and $15 per child. The sails are popular with families, school groups, scout troops, and others. The center also offers three-hour sunset sails for $30 per person.

# Fishing

The state Department of Environmental Protection (www.dep.state.ct.us/burnatr/fishing) maintains updated fishing reports, lists of fishing access sites, and angling rules and regulations. Fishing piers in Fairfield County include the Bonds Dock Fishing Pier on Ferry Boulevard in Stratford; the North Water Street Park Fishing Pier on Allen Road in Norwalk; and the Squantz Pond State Park fishing pier in New Fairfield, which is wheelchair-accessible.

Fly-, fresh-, and saltwater fishing supplies are available at the following locations: The Bait Shop in Rowayton (99 Rowayton Avenue; 203-853-3811); Compact Fishing Gear & Bait Tackle Shop in Westport (170 Post Road West; 203-227-4377); Dockside Bait & Tackle in Stratford (638 Stratford Avenue; 203-378-5446); Fairfield Fly Shop in Fairfield (917 Post Road; 203-255-2896); the Compleat Angler in Darien (987 Post Road; 203-655-9400); Stratford Bait & Tackle Shop in Stratford (1076 Stratford

*In the state of Connecticut, fishing licenses are required for any angler in inland waters such as rivers, ponds, lakes, or streams. Licenses are available for $20 at any town hall, city hall, or tackle shop.*

Avenue; 203-377-8091); Fisherman's World in Norwalk (Liberty Square; 203-866-1075); and Ted's Bait & Tackle in Bridgeport (2439 Fairfield Avenue; 203-366-7615).

### Coastal Atlantic Striper Hunters
**Norwalk Cove Marina, Norwalk**
**(203) 655-5918**
**www.middlebank.tv**
Between April and December, the *Middlebank* sails daily from the Norwalk Cove Marina for six-hour day fishing trips and four-hour sunset trips. Depending on the month, you can expect to find bluefish, blackfish, fluke, striped bass, and porgy.

### Helen B. Charters
**Captain's Cove Marina, Bridgeport**
**(203) 615-0070**
Helen B. Charters operates the *Daystar,* a 34-foot vessel equipped with radar, a fish finder, and a full galley. The fishing boat travels throughout western Long Island Sound to help passengers catch striped bass, spring flounder, bluefish, and more. Up to six anglers can fit on a charter; all bait and tackle are supplied.

### My Bonnie Charters
**7 Outer Road, Norwalk**
**(203) 866-6313**
**www.mybonniecharters.com**
Anglers can take full advantage of Captain Sal Tardella's expertise on My Bonnie Charters fishing trips. Expect to find bluefish, striped bass, and other species. Bait and tackle are provided on all charters, and the 25-foot vessel is equipped with electronic navigation systems.

**North Coast Charters**
**40 San Pedro Avenue, Stratford**
**(203) 378-1160**
www.northcoastcharters.com
Providing charter services for fly fishing and sight fishing, North Coast Charters also provides casting instruction and onboard tackle. The service operates throughout the year from Rhode Island to the Norwalk Islands in search of striped bass, bluefish, false albacore, and other species.

**Northeast Saltwater Flyfishing and Westport Outfitters**
**44 Calf Pasture Beach Road, Norwalk**
**(203) 831-8036**
www.saltwater-flyfishing.com
In addition to providing guided fly-fishing charters on Hewes and Maverick skiffs, Northeast Saltwater Flyfishing and West-port Outfitters is also a place where anglers can stock up on rods, reels, tackle, flies, and rigging. Fishing boats are available for sale.

# Hiking

**Audubon Center of Greenwich**
**613 Riversville Road, Greenwich**
**(203) 869-5272**
This ample 686-acre site, a preserve of the National Audubon Society, offers more than 15 miles of trails for hikers and bird-watchers to enjoy. (Bicycles are not permitted.) For more information about the center, see the listing in the Attractions chapter.

**Bear Mountain Reservation**
**17 Bear Mountain Road, Danbury**
**(203) 743-0546**
If you enjoy secluded and rustic hiking spots, 140-acre Bear Mountain is for you. Visitors will find posted park rules and hiking trail maps at the entrance gate at the end of the parking lot. The blazed trails are identified by color, including the Red, Yellow, Orange, Violet, and White Trails. The Red Trail circles the entire property.

The Yellow Trail climbs to the summit, where hikers will be rewarded for their efforts with expansive views. The Orange Trail reaches down to Candlewood Lake. Other trails wind past sunny meadows, wooded areas, huge boulders, and stands of birch trees. Bird-watchers will want to bring their binoculars for views of wood-peckers and other species. Picnic tables are also available.

**Bradley Park**
**Oakledge Lane, Wilton**
**(203) 834-6234**
Hikers can relish a nice walk or two in Bradley Park's 82 acres of winding trails, including one boardwalk that passes over a beautiful wetlands area. For more information about mountain biking in the park, see the listing under Biking.

**Collis P. Huntington State Park**
**Sunset Hill Road, Redding/Bethel**
**(203) 938-2285**
This is not a challenging hike, perhaps, but it is definitely a pleasurable one. There is one fairly steep climb between the parking area and trails; after that, the gravelly walkways are level and smooth enough to accommodate strollers and even wheel-chairs. This is an especially popular site for dog walkers. For more information see the listing in the Parks section.

**Devil's Den Preserve**
**The Nature Conservancy**
**33 Pent Road, Weston**
**(203) 226-4991**
Favored by backwoods hikers for its pristine and lush trails, Devil's Den (not to be confused with Devil's Glen in Weston) is one of the few places in crowded Fairfield County where you can truly "get away from it all." For more information about the park, see the listing in Parks, above.

**Mianus River Park and Glen**
**Westover Road, Stamford**
**(203) 977-4688**
The "glen" of this park's name encompasses 185 acres, with plenty of fairly easy

hiking trails to enjoy. Stop along the way for a picnic, a fishing expedition, or a nap in the shade. Complete trail maps are available from the Stamford Parks and Recreation Department. There are no snacks or water on-site, so bring your own.

### Paugussett State Forest
### Echo Valley Road, Newtown
### (860) 485-0226
The 6.5-mile Lake Zoar Trail in Paugussett State Forest winds through the forest and along the water. Another good choice is the Lillinonah Trail, which has some steep inclines and plenty of lake views. The forest is managed by the Connecticut Department of Environmental Protection. Parking is available on Echo Valley Road and at the Pond Brook Boat Launch.

### Pootatuck State Forest
### New Fairfield
### (860) 485-0226
You'll hear a lot about Squantz Pond in Fairfield, but this "other" New Fairfield forest area manages to stay just below the radar. That's just fine with the hikers who cherish the spot's secluded and quiet trails, which are located on former charcoal wagon roads. (Some of the trails also connect with Squantz Pond, so it's possible to get the best of both worlds.) The protected forest has three primary regions: the southern (Woods Road), the northern (Pine Hill Road), and the western (Beaver Bog Road).

### Saugatuck Valley Hiking Trail System
### Route 53, Redding
### (203) 452-3510
The nearly 65 miles of rustic trails in this system include portions of the Devil's Den Preserve, Redding Land Trust properties, and other areas in Easton and Weston. All the trails are connected and offer glimpses of the reservoir, towering cliffs, deep woods, and open spaces. The land was acquired and preserved by The Nature Conservancy, the Connecticut Department of Environmental Protection, and the Aquarion Water Company of Con-

necticut. A trail map is required for access; you can get one by calling the Aquarion Water Company at the above number or by visiting the Mark Twain Library or the Redding Town Clerk's office. The trails are open daily from sunrise to sunset. Fishing is permitted; dogs and swimming are not.

---

*The Connecticut Forest and Park Association is one of the best local resources for hikers and other outdoors enthusiasts. The 108-year-old conservation group helps maintain trails, distribute trail maps, and organize hiking trips throughout the state. For more information call (860) 346-2372 or www.ctwoodlands.org.*

---

### Squantz Pond State Park
### 178 Shortwoods Road, New Fairfield
### (203) 797-4165
Climb rocks, walk along gravel paths, and enjoy views of the forest and pond at this scenic park, which is particularly beautiful in fall. See the Beaches listings, above, for more information about Squantz Pond.

### Wilton Town Forest
### Patrick Lane, Wilton
### (203) 563-0180
Hikers enjoy the up-and-down trails at Wilton Town Forest, which are marked by color and pass a pond, thick woods, and open areas. Parking is available near the intersection of Partrick and Bogus Lanes. Plant life here includes ferns, grasses, herbs, vines, sedges, and tree species such as red oak, yellow birch, and eastern hemlock. Camping is available at the 190-acre preserve; call the Conservation Department for more information.

## Horseback Riding

Horseback riding is a popular sport throughout the county. Many private homes and country clubs in the southern region are equipped with their own stables and pastures, and peacefully grazing equines are common sight along country roads. But owning a horse is not a prerequisite for learning how to ride: Northern towns like Ridgefield and Newtown provide plentiful public access to the sport, with numerous farms and stables offering riding lessons, arenas, paddocks, and boarding for the general public. Private and group lessons are common, as are clinics, children's programs, seminars, and a variety of other training and riding programs. Local schools, including Sacred Heart University, also boast equestrian teams that practice at these nearby facilities. All you need to get started is a helmet, heeled shoes, long pants, and a sense of adventure. Contact one of these local horse farms for more information.

**Canterbury Tails Farm**
**Canterbury Lane, Ridgefield**
**(203) 790-0604**

**Crickerbrook Farm**
**153 Bagburn Road, Monroe**
**(203) 268-6676**

**Epona Stables**
**550 Riversvilles Road, Greenwich**
**(203) 552-0877**

**Fox Ridge Farm**
**39 Aunt Park Lane, Newtown**
**(203) 270-8329**

**Gray Gables Farm**
**62 Mopus Bridge Road, Ridgefield**
**(203) 438-9065**

**Lion Hill Farm**
**1020 Sport Hill Road, Easton**
**(203) 268-0089**

**Meadowbrook Farms**
**34 Meadowbrook Road, Newtown**
**(203) 270-2953**

**New Canaan Mounted Troop**
**22 Carter Street, New Canaan**
**(203) 966-0634**

**Redgate Farm**
**50 Poverty Hollow Road, Newtown**
**(203) 270-1430**

**Ridge Equestrian Center**
**163 Papoose Hill Road, Newtown**
**(203) 426-8212**

**Ridgefield Equestrian Center**
**258 North Street, Ridgefield**
**(203) 438-7433**

**Silvermine Horse Farm**
**80 Comstock Hill Road, Norwalk**
**(203) 846-2098**

**Stepping Stone Farm**
**20 Mopus Bridge Road, Ridgefield**
**(203) 438-7749**
**www.horserentals.com**

**Sunset Hill Riding Academy**
**160 Sunset Hill Road, Redding**
**(203) 938-8709**

# Ice-Skating

**Danbury Ice Arena**
**1 Independence Way, Danbury**
**(203) 794-1704**
**www.danburyice.com**
The much-anticipated Danbury Ice Arena has made its presence known with sparkling new facilities and a wide variety of sports programs for all ages. Adult, children's, and women's hockey leagues are all available, as are public skating hours, children's birthday parties, summer camps, and lessons for all abilities. High school teams, the Western Connecticut University Colonials, and the Danbury Speedskating Club all practice here.

**Darien Ice Rink**
**55 Old King's Highway North, Darien**
**(203) 655-8251**
**www.darienicerink.com**
Open year-round, the Darien Ice Rink provides summer hockey camps, winter figure-skating programs, and a variety of

lessons and activities for children and adults no matter the season. Local adult hockey leagues also practice here.

### Dorothy Hamill Skating Rink
### Sherman Avenue, Greenwich
### (203) 531–8560

Managed by the Greenwich Parks and Recreation Department, this ice rink is the home of figure-skating competitions, hockey leagues for kids and adults, private and group lessons, hockey camps and clinics, and public skating hours. Use of the Dorothy Hamill Ice Rink is limited to Greenwich residents.

### Stamford Twin Rinks
### 1063 Hope Street, Stamford
### (203) 968–9000
### www.icecenter.com

Figure skating, hockey, and public skating are key components of the Stamford Twin Rinks' offerings. In addition to the rinks, the facilities include locker rooms, private function rooms, a cafe, a bar and grill, a pro shop, a ballet studio, and a New York Sports Club fitness center. Visitors can learn how to skate in private or group lessons, join a hockey league, plan a birthday party, or just spend an afternoon with family and friends.

### Winter Garden Arena
### 111 Prospect Ridge, Ridgefield
### (203) 438–4423
### www.wintergardenarena.com

Winter Garden provides an opportunity for locals to take a skating lesson, play hockey, attend a special event, or relish the moment of Junior's first wobbly attempts on the ice. The arena offers seasonal skating passes, hockey camps, seminars, birthday parties, a training center, figure-skating lessons, youth programs, and adult hockey leagues. The on-site pro shop provides blade sharpening and other services and equipment.

### Wonderland of Ice
### 123 Glenwood Avenue, Bridgeport
### (203) 576–8110
### www.wonderlandofice.com

Learn-to-skate programs, birthday parties, rental skates, and public skating hours are all part of the fun at Wonderland of Ice. The rink also offers "Beat the Heat" summer camps, hockey schools, the Mighty Mites preschool program, the Connecticut Cobras youth hockey team, and the annual Central Eastern Regional Figure Skating Competition hosted by the Bridgeport Skating Club.

# GOLF

It might be an understatement to say that you'll have no problem hitting the links in Fairfield County, a place that is generously sprinkled with well-clipped greens, water hazards, and enough golf carts to transport a well-heeled army. (Greenwich alone has eight courses.) On the downside, the average Joe will be disappointed to learn that most greens are private. But the region does offer a handful of good public courses. One of the best is Danbury's Richter Park, which is usually picked as a favorite in local, state-wide, and even national polls. Each course has its own personality, so shop around to find the one that best suits your style. Whether you're looking for a tough test, a fast pace, great views, or a long, leisurely walk, the county most likely has a course you'll like.

## PUBLIC COURSES

### D. Fairchild-Wheeler Golf Course
**2390 Easton Turnpike, Fairfield**
**(203) 373-5911**
"The Wheel" has two 18-hole golf courses in one: the Black and the Red, both created in 1934. Both have wide-open fairways and a relatively fast pace, appealing to those who like to keep things moving. Some golfers have complained about the condition of the municipal course, which might be somewhat less imaginatively designed than others nearby. (Most diehards argue that the Black is the better of the two layouts.) Fairchild-Wheeler also has a putting green, a restaurant, and a pro shop. Weekday greens fees are $8.00 to $16.00 for 9 holes ($18 cart fee) and $10.00 to $26.00 for 18 holes ($26 cart fee). Weekend golfers will pay $9.00 to $22.00 for 9 holes and $12.00 to $32.00 for 18 holes. Cart prices remain the same on weekends. The prices on the lower end

of the scale reflect fees for juniors and seniors. Fairfield residents pay less than nonresidents, whose fees are reflected on the higher end of the scale.

### E. Gaynor Brennan Municipal Golf Course
**451 Stillwater Road, Stamford**
**(203) 356-0046**
**www.brennangolf.com**
Not as popular as nearby Sterling Farms, the E. Gaynor Brennan Municipal Golf Course nonetheless provides another welcome public golf opportunity in the city of Stamford. The 18-hole course has numerous elevated (and fairly small) greens. You'll also find an on-site restaurant and a pro shop offering club rentals and lessons. For tee times feel free to call or make a cyberrequest for a slot on the Web site. Weekend slots are determined by separate lotteries for residents and nonresidents. Fees range from $7.00 to $24.00 for 9 holes and $7.00 to $36.00 for 18 holes on weekdays. Weekend fees are for 18 holes only and range from $8.00 to $40.00. Golfers are welcome to walk or rent a cart ($16 for 9 holes, $24 for 18 holes). Nonresidents pay more than twice as much as Stamford residents for greens fees; children and seniors enjoy considerable discounts.

### Griffith E. Harris Golf Club
**1300 King Street, Greenwich**
**(203) 531-7261**
Although Greenwich has about a kajillion golf courses, this is the only one that is open to the general public. That fact alone makes it popular, although there are a few caveats: The "general public," by and large, refers to Greenwich residents, who always have priority for weekday tee times and weekend lotteries. (Nonresidents can request same-day play if any tee times are available.) Robert Trent Jones, the late king of golf-course

architecture, designed the 18-hole course in 1965. Other features include a driving range, a putting green, a restaurant, and a pro shop. On weekdays residents pay $8.00 to $12.00 for 9 holes and $8.00 to $15.00 for 18 holes. Weekend greens fees are $12 for 9 holes and $16 for 18 holes for residents. Nonresidents pay $40 for either 9 or 18 holes on both weekdays and weekends. Carts are available for $16 for 9 holes and $23 for 18 holes. Resident golfers who are under 17 years of age or over 65 receive a discount on weekdays only.

### H. Smith Richardson Golf Course
### 2425 Morehouse Highway, Fairfield
### (203) 255-7300

Golfers love Richardson—when they can get a tee time. The public course attracts scores of locals and visitors alike, so plan to wait your turn. You'll probably find it worth the extra effort as you stroll the par-72, 18-hole course with a back tee slope of 127 and a front tee slope of 129. The back nine greens are especially challenging. You'll also find a driving range and a clubhouse on-site. Fairfield residents pay $15 per round on weekdays and $20 per round on weekends. For nonresidents the greens fees are $30 on weekdays and $40 on weekends. Discounts are given to golfers over the age of 62 and under the age of 17. Season passes are also available for both residents and nonresidents. Call one week in advance for weekday reservations and three days in advance for weekend reservations.

### Longshore Club Park
### 260 Compo Road South, Westport
### (203) 222-7535

The 18-hole Longshore is short, highly walkable, and a whole lot of fun with a great location on the waterfront. Longshore Club Park is public only in the sense that Westport residents are welcome: A photo ID, known as a handpass, is required for admittance. Nonresidents can play residents as guests, although there is a limit of one guest per foursome during

peak hours. Greens fees per 18 holes are $14 to $18 for residents and $27 to $44 for guests. For 9 holes the fees are $10 to $16 for residents and $25 to $32 for guests. The lower end of the fee scale represents reduced rates for seniors and juniors. The on-site Inn at Longshore (see Accommodations for more information) also offers a bar and restaurant with outdoor dining and views of Long Island Sound. Overnight inn guests receive a pass that allows them to play the course if they wish. The road that runs through the course is also popular with runners, dog-walkers, and in-line skaters.

*For those who want to venture outside county lines, nearby public courses such as Yale Golf Course (200 Conrad Drive in New Haven, 203-432-0895); the Great River Golf Club (130 Coram Lane in Milford, 203-876-8051); and the Candlewood Valley Country Club (401 Danbury Road in New Milford, 860-354-9359) are all within a reasonable driving distance and are usually cited as favorites by local enthusiasts.*

### Oak Hills Golf Club
### 165 Fillow Street, Norwalk
### (203) 853-8400
### www.oakhillsgc.com

The high season runs from April through November at Oak Hills, a quirky municipal course with 18 holes, a back tee yardage of 6,407, and a front tee yardage of 5,221. The course was designed by Alfred Tull in 1969. Walking is unrestricted; carts are also available ($24). Norwalk residents receive discounted rates but must show town ID cards ($32 per year). The weekday golf fees at Oak Hills are $16 for residents and $40 for nonresidents. On weekends, residents will pay $17 per round; nonresidents pay $45. Senior citizens and junior golfers pay less on weekdays ($8.00 to $9.00 per round) but do not receive discounts on weekends.

**GOLF**

Golfers who play after 4:00 P.M. on weekdays will also enjoy a slight discount.

### Richter Park Golf Club
### 100 Aunt Hack Road, Danbury
### (203) 792–2550
### www.richterpark.com

Consistently ranked one of the best golf courses in Connecticut (and the country), Richter Park is scenic, challenging, and accessible to all. The 18-hole course was designed by Edward Ryder and opened in 1971. Golfers will find lots of trees and water, a back tee yardage of 6,740, a front tee yardage 5,627, and a walk that provides plenty of exercise. (Carts are another option at $16 for 9 holes and $26 for 18 holes.) Because the course is so popular, getting a tee time can be difficult. Visitors will also find a clubhouse, a restaurant, a putting green, two tennis courts, hiking trails, basketball courts, and a chipping area on-site. To receive discount rates, Danbury residents must show a valid photo ID issued by the city ($20 per year). Resident greens fees are $21 for regular play and $15 for twilight play. Nonresidents pay $57 per regular round and $35 for each twilight round. Resident seniors and juniors enjoy discounted rates, paying about $10.00 to $18.00 for regular play and $8.00 to $13.00 for twilight play. Club rentals and lessons are available at Richter Park's pro shop.

### Ridgefield Golf Course
### 545 Ridgebury Road, Ridgefield
### (203) 748–7008

Designed by George and Tom Fazio, the Ridgefield Golf Course has 18 holes (including a new sixth hole) and a tricky back nine. Walking is unrestricted; or choose a cart ($12 for 9 holes and $24 for 18 holes). Other amenities include a grass driving range, a putting green, a restaurant, and a pro shop. Ridgefield residents pay $18 per round all week long, while nonresidents can expect to pay $40 per round on weekdays and $45 per round on weekends. Discounts are given to juniors, seniors, and golfer who play after 4:00 P.M. weekdays. Town residents can also participate in the Ridgefield Ladies Golf Association (203–431–0520) and the Ridgefield Men's Golf Club (203–431–2764).

### South Pine Creek Golf Course
### Old Dam Road, Fairfield
### (203) 256–3173

This par-27, nine-hole course is often described as "relaxing" and a good spot for families. Fairfield residents will pay $7.00 on weekdays and $9.00 on weekends for a round. Nonresidents pay $14 on weekdays and $18 on weekends. Seniors (over age 62) and juniors (under age 17) can expect to pay a few dollars less per round. A season pass ($100 for residents and $200 for nonresidents) gives golfers a $2.00 discount per round all season long. To schedule tee times, residents can call five days in advance between 7:00 and 10:00 A.M. Nonresidents are free to do the same but must wait until after 10:00 A.M. to call.

### Sterling Farms Golf Club
### 1349 Newfield Avenue, Stamford
### (203) 329–7888
### www.sterlingfarmsgc.com

Sterling Farms might have a somewhat slower pace than other public courses in the area, but golfers nonetheless enjoy its easily accessible, well-maintained 18 holes. The course is also fairly short, making it a good choice for those who aren't looking for an all-day trek. The club also offers a pro shop, a restaurant, a driving range, tennis courts, club-fitting services, golf schools, and private lessons for adults and children. For 18 holes Stamford residents pay $16 all week long and $12 if playing after 4:00 P.M. Nonresidents pay $50 per 18-hole round all week long and $30 per round if playing after 4:00 P.M. For 9-hole play, residents pay $12 all week long; nonresidents pay $30 (no twilight discounts). Stamford residents must show a valid town permit ($25 per year) to receive discounted rates. Resident senior and junior golfers enjoy additional discounts, paying $10 to $16 for 18 holes and $10 to $12 for 9 holes.

**Tashua Knolls Golf Club**
**40 Tashua Knolls Lane, Trumbull**
**(203) 261-5989**
**www.tashuaknolls.com**
This highly enjoyable, par-72 Al Zikorus–designed course has 18 holes over rolling woodlands, water hazards, a back tee rating of 71.9, and a front tee rating of 71.7. Other club features include a putting green, locker rooms, a pro shop, a restaurant, tournaments, special events, and several active club organizations for men and women. Trumbull residents must carry a town ID pass ($15 per season) to take advantage of discounted greens fees. Resident fees are $18 on weekdays and $20 on weekends for 18 holes and $11 on weekdays and $13 on weekends for 9 holes. Nonresidents pay $36 on weekdays and $40 on weekends for 18 holes and $22 on weekdays and $26 on weekends for 9 holes. Cart rentals are available for $27 for 18 holes and $18 for 9 holes. Resident senior and junior golfers pay $14.00 per round for 18 holes and $9.00 per round for 9 holes. Extremely popular with Trumbull residents, this course is always busy.

**Whitney Farms Golf Course**
**175 Shelton Road, Monroe**
**(203) 268-0707**
**www.design-street.com/whitneyfarms**
A bit pricey, perhaps, but fun and well-maintained: That's the general consensus of Fairfield County golfers who patiently wait their turn for a shot at this 18-hole course designed by Hal Purdy. Most don't

come to Whitney Farms looking for exercise. Carts are mandatory, and cart rental is included in the greens fees. Golfers will also find a driving range, a pro shop, and a restaurant with banquet facilities. Monroe residents and nonresidents pay the same greens fees: $50 on weekdays and $60 on weekends for 18 holes and $27 on weekdays and $30 on weekends for 9 holes. Golfers over age 60 enjoy discounted play ($40 per 18 holes) Monday through Thursday. Call seven days in advance when booking weekday play and two days in advance when booking weekend and holiday tee times.

*With so many golf courses and enthusiasts around, it's no wonder that* Golf Digest *is headquartered right here in Fairfield County. The national magazine, considered somewhat of a "bible" for golfers of all abilities, is located on Westport Road in Wilton (203-761-5100; www.golfdigest.com).*

## PRIVATE COURSES

Membership is usually required to play at one of the numerous private courses found in Fairfield County.

# Southern Fairfield County

**Aspetuck Valley Country Club**
**67 Old Redding Road, Weston**
**(203) 226-4701**

**Birchwood Country Club**
**25 Kings Highway South, Westport**
**(203) 221-3280**

**Brooklawn Country Club**
**500 Algonquin Road, Fairfield**
**(203) 334-5116**

*Share and share alike: If you show up as a single either very early or late in the day at any local course, you might be paired up with a threesome.*

Burning Tree Country Club
120 Perkins Road, Greenwich
(203) 869-9010

Connecticut Golf Club
915 Black Rock Turnpike, Easton
(203) 261-2544

Country Club of Darien
300 Mansfield Avenue, Darien
(203) 655-9726

Country Club of Fairfield
936 Sasco Hill Road, Fairfield
(203) 259-1601

Country Club of New Canaan
95 Country Club Road, New Canaan
(203) 966-3513

Fairview Country Club
Kings Street, Greenwich
(203) 531-6200

Greenwich Country Club
19 Doubling Road, Greenwich
(203) 869-1000

Innis Arden Golf Club
120 Tomac Avenue, Greenwich
(203) 637-3677

Milbrook Club
61 Woodside Drive, Greenwich
(203) 869-4540

Mill River Country Club
4567 Main Street, Stratford
(203) 375-9001

Oronoque Country Club
385 Oronoque Lane, Stratford
(203) 375-4293

Patterson Club
1118 Cross Highway, Fairfield
(203) 259-5244

Rockrimmon Country Club
2949 Long Ridge Road, Stamford
(203) 322-3408

Rolling Hills Country Club
333 Hurlbutt Street, Wilton
(203) 762-8381

Round Hill Club
33 Round Hill Club Road, Greenwich
(203) 869-2350

Shorehaven Golf Club
Canfield Avenue, Norwalk
(203) 866-5528

Silvermine Golf Club
95 North Seir Hill Road, Norwalk
(203) 847-4020

Stanwich Club
888 North Street, Greenwich
(203) 869-0555

Wee Burn Country Club
410 Hollow Tree Ridge Road, Darien
(203) 655-1477

Woodway Country Club
412 Hoyt Street, Darien
(203) 322-1661

# Northern Fairfield County

Candlewood Lake Club
P.O. Box 289, Brookfield 06804
(203) 354-4004

Highland Golf Club
Wooster Street, Shelton
(203) 924-9754

Newtown Country Club
2 Country Club Road, Newtown
(203) 426-9311

Redding Country Club
109 Lonetown Road, Redding
(203) 938-2567

Ridgewood Country Club
119 Franklin Street, Danbury
(203) 743-4491

Rock Ridge Country Club
P.O. Box 116, Route 302
Newtown 06470
(203) 426-2658

*The Connecticut State Golf Association is the oldest state golf association in America. The group hosts about 50 competitions each season and provides course rankings, newsletters, and a scholarship program. For more information visit www.csgalinks.org, call (860) 257-4171, or write the association at 35 Cold Spring Road, Suite 212, Rocky Hill 06067.*

Silver Spring Country Club
439 Silver Spring Road, Ridgefield
(203) 438-2671

Sunset Hill Golf Club
13 Sunset Hill Road, Brookfield
(203) 740-7800

# SPECTATOR SPORTS

Nearby New York City offers plenty in the way of professional sports thrills—just ask any Yankee, Mets, or Islanders fan. And football enthusiasts don't have too far to go to Foxboro, Massachusetts, if they want to catch the New England Patriots in action. But the past few years have made high-quality, heart-stopping sports events even more accessible in Fairfield County, most notably with the opening of the Arena at Harbor Yard and the Ballpark at Harbor Yard, located next to each other in downtown Bridgeport. The sports complex has brought a much-needed shot of energy to the city, and fans from New Canaan to Brookfield are heeding the siren call by buying up hockey and baseball tickets in droves. (Those cute mascots don't hurt, either.) Hot dog, anyone?

## BASEBALL

**Bridgeport Bluefish**
**500 Main Street, Bridgeport**
**(203) 345-4800**
**www.bridgeportbluefish.com**
"Get hooked on the Blues!" So goes the official jingle for Connecticut's only minor-league baseball team—and the public seems to be gobbling it up hook, line, and sinker. The team played its first game in the brand-new Ballpark at Harbor Yard on May 21, 1998. During that first season, the Bluefish led the league in attendance and wins. Today attendance hovers around the 250,000 to 300,000 fans-per-season mark, and the Bluefish entered their fifth season as the only Atlantic League team to have welcomed more than one million fans.

The charm of the Ballpark at Harbor Yard has had a lot to do with the team's success. The tickets and concessions are affordable; the games are a heck of a lot easier to get to than those of the major-league teams in New York; and the sta-

dium is large enough to hold a good-size crowd but small enough to feel accessible. Add to that the appeal of kids' programs, myriad family festivities, and an appreciated shot of hometown pride, and you can see why the Bluefish have caught on with locals. (For more information about the team's child-friendly policies and programs, see the Kidstuff chapter.)

Other Atlantic League baseball teams include the Pennsylvania Road Warriors, the Somerset Patriots, the Atlantic City Surf, and the Nashua Pride. Ticket prices vary depending on the game, your seats, and the ticket plan you choose. Individual seats are available for $6.00 to $18.00. Or you might opt for season passes for reserved seating ($310 for adults and $125 for kids and seniors); loge box seats ($486); field box seats ($710); club seats ($1,100); or Harbor Club seats ($1,100). The club and Harbor Club sections are located behind home plate and feature private bars and a waitstaff. The Hi-Ho D'Addario Kids Cove is another reserved section, set aside for children's parties.

## BASKETBALL

**The Colonials (Men's and Women's)**
**Western Connecticut State University**
**Department of Athletics**
**181 White Street, Danbury**
**(203) 837-9015**
**www.wcsu.edu/sports**
WestConn's men's and women's basketball teams have done well in National Collegiate Athletic Association (NCAA) competitions: The women's team qualified for postseason play in 10 of the last 16 seasons; the men's team qualified for the same in 8 of the last 15 seasons. Both teams play at a Division III level. The men's team plays opponents like Albertus Magnus, Trinity College, Southern Maine, and the University of Massachusetts at Dartmouth. (Head coach Bob Campbell

is the "winningest" coach in the school's history, with 284 victories since he arrived on the scene in 1984.) The women's team regularly goes up against teams from Westfield State, the University of Massachusetts at Boston, Southern Maine, and Plymouth State. Coach Kimberley Rybczyk, a WestConn alum, is relatively new on the scene, having previously coached at Southwestern University and Rensselaer. The teams play in the Feldman Arena in the O'Neill Center, located on the Westside Campus (exit 4 off I-84).

**The Stags (Men's and Women's)**
**Fairfield University**
**Department of Athletics**
**1073 North Benson Road**
**Fairfield**
**(203) 254-4216**
**www.fairfieldstags.com**
The Fairfield University Division I NCAA basketball teams are fortunate enough to play all of their games in the brand-new Arena at Harbor Yard in Bridgeport. Many of the Stags' games are broadcast on ESPN 2. Under the direction of Head Coach Tim O'Toole, the men play against teams from Harvard, St. John's, Duke, George Washington, Loyola, Manhattan College, and other schools. The women battle such opponents as Villanova, Seton Hall, Brown, Northeastern, and St. John's with the leadership of their head coach, Dianne Nolan. The Fairfield University Athletic Ticket Office is located at 1073 North Benson Road in Fairfield. Fans can buy tickets there in person Monday through Friday from 9:00 A.M. to 5:00 P.M. or call (203) 254-4103. Group sales and season-ticket packages are also available.

## FOOTBALL

**The Colonials**
**Western Connecticut State University**
**Department of Athletics**
**181 White Street, Danbury**
**(203) 837-9015**
**www.wcsu.edu/sports/football**

Head Coach John Burrell continues to lead his Colonials in Division III football. In 2002 the team had 14 of its players voted to the All-FFC (Freedom Football Conference), and one was named rookie of the year. The team typically plays on Saturday afternoon during the fall season. Opponents include Salve Regina, the United States Coast Guard, Plymouth State University, Kean College, and William Paterson. All home games are played in the new Westside Stadium, located on the Westside Campus of the University (exit 4 off I-84). If you can't attend the game, you can listen in to the action on WLAD-Radio 800 AM. All upcoming schedules are listed on the Web site.

## HOCKEY

**Bridgeport Sound Tigers**
**600 Main Street, Bridgeport**
**(203) 334-GOAL**
**www.soundtigers.com**
More than 8,000 fans at a time can cheer for their favorite American Hockey League (AHL) hockey team, the Bridgeport Sound Tigers, at the Arena at Harbor Yard. Both the team and the arena are relatively new: An affiliate team of the New York Islanders, the Sound Tigers played their first game on October 10, 2001, shortly after the builders put the finishing touches on the arena. The team got its name after a region-wide "Name the Team" contest, in which Bridgeport's affiliations with P. T. Barnum's circus animals and the Long Island Sound were repeatedly referenced. Combining the two seemed logical, and so the Sound Tigers were born.

Today the Sound Tigers battle rivals like the Philadelphia Phantoms, the Utah Grizzlies, and the Hartford Wolf Pack in high-intensity games throughout the fall and winter. AHL season tickets are available for $495 to $1,295 per person. Fans can also buy 40-game, 20-game, and 10-game plans and individual tickets. Those who choose multigame plans receive added benefits such as "meet the players" events, ticket discounts, unused ticket exchanges, a newsletter, a souvenir ticket book, a parking pass, and other extras, depending on the plan purchased. During the 2003–2004 season, box office prices were $16.50 to $25.00 per ticket for adults and $12.50 per ticket for children and seniors. AHL standings and statistics are available on the team's Web site, as is the complete game schedule. The team mascot, a blue tiger named Storm, is a popular spectator at games and kids' parties and even has his own Web site (www .soundtigers.com/kids/storm).

The arena itself has a private club lounge, 33 luxury executive suites, 3 "party suites," 6 concession areas, huge video screens for replays, and an adjacent parking garage (used by commuters during the week). In addition to hosting hockey games, the venue is used throughout the year for consumer expos, ice-skating competitions, concerts, and numerous other events. For more information about the Arena at Harbor Yard, see the Attractions chapter.

# POLO

**Greenwich Polo Club**
**Conyers Farm, Greenwich**
**(203) 863–1213**
**www.greenwichpolo.com**
Come summertime, the ponies are flying at Greenwich Polo Club, where spectators can enjoy fast-paced competitions amid beautiful scenery. Enthusiasts can start setting up blankets and picnics after 1:00 P.M. on match day, when the gates open. Matches typically begin at 3:00 P.M., and the gates close at 6:00 P.M. The U.S. Polo Association Gold Cup, the U.S. Open Polo Championship, and the Thomas B. Glynn Memorial Cup are some of the tournaments you can expect to see from season to season. The club opened the Greenwich Polo School in 2001 to commemorate its 20th anniversary. The polo season runs June through September.

# DAY TRIPS AND GETAWAYS

One of the best features of Fairfield County is its location. Few residents fail to take advantage of the short driving distance between their hometowns and some of the best-known attractions in the Northeast—if not the world. Some of those spots, like New York City, need no introduction. Others, like the Litchfield Hills' small towns and Catskill Mountain hideaways, are best-kept-secrets with the unsurpassed advantage of being close, close, close. Visit a living-history museum, shop for antiques, sample world-famous pizza, browse a vineyard, tour a mansion, or relax on the beach—and still be home by dinnertime. Or take a weekend and explore slightly more distant destinations. Whatever the length of your trip, you won't want to miss the playground that lies just beyond your front door.

## CONNECTICUT

## The Litchfield Hills

Sandwiched between Fairfield County and western Massachusetts, this idyllic region offers mesmerizing autumn leaves, small towns overflowing with history and charm, and cozy inns and B&Bs providing comfort food and accommodations. Many state residents associate the area primarily with antiques: No matter where you roam in the Litchfield Hills, the roadsides are lined with antiques shops and dealers selling everything from furniture to maps, books, and collectibles. The quaint town of Woodbury, in particular, features more than 25 antiques shops, earning it the unofficial title of "the antiques capital of Connecticut."

If you're planning a one-day trip, it's probably best to limit yourself to just one Litchfield Hills destination at a time. In Kent, for example, visitors can hike, go window-shopping downtown, enjoy a delicious dinner, relax with a coffee on a sidewalk bench, or spend the night at a local inn. Or you might want to head instead toward Litchfield, a refined spot with a legendary town green, one of the world's most-photographed churches (the First Congregational, located at the intersection of Route 118 and U.S. Route 202), gourmet food shops, and upscale boutiques and restaurants. Another popular Litchfield Hills destination is Washington, a culturally rich locale offering art galleries, a winery, scenic **Lake Waramaug,** and upscale accommodations such as the **Mayflower Inn** (860–868–9466); the **Birches Inn** (860–868–1735); and the **Lakeview Inn** (860–868–1000). No matter where you go in the Hills, you're sure to find plenty of opportunities for wining, dining and relaxing.

But not every visitor to the Litchfield Hills wants to take it easy. For sportsmen and -women, well-known outfitter **Clarke Outdoors** in West Cornwall (860–672–6365; www.clarkeoutdoors.com) can arrange exciting white-water rafting trips, kayaking journeys, and fishing expeditions along the **Housatonic River.** The town of Cornwall attracts fly-fishing enthusiasts from all over with its great on-the-river location and local guide services like **Housatonic River Outfitters** (860–672–1010) and **Housatonic Anglers** (860–672–4457). In Lakeville, **Lime Rock Park** (860–435–5000; www.limerock.com) appeals to those with a need for speed. The motor-sports racetrack has Grand Prix events, vintage car festivals, Ferrari Racing Days, SCCA Regional and National Championship races, a gift shop, and the

**Skip Barber Racing School** for aspiring NASCAR champions.

If history lessons are more your speed, include a visit to one of the Litchfield Hills' many museums in your itinerary. The **American Clock and Watch Museum** in Bristol (860–583–6070) has a garden, a gift shop, and more than 3,000 antique timepieces. The **New England Carousel Museum,** also in Bristol (860–585–5411), offers a colorful collection of carousel memorabilia. In Riverton, the **Hitchcock Museum** (860–738–4950) specializes in 19th-century hand-painted furniture. And the **Sloane-Stanley Museum** in Kent (860–927–3849) showcases 17th-century woodworking tools and the remains of the original Kent Furnace.

One of the most popular Litchfield County spots for locals and visitors is **Kent Falls State Park** in Kent (860–927–3238). As the name implies, the park features an impressive waterfall—hardy visitors can even climb a steep path/staircase beside the falls to see the view from the top as well as the bottom. Other great regional parks for picnics, hikes, camping, and wildlife-watching include the **American Legion State Forest** in Barkhamstead (860–379–2469); **Haystack Mountain State Park** in Norfolk (860–482–1817); **Housatonic Meadows State Park** in Sharon (860–927–3238); **Kettletown State Park** in Southbury (203–264–5169); **Mohawk State Park** in Cornwall (860–672–6464); and **Mt. Tom State Park** in Litchfield (860–868–2592).

The region is also well known among music fans, who appreciate the many festivals that brighten the bucolic hills with music each year. For a day of entertainment and harmony, try one of these: the annual **Litchfield Jazz Festival** at the **Goshen Fairgrounds** (860–567–4162; www.litchfieldjazzfest.com); the annual **Morris Bluegrass Festival** at the **Bethlehem Fairgrounds** (860–567–3066); the annual **Music Mountain Festival** in Falls Village (860–824–7126; www.musicmountain.org); and the annual **Norfolk**

**Chamber Music Festival** at the **Ellen Battell Stoekel Estate** in Norfolk (860–542–3000).

If you plan to visit the Litchfield Hills during "leaf-peeping" season and want to stay overnight, be sure to book far in advance: The hotels, motels, and B&Bs here fill up quickly during fall. For more information about accommodations, shopping, restaurants, and attractions, contact the Litchfield Hills Visitor Bureau at P.O. Box 968, Litchfield, CT 06759, call (860) 567-4506, or visit www.litchfieldhills.com. The bureau offers a free visitor's guide to the area. For more information about Litchfield County's state parks, including camping reservations and maps, call the Connecticut Department of Environmental Protection at (860) 424-3200 or visit www.dep.state.ct.us/stateparks.

# Mystic

New England's maritime history, in all its charming glory, is on full display at this popular destination. If you like seafood, shopping, marine animals, ice-cream cones, holiday finery, and sailboat-watching, Mystic and its neighboring villages can provide the perfect backdrop for a day trip or weekend getaway.

The highlight of any visit is **Mystic Seaport** (860–572–0711; www.mysticseaport.org), a re-created fishing village complete with winding walkways, flower gardens, horse-drawn carriages, and more than 40 historic buildings, including a one-room schoolhouse, family homes, a "chemist," and a smithy. Huge clipper ships were once built on the docks here; today you can tour an authentic whaling ship and replicas of other majestic vessels and watch new ones being built. The living-history museum also offers a planetarium, classes and programs, guided tours, a gift shop, a restaurant, and vast collections of seafaring artifacts and memorabilia. Admission fees are $17.00 for adults and $9.00 for children ages 6 to 12.

Just down the street from Mystic Seaport is another family-friendly attraction, the **Mystic Aquarium Institute for Exploration** (860-572-5955; www.mystic aquarium.org). Visitors of all ages can get their hands wet in touch tanks, learn the latest information about current deep-sea explorations, shop in the gift store, enjoy lunch or dinner, explore different underwater habitats, and observe the behavior of such marine creatures as sea lions, jellyfish, penguins, whales, sharks, frogs, and countless others. General admission at the aquarium is $16 for adults, $15 for seniors, and $11 for children ages 3 to 12.

When all that exploring makes your stomach growl, the downtown area is full of snack stands and full-blown restaurants sure to satisfy any craving. The most famous is **Mystic Pizza** (56 West Main Street; 860-536-3700), which inspired the popular 1988 movie of the same name. Grab some lunch, stroll across the bridge, and then browse in one of the many gift and novelty shops along Main Street and its adjoining roads. Serious shoppers will also want to head to **Olde Mistick Village,** an outdoor mall of sorts with a duck pond, walking paths, gardens, and quaint buildings full of clothing boutiques, gift shops, restaurants, toy stores, and more. The nearby villages of Noank and Stonington also make for picture-perfect side trips, complete with white church steeples, town greens, lighthouses, craft fairs, marinas, eateries, and other attractions.

Many visitors like to combine a Mystic trip with a visit to one (or both) of the nearby casinos. For more information about the **Foxwoods** and **Mohegan Sun** gaming centers, see the Roll of the Dice Close-up. For more information about Mystic lodging and local attractions, visit the Mystic Chamber of Commerce at 14 Holmes Street, call them at (860) 572-9578, or visit www.mysticchamber.org. The Connecticut Department of Tourism (www.ctbound.org) is another helpful travel resource.

*Feeling a bit uneasy about your gaming* ℹ️ *skills? Before you head out to one of the casinos, visit the Foxwoods Web site (www.foxwoods.com) for complete instructions on how to play poker, roulette, and other popular table games.*

# New Haven

Connecticut's third-largest city is perhaps best known as the home of world-renowned Yale University. Although the school and its programs undoubtedly enrich the area, New Haven's history, nightlife, and cultural diversity reach far beyond its student population to create a place that is at once exciting and laid-back, historic and cutting-edge. (Lollipops are rumored to have been invented here, along with the first "American" pizza and hamburger.) Best of all, the city's many attractions, restaurants, nightclubs, museums, boutiques, and parks are all located within an hour's drive of most Fairfield County locations.

On Wooster Street, otherwise known as **New Haven's Little Italy,** mouthwatering smells waft out of the many Italian restaurants and bakeries. **Pepe's** (203-865-5762), the best known of them all, is the unofficial site of the first American pizza pie. The eatery still makes its pizzas in old-fashioned coal-fired ovens, as do most of the other pizzerias on the street. Other renowned Wooster Street spots include **Sally's** (203-624-5271) and **Tony and Lucille's** (203-787-1620). The long waits for a table at Wooster Street restaurants (up to two or three hours, in some cases) are almost as famous as the food. Your best bet is to arrive on a weekday or during off-hours.

If you're not in the mood for pizza, downtown New Haven is awash with other dining choices, including Malaysian, Spanish, Japanese, Indian, continental, del-

## CLOSE-UP

# Roll of the Dice: Connecticut's Casinos

Feeling lucky? Connecticut's two Native American–owned casino complexes—Foxwoods in Ledyard and Mohegan Sun in Uncasville—are a lure that few gaming enthusiasts can ignore. But as enticing as the casino floors may be, both sites offer much more than gambling, including museums, gourmet restaurants, upscale shops, and health spas. Starting from somewhat humble beginnings, the casinos have quickly developed into the state's top tourist attractions.

Mohegan Sun, owned and managed by the Mohegan Tribe, encompasses 240 acres and 300,000 square feet of gambling space—making it the second-largest casino in the world. The Casino of the Earth section includes the Spring, Summer, Autumn, and Winter casinos with a smoke-free slot area, a smoke-free poker area, a high-limit slot area, general gaming areas, and a food court. In the Casino of the Sky, visitors will find an indoor waterfall, a 10,000-pound glass "mountain," massive sculptures, a planetarium dome, and murals. The casino complex also offers more than 29 casual and upscale restaurants, including Michael Jordan's Steak House, Todd English's Tuscany, the Sunburst Buffet, Bamboo Forest, Granny Squannit's, and Big Bubba's BBQ. The Shops at Mohegan Sun, including unique vendors and well-known brand names, encompass more than 130,000 square feet of space. The Elemis Spa and the 34-story Mohegan Sun Hotel attract gamblers and nongamblers alike with luxurious accommodations and pampering

icatessens, coffee shops, grilles, cafes, and more. While you're there, take advantage of the shopping scene: Whimsical gifts, housewares, artwork, furniture, and antiques are all available along Chapel and College Streets. In addition, the **Yale Bookstore** on Broadway (203-777-8440) houses just about every book and magazine you could hope to find—and if they don't have it, they can find it. At night, club-hop over to **Toad's Place** on York Street (203-624-TOAD), the best local spot for live music; **Gotham Citi** on Crown Street (203-498-CITI), a dance club that attracts both gay and straight patrons; or **Anna Liffey's** on Whitney Avenue (203-773-1776), an Irish pub.

Perhaps the best-loved park in New Haven is the city's green, a vast square swath of grass that plays host to outdoor concerts, festivals, and other gatherings throughout the year. But it's far from the only game in town: Other spots for walks, sightseeing, and picnics include **Lighthouse Point** on Townsend Avenue, **East Shore Park** on Woodward Avenue, and 426-acre **East Rock Park** on East Rock Road.

When you've had enough of the great outdoors, venture inside for some culture. The **Peabody Museum of Natural History** at **Yale University** (203-432-5050; www.peabody.yale.edu) offers an impressive collection of dinosaur skeletons along with natural history and wildlife dioramas, Egyptian mummies, a gift shop, special events, and a variety of rotating exhibits. The **Shubert Performing Arts Center** (203-562-5666; www.shubert.com) stages such popular plays as *Rent, Oliver, Les Miserables, A Christmas Carol,* and services. The Mohegan Sun Arena and the Wolf Den (free concerts) welcome big-name musicians, singers, comedians, and other acts throughout the year.

Foxwoods, which began as a bingo hall and then a small gaming facility with a few shops and restaurants, is all grown up now. The resort is managed by the Mashantucket Pequot Tribe and offers 6,400 slots, more than 350 table games, keno, bingo, Ultimate Race Book, and other gambling diversions. A huge waterfall marks the entrance of the two-level casino space, called Rainmaker Country. Smoking and nonsmoking gaming areas are provided throughout the property. Visitors can but tickets to see acts like B. B. King, the Dixie Chicks, and Bill Cosby in the Foxwoods Arena or take in a free concert at the Atrium and Intermezzo. When all that gambling and entertainment makes you hungry, choose from gourmet restaurants like Han Garden,

Paragon, and Cedars Steak House or more casual cafes, bistros, delis, and buffets. Three hotels—the Grand Pequot Tower, the Two Trees Inn, and the Great Cedar Hotel—provide more than 1,400 rooms. And if you need a break from gambling, the Grand Spa and Salon, the Mashantucket Pequot Museum and Research Center, and the Foxwoods Golf and Country Club offer a change of pace.

Weekenders might want to consider combining a visit to the casinos with a trip to the nearby nautical community of Mystic. (Foxwoods, in particular, is right up the road from Mystic's attractions.)

For more information about Mohegan Sun, including directions and parking information, contact the casino at (860) 862-8000 or visit www.mohegansun.com. More information about Foxwoods is available at www.foxwoods.com or by calling (800) FOXWOODS.

Fame, as well as New Haven Symphony concerts. At the **Long Wharf Theatre** (203-787-4282; www.longwharf.org), the season includes professional productions with stars like Al Pacino, Lynn Redgrave, and Mia Farrow, and a wide variety of less famous but equally talented actors. At the **Yale Repertory Theater** (203-432-1234; www.yale.edu/yalerep), better known as "Yale Rep," actors join to perform such shows as The Taming of the Shrew, Kingdom of Earth, and The Black Dahlia.

For more information about staying and playing in New Haven, stop by the Greater New Haven Convention and Visitors Bureau at 59 Elm Street in New Haven, call (203) 777-8550, or visit www.newhavencvb.org. For more information about the city's parks and outdoor activities, contact the New Haven Department of

*Watch for "secret" symbols and designs in the decor of the Mohegan Sun casino complex. They provide information about tribal history. The Trail of Life, for example, is a winding path in the flooring of the Casino of the Sky that depicts the Mohegan journey across the Connecticut River. Custom-designed carpeting in the concourse of the Casino of the Earth reveals the 13 moons (lunar months) in the Native American year, including the Moon of Snow Wading, the Harvest Moon, the Moon of Falling Leaves, and the Moon of the Peeping Frogs.*

Parks & Recreation at (203) 946-8019 or visit www.cityofnewhaven.com/parks.

## MASSACHUSETTS

# The Berkshires

The Berkshires region is an underexplored gem, too often overshadowed by Massachusetts's better known destinations on the eastern shore. But that can work to your advantage as you explore uncrowded parks, climb mountains, take in some culture, and sample a surprising variety of foods at the region's many restaurants. The area is an especially good choice for leaf-peeping jaunts, as it tends to be less expensive and congested than better known autumn-vacation locales like Vermont.

Don't let the rural surroundings fool you: Western Massachusetts is a haven for highbrow pursuits in music and the arts. It all begins at **Tanglewood** (297 West Street, Lenox; 413-637-1600; www.bso.org), where the Boston Symphony Orchestra hangs out during the summer. Visitors at this music center can enjoy string quartets, jazz festivals, chamber music, the Boston Pops, and other concerts under the stars or indoors at Seiji Ozawa Hall. Downtown Lenox caters to discriminating visitors with a plethora of galleries, antiques shops, gourmet restaurants, and boutiques. Venture just south of Lenox and you'll find the popular **Norman Rockwell Museum** (Massachusetts Highway 183, Stockbridge; 413-298-4100; www.nrm.org), a venue dedicated to showcasing the collection of one of America's favorite illustrators.

A bit farther east, the college towns of Amherst and Northampton are home to the **University of Massachusetts, Amherst College, Hampshire College, Smith College,** and **Mount Holyoke College**—all home to fine arts centers, theaters, extensive library collections, art galleries, festivals, and seasonal special events. Downtown Northampton, in particular, seems custom-made for a day or weekend visit. The area is always hopping with fun shops, a good variety of eateries, and plenty of opportunities for people-

watching. Another fun nearby destination is the flagship store of the **Yankee Candle Company** (U.S. Highway 5 and Massachusetts Highway 10, South Deerfield; 877-636-7707; www.yankeecandle.com). Here you can spend hours watching candles being made, taking tours, making crafts, and browsing the seemingly endless rooms of candles, holiday ornaments, and home decor.

Another well-known feature of western Massachusetts is the **Mohawk Trail,** 100 miles of highway (Massachusetts Highway 2) stretching between Williamstown and Shirley. Popular stops along the trail include **Old Greenfield Village,** the **Shelburne Falls Trolley Museum,** the **Bridge of Flowers in Shelburne Falls,** the **Massachusetts Museum of Contemporary Art,** antiques shops, wineries, craft fairs, the famous hairpin turn in North Adams, and the Mount Greylock summit. The byway, which began as a footpath trade route for Native Americans, is also one of the state's best spots to admire autumn leaves.

Outdoorsy types, take note: When it comes to public parks, state parks, and camping facilities, few areas in Massachusetts can rival the Berkshires. Try to make time to visit one of these: **Mohawk Trail State Forest** (Tida Hill Road, Monroe); **Mount Greylock State Reservation** (Rockwell Road, Lanesborough); **Natural Bridge State Park** (Massachusett's Highway 8, North Adams); **October Mountain State Forest** (Woodland Road, Lee); **Beartown State Forest** (Blue Hill Road, Monterey); **Pittsfield State Forest** (Cascade Street, Pittsfield); **Tolland State Forest** (Tolland Road, East Otis); **Mount Sugarloaf State Reservation** (Massachusetts Highway 116, South Deerfield); and **Mount Tom State Reservation** (US 5, Holyoke).

For more information about visiting western Massachusetts, contact the Berkshires Visitors Bureau (Berkshire Common, Pittsfield; 800-237-5747; www.berkshires.org) or the Massachusetts Office of Travel and Tourism (10 Park

Plaza, Boston; 800–227–MASS; www.mass-vacation.com). For more information about local state parks and forests, including camping fees and reservations, contact the Massachusetts Department of Conservation and Recreation (251 Causeway Street, Boston; 617–626–1250; www.state.ma.us/dem/park).

# Boston

Chowdah, anyone? Boston, the bustling capital city of Massachusetts, is located roughly three hours from most Fairfield County locales. This short highway trip brings visitors far into America's past, chronicling the sites and characters that defined a young nation's beginnings. But Boston's future—marked by the ongoing "Big Dig" revitalization project—promises to be just as vibrant as its colorful past.

For first-time visitors and history buffs, the **Freedom Trail** (www.thefreedomtrail .org) is usually near the top of any Boston to-do list. Winding through the city streets, the trail is marked by red bricks (or paint) and passes 16 landmarks, including the **Old South Meeting House,** the **Paul Revere House,** and the **site of the Boston Massacre.** The self-guided trail starts at the visitor center at Boston Common and ends at the **Bunker Hill Monument.** A similar walking tour known as the **Black Heritage Trail** (www.afroammuseum .org) winds past 19th-century sites that were significant in the history of Boston's African-American residents.

A fun outdoor and indoor market area known as **Faneuil Hall** (or **Quincy Market**) also attracts tourists and locals by the thousands. The market features hundreds of free-standing carts and vendors, along with indoor shopping malls. In addition to the many available bars and restaurants in Faneuil Hall, the site also features a vast building filled with counter after counter of mostly take-out eateries selling everything from seafood to smoothies, cookies, pizza, fruit, and sandwiches. In the unlikely event that you can't find anything here to please your palate, head just a few blocks away to the North End, the Italian capital of the city, where pasta, pastries, and pepperoni rule.

Once your belly is full, the **Boston Common** beckons with paved paths, playgrounds, fountains, benches, flowers, and wide expanses of green. The **Public Garden's Swan Boats** have been a favorite with Bostonians since the 1870s; today they are still ferrying visitors around the park's waterways. Another well-known fixture of the Common is the cute *Make Way for Ducklings* statues, inspired by a children's story by Robert McCloskey.

Other don't-miss sights include the **Beacon Hill** neighborhood, the **State House,** the **Boston Harbor Islands,** the **"Cheers" bar** on Beacon Street, **Fenway Park,** the **Kennedy Library and Museum, Harvard Square** (located in Cambridge, just across the bridge), **Kenmore Square,** and a variety of harbor tours and whale-watch trips. The **Museum of Science** (617–723–2500; www.mos.org) has plenty of activities and exhibits for kids and adults, including a planetarium, the 180–degree Omni Theater, and live shows. The **New England Aquarium** (617–973–5200; www.neaq.org) gives marine-life buffs the chance to see seals, penguins, sea otters, sharks, turtles, and thousands of fish. And those traveling with kids won't want to miss the **Children's Museum** (617–426–8855; www.bostonkids.org), a hands-on kind of place with hundreds of learning exhibits, play areas, and fun activities.

For the most part, a car is unnecessary once you reach the city itself. Taxis and the public transportation system, known affectionately as "the T," can get you anywhere you need to go. For more information about visiting Boston, including accommodations guides and maps, write to the Greater Boston Convention & Visitor's Bureau at 2 Copley Place, Suite 105, Boston, MA 02116; call (800) SEE-BOSTON, or visit www.bostonusa.com.

# Cape Cod and the Islands

Far and away Massachusetts's most popular tourist destinations, Cape Cod and its sister islands, Nantucket and Martha's Vineyard, beckon with every amenity a traveler could hope for. Located south of Boston and east of Rhode Island, the three locales are overflowing with charm, lighthouses, friendly faces, beaches, shops, and plenty of clam shacks.

They're also, unfortunately, overflowing with crowds as soon as the days get longer and the air gets warmer. Cape Cod, connected to the mainland and stuck with only a few main roadways, suffers the worst traffic jams (particularly on Friday and Sunday). But once you arrive, the Cape's attractions make it worth the extra effort. Once a strictly summer destination, the region is quickly becoming a year-round home for locals and enthusiasts from around New England.

When you first cross the bridge into the "Upper Cape," towns like Sandwich, Falmouth, and Mashpee offer town parks, beaches, plentiful shopping districts and restaurants, resort communities, tiny cottages, ocean views, and seasonal ice-cream stands. The harbor town of Woods Hole is home to the renowned **Woods**

---

**i** | *Great child-friendly day-trip destinations include: Dinosaur State Park (400 West Street, Rocky Hill; 860–257–7601); Gillette Castle State Park (River Road, East Haddam; 860–526–2336); and the Dr. Seuss National Memorial sculpture garden (State and Chestnut Streets, Springfield, Massachusetts). Or try a living-history history museum: Two of the most popular are Old Sturbridge Village in Sturbridge, Massachusetts (508–347–3362; www.osv.org) and Plimoth Plantation in Plymouth, Massachusetts (508–746–1622; www.plimouth.org).*

---

**Hole Oceanographic Institution,** where scientists from around the world gather to research and share scientific findings about the ocean environment. Continuing further along, the "Mid-Cape" region includes miles of shoreline, village greens, and welcoming public parks, along with less-pleasant features like strip malls, urban sprawl, and busy intersections. The main towns in this area are Hyannis, Yarmouth Port, Dennis, and Barnstable.

The "Outer Cape" benefits from its distance: Here, towns like Orleans, Wellfleet, Chatham, and Brewster are slightly quieter and more genteel than those located closer to the mainland. Antiques shops are common, as are preserved nature trails, cranberry bogs, fishing charters, seaside villages, lighthouses, and seafood. **Provincetown,** an arts colony known for its open attitude and gay population, is one of the best-known Cape destinations. Tourists come to Provincetown from all over to wander the busy downtown streets, visit art galleries, eat at outdoor cafes, and enjoy the "anything goes" atmosphere.

You'll have to take a ferry, plane, or private boat to reach the Cape's two popular islands, where quaint buildings, narrow streets, and lively marinas call to mind a simpler time in America's past. **Nantucket,** a bit smaller and farther away, is the less crowded of the two, but that doesn't mean you'll find yourself alone. The guest houses, B&Bs, museums, guided tours, antiques shops, and cobblestone streets offer a glimpse of Nantucket's formerly dominant whaling industry; high-end shopping and restaurants bring you back into the present. As you might expect, much of the activities here focus on the water. You won't have any trouble finding a fishing charter, sunset sail, marina, beach, or beautiful ocean view. Island shuttle buses, taxis, and bicycles will help you get around; in most cases, there's no need for a car.

Located less than 10 miles off the coast of Cape Cod, the island of **Martha's Vineyard** offers six towns, postcard-ready views from every angle, and a thriving tourist trade. Those Black Dog T-shirts you see everywhere originate here, at the **Black Dog Bakery** and restaurant in Vineyard Haven. You'll also find lavish summer estates, tiny cottages, quiet country roads, nature sanctuaries, huge hotels and tiny B&Bs, dramatic cliffs, lighthouses, classic New England churches, flower gardens, gingerbread-style Victorian houses, farmers' markets, seasonal parades and festivals, and plenty of shopping and eateries. The island has its busy spots (like the harbor) and quieter, more secluded areas (like Chilmark). Summer is the most congested time of year, owing to the island's incredible beaches and wonderful cool breezes. But visitors shouldn't discount a trip to Martha's Vineyard in fall, spring, or even winter, when the island reveals sides of itself that few visitors see.

For more information about visiting the Cape (including maps and updated traffic reports), contact the Cape Cod Chamber of Commerce at (888) CAPE–COD or visit www.capecod.com. Additional Nantucket tourism information can be found at the Town of Nantucket's Web site: www.nantucket-ma.gov. (Visitors' information kiosks are also located at Straight and Steamboat Wharfs.) Those planning a visit to Martha's Vineyard will want to contact the Martha's Vineyard Chamber of Commerce at (508) 693-0085 or www.mvy.com/chamber for information about ferries, accommodations, and activities.

# NEW YORK

# Hudson Valley and the Catskill Mountains

Just a quick hop over the state line, the Hudson Valley is well known for its historic sites, including the Sleepy Hollow–Tarrytown area made famous in Washington Irving's tall tale. The region is also awash in towering estates sure to impress

any history buff or casual observer: The **Vanderbilt Mansion National Historic Site** (New York Highway 9, Hyde Park; 845–229-9115); the Victorian manor known as **Wilderstein** (Morton Road, Rhinebeck; 845-876-4818); the castlelike **Lyndhurst** (South Broadway, Tarrytown; 914-631-4481); and **Mills Mansion** (Old Post Road, Staatsburg; 845-889-8851) all call to mind lavish lifestyles of the gilded age. The **Franklin D. Roosevelt Home National Historic Site** (845-229-9115) and the **Franklin D. Roosevelt Presidential Library and Museum** (800-FDR-VISIT), both located on Albany Post Road in Hyde Park, commemorate the life of America's only four-term president.

When you're ready to return to the present, the Hudson Valley offers plenty of indoor and outdoor adventures to keep every member of the family busy. The tony area of Westchester County offers some of the best boutique and antiques shopping around, and golf courses are plentiful throughout the region. Paddling, fishing, and sailing down the Hudson River are popular pursuits, as are visits to one of the valley's seven lighthouses. **Taconic State Park** (New York Highway 62, Millerton; 518-789-3059); **Margaret Lewis Norrie State Park** (Old Post Road, Staatsburg; 845-889-4646); the **Old Croton Aqueduct Trail** (914-693-5259); **Bear Mountain State Park** (Palisades Parkways and New York Highway 9W, Bear Mountain; 845–786-2701); and **Ward Pound Ridge Reservation** (New York Highways 35 and 121, Cross River; 914-864-7317) are all popular spots for hiking, camping, fishing, and wildlife-watching.

Venture a bit farther west and you'll enter the Catskill region, home of renowned 300,000-acre **Catskill Park.** Rustic retreats and campgrounds are plentiful here, offering a taste of the great outdoors in addition to numerous family-friendly attractions and activities. Miniature golf courses, farmers' markets, fishing preserves, festivals, skiing, museums, theaters, bike tours, kayaking trips, train rides, and covered bridges are all part of the fun. In Bethel you'll find the site of the original Woodstock Music and Arts Festival of 1969 on Hurd Road. You might want to also visit **Huguenot Street** in New Paltz, one of America's oldest remaining streets. A walk on the historic road will take you past a 300-year-old burial ground and intact homes built by French refugees in the 1600s.

One of the region's best known parks is **Devils' Tombstone State Park** (New York Highway 214, Hunter; 845–688–7160). According to local legend, the massive boulder that sits within park grounds was placed there by the devil himself. Other popular outdoors destinations include **Kenneth L. Wilson Park** (Wittenberg Road, Mount Tremper; 845–679–7020); **Lake Superior State Park** (New York Highway 55, Monticello; 845–794–3000); and The Nature Conservancy's **Sam's Point Dwarf Pine Ridge Preserve** (off New York Highway 52, Wawarsing; 845–647–7989). And don't miss Saugerties and Woodstock, where you'll find sidewalk cafes, cute stores, and the "environmental sculpture" *Opus 40.*

Two good resources for Catskills travel and tourism information are the Sullivan County Visitor's Association (North Street, Monticello; 845–794–3000; www.scva.net) and the Ulster County Tourism Department (Westbrook Lane, Kingston; 845–334–8687; www.ulstertourism.info). For more information about visiting the Hudson Valley, contact Dutchess County Tourism

---

*The Long Island Sports Commission is a good source for information about big sporting events on Long Island, including the Belmont Stakes, U.S. Open Championships, the annual Hampton Classic Horse Show, and the annual Long Island Marathon. Volunteers at the events get free admission—and great seats, to boot. To learn more, visit www.licvb.com/commission or call (631) 951-3440.*

---

(Neptune Road, Poughkeepsie; 845–463–5446) or the Westchester County Office of Tourism (Mamaroneck Avenue, White Plains; 914–995–8500; www.westchesterny.com).

# Long Island

Long Island may seem like a somewhat faraway destination for a day or weekend trip, but the oh-so-convenient Bridgeport–Port Jefferson ferries (Water Street Dock, Bridgeport; (203) 335–2040; www.bpjferry.com) bring Long Island's shoreline communities as close as a one-hour boat ride. (Cars and dogs are welcome on board.) The ferry docks in **Port Jefferson,** a quaint town that serves as a day-trip destination in itself with gift shops, cafes, marinas, antiques stores, and more.

If you want to venture out a little farther, the **North Fork** area, known as "wine country," offers a plentiful collection of vineyards. Visitors are welcome at most wineries for tastings and tours. Horses, farm stands, and laid-back eateries are common here. On the **South Fork,** ritzy "Hamptons" communities like Southampton, Bridgehampton, Easthampton, Montauk, and Hampton Bays beckon with extravagant boutiques, great beaches, gourmet restaurants, B&Bs, hotels, and a hopping nightlife scene.

**Fire Island,** located on the southern shore, is a barrier-island resort area with miles of beaches (including a few nude beaches), cozy summer communities, a restored historic lighthouse, a designated wildlife preserve, and an anything-goes attitude that welcomes visitors of every race, creed, and sexual orientation. The north shore has a more conservative nature and offers numerous historic sites, harbors, restaurants, gardens, and "Gold Coast" estates that were once home to Vanderbilts and Gueggenheims.

Summer is the most popular time for visiting Long Island, although the region offers fewer crowds, less traffic, and similarly beautiful scenery in the other seasons. (In some areas, like Fire Island, you might have trouble finding accommodations during winter.) The Long Island Convention & Visitors Bureau can provide more information about accommodations, restaurants, and attractions: Contact the bureau at (877) FUN–ON–LI or visit www.licvb.com.

# New York City

It would take a lot more than one day to explore every attraction in the Big Apple, although Fairfield County residents certainly live close enough to make quick daylong visits whenever the mood strikes. The easiest way to reach the city is to hop on board the Metro-North train at one of the many local stops (see the Getting Here, Getting Around chapter). Some trains are express; some make a switch in Stamford. No matter where you board, you'll disembark at **Grand Central Station**—a New York landmark that could almost serve as a destination in itself. From here you can take the subway, a bus, a taxi, or just walk. Not sure where to start? Try one of these "first-timer" itinerary suggestions, create your own, or just wander. Keep in mind that when outsiders talk about "New York City," they are most often referring to one borough in particular: Manhattan. While it's true that the vast majority of NYC's famous tourist attractions are located in Manhattan, the city's other four boroughs—the Bronx, Brooklyn, Staten Island, and Queens—also offer attractions and appeal for visitors.

## ARCHITECTURAL HIGHLIGHTS

Few cities offer better building-gawking opportunities than New York. Some of the best include **St. Patrick's Cathedral** (Fifth Avenue and 51st Street), America's largest Catholic cathedral; the **Empire State Building** (350 Fifth Avenue), which offers Art Deco design as well as a chance to get a great bird's-eye view of the entire

*If you're planning a day trip to New York City and don't have any particular timetable to follow, try to keep your schedule flexible. You'll pay much less for your Metro–North train ticket if you travel on a weekend day or during off-peak weekday hours.*

city; the **Cathedral of St. John the Divine** (1047 Amsterdam Avenue), an example of Romanesque and Gothic architecture; Grand Central Station (42nd Street at Park Avenue), a spectacular and busy spot complete with a constellation-painted ceiling; **St. Bartholomew's Church** (109 50th Street), a Byzantine structure; and the **Morris-Jumel Mansion** (65 Jumel Terrace), which served as George Washington's headquarters in 1765.

## LIBERTY ISLAND AND ELLIS ISLAND

Liberty Island is home to the **Statue of Liberty.** A gift from France, Lady Liberty has been standing guard over America's shores since 1886—she was the first glimpse of the country that most immigrants saw as they completed their journey across the ocean. You can always walk around the island and the base of statue, but you may or may not be able to get inside; the statue is periodically closed due to renovation and safety concerns. Nearby, **Ellis Island National Monument** chronicles the arrival of nearly 12 million immigrants at the island's inspection station between 1892 and 1954. To get to both islands, you'll have to board a Circle Line–Statue of Liberty Ferry vessel: Round-trip tickets cost $10.00 for passengers ages 13 to 62, $4.00 for children ages 3 to 12, and $8.00 for seniors age 62 and older. All ferries depart from **Battery Park,** located on the southern tip of Manhattan. When you're done visiting these all-American locales, take a short walk over to the hallowed-ground site of **Ground Zero,** where the World Trade Center's

Twin Towers once stood. The site is located near the intersection of Liberty and Church Streets.

## LITTLE ITALY, CHINATOWN, AND SOHO

Located primarily around the Mulberry Street area, **New York's Little Italy** is home to a plethora of Italian restaurants, pastry shops, food stores, gift stores, and other venues celebrating the Italian culture. The area has also hosted the much-loved Feast of San Gennaro—usually held in mid-September—for more than 75 years, bringing a festival atmosphere to the neighborhood with music, parades, games, and (of course) more food. If you had Italian for lunch, try Chinese for dinner: The **Chinatown** district bumps right into Little Italy and offers a similar experience of ethnic-specific eateries and shops. On the other side of Little Italy is **SoHo** (meaning "south of Houston"), a neighborhood that also borders **Greenwich Village** and provides some of the most funky and eclectic shopping in the city. From handbags to jewelry, fashion, furniture, toys, and consignment, you'll find it all in the SoHo byways between Houston and Canal Streets.

## MUSEUM HOPPING

New York City's museums run the gamut from quirky to world renowned. Try to fit in one of these during your next visit: The **Museum of Modern Art,** or MoMA (212-708-9400; www.moma.org), offers a permanent collection and numerous rotating exhibits that highlight the best of modern art. MoMA is scheduled to reopen at its newly renovated Manhattan location (11 West 53 Street, between Fifth and Sixth Avenues) on November 20, 2004. The **Metropolitan Museum of Art,** aka "The Met" (1000 Fifth Avenue; 212-535-7710; www.metmuseum.org), boasts a dizzying array of artifacts, sculptures, paintings, drawings, and decorative arts from Egyptian, Medieval, Islamic, Greek, Roman, Asian, Near East, and South American cultures. The **American Museum of Natural History** (Central Park West and 79th Street; 212-313-7278; www.amnh.org) has something to interest every kid and adult. The **Solomon R. Guggenheim Museum** (1071 Fifth Avenue; 212-423-3500; www.guggenheim.org) is an art museum displaying the works of the masters as well as up-and-comers. The **Jewish Museum** (1109 Fifth Avenue; 212-423-3200; www.jewishmuseum.org) has permanent exhibits on its top floors and rotating exhibits below. And let's not forget the **Museum of Sex** (233 Fifth Avenue; 212-689-6337), a unique institution dedicated to chronicling human sexuality.

## FIFTH AVENUE, ROCKEFELLER CENTER, AND CENTRAL PARK

The best window-shopping opportunities in New York are on **Fifth Avenue** between 59th and 72nd Streets, including Tiffany & Co., Saks Fifth Avenue, Cartier, Gucci, Versace, Harry Winston, Bulgari, Bergdorf Goodman, Prada, and Louis Vuitton, to name just a few. When all that gawking works up your appetite, take a break for lunch at the **Plaza** or the **Ritz-Carlton. Rockefeller Center,** a tourist attraction and business complex famous for its giant holiday tree, ice-skating, and sidewalk-window views into NBC shows, is located between 48th and 51st Streets. This might also be a good time to fit in a walk in nearby **Central Park,** the fabled green space designed by Frederick Law Olmstead and Calvert Vaux in 1858. Visitors will find walking paths, flower gardens, ponds, fountains, dog-walkers, joggers, lemonade vendors, wildlife, open fields, and lots of surprisingly tucked-away spaces for contemplation. This is also the best place to enjoy a ride in a horse-drawn carriage: You can find the empty carriages waiting for customers at the intersection of Fifth Avenue and 59th Street.

## TIMES SQUARE AND BROADWAY

Lights, lights, lights: This is where the action's at after the sun goes down. Filled with blinding, blinking bulbs at every turn, **Times Square** attracts millions of visitors each year with its restaurants, shops, and frenzied crowds that gather for the filming of popular MTV shows and other media circuses. The most popular time to visit Times Square of course is New Year's Eve, when Dick Clark arrives and everyone watches the sparkling ball drop into the new year. For more information, travelers can stop by the Times Square Visitors Center at 1560 Broadway. Another huge attraction of this area is its theaters—more than 35 in all, offering hits like *The Lion King, Rent, 42nd Street, The Producers,* and countless "off-Broadway" and "off-off-Broadway" productions.

## FUN FOR KIDS

New York City's attractions are definitely not just for adults. Check out some of these popular stops for the younger set: the **Children's Museum of Manhattan** (212 West 83rd Street; 212-721-1234; www.cmom.org), with exhibits, workshops, and live demonstrations; the **Children's Museum of the Arts** (182 Lafayette Street; 212-941-9198), where kids can make a mess, experiment, play, and enjoy participatory exhibits; the **Brooklyn Children's Museum** (145 Brooklyn Avenue, Brooklyn; 718-735-4400), with galleries focused on science, culture, and the arts; the **Central Park Zoo** (830 Fifth Avenue; 212-439-6574), where monkeys, sea lions, and even polar bears make their home; the **New York Aquarium** (West Eighth Street, Brooklyn; 718-265-3428), offering 14 acres of marine-life exhibits; **Toys Я Us Times Square** (1514 Broadway; 646-366-8855); and the **Bronx Zoo and Wildlife Conservation Park** (2300 Southern Boulevard, the Bronx; 718-367-1010), America's largest urban zoo and wildlife center. And don't forget the annual **Macy's Thanksgiving Day Parade** (212-494-4495), which

*Balking at the high cost of Broadway theater tickets? Same-day tickets can be had at considerable discounts at most Broadway and off-Broadway theaters; just stop by the individual theaters' box offices or the Broadway Ticket Office at the Times Square Visitors Center, 1560 Broadway.*

features marching bands, dancers, fire engines, police cars, and giant helium balloons shaped like kids' favorite characters.

## FOUR-LEGGED NYC

There's no need to leave Fido at home when you explore New York City. As long as he's leashed and picked up after, your dog will be able to join you on many urban rambles. In addition to the superb **Central Park** (a must-visit locale), the city also offers numerous dog runs designed exclusively for pooches and people. Try **Theodore Roosevelt Park** at 81st and Columbus; **Tompkins Square Park** at East Ninth and Avenue B; **Union Square Park** at 15th and Union Square West; and **Washington Square Park** at Fifth Avenue and Washington Square North. You might also want to try one of the **Dog-Friendly Walking Tours of New York City** led by Zuckerman Family Travel (914-633-7397; www.zuckermanfamilytravel.com) or take part in the **Blessing of the Animals** festival held each year in early October at **St. John the Divine** (1047 Amsterdam Avenue). The event is held on the Feast Day of St. Francis, the patron saint of animals. Dogs are also welcome at **Staten Island Botanical Garden** (1000 Richmond Terrace, Staten Island; 718-273-8200), **Socrates Sculpture Park** (32 Vernon Boulevard, Long Island City, Queens; 718-956-1819), and one of the hottest spots for pooches in the city: Brooklyn's **Prospect Park** (Flatbush Avenue; www.prospectpark.org). And don't miss the **William Secord Gallery** (52 East 76th Street; 212-249-0075), where all the art exhibits feature dog-related subjects and your well-behaved pup is welcome to join you in the galleries.

For more information about visiting New York City, enlist the help of the Convention and Visitors Bureau, otherwise known as NYC & Company. You can visit the bureau at 810 Seventh Avenue, call (212) 484-1200, or check out the organization's Web site at www.nycvisit.com. Free travel guides are available.

## RHODE ISLAND

# Block Island

You'll have to take a ferry (or private boat) to reach this secluded, serene spot off the coast of Rhode Island. It's a bit far for a day trip, perhaps, but well worth the effort for a weekend jaunt. Despite its small size (roughly 6.5 by 3.5 miles), the tiny island attracts more than 15,000 visitors each year—most of whom arrive during summer.

If you expect gaudy T-shirt stands and bright lights, you'll be surprised. This is a quiet and stately place, dotted with weathered-shingle cottages, beach roses, lighthouses, and miles of sand. One of the most popular activities here is walking, either on the beach or along the 30 miles of trails managed by the Nature Conservancy (Ocean Avenue and Legion Way; 401-466-2129; www.nature.org) and the Block Island Land Trust. You won't need a car to get around; bikes and feet usually suffice.

The ferries dock in **Old Harbor,** the busiest area of the island, with restaurants, marinas, old-fashioned hotels, shops, and beaches. One of the better known accommodations in town is the 1888 **National Hotel** (Water Street; 401-466-2901). Smaller B&Bs, inns, and hotels abound as well, although most fill up far in advance of the warmer months. You shouldn't have any problems satisfying a sweet tooth or a gourmand's cravings, considering the

plethora of seafood restaurants, cafes, ice-cream parlors, and other eateries that provide sustenance in Old Harbor.

Island visitors will also find nightclubs and taverns, theaters, antiques shops, outfitters for anglers and bikers, art galleries, harbor cruises, kayak rentals, and a host of other diversions. The Nature Conservancy recently called Block Island one of the 12 "Last Great Places" in the Western Hemisphere, a tribute to the preservations efforts of local residents and other admirers of the island. With the salt air blowing through your hair and the birdsong ringing in your ears, you're likely to agree with the assessment.

For more information about visiting this pristine corner of New England, contact the Block Island Tourism Council at (800) 383-BIRI or visit www.blockisland .com. Ferries to Block Island are available from New London, Connecticut (Nelseco Navigation, 401-783-4613); Point Judith and Newport, Rhode Island (877-733-9425; www.islandhighspeedferry.com); and Montauk, New York (Viking Ferry Lines, 631-668-5700). For more information about the ferries, including prices and schedules, contact each company directly, or visit the Block Island Tourism Council's Web site.

# Newport

Continuing past Mystic along I-95, travellers soon roll into the tiny state of Rhode Island. Small in size but big in reputation, Rhode Island's most popular tourist destination is the swanky and historic town of Newport. This is where some of the country's grandest estates and mansions—the summer "cottages" of magnates like the Astors, Vanderbilts, and Oelrichs—still stand guard over the wide expanse of the Atlantic Ocean.

Many of the estates are now owned and managed by the Preservation Society of Newport County (401-847-1000;

www.newportmansions.com). The society offers guided tours, rentals for weddings and other private parties, and special holiday events at the stately homes—most of which have to be seen to be believed. Perhaps the best known mansion is **the Breakers,** a 70-room palace with soaring ceilings, designed to mimic a European castle. Other mansion hot spots include **the Elms, Rosecliff, Marble House,** and **Chateau-sur-Mer.** Ticket prices ($10 to 15 per person) vary by location; combination tickets allow visitors to view more than one mansion at a slightly discounted price. Most of the notable mansions are located along famed **Ocean Drive.** Even if you're not planning to tour any of the homes, a drive along this winding, scenic road is a real treat.

Another way to get a great view of the mansions, not to mention the ocean, is to take a stroll along the **Cliff Walk.** This 3.5-mile paved path winds between the water and the waterfront properties, starting at Memorial Boulevard. You can jump in or out at Narragansett Avenue, Webster Street, Sheppard Avenue, Ruggles Avenue, Marine Avenue, Ledge Road, and Bellevue Avenue.

Sooner or later, every Newport visitor ends up at the waterfront shopping district, where touristy gift shops blend with upscale boutiques, seafood restaurants, and sidewalk vendors. There's something to do here in every season: In winter, holiday lights and music brighten the district

*Pet owners have several options for boarding animals locally, including Marta's Vineyard Pet Resort in Brookfield (203-775-4404); Best Friends Pet Resort and Salon in Norwalk (203-849-1010); and Town House for Cats and Dogs in Westport (203-227-3276). Many veterinarians' offices also provide overnight boarding. To locate an in-home pet-sitter, visit the Web site for Pet Sitter International: www.petsit.com.*

as Santa arrives for a visit (by boat, of course). In summer, crowds of beachgoers relax and mingle here after a day in the sun. And speaking of beaches, Newport and its neighboring towns are home to more than 12 public sandy shores, many of which have snack bars, changing areas, and restrooms.

The narrow, historic streets of Newport are crowded with cozy B&Bs and inns. You can also find larger chain-style hotels closer to the main roads and highways. Although accommodations are plentiful, they fill up quickly, especially in the summer months. Book your room as early as possible. For more information about Newport getaway planning, contact the Newport County Convention and Visitor's Bureau at 23 America's Cup Avenue, visit the bureau's Web site at www.go newport.com, or call (800) 976-5122.

# NONPROFITS AND VOLUNTEERING

If Fairfield County residents have a reputation for affluence, they also enjoy an equal reputation for generosity. The region is full of nonprofit organizations that depend on the help of volunteers and donors for their survival. Some agencies feed the hungry; others fight disease, rescue homeless pets, or provide mentors for children. The missions vary, but the spirit of giving and optimism remains the same.

If you're wondering how you can help, all the organizations profess a need for cold, hard cash. Many can also use specific items like office supplies, canned food, and "gently used" clothing. (Contact each individual agency for details about their needs, which often change as the year goes on.) Volunteers are also usually needed to provide a variety of services, from reading to the blind to organizing fund-raisers and counseling victims of violence. In most cases, you don't need any special skills to get involved—just bring a smile, a friendly attitude, and a desire to help. Here are some descriptions of the county's long-standing nonprofits; with such a wide range of agencies, you're sure to find one that piques your interest.

## Adopt-A-Dog
**Greenwich**
**(203) 629-9494**
**www.adoptadog.org**
This unusual animal welfare organization has no building or headquarters. Instead, groups of volunteers work to find shelter animals new homes by placing ads in local newspapers and answering telephone inquiries about the animals. Each year the group places more than 500 pets in new homes. Hotline operators are always needed, and donations of canned dog food, pet bedding, and other items are always welcome.

## American Cancer Society
**Southern New England Regional Office**
**372 Danbury Road, Wilton**
**(203) 563-0740**
**www.cancer.org**
This well-respected national organization provides medical information, support, newsletters, advocacy, and direct assistance to cancer patients and their friends and families. Volunteers can plan special events, help with fund-raising, manage office tasks, or even drive patients to and from doctors' appointments.

## American Red Cross
**Various locations, Fairfield County**
**www.redcross.org**
Volunteers can help with emergency disaster aid and blood-donation services in these Fairfield County American Red Cross locations: Bridgeport (158 Brooklawn Avenue; 203-576-1010); Danbury (2 Terrace Place; 203-792-8200); Darien (39 Leroy Avenue; 203-655-2586); Greenwich (231 East Putnam Avenue; 203-869-8444); New Canaan (51 Main Street; 203-966-1663); Stamford (112 Prospect Street; 203-363-1041); and Westport (36 Church Lane; 203-227-3954).

## AmeriCares
**88 Hamilton Avenue, Stamford**
**(800) 486-HELP**
**www.americares.org**
This disaster-relief organization provides medical supplies and services, clothing, blankets, and other necessities throughout the world, reaching sufferers in more than 137 countries since its inception in 1982.

AmeriCares also runs a variety of domestic programs to help sick and impoverished children and adults in the United States. Financial donations are needed to keep the programs running.

## Animal Adoption Network
**359 Spring Hill Road, Monroe**
**(203) 445-9978**
**www.animaladoptionnetwork.org**
The volunteers and staff members at this shelter facility rescue dogs and cats from local pounds, provide medical care and loving attention, and work to find each animal a new, permanent home. Donations of food, treats, and supplies are welcome, and volunteers can help with tasks like direct care, fund-raising, dog-walking, and transporting animals to various pet-adoption events throughout the region.

## Ann's Place, The Home of I CAN
**103 Newtown Road, Suite 1-B, Danbury**
**(203) 790-6568**
**www.annsplace.org**
Those who receive a cancer diagnosis can turn to Ann's Place for information, support, and comfort. The nonprofit organization provides counseling, resource materials, support groups, and even prescription assistance—all free of charge. Clinical volunteers have master's degrees in social work or counseling; other volunteers help with fund-raising, special-events planning, and other tasks.

## Building with Books
**P.O. Box 16741, Stamford 06905**
**(203) 961-5087**
**www.buildingwithbooks.org**
With an aim to spread education and cultural enrichment around the globe, this nonprofit organization helps build schoolhouses in impoverished areas. In 2003 the group built its 100th school. Volunteer "club members" (often students) raise money, travel overseas, participate in local cultural enrichment programs, and learn teambuilding skills.

## CancerCare of Connecticut
**120 East Avenue, Norwalk**
**(203) 854-9911**
**www.cancercare.org**
Counseling, information, financial assistance, and support are all available at CancerCare of Connecticut, a nonprofit that utilizes volunteers in office work, special-events planning, and other areas. Donations of money, wigs, and breast prosthetics are always welcome. The organization has a satellite office at 111 Beach Road in Fairfield (203-255-5300).

## Center for Women and Families of Eastern Fairfield County
**753 Fairfield Avenue, Bridgeport**
**(203) 334-6154**
**www.cwfefc.org**
This nonprofit group helps women and families coping with a variety of crisis situations, including homelessness, domestic violence, and sexual assault. Available services include the Family Violence Outreach Program, support groups, the Safe Start initiative, and programs for at-risk pregnant women and mothers. All services are free and confidential. Contact the center for information about volunteer opportunities.

## CLASP Homes
**246 Post Road East, Westport**
**(203) 226-7895**
**www.clasphomes.org**
CLASP aims to provide housing, assistance, and opportunities for people with mental retardation and similar disabilities. The agency accomplishes this goal with

*If you can't volunteer your time, you can always help out a local nonprofit by buying a ticket to one of the many scheduled fund-raising events throughout the year. Activities often include golf tournaments and other sporting events, galas, picnics, tag sales, bake sales, carnivals, and pancake breakfasts.*

career training, group homes, apartments, recreational opportunities and outings, and even a Pet Companion Program. Financial contributions are always needed.

*Potential volunteers needn't worry about making a long-term commitment to any organization. Most Fairfield County agencies listed here will welcome help on a long-term, short-term, or even one-time basis.*

### Covenant to Care
**96 Chapel Street, Stratford**
**(203) 377-4037**
Working with religious communities in every local denomination, Covenant to Care's primary goal is to provide services and care to abused and neglected children. Available services include a food bank, a foster-care and adoption program, and a mentoring program. Volunteers are always needed in a variety of areas.

### Danbury Animal Welfare Society (DAWS)
**P.O. Box 971, Danbury 06813**
**(203) 798-5816**
**www.daws.org**
In addition to providing care and adoption services for homeless pets in its Bethel shelter, DAWS volunteers also work to supply low-cost vaccination, subsidized spay/neuter programs, and animal rescue services. Volunteers are needed to walk dogs, play with and socialize the in-house animals, and help out with special events and office work.

### Darien Book Aid Plan
**1926 Post Road, Darien**
**(203) 655-2777**
**www.dba.darien.org**
When local residents donate books to Darien Book Aid Plan, the organization wraps and sends the materials to impoverished communities, libraries, schools,

prisons, and hospitals throughout the United States and around the world. Books must be in good condition. Science textbooks, classic literature, children's books, how-to books, English dictionaries, and books with health and medical topics are especially needed.

### Domestic Violence Crisis Center
**5 Eversley Avenue, Norwalk**
**(203) 853-0418**
DVCC's free services include a 24-hour hotline, advocacy in the court system, counseling, education, emergency shelter housing, support groups, and children's programs. Staff members and volunteers work together toward a common goal of preventing and ending domestic violence and helping victims of sexual assault and violence in the home.

### Family & Children's Agency
**9 Mott Avenue, Norwalk**
**(203) 855-8765**
**www.fcadopt.org**
The Family & Children's Agency provides a variety of programs and services in the community, including adoption and foster-care programs, pregnancy counseling, aid and support for senior citizens, after-school services, fund-raising special events, and youth mentoring programs. Volunteers are needed to help with all aspects of the group's work.

### Family ReEntry
**9 Mott Avenue, Suite 104**
**(203) 838-0496**
**www.familyreentry.org**
In an effort to reduce the prison reincarceration rate and create safer communities, Family ReEntry provides substance-abuse treatment, counseling, anger-management programs, and mentoring for inmates at two prison facilities as well as for members of the general public. Volunteers experienced in mentoring, public relations, and clinical service, as well as those who want to help with general tasks, are always appreciated.

## Good Friend
**185 Main Street, Danbury**
**(203) 790-0032**
**www.good-friend.org**
A program of Green Chimneys Children's Services, this downtown Danbury nonprofit matches mentors with children ages 7 to 14 who come from homes where parent-child contact is limited, often homes without a father. Volunteers simply spend time with the children to play, learn, explore, and create a much-needed caring, mentoring relationship.

## Habitat for Humanity of Greater Bridgeport
**1470 Barnum Avenue, Bridgeport**
**(203) 333-2642**
**www.bridgeporthabitat.org**
The Bridgeport chapter of this international Christian housing ministry works to renovate run-down homes and build new homes in impoverished local areas, creating a sense of community pride and raising the standard of living for local families. Volunteers can organize teams of homebuilders, join an already established team, help with office work, raise funds, or collect donated materials.

## Interfaith AIDS Ministry
**46 Main Street, Danbury**
**(203) 748-4077**
**www.danbury.org/interfaith**
Supported by local churches and synagogues, the Interfaith AIDS Ministry provides free information, referrals, counseling, outreach, advocacy, support groups, and retreats for those diagnosed with AIDS. Volunteers help with a variety of tasks, including shopping, office work, cooking, public speaking, planning fundraisers, sorting mailings, and driving patients to doctors' appointments.

## Interlude
**60 West Street, Danbury**
**(203) 797-1210**
The mission of this mental health agency is to provide support, advocacy, and housing to persons with mental illness, thereby providing them with the tools to become independent and productive community members. In-house residential support programs, outreach, and intensive treatment programs are all available. Interlude welcomes donations of money, office equipment, gift certificates to local stores, appliances, and bedding.

## International Institute of Connecticut
**670 Clinton Avenue, Bridgeport**
**(203) 336-0141**
"Helping new Americans help themselves" is the goal of this agency that serves approximately 7,000 immigrants each year. Services include citizenship counseling, court representation, interpreter and translation services for more than 40 languages, employment assistance, and refugee resettlement. The organization also has a satellite location at 22 Grove Street in Stamford (203-965-1790).

## The Kennedy Center
**2440 Reservoir Avenue, Trumbull**
**(203) 339-3034**
**www.thekennedycenterinc.org**
The Kennedy Center's mission is to empower men and women with disabilities, enabling them to become active community participants and live independently. Programs include vocational training, behavioral counseling, recreational outings and opportunities, and other services for those with mental retardation, autism, hearing and visual impairments, cerebral palsy, and other illnesses and injuries.

## Kids in Crisis
**1 Salem Street, Cos Cob (Greenwich)**
**(203) 622-6556**
**www.kidsincrisis.org**
This is the only organization in the state that provides free crisis care for children 24 hours per day. Children who use Kids in Crisis's services are often abused or neglected or need a place to temporarily escape family conflicts like domestic violence, homelessness, or parental substance abuse. Volunteers help with direct

care of children, office work, special programs, maintenance, and other tasks.

## Literacy Volunteers of Southeastern Fairfield County
### 1 Belden Avenue, Norwalk
### (203) 853-2714

Literacy Volunteers matches volunteers with clients who are interested in learning to read English. Volunteer opportunities include direct tutoring, training other tutors, working in the office, and editing the newsletter. The agency's mission includes promoting literacy through a variety of programs for adults from all cultures and walks of life.

## Make-A-Wish Foundation of Connecticut
### 940 White Plains Road, Trumbull
### (203) 261-9044
### www.wish.org

The internationally respected Make-A-Wish organization specializes in granting wishes to terminally ill children. Much of the work is done by volunteers, who coordinate special events, complete office work, raise funds, and directly grant wishes by making travel arrangements, contacting businesses and organizations, and communicating with "wish children" and their families.

## Meals on Wheels of Stamford-Darien
### 945 Summer Street, Stamford
### (203) 323-3294
### www.getmealsonwheels.org

Contributions and volunteers are always needed at Meals on Wheels, a program that delivers hot meals to anyone in the community who needs them—including senior citizens, invalids, new parents, and those recovering from trauma or illness. Packers, drivers, and delivery volunteers can work with a friend or be paired up.

## Mid-Fairfield AIDS Project
### 16 River Street, Norwalk
### (203) 855-9535
### www.mfap.com

Volunteers working with the Mid-Fairfield AIDS project organize food drives, complete office tasks, drive patients to doctors' appointments, plan special events, help with fund-raising, and more. The project provides counseling, financial assistance, food, transportation, information, housing, and other services for people who have been diagnosed with the AIDS virus.

## Norwalk Emergency Shelter
### 4 Merritt Street, Norwalk
### (203) 866-1057
### www.norwalkemergencyshelter.org

Open 365 days a year, the Norwalk Emergency Shelter provides food and housing for homeless men, women, and families, as well as counseling, job training, job placement, and outreach programs. Volunteers are always needed to help with maintenance and repairs of the shelter building, newsletter mailings, special events, and holiday decorating and gift-wrapping. Donations of toys, bedding, clothing, and other items are welcome.

## PAWS
### 504 Main Avenue, Norwalk
### (203) 750-9572
### www.pawsct.org

The staffers and volunteers at PAWS provide loving attention, medical care, food, and shelter to homeless animals (mostly dogs and cats) in the greater Norwalk area. Whenever possible, the group also places the animals in new homes. The Web site includes "wish list" items, volunteer opportunities, and pet sponsorship program information.

## Person-to-Person
### 1864 Post Road, Darien
### (203) 655-0048
### www.p2p.darien.org

A program of St. Luke's parish, Person-to-Person provides food, clothing, eviction mediation, loans and grants for rent and utility payments, and other services for local families in need. Volunteers can help out in the food pantry, answer phones, pick up donations, organize seasonal projects, sort clothing, deliver food to shut-ins, and provide a variety of other services.

### Salvation Army of Greater Bridgeport
### 30 Elm Street, Bridgeport
### (203) 334-0995
### www.1salvationarmy.org

This Christian organization works to provide food, clothing, furniture, emergency disaster services, children's camps, AIDS ministry programs, and more for local residents. The Bridgeport location is one of 24 service centers in Connecticut and Rhode Island managed by the Salvation Army's Southern New England Division (860-543-8400). Call the local or regional offices to find out what donation items are most needed.

### Save the Sound
### 18 Reynolds Street, East Norwalk
### (888) SAVE-LIS
### www.savethesound.org

Staffers, volunteers, and members of Save the Sound are working to protect and restore the wildlife and ecosystems along Long Island Sound through a combination of research projects, outreach education, and advocacy. Volunteers provide administrative support, photography and photo scanning, legislative lobbying, special-events planning, data collection, beach cleanups, library research, and other services.

### SoundWaters
### 1281 Cove Road, Cove Island Park
### Stamford
### (203) 323-1978
### www.soundwaters.org

The natural beauty and fragility of Long Island Sound's habitats are the focus of the work done at SoundWaters, a nonprofit dedicated to education, conservation, and advocacy on behalf of the Sound. Interested visitors and members can take a class, attend a lecture, participate in research programs, take an ecology sail aboard the *SoundWaters* vessel,

or volunteer to help out with the group's services, research, and outreach programs.

### Shelter for the Homeless
### 597 South Pacific Street, Stamford
### (203) 348-2792
### www.shelterforhomeless.org

Serving homeless adults throughout greater Stamford, the Shelter for the Homeless provides emergency housing, transitional housing, meals, career development training, education services, mental-health treatment programs, outreach services, and training in independent living skills. Volunteers are needed to keep the shelter programs running.

### St. Luke's Lifeworks
### 141 Franklin Street, Stamford
### (203) 388-0100
### www.stlukeslifeworks.org

St. Luke's Lifeworks helps local residents in crisis situations by providing shelter, clothing, food, information, advocacy, and support. Volunteers can help with all aspects of day-to-day life at shelter, donate goods and services, and help organize golf tournaments, musical concerts, and other fund-raising events.

### Strays and Others
### P.O. Box 473, New Canaan 06840
### (203) 966-6556

This all-volunteer organization works to help homeless dogs and cats find medical care, foster homes, and eventually permanent placement with a new family. Some Strays and Others programs include low-cost spaying and neutering, humane education, emergency rescues, lost-and-found services, pet adoptions, and pet foster-care placement.

### Voluntary Services for the Blind
### 945 Summer Street, Stamford
### (203) 324-6611

Founded in 1993, this former offshoot of the Darien Lions Club quickly developed into a full-fledged nonprofit organization of its own. The agency works to help visu-

*The Volunteer Center of Southwestern Fairfield County is a great resource for those who want to investigate volunteer opportunities in the area. The organization catalogs and lists volunteer jobs, including everything from one-hour tasks to yearlong assignments. The listings are updated regularly. For more information visit the Volunteer Center at 62 Palmer's Hill Road in Stamford, call (203) 348-7714, or visit www.ucanhelp.org.*

ally impaired local residents gain independence and follow their dreams. Volunteers help with such tasks as reading, driving, shopping, visiting, and helping to complete paperwork.

**The Wildlife Orphanage**
**P.O. Box 4706, Stamford 06907**
**(888) 727-ORPHAN**
**www.wildlifeorphanage.org**

This nonprofit animal welfare organization is dedicated to rescuing, rehabilitating, and releasing injured and orphaned wildlife species, including squirrels, ducks, birds, chipmunks, raccoons, and deer. Volunteer positions include wildlife rehabilitator, animal transporter, nut gatherer, and nest-box builder, to name a few. The Web site includes a "wish list" of much needed donation items.

**Women's Center of Greater Danbury**
**2 West Street, Danbury**
**(203) 731-5200**
The Women's Center provides free counseling, court advocacy, transitional housing, children's programs, and outreach for victims of domestic violence and sexual assault. The agency also staffs a 24-hour domestic violence hotline (203-731-5206) and a sexual assault hotline (203-731-5204). Volunteers undergo a one-time training program before delving into counseling or hotline work.

# REAL ESTATE 🏠

Spend any time at all at a neighborhood party, PTA meeting, or hair salon and the subject is bound to come up: Did you see the new house on Main Street? Can you believe what the Joneses got for their house? Are you planning on selling? Buying? Building an addition? How did they manage to shoehorn another housing development into this town?

Real estate continues to be *the* hot topic in Fairfield County, touching nearly every aspect of local life. From schools to taxes, traffic, and the environment, everything seems to depend on the number of houses, the price of houses, and the availability (or lack thereof) of houses in the county's 23 towns and cities. Some say there are too many houses already; others argue that the supply is too low. Certain areas, like Black Rock in Bridgeport, can quickly jump in and out of favor as up-and-coming real estate investment sites. Other areas, like the quiet suburbs of Greenwich, Darien, and New Canaan, seem to remain in constant demand—with accompanying constant high prices. Apartments and small homes, meanwhile, are hard to come by, making things difficult for those who are struggling to make ends meet.

If you're hoping to buy a home in Fairfield County, be prepared for a wild ride. It's not uncommon for listings to be sold within days or hours—sometimes sight unseen. Towns along the Metro-North Railroad commuter line into New York City continue to command the highest prices: The closer you are to the city and the waterfront, the more you can expect to pay for housing. That's especially true in the coastline's "trophy" towns, where million-dollar homes are considered the low end of the spectrum in many cases. But as commuters get more flexible and employment opportunities improve in places like Stamford, Danbury, Waterbury,

and Hartford, house prices in the inland areas of the county have continued to rise as well. Locals complain about the costs but at the same time seem willing to pay a premium for the county's location, ambience, and renowned school systems.

All this demand is nothing new: Fairfield County real estate has been a much-desired commodity for decades, and the most sought-after areas have very little available land on which to build new homes. The result? Older, smaller, and sometimes historic homes are being razed to make way for new, larger, modern homes with hot tubs, central air, and the other conveniences that many homebuyers desire. The practice has pitted neighbors against neighbors and preservationists against contractors in places like Rowayton but nevertheless seems likely to continue into the near future. The ever-increasing spate of housing developments has replaced forests and wetlands throughout the area, leading to battles in Ridgefield and other towns over the importance of preserving open space.

The controversies continue to rage, and the housing prices continue to climb. But as long as Fairfield County keeps attracting new residents, real estate will maintain its status as the most popular topic around.

## THE $500,000 QUESTION

What will your money buy in Fairfield County? Fairfield County surpasses all other Connecticut counties when it comes to home prices. According to the National Association of Realtors, the median price in all other counties ranged from $171,000 to $281,000 in 2003. The median selling price for a home in Fairfield County during the third quarter of 2003 was $476,000. That means half the houses sold for more than that amount, and half sold for less. Rounding that figure off to $500,000, let's take a look at what the median amount could have garnered a home buyer in different parts of the county in late 2003.

In Greenwich, arguably the most expensive town in the county, you'll primarily find a $500,000 price tag only on condominiums, town houses, and small in-town homes on a quarter acre or less. If you're looking for the typical three- or four-bedroom house with a big yard, expect to pay closer to $1.2 million. And for an estate on the water or in one of Greenwich's posh gated neighborhoods? Stratospheric.

Stamford has a huge variety of real estate offerings, from tiny city apartments to plush suburban homes. At the half-million-dollar mark, available options include three-bedroom condos and older Cape-style homes or ranches on one-quarter acre of land or less. Your options are more limited next door in Darien and New Canaan, more exclusive towns where a $500,000 home is in the minority. In these areas, the few homes available in that price range include older houses with two or three bedrooms and a limited amount of property.

Norwalk is another diverse area where your housing price will depend largely on what part of the city you're looking in. In late 2003 several multifamily properties were selling in downtown areas for between $450,000 and $500,000. Single-family homes were also available with three or four bedrooms, backyards, and two-car garages. In Norwalk's waterfront Rowayton district, however, most house prices far surpassed that amount. To the immediate north in Wilton, houses were considerably more pricey as well. Here your options in the given price range are limited to a few very small single-family houses, as well as condominiums and town houses.

In Westport houses are being built, razed, and/or remodeled faster than ever before. The town is a mecca for families

and commuters, a phenomenon that is reflected in the home prices. For $500,000 Westport home shoppers won't find many listings to choose from. The homes that are available in that range are typically 1,000- to 1,800-square-foot ranches or condos with two or three bedrooms. Neighboring Weston and Easton share similar price ranges: In Weston, for example, only one of the 126 available listings was priced between $450,000 and $550,000—and that was property only, featuring 2.6 acres but no house. In these two rural towns, houses are set on large plots and usually are larger than average in size.

Fairfield accommodates its many college students and university employees with apartments and condos, making this one of the better locales for locals looking for rental housing. If you're looking to buy a house here, your $500,000 can garner a three- or four-bedroom ranch or Cape, usually built prior to 1960. In more exclusive areas of Fairfield, such as coastal Southport or the estate-filled Greenfield Hills, few houses can be found in that range. On the other hand, the city of Bridgeport, located next to Fairfield, offers the most affordable coastal housing in the county. The city's tough reputation means that your half million dollars will stretch far to buy waterfront properties and large homes.

Trumbull and Stratford, both neighbors of Bridgeport, are also good options for those who want to save some money, be close to the water, and even commute into New York City. In both towns, $500,000 listings typically include three- and four-bedroom homes with large lots (sometimes an acre or more), central air-conditioning, two-car garages, and other features.

In the northern region of the county, Ridgefield and Redding have the highest home prices. Both towns have historic homesteads, older estates, and lots of new construction. While $500,000 won't grant you access to some of the fanciest homes in town, it will buy an older single-

family home with such amenities as a half acre or more, three or four bedrooms, master bathrooms, and hardwood floors.

Monroe and Shelton, located to the east of Redding, offer more affordable listings. Both towns are suburban, with a generous smattering of small businesses and some industry. A half-million-dollar house in this area will have lots of land (usually an acre or more) and three or four bedrooms and might be part of a newly built housing development. Just north of Monroe is Newtown, which straddles I–84 and offers houses with slightly higher prices. The $500,000 listings in Newtown include antique homes, colonials, and raised ranches built in the '60s and '70s, and a few large town houses.

Next to Newtown is tiny Bethel, which was once part of the city of Danbury. Half a million dollars buys a lot of house in Bethel, where listings in that price range include antique farmhouses and large colonials with fireplaces, garages, and central air. Because land is at a premium in most parts of town, you won't find many lots larger than a half acre or so. In Danbury housing options include duplexes, small older homes, and large suburban homes to the north of the downtown area. As you might expect, your money will go further in the high-density areas than in the suburban areas. Nevertheless, Danbury offers the best bargains around for those who are seeking a large house on a large lot with plenty of extras. One typical $499,000 listing, offered in late 2003, had such amenities as a lakefront location, four bathrooms, four bedrooms, cathedral ceilings, a deck, and one acre of land. You won't find a much better deal than that for a suburban home in all of Fairfield County.

Some Danbury employees also choose to commute from the nearby towns of New Fairfield and Brookfield. Both have well-respected school systems and more expensive housing than that found within city limits. That $500,000 will buy you a three- or four-bedroom split-level, contemporary, or colonial house: Go slightly

*Rental units are extremely difficult to come by in the region, particularly in the northern part of the county. Real estate agents sometimes list full-size homes for rent, usually with long-term leases of a year or more. If all you need is an apartment, however, your best bet is the local newspaper in the town or city you're looking in. Few apartment complexes exist, so don't be surprised to find yourself looking at duplex rentals and similar arrangements.*

higher than that and you can peruse new four-bedroom homes built between 2000 and 2002. And then there is Sherman, the northernmost locale in the county, with a rural atmosphere, older farmhouses, and quite a bit of new construction. Here your half-a-million price tag is dangling on brand-new 2,500-square-foot homes in subdivisions offering two-acre plots, whirlpool tubs, porches, vaulted ceilings, and two-car garages.

## REAL ESTATE AGENCIES

No matter where in the county you decide to shop for a home, your search will most likely begin at a local real estate office. Some specialize in high-end homes and estates, especially in the southern part of the county. Others choose to concentrate on just one town, while still others spread their listings around several towns or a general region of the county. Before beginning your search, try to narrow down the list of towns and cities you'd like to consider and the housing features you'd like to have: This will make it easier to choose a Realtor and will help him or her find the best house for your lifestyle and price range.

Here is a sampling of real estate agents throughout the county (listed alphabetically) who would be happy to help you find your dream home:

## Alberti Realty Associates
## 170 Post Road, Fairfield
## (203) 256-1239

Offering "million dollar service in every price range," Alberti Realty Associates allows buyers to conduct thorough home searches and sellers to get up-to-the-minute information about their home's true market value. This is a small, independently owned company.

## American Realty Associates
## 11 Saw Mill Road, New Fairfield
## (203) 746-1717

American Realty lists all types of houses for sale, although the agency specializes in homes on or near Candlewood Lake. Real estate in New Fairfield, Brookfield, Danbury, and Kent is often highlighted. Owner Kevin Bendler is a member of the Northern Fairfield County Association of Realtors.

## Ameriland Real Estate
## 85 Albermarle Street, Bridgeport
## (203) 372-2722
## www.amerilandrealty.com

Ameriland is a 10-year-old Bridgeport company helping families and businesses with their real estate needs. The five-member staff includes agent and Realtors who showcase home and companies in the Greater Bridgeport area.

## Anderson Associates Real Estate
## 164 Mason Street, Greenwich
## (203) 629-4519

Focusing on luxury residential sales, Anderson Associates specializes in Green-wich properties. Typical listings include a $5 million country estate, a $1 million condominium, a $500,000 two-acre plot of land, and a $2 million family compound. The company employs eight agents.

## Blue Sky Realty
## 92 Park Avenue, Danbury
## (203) 743-1000

This independently owned agency helps newcomers find rental properties and single-family homes in the city of Danbury and its surrounding communities. Co-owners Jocelyn May and Raymond Neville run a small company and aim to provide lots of personal attention to each client.

## Bob Tendler Real Estate
## 17 Church Hill Road, Newtown
## (203) 426-5679
## www.bobtendler.com

The Bob Tendler agency focuses its attention on Newtown listings, helping home-buyers as well as sellers with all their relocation needs. The company is involved in approximately 4 out of every 10 home sales in the town. In addition to Bob Tendler himself, the company employs an additional 14 brokers and agents.

## Brotherhood & Higley Real Estate
## 161 Elm Street, New Canaan
## (203) 966-3507

The agents at Brotherhood & Higley have been managing New Canaan real estate sales since 1926. Independently owned, the agency employs local Realtors who are familiar with the town's schools, businesses, and personality. The company is an affiliate of Sotheby's International Realty.

## Century 21 Access America
## 27 Strawberry Hill Avenue, Stamford
## (203) 326-3399
## www.century21.com

This Century 21 office specializes in "fine homes and estates" and has won several Quality Service Awards from its parent company. Century 21 also has locations in Bridgeport (see listing below) and other towns around the county. Log on to the

*County homebuyers purchase approximately twice as many four (or more)-bedroom homes as three-bedroom homes, with two-bedroom homes coming in last in a popularity contest. This contrasts sharply with homebuying habits in other counties, where two-, three-, and four-bedroom home sales are much closer in number.*

Web site for more information and directions to each office.

## Century 21 Greengarden Realty
**4942 Main Street, Bridgeport**
**(203) 374-0295**
This office beat out more than 100 other New England Century 21 offices in 2003, earning the No. 1 spot for units sold and other industry measures of performance. Based in Bridgeport, the agency has Realtors based around Fairfield County, mainly selling private homes.

## Coldwell Banker
**185 East Avenue, Norwalk**
**(and other locations)**
**(203) 853-3700**
**www.coldwellbanker.com**
In addition to this Norwalk office, Coldwell Banker also offers offices in Bethel, Greenwich, New Canaan, Danbury, Westport, Stamford, Trumbull, Wilton, New Fairfield, Monroe, and Ridgefield. Homes are offered in every price range. Log on to the Coldwell Banker Web site for more information on all local offices and agents.

## Country Living Associates
**98 East Avenue, Norwalk**
**(203) 838-3737**
**www.country-living.com**
Although its corporate office is located in Norwalk, Country Living Associates has 12 offices and 165 agents throughout southern Fairfield County. The company's offerings include "premier properties" and other private homes in Darien, Greenwich, and New Canaan.

## Curtiss & Crandon Realtors
**45 South Main Street, Newtown**
**(203) 426-8104**
**www.curtisscrandon.com**
Curtiss & Crandon has been offering real estate listings in Newtown and surrounding communities like Ridgefield, Fairfield, Southbury, and Danbury for more than 30 years. Expect to find all price ranges and types of homes. The agency makes use of extensive Internet marketing.

*It's not uncommon for local homeowners of all faiths to bury a statue of St. Joseph in their yard before attempting to sell a home. The practice is said to bring good luck in the home-selling process, and some local Realtors even provide the statues for their clients. You can also buy the statues at religious stores throughout the area.*

## Davis & Hoyt Realtors
**801 Federal Road, Brookfield**
**(203) 775-4561**
Betty and Tom Hensal, owners of Davis & Hoyt Realtors, manage a staff of sales associates who specialize in the communities of Brookfield, Bethel, Danbury, Redding, Newtown, and New Fairfield. In addition to showing you houses, they can tell you all about your commute, the local school system, and more.

## ERA Shays Real Estate
**680 Main Street, Stamford**
**(203) 359-4425**
This agency can help you find a condo, a house, or even a rental unit in the city of Stamford. The 18 ERA agents on staff speak numerous languages and can help you sort through listings, host an open house, or smooth out a relocation to the area. ERA has another Stamford location (680 Main Street) and an office in Westport (991 Post Road).

## Fairfield County Real Estate
**200 Mill Plain Road, Fairfield**
**(203) 259-9999**
**www.fairfieldcountyrealestate.net**
Serving nine local towns, Fairfield County Real Estate helps buyers, sellers, renters, and landlords with nearly 30 agents and brokers. Listings run the gamut from $100,000 condos to million-dollar estates. The company also manages a mortgage service.

## Kelly Associates Real Estate
**780 Post Road, Darien**
**(203) 655-8238**

This independently owned agency is one of the busiest real estate offices in Darien, listing single-family homes that typically range from $500,000 to more than $9 million. Kelly also has more than 50 agents on staff to keep its clients on top of the ever-changing market.

## Landmark Properties
**398 Main Street, Ridgefield**
**(203) 431-0000**
**www.c21landmark.com**
A Century 21 affiliate, Landmark Properties specializes in single-family houses, condos, new construction, and waterfront homes in the greater Ridgefield area, including Redding, Wilton, Bethel, Weston, and Danbury. Virtual tours and complete listings are available on the company's Web site.

## Lombardi Realtors
**88 Mill Plain Road, Danbury**
**(203) 791-1666**
Started in 1986, Lombardi began as an independent company and joined Century 21 in 1989. Specializing in single-family homes and VIP office space, the agency employs 10 staffers with typical listings in the $250,000 to $600,000 range. Home sellers can also take advantage of the agency's services.

## Mizak Realtors
**5277 Main Street, Trumbull**
**(203) 261-3659**
**www.donnasoldmine.com**
Donna Mizak raised her children in Trumbull and worked as a full-time Realtor in the town for more than 30 years. She and her staff can help you buy or sell a home in Trumbull, Monroe, Bridgeport, Easton, Fairfield, Shelton, or Stratford. The agency can also provide you with mortgage information, school reports, and more.

## Neumann Real Estate
**395 Main Street, Ridgefield**
**(203) 438-0455**
Neumann Real Estate, an independently owned realty company, has been offering home listings in the greater Ridgefield and New Fairfield areas for more than 35 years. Listings often include new construction and antique homes in towns like Newton, Redding, and Ridgefield. Neumann also has a New Fairfield office on Route 37.

## Pandolfi Properties
**82 Route 55 West, Sherman**
**(860) 355-3118**
**www.pandolfi-properties.com**
The slogan of this independently owned agency is "big enough to compete, small enough to care." Pandolfi Properties' seven agents showcase homes in the northern region of the county. The company also has a Danbury office at 46 North Street.

## Preferred Properties
**177 West Putnam Avenue, Greenwich**
**(203) 869-5975**
Preferred Properties also has office locations in Westport, Darien, Danbury, New Canaan, Norwalk, and Stamford. The Greenwich office and headquarters was the first location, before expansion began in the 1960s. The company primarily specializes in residential sales.

## Prudential Connecticut Realty
**455 Post Road, Darien**
**(and other locations)**
**(203) 655-5114**
**www.prudentialct.com**
This is just one of Prudential Connecticut Realty's locations in southern Fairfield County. The others can be found in Fairfield, Greenwich, New Canaan, Norwalk, Ridgefield, Stamford, Stratford, Trumbull, Westport, and Wilton. With hundreds of agents, the company showcases residential and commercial properties throughout the area.

## Real Estate Two
### 100 Huntington Street, Shelton
### (203) 926-1122
Located on the border of Fairfield and New Haven Counties, Real Estate Two specializes in helping homebuyers and sellers in both areas. The agency's name was derived from the teamwork of its owners, Susan Coyle and Linda Schauwecker, who work with a staff of more than 25 agents.

## Realty Seven
### 250 Danbury Road, Wilton
### (203) 762-5548
Realty Seven is an independently owned agency with a sales staff of more than 20. Focused on the town of Wilton, the agency can help newcomers with buying a home and relocating and help sellers determine fair market value and smooth the selling process.

## Re/Max Heritage
### 1835 Post Road East, Westport
### (203) 254-0665
Mother-daughter agents Carrie Perkins and Virginia Klein specialize in helping homebuyers and sellers in the greater Westport area, including Weston, Wilton, Darien, New Canaan, and Southport. In addition to the Westport office, Re/Max Heritage has locations in Greenwich and Fairfield.

## Richter Real Estate
### 458 Monroe Turnpike, Monroe
### (203) 459-9101
This agency helps buyers and sellers in the towns of Monroe, Shelton, Stratford, Bridgeport, Huntington, and several New Haven County areas. Buyers will find listings for single-family homes, estates, office space, and even senior housing. Richter Real Estate is part of the Century 21 real estate network.

## Settlers & Traders Real Estate
### 215 Post Road West, Westport
### (203) 226-0000
### www.settlers.com

This local real estate company specializes in Fairfield County homes. Agents have a wealth of information about schools, commutes, shopping, and anything else a newcomer might need to know. In addition to its Westport location, the company has offices in Redding, Danbury, Brookfield, Wilton, and Ridgefield.

*If you're just starting your home search and are not sure which areas or Realtors interest you the most, try visiting www.realtor.com. This site lists all MLS listings in all towns and all price ranges and can give you a head start.*

## Scalzo Realty
### 2 Stony Hill Road, Bethel
### (800) 553-2100
### www.scalzo.com
Now a part of the Century 21 real estate network, Scalzo Realty started out as an independent company and has been helping homebuyers and sellers in Fairfield County for more than 45 years. Listings include homes throughout the greater Bethel area, including Danbury, Brookfield, and Newtown.

## Weichert Realtors
### 25 Field Point Road, Greenwich
### (203) 661-5400
### www.weichert.com
The 58 sales associates at Weichert cover all southern Fairfield County and parts of Westchester County, New York, primarily showing residential listings. Buyers can expect to browse houses ranging from $250,000 to well over $10 million. The agents also regularly offer open houses at properties for sale.

## William Pitt Real Estate
### 1266 East Main Street, Stamford
### (800) 229-7488
### www.williampitt.com
This Connecticut-based real estate company is headquartered in Stamford,

> *The average Fairfield County home stays on the market for about a month before being sold, although that can increase or decrease dramatically depending on the house. Homes that are unusual in their location or style, for example, can take a bit longer to find that "perfect" buyer. On the other hand, houses that appeal to a wider number of buyers can be snapped up in a matter of days.*

although it has 21 other offices throughout Fairfield County. William Pitt agents can help you find a new home and assist with insurance, finances, relocation, auctions, and numerous other services. Properties in every price range are offered throughout the county.

**William Raveis Real Estate**
**2525 Post Road, Southport (Fairfield)**
**(203) 255-6841**
**www.raveis.com**
This well-known company was founded by its namesake in Fairfield in 1974. Today its associates work in 45 offices throughout New England and New York. The company's other Fairfield County offices are located in Danbury, Greenwich, Monroe, New Canaan, Norwalk, Ridgefield, Shelton, Stamford, Stratford, Trumbull, Westport, and Wilton.

# RELOCATION 🏠

So you're moving to Fairfield County: Welcome! As you get settled, the following contact information and tidbits can help you get your phone line connected, dispose of your trash, get a new driver's license, buy stamps, and perform the countless other tasks of daily life.

Every town and city in the region has a public library and at least one U.S. Post Office. Department of Motor Vehicles (DMV) locations are a bit less convenient, but you should still be able to locate one not too far away from home or work. When seeking any type of information about your municipality, town and city halls are usually the best places to start. Some towns and cities also host Web sites where you can skim through lists of "Frequently Asked Questions" to save yourself some time and hassle. If you're looking for a particular type of business, your local chamber of commerce is always a good bet. The chambers typically have hundreds of members offering nearly every service you might need, from child care and beauty services to dog training, floral design, and roofing. And then of course there are the local residents, who are usually more than willing to offer advice, recommendations, and help to their neighbors.

Like any other locale, our community has its challenges and shortcomings. But the friendly faces, impressive resources, beautiful landscape, and Yankee spirit of Fairfield County have long made it stand out as a wonderful place to live and work. We welcome you to the family.

## UTILITIES

### Electricity

**Connecticut Light and Power/ Northeast Utilities**
P.O. Box 270, Hartford 06141
(800) 286-2000, (800) 286-2828
www.nu.com

### Gas

**Connecticut Natural Gas Corporation**
(203) 869-6900, (203) 869-6913

**Iroquois Gas**
(203) 925-7200

**Southern Connecticut Gas Company**
(203) 334-1061, (203) 382-8111
www.soconngas.com

**Yankee Gas Services**
(800) 989-0900

### Water

**Aquarion Water Company**
(203) 445-7310, (800) 732-9678
www.aquarionwater.com

**Conn-Am Water Company**
(800) 292-2938

**Rural Water Company**
(203) 744-5459

ℹ️ *All county phone numbers have a 203 area code with the exception of those in Sherman, which have an 860 area code. You'll have to dial the area code to reach another number in the county if it's outside your local calling area.*

# Useful Telephone Numbers in Connecticut

| | |
|---|---|
| Emergency | 911 |
| Connecticut Infoline | 211 |
| Poison Control Center | (800) 222-1222 |
| | |
| Better Business Bureau | (203) 269-2700 |
| Child Abuse and Neglect Hotline | (800) 842-2288 |
| Department of Environmental Protection | (860) 424-3000 |
| Department of Social Services | (800) 385-4052 |
| Department of Veteran's Affairs | (800) 827-1000 |
| Domestic Violence Crisis Hotline | (888) 774-2900 |
| Medicaid Information | (800) 285-4052 |
| Medicare Advocacy | (800) 262-4414 |
| Mental Health Association | (800) 842-1501 |
| Sexual Assault Crisis Hotline | (888) 999-5545 |
| Statewide Legal Services | (800) 453-3320 |
| Suicide Crisis Hotline | (800) 784-2433 |
| Wildlife Rescue | (860) 424-3011 |

United Water Connecticut
(203) 426-2430

## Telephone and Internet Service Providers

AT&T
(800) 222-0300
www.att.com

B.A.C. Company
(866) 392-3547
www.1-866-excelir.com

Brooks Fiber Communications
(203) 399-1000

Choice One Communications
(888) 832-5801
www.choiceonecom.com

Frontier Communications
(203) 926-9899
www.frontieronline.com

Hi-Tech Communications
(203) 363-0639

MCI Telecommunications
(203) 967-9022
www.mci.com

Paetec Communications
(800) 946-1233
www.paetec.com

SBC
(800) 453-7638
www.sbc.com

Sprint
(800) 877-7746
www.sprint.com

## CABLE/SATELLITE TELEVISION

Cablevision (cable service)
(203) 336-2225
www.cablevision.com

Charter Communications (cable service)
(203) 270-8665
www.charter.com

Comcast Cable (cable service)
(866) 200-6670
www.comcast.com

DIRECTV (satellite service)
(888) 238-7177
www.directv.com

Dish Network (satellite service)
(800) 333-3474
www.dishnetwork.com

## MOTOR VEHICLE AND LICENSING INFORMATION

## Motor Vehicle Registration

Drivers have a 60-day grace period after moving to Connecticut to register their vehicle. Before that time expires, visit one of these full-service Connecticut DMV sites to register your car or truck. All vehicles must pass yearly Connecticut emissions inspections in order to legally stay on the road. (At the time of this writing, the emissions-testing program was temporarily suspended for renovations.)

**Bridgeport DMV Office**
**95 Sylvan Avenue, Bridgeport**
Tuesday, Wednesday, and
Friday: 8:00 A.M. to 4:30 P.M.
Thursday: 8:00 A.M. to 7:00 P.M.
Saturday: 8:00 A.M. to 12:30 P.M.

**Danbury DMV Office**
**2 Lee Mac Avenue, Danbury**
Tuesday, Wednesday, and
Friday: 8:00 A.M. to 4:30 P.M.
Thursday: 8:00 A.M. to 7:00 P.M.
Saturday: 8:00 A.M. to 12:30 P.M.

*Waits can be long at DMV offices, so make sure you have all the required paperwork before you get in line. To replace a lost or stolen license, for example, you need two forms of identification, one of which must come from the "primary list" (including passports, military IDs, and adoption papers). For complete listings of required paperwork for all transactions, visit the DMV Web site at www.ct.gov/dmv.*

**Norwalk DMV Office**
**540 Main Avenue, Norwalk**
Tuesday, Wednesday, and
Friday: 8:00 A.M. to 4:30 P.M.
Thursday: 8:00 A.M. to 7:00 P.M.
Saturday: 8:00 A.M. to 12:30 P.M.

## Driver's Licenses

When you move to this area from another state, you must obtain a valid Connecticut Driver's License within 30 days of your arrival. All drivers must be 16 years or older with a completed driver's education course certificate or 18 years or older without a completed course certificate. In addition to the full-service DMV locations listed above, you can also renew your driver's license at a DMV renewal bus or at a photo license center.

**DMV License Renewal Buses**
www.ct.gov/dmv
These mobile renewal stations make stops in Greenwich, Trumbull, and Westport. For complete updated travel schedules, visit the DMV Web site.

**Derby Photo License Center**
**12 Main Street, Derby**
**(Derby is located just outside the county, next to Shelton.)**
Wednesday and Friday:
8:00 A.M. to 5:00 P.M.

ℹ️ *Some local DMV offices have adopted the strange practice of not providing pens for filling out paperwork. If you don't have a pen with you, you'll have to buy one at the office.*

**Stamford DMV Satellite Office**
**888 Washington Boulevard, Sixth Floor**
**Stamford**
Tuesday, Wednesday, and
Friday: 8:00 A.M. to 4:30 P.M.

## TRASH DISPOSAL AND RECYCLING

# Trash Collection

In some locales, such as Stamford, Norwalk, and Stratford, residents of the community enjoy weekly trash pickup as part of their city services. In most towns, however, expect to have one of two choices when it comes to your garbage: You can either take it yourself to the local transfer station (aka "the dump"), or you can hire a private company to haul your trash away from your curb, usually once a week. The majority of towns require a valid resident permit to enter the transfer station. Some charge no fees for residents dropping off a reasonable amount of garbage; others charge a per-pound fee. Almost all charge fees for appliances, extra-large loads, and other heavy-duty disposals. A call to the town hall (see listings later in this chapter) will help you get information about your town's trash pickup—or lack thereof—as well as the specifics about the local transfer station's rules and hours.

If you would prefer to hire a private company, the phone book is chock-full of businesses that would be more than happy to haul away your trash for a yearly fee. It usually helps to talk to your neighbors before hiring someone: If everyone in your neighborhood works with the same company, it often makes sense just to add your house to the already established route. (If a truck has to make a special trip across town just to get to your house, you might find yourself paying higher fees than your neighbors.) In addition, having the same "trash day" as your neighbor can be especially useful if seeing your neighbor's cans at the curb will remind you to set yours out as well.

# Recycling

Currently, Connecticut produces about one ton of trash per person, per year; recycling can help dramatically reduce that output. Recycling can also help reduce your garbage drop-off costs, especially in towns where you pay a per-pound trash fee. Many municipalities, such as Monroe, Norwalk, Stratford, and Stamford, offer curbside recycling. You can also visit recycling centers in Bethel (off of Route 53, Monday, Tuesday, and Thursday); Bridgeport (transfer station on Asylum Street); Darien (126 Ledge Road, permit needed); Fairfield (transfer station at 1 Rod Highway); Redding (Hopewell Woods Road, Monday through Saturday); New Canaan (Volume Reduction Plant on Route 123); New Fairfield (41 Bigelow Road, Tuesday and Saturday); Newtown (Ethan Allen Road, Monday through Saturday); Stratford (Transfer Station on Spring Hill Road); Westport (300 Sherwood Island Road); and Wilton (Transfer Station on Mather Street). For complete information about recycling in your town or city, contact your local town or city hall (see listings later in this chapter).

## TOWN AND CITY HALLS

The county's town and city halls usually contain such offices and departments as the board of education, the comptroller, parks and recreation, health department, board of elections, public works, town clerk, and tax collector. These are the places where you'll get a license for your dog, register to vote, apply for a marriage license, visit elected officials, learn about local zoning restrictions, and perform other vital tasks. If you're not sure which department to contact, call the main number and ask for assistance.

# Southern Fairfield County

**Bridgeport City Hall**
45 Lyon Terrace, Bridgeport
(203) 576-7081

**Darien Town Hall**
2 Renshaw Road, Darien
(203) 656-7300

**Easton Town Hall**
225 Center Road, Easton
(203) 268-6291

**Fairfield Town Hall**
611-725 Old Post Road, Fairfield
(203) 256-3000

**Greenwich Town Hall**
101 Field Point Road, Greenwich
(203) 622-7799

**New Canaan Town Hall**
77 Main Street, New Canaan
(203) 594-3000

**Norwalk City Hall**
125 East Avenue, Norwalk
(203) 854-7746

**Stamford Government Center**
888 Washington Boulevard, Stamford
(203) 977-4140

**Stratford Town Hall**
2725 Main Street, Stratford
(203) 385-4020

**Trumbull Town Hall**
5866 Main Street, Trumbull
(203) 452-5037

**Weston Town Hall**
56 Norfield Road, Weston
(203) 222-2656

**Westport Town Hall**
110 Myrtle Avenue, Westport
(203) 341-1000

**Wilton Town Hall**
238 Danbury Road, Wilton
(203) 563-0100

# Northern Fairfield County

**Bethel Municipal Center**
1 School Street, Bethel
(203) 794-8501

**Brookfield Town Hall**
Pocono Road, Brookfield
(203) 775-3087

**Danbury City Hall**
155 Deer Hill Avenue, Danbury
(203) 797-4500

**Mallory Town Hall**
9 Route 39 North, Sherman
(203) 355-1139

**Monroe Town Hall**
7 Fan Hill Road, Monroe
(203) 452-5421

**New Fairfield Town Hall**
4 Brush Hill Road, New Fairfield
(203) 312-5616

*To register to vote, visit your local town or city hall or use a mail-in registration form. The forms are available at all local libraries, DMV offices, and Armed Forces recruitment offices.*

Newtown Town Hall
45 Main Street, Newtown
(203) 270-4200

Redding Town Hall
Route 107, 100 Hill Road, Redding
(203) 938-2002

Ridgefield Town Hall
400 Main Street, Ridgefield
(203) 431-2783

Shelton City Hall
54 Hill Street, Shelton
(203) 924-1555

## U.S. POST OFFICES

# Southern Fairfield County

The U.S. Postal Service has branches throughout southern Fairfield County: Bridgeport (2253 Fairfield Avenue, 2741 Main Street, 120 Middle Street, and 934 East Main Street); Darien (30 Corbin Drive and 140 Heights Road); Easton (295 Center Road); Fairfield (357 Commerce Drive, 402 Pequot Avenue, and 1262 Post Road); Greenwich (152 East Putnam Avenue, 29 Valley Drive, 310 Greenwich Avenue, and 25 Glen Ridge Road); New Canaan (2 Pine Street); Norwalk (2 Belden Avenue, 16 Washington Street, 144 Rowayton Avenue, and 190 East Avenue); Stamford (421 Atlantic Street, 24 Camp Avenue, 370 Hope Street, 79 Atlantic Street, 60 Sixth Street, 320 Shippan Avenue, 427 West Avenue, and 1 Barry Place); Stratford (3100 Main Street and 411 Barnum Avenue Cutoff); Trumbull (50 Quality Street); Weston (190 Weston Road); Westport (154 Post Road East, 615 Riverside Avenue, and 4 Post Office Lane); and Wilton (15 Hubbard Road).

# Northern Fairfield County

In the northern end of the county, look for these U.S. Post Office locations: Bethel (10 Library Place); Brookfield (115 Pocono Road); Danbury (23 Backus Avenue and 265 Main Street); Monroe (270 Monroe Turnpike); New Fairfield (7 Brush Hill Road); Newtown (1 Botsford Hill Road and 5 Commerce Road); Redding (268 Simpaug Turnpike, 63 Redding Road, 10 Lonetown Road, and 109 Black Rock Turnpike); Ridgefield (26 Catoonah Street); Shelton (41 Church Street and 83 Bridge Street); and Sherman (29 Route 37).

## LIBRARIES

# Southern Fairfield County

Bridgeport Public Library
925 Broad Street, Bridgeport
(203) 576-7777

Darien Library
35 Leroy Avenue, Darien
(203) 655-1234

Easton Public Library
691 Morehouse Road, Easton
(203) 261-0134

Fairfield Public Library
1080 Old Post Road, Fairfield
(203) 256-3155

ℹ️ *The Connecticut Infoline provides a wealth of information about state services and programs such as Alcoholics Anonymous, elder assistance, child care, counseling, volunteering, transportation assistance, lawyer referrals, suicide prevention, food pantries, blood donation, support groups, and much more. To reach the Infoline, simply dial 211.*

Greenwich Library
101 West Putnam Avenue, Greenwich
(203) 622-7900

New Canaan Library
151 Main Street, New Canaan
(203) 594-5000

Norwalk Public Library
1 Belden Avenue, Norwalk
(203) 899-2780

Stamford Public Library (Ferguson Library)
1 Public Library Plaza, Stamford
(203) 964-1000
Other branches:
South End Branch, 34 Woodland Avenue
Weed Branch, 1143 Hope Street
Harry Bennett Branch, 115 Vine Road

Stratford Library Association
2203 Main Street, Stratford
(203) 385-4161

Trumbull Library
33 Quality Street, Trumbull
(203) 452-5197

Weston Public Library
56 Norfield Road, Weston
(203) 222-BOOK

Westport Public Library
Arnold Bernhard Plaza
20 Jesup Road, Westport
(203) 291-4840

Wilton Library Association
137 Old Ridgefield Road, Wilton
(203) 762-3950

# Northern Fairfield County

Bethel Public Library
189 Greenwood Avenue, Bethel
(203) 794-8756

Brookfield Library
182 Whisconier Road, Brookfield
(203) 775-6241

C. H. Booth Library
25 Main Street, Newtown
(203) 426-4533

Danbury Public Library
170 Main Street, Danbury
(203) 797-4505

Mark Twain Public Library
Route 53 and Diamond Hill Road
Redding
(203) 938-2545

Monroe Library
7 Fan Hill Road, Monroe
(203) 452-5458

New Fairfield Public Library
2 Brush Hill Road, New Fairfield
(203) 312-5679

Plumb Memorial Library
65 Wooster Street, Shelton
(203) 924-1580

Ridgefield Library
472 Main Street, Ridgefield
(203) 438-2282

Sherman Library
1 Sherman Center, Sherman
(860) 354-2455

# CHAMBERS OF COMMERCE

Bridgeport Regional Business Council
10 Middle Street
P.O. Box 999, Bridgeport 06601
(203) 335-3800

Danbury Chamber of Commerce
39 West Street, Danbury
(203) 743-5565

Darien Chamber of Commerce
17 Old Kings Highway, Darien
(203) 655-3600

Fairfield Chamber of Commerce
1597 Post Road, Fairfield
(203) 255-1011

Greater Norwalk Chamber of Commerce
P.O. Box 668, Norwalk 06856
(203) 866-2521

Greater Valley Chamber of Commerce
900 Bridgeport Avenue, Shelton
(203) 925-4981

Greenwich Chamber of Commerce
21 West Putnam Avenue, Greenwich
(203) 869-3502

Monroe Chamber of Commerce
477 Main Street, Monroe
(203) 268-3337

Newtown Chamber of Commerce
P.O. Box 314, Newtown 06470
(203) 426-2695

Ridgefield Chamber of Commerce
9 Bailey Avenue, Ridgefield
(203) 438-5992

Southwestern Area Commerce and
Industry Association
1 Landmark Square, Stamford
(203) 359-3220

Trumbull Chamber of Commerce
571 Church Hill Road, Trumbull
(203) 261-4533

Westport Chamber of Commerce
60 Church Lane, Westport
(203) 227-9234

Wilton Chamber of Commerce
211 Town Green, Wilton
(203) 762-0567

# EDUCATION

Connecticut consistently ranks among the top in the nation for educational assessments, often joining Massachusetts, New Hampshire, and New Jersey to earn the highest overall rankings for test scores, graduation rates, percentage of students going on to college, and quality of educational institutions. And although disparities still exist among lower income students, females, and minorities, the fact remains that there are few better spots in America to send your child to school.

Fairfield County parents value that advantage. Many are willing to pay a premium for housing in places like Newtown, Greenwich, Weston, and Ridgefield in order to access the towns' much-touted school systems. Local schools offer more Advanced Placement courses than others in the nation, and local students tend to earn higher scores on AP tests than students in most other states. About 80 percent of all Connecticut teachers have a master's degree or higher level of education. In addition, the rate of absenteeism is low, one computer is available for every 4.7 public-school students, and the National Center for Public Policy recently gave Connecticut a perfect score of 100 for its methods of preparing high-school students for college.

Unfortunately, some local schools are having a harder time keeping up than others. In 2001–2002 the Connecticut Department of Education identified 38 school districts in the state as "not making adequate yearly progress." Six of those districts were located in Fairfield County—Bridgeport, Danbury, Norwalk, Stamford, Stratford, and Westport (Bedford Middle School only). In some cases, only some of the schools in a district were identified as lacking. The assessment was based on the results of the 2002 Connecticut Mastery Test, required by the new No Child Left Behind legislation. It is perhaps not surprising that most of the lower test scores were found in cities with high population densities and a lower overall income level—both of which too frequently combine to create overcrowded classrooms and overburdened districts. The state is currently researching ways to make education more equitable throughout all regions. As it stands now, however, the Fairfield County disparity between school spending in wealthy and poor districts ranks as one of the widest in the United States.

The state Department of Education frowns upon pitting districts against one another with "rankings," so no list exists to compare the schools from town to town. But local residents—and real estate agents—certainly have their own opinions about which town and city schools rate the best. Although it's impossible to make generalizations about such a complex topic as education, a glace at housing prices in each town will give you an idea about which contain the most sought-after schools. That said, however, great teachers and motivated administrators exist in even the most poorly funded schools, as do parents who are willing to do what it takes to improve their child's classroom experiences.

And for those parents who don't want to limit their choices to the public schools (no matter what town or city they live in), the region also offers a larger-than-usual selection of private high schools, day schools, prep schools, and academies. Some of the schools are affiliated with a religious denomination; others promise smaller classroom size, a more diverse student body, more individualized attention for each child, school uniforms, advanced academic programs, and a wide array of extracurricular activities. Tuition costs vary from school to school.

A popular alternative to conventional public schools is the burgeoning magnet-school system, which emphasizes a diverse student body and specialized instruction. In most cases, the school's students are equally divided along racial, economic, and gender lines, coming from neighborhoods in the cities as well as the suburbs. Although regional magnet schools are public, parents must use a lottery system to try and gain entry. Typically the schools receive twice as many applications as they can accommodate: If you're determined to have your child attend a magnet, it pays to be persistent. In addition to the magnet schools listed in this chapter, many county towns and cities have plans to open more magnet schools in the near future.

The county's colleges and universities, including two community colleges, three private universities, and two state universities, attract local high-school students as well as students from other areas of the country and the world. Local working adults often take advantage of the schools' night classes, seminars, and cultural programs to enrich their professional abilities, pursue a new career, or simply learn a new skill. From preschool to graduate school and beyond, Fairfield County's educational systems seem to have the three R's covered.

## PUBLIC SCHOOLS

# Southern Fairfield County

### BRIDGEPORT

This large and diverse school district encompasses 45 schools that serve students from a wide variety of ethnic and socioeconomic backgrounds. The city supports 18 elementary schools, 12 middle schools, and 5 high schools. Students will also find an Alternative Education high school, an Aquaculture School, two voca-

tional-technical schools, five magnet schools, and even a high school that specializes in preparatory education for health careers.

### DARIEN

Darien children start out their school careers at one of five elementary schools: Hindley, Holmes, Ox Ridge, Royle, and Tokeneke. The town's Middlesex Middle School serves students before they move on to Darien High School, home of the "Blue Wave." New construction, scheduled to be completed in 2005, will provide the town with a brand-new high school building. A continuing education program allows older members of the community to pursue educational interests.

### EASTON

This rural town offers two public schools: Samuel Staples Elementary, which boasts a computer lab, a media center, and music and fine-arts specialists; and Helen Keller Middle School, which has a diverse curriculum and a wide variety of extracurricular activities and special programs. Easton students in grades 9 through 12 attend Joel Barlow High School in the neighboring town of Redding (see listing below in Northern Fairfield County).

### FAIRFIELD

Dwight, Holland Hill, Jennings, McKinley, Mill Hill, Osborn Hill, Riverfield, Roger Sherman, and Stratfield are the public elementary schools supported by the town of Fairfield. As students get older, they move on to one of three middle schools: Fairfield Woods, Roger Ludlowe, or Tomlinson. Fairfield High School offers a curriculum that includes advanced learning courses, business education, family and consumer science, independent studies, and even a student-run restaurant.

### GREENWICH

Greenwich has a multitude of public elementary schools and preschools, including

Cos Cob School, Glenville, Greenwich Public Preschool, Hamilton Avenue School, Julian Curtiss, New Lebanon, North Mianus, North Street School, Old Greenwich School, Parkway, and Riverside. Central, Eastern, and Western Middle Schools serve students before they all move on to Greenwich High School, which serves more than 2,600 students in grades 9 to 12.

## NEW CANAAN

In addition to offering several private schools, New Canaan has a public school system with the East, South, and West Elementary Schools; Saxe Middle School; and New Canaan High School. The curriculum at all schools includes a focus on math, science, technical education, assessment, language arts, health and physical education, social studies, foreign languages, special education, and the arts.

## NORWALK

The city of Norwalk has a big educational system, encompassing 18 schools. In the elementary arena, students will find themselves learning the three R's at Brookside, Columbus, Cranbury, Fox Run, Jefferson, Kendall, Marvin, Naramake, Silvermine, Tracey, and Wolfpit. The city also offers four middle schools—Nathan Hale, Ponus Ridge, Roton, and West Rocks—as well as three high schools: Brien McMahon, Briggs, and Norwalk High. The Columbus Magnet School also serves local students.

## STAMFORD

Stamford has good representation of both private and public schools to serve its thousands of students. In the public forum, options include the William Pitt Child Development Center (a preschool), 12 elementary schools (including 4 magnets), 5 middle schools (including 1 magnet), 2 high schools, and the Academy of Information Technology—a "prodigy" high school for students interested in specializing in technology, architecture, engineering, or digital arts.

## STRATFORD

The Stratford public school system includes two high schools, Frank Scott Bunnell High and Stratford High, as well as two middle schools, Harry B. Flood and David Wooster. For the little ones, nine elementary schools fill the academic need: Center, Chapel Street, Franklin, Lordship, Nichols, Second Hill Lane, Stratford Academy (a magnet school), Eli Whitney, and Wilcoxson. A variety of district programs include Saturday Academy, ALPHA (for students with special needs), and technology classrooms.

*The Stratford School for Aviation Maintenance Technicians takes full advantage of its town's rich aviation history. The vocational school is located at Sikorsky Memorial Airport and offers a 30-month Aircraft Maintenance Technician certification program as well as a 20-month Aircraft Electronic Technician program. For more information call (203) 381–9250 or visit www.cttech.org/ssamt.*

## TRUMBULL

Trumbull's children start their academic careers at one of six elementary schools: Booth Hill, Daniels Farm, Frenchtown, Jane Ryan, Middlebrook, or Tashua. Students then move on to either Hillcrest or Madison Middle School, and all eventually end up at Trumbull High. The town employs about 450 teachers and administrators to educate the approximately 6,000 children in the school system.

## WESTON

For residents of this bucolic town, school choices are simple: Each Weston child attends Hurlbutt Elementary, then Weston Middle School, then Weston High School. The current Building Plan for the town includes new construction and renovations at the high school, a new auditorium for the middle school, and construction of a new elementary school in the near future.

## WESTPORT

Westport offers four elementary schools for its youngest students: Coleytown, Greens Farms, Kings Highway, and Long Lots. Middle school–age children attend Coleytown Middle School and then move on to Staples High School in the ninth grade. At the time of this writing, overcrowding conditions in the high school had led to the planning of major renovations to the current site. The new school will be expanded to three stories but keep the pool, gym, field house, music wing, and auditorium intact.

*One of the hottest topics in local education is school overcrowding. As Fairfield County towns become more popular and new housing developments continue to appear, many districts are finding themselves facing a dilemma: Build more public schools, expand current schools, or make do with more crowded classrooms? Watch for the controversial topic to continue to dominate school board and budget meetings in the near future.*

## WILTON

In the town of Wilton, children in kindergarten through grade 2 attend either the Tilford W. Miller School or the Ina E. Driscoll School. The Cider Mill School serves students in grades 3 through 5; the Middlebrook School provides education for grades 6 through 8. From grade 9 on, all students attend Wilton High School, where they'll find courses in business, math, health, social studies, consumer and life sciences, fine arts, foreign language, science, English, and technology.

# Northern Fairfield County

## BETHEL

Bethel parents send their youngest students to one of three elementary schools: Berry, Johnson, and Rockwell. Bethel Middle School and Bethel High School serve all the town's older children. The high school's departments include mathematics, technology education, languages, science, social studies, English, and health. The sports and student activities departments provide a range of extracurricular activities.

## BROOKFIELD

Brookfields High School (home of the Bobcats) offers a media center, an athletics department, computer labs, and a varied educational curriculum. The town also offers one middle school, Whisconier, and one elementary school, Huckleberry Hill. Center School, located in a historic building that is the only remaining all-wooden school in Connecticut, serves children in preschool, kindergarten, and first grade.

## DANBURY

The Danbury school system is the largest in the northern part of the county, offering 13 elementary schools, 2 middle schools (Broadview and Rogers Park), and the large Danbury High School. In addition, the city supports an Alternative High School, Henry Abbott Vocational-Technical School, a institution that provides traditional coursework as well as training in subjects like culinary arts, electronics, carpentry, automotive mechanics, and cosmetology.

## MONROE

The relatively small town of Monroe nonetheless has three elementary schools (Fawn Hollow, Monroe Elementary, and Stepney Elementary) as well as two middle schools (Chalk Hill and Jockey Hollow). All students join together in ninth grade at Masuk High School, named for the donor who originally provided the building site. The high school enrolls approximately 1,250 pupils, with classes in science, languages, business, social studies, and other areas.

## NEW FAIRFIELD

All New Fairfield students progress together through a series of schools, starting with the Consolidated School for kindergarteners, first-graders, and second-graders. The Meeting House Hill School serves children in grades 3 through 5; students then move on to New Fairfield Middle School and finally New Fairfield High School. During the 2003–2004 school year, New Fairfield High enrolled a total of 915 students.

## NEWTOWN

Newtown High School's updated facilities, academics, and athletics are well respected in the region. Students at the school participate in Cooperative Work Experience Program, choose from a variety of extracurricular activities, and more often than not go on to attend two- and four-year colleges. The town also offers Newtown Middle School, the Reed Intermediate School, and four elementary schools: Hawley, Head O'Meadow, Middle Gate, and Sandy Hook.

## REDDING

Redding is a spread-out, rural community with one elementary school, Redding Elementary; one middle school, John Read; and one high school, Joel Barlow. At the high school, Redding students join up with those from Easton for classes in chemistry, art, environmental biology, writing, and a variety of other subjects. The school also offers a media center, special-education programs, athletics, and extracurricular activities like the Acapella Choir, Fencing Club, and Photo Club.

## RIDGEFIELD

Ridgefield High is a large, well-regarded facility near the New York border, offering a plethora of academic, athletic, and extracurricular programs. Before enrolling at the high school, students attend East Ridge or Scotts Ridge Middle School and one of six elementary schools: Barlow Mountain, Branchville, Farmingville, Ridgebury, Scotland, or Veteran's Park. Continuing education programs are offered for Ridgefield's adult learners.

## SHELTON

This town has no shortage of elementary schools, offering seven in all: Booth Hill, Elizabeth Shelton, Lafayette, Long Hill, Mohegan, Ripton, and Sunnyside. After finishing up the early grades, students attend the Shelton Intermediate School and then Shelton High School. Shelton High's departments include science, languages, English, business education, mathematics, art, technology education, and social studies.

## SHERMAN

The tiny town of Sherman supports one school, called the Sherman School, which encompasses all the elementary and middle school grades. Representative courses include music, art, writing, science, Spanish, and mathematics. When they reach the ninth grade, students are free to attend any high school in the state, although most opt for one of two nearby high schools in New Fairfield and New Milford.

# PRIVATE SCHOOLS

# Southern Fairfield County

## BRIDGEPORT

Kolbe Cathedral High School, a Catholic coed school serving about 315 students

(33 Calhoun Place; 203-335-2554), is an option for private education in Bridgeport. Parents might also want to consider the Bridge Academy (P.O. Box 2267, Bridgeport 06608; 203-336-9999). Although it is public, the academy is a charter high school and accepts students by a lottery method.

## DARIEN

Parents looking for a private school in Darien can explore their options at the Pear Tree Point School, a day school serving students in kindergarten through fifth grade (90 Pear Tree Point Road; 203-655-0030; www.ptpschool.org).

## FAIRFIELD

Parents can choose from a huge variety of private schools in Fairfield, including these: Eagle Hill, a coed school serving children ages 6 to 16 with learning disabilities (Main Street; 203-254-2044; www.eaglehillsouthport.org); Fairfield College Preparatory School, affiliated with Fairfield University (1073 North Benson Road; 203-254-4200; www.prep.fairfield.edu); Fairfield Country Day School, a boys' prep school encompassing kindergarten through grade 9 (2970 Bronson Road; 203-259-2723; www.fairfieldcountryday.org); Hillel Academy, a Hebrew day school (1571 Stratfield Road; 203-374-6147; www.hillelacedemy.org); Holy Family School, a Catholic facility for children in preschool through grade 8 (140 Edison Road; 203-367-5409); Notre Dame High School, a coed Catholic high school (220 Jefferson Street; 203-372-6521; www.notredame.org); Our Lady of the Assumption, a regional Catholic school (545 Stratfield Road; 203-333-9065); Phoenix Academy, a coed school for kindergartern through grade 8 (834 Brookside Drive; 203-254-1134; www.phoenixacademy.org); St. Thomas Aquinas, a Roman Catholic school serving students in kindergarten through grade 8 (1719 Post Road; 203-255-0556); and Unquowa School, the oldest coed day school in Connecticut (981 Stratfield Road; 203-336-3801; www.unquowa.com).

## GREENWICH

In addition to its highly regarded public schools, Greenwich also offers these private school choices: Brunswick School, a boys preparatory school (100 Maher Avenue; 203-625-5800; www.brunswickschool.org); Convent of the Sacred Heart, a girls' Catholic school (1177 King Street; 203-531-6500; www.cshgreenwich.org); Eagle Hill School, which accepts students ages 6 to 13 with diagnosed learning disabilities (45 Glenville Road; 203-622-9240); Greenwich Academy, a prep school for girls in kindergarten though grade 12 (200 North Maple Avenue; 203-625-8900; www.greenwichacademy.org); Greenwich Catholic School, a coed day school (471 North Street; 203-869-4000; www.greenwichcatholicschool.org); Greenwich Country Day School, a coed program serving children in preschool through grade 9 (P.O. Box 623, Greenwich 06836; 203-863-5600; www.greenwichcds.org); Greenwich Japanese School (15 Ridgeway; 203-629-9039; www.gwjs.org); the Stanwich School, an independent coed day school (257 Stanwich Road; 203-869-4515; www.stanwichschool.org); and the Whitby School, a Montessori elementary school (969 Lake Avenue; 203-869-8464; www.whitbyschool.org). At the time of this writing, a new private school, the Downtown School, was scheduled to open in 2004 on Greenwich Street.

## NEW CANAAN

New Canaan is home to three private schools: New Canaan Country Day School, a coed school for children in preschool through grade 9 (545 Ponus Ridge; 203-972-0771; www.nccs.pvt.k12.ct.us); St. Aloysius School, a regional Catholic facility (33 South Avenue; 203-966-0786); and St. Luke's School, a coed institution for grades 5 through 12 (377 North Wilton Road; 203-966-5612; www.stlukesct.org).

## NORWALK

Local parents looking for private schools in Norwalk will find All Saints Catholic School (139 West Rocks Road; 203-847-3881; www.ascs.net) and the Parkway Christian Academy (260 New Canaan Avenue; 203-847-9566). Another option is the the Side-by-Side Community School, a public charter school striving for diversity with students in preschool through grade 8 (203-857-0306; www.sidebysideschool.org).

## STAMFORD

Stamford's private educational institutions include the Bi-Cultural Day School, a school for Jewish students (2186 High Ridge Road; 203-329-2186; www.bcds.org); the J. M. Wright Regional Vocational-Technical School (P.O. Box 1416, Stamford 06904; 203-324-7363; www.cttech.org); King & Low-Heywood Thomas School, a coed day school for kindergarteners through high-school seniors (1450 New-field Avenue; 203-322-3496; www.klht.org); Sacred Heart Academy, a prep school for girls (200 Strawberry Hill Avenue; 203-323-3173; www.shastamford.org); the Children's School, a primary school for ages 3 through 8 (12 Gary Road; 203-329-8815; www.childrensschool.org); Long Ridge School, a coed program for children age 2 through grade 5 (478 Erksine Road; 203-322-7693; www.longridgeschool.org); and the Mead School, which serves children in preschool through grade 12 (1095 Riverbank Road; 203-595-9500; www.meadschool.com).

## STRATFORD

The two private schools located in Stratford are the St. James Regional School, a Catholic regional school for kindergarten through grade 8 (1 Monument Place; 203-375-5994; www.stjamesstratford.org), and St. Mark School, a Catholic regional school (500 Wigwam Lane; 203-375-4291; www.stmarkschool.org).

## TRUMBULL

Nonpublic schools in Trumbull include the Christian Heritage School, a coed day school with 550 students (575 White Plains Road; 203-261-6230; www.kingsmen.org); St. Catherine of Siena, a private elementary school (190 Shelton Road; 203-375-1947; www.student.stcatherineschool.org); St. Joseph High School, a Roman Catholic prep school (2320 Huntington Turnpike; 203-378-9378); and St. Teresa School, a Catholic program for children in preschool through grade 8 (55 Rosemond Terrace; 203-268-3236).

## WESTPORT

Greens Farms Academy, a coed preparatory day school, is one of Westport's private educational options (35 Beachside Avenue; 203-256-0717; www.gfacademy.org). The other is the Hall-Brooke School, a small alternative learning center for students in grades 4 through 12 (47 Long Lots Road; 203-227-1251).

## WILTON

Private school options in Wilton include Connecticut Friends School, a Quaker school for children in kindergarten through grade 8 (317 New Canaan Road; 203-762-9860; www.ctfriendsschool.org); Our Lady of Fatima Regional School, a Catholic school for children in kindergarten through grade 8 (225 Danbury Road; 203-762-8100; www.olfrs.org); and the Wilton Montessori School (34 Whipple Road; 203-834-0440).

# Northern Fairfield County

## DANBURY

The city of Danbury provides local residents with multiple private schools, including Immaculate High School, a coed Catholic facility (73 Southern Boulevard;

203-744-1510; www.immaculatehs.org);
Maimonides Academy of Western Connecticut, a Jewish day school (103 Miry
Brook Road; 203-748-7129; www.mawc
school.org); New Hope Christian Academy,
an outreach program of Bright Clouds Min-
istries (18 Clapboard Ridge Road; 203-
798-1553; www.brightclouds.org); St.
Joseph School, a Catholic school serving
kindergarten through grade 8 (370 Main
Street; 203-748-6615); the St. Peter School,
a Roman Catholic facility with a preschool
and eight grades (98 Main Street; 203-
748-2895); and Wooster School, a coed
school offering academics for children in
kindergarten through grade 12.

## NEWTOWN

Newtown's private schools include the
Frasier-Woods School, a program for students in preschool through grade 8 formerly known as the Newtown Montessori
School (173 Main Street; 203-426-3390;
www.fraserwoods.com), and the St. Rose
School, a Christian school for students in
kindergarten through grade 8 (40 Church
Hill Road; 203-426-5102; www.strose
school.com).

## RIDGEFIELD

The town of Ridgefield offers two private-
school facilities: Ridgefield Academy, a
coed school for children in preschool
through grade 8 (223A West Mountain
Road; 203-894-1800; www.ridgefield
academy.com), and St. Mary's School, a
regional Catholic high school (183 High
Ridge Avenue; 203-438-7288).

## SHELTON

In addition to its many public schools,
Shelton is home to one private school: St.
Joseph's School, which serves children in
kindergarten through grade 8 (420 Coram
Avenue; 203-924-9677).

# COLLEGES AND UNIVERSITIES

**Fairfield University**
**1073 North Benson Road, Fairfield**
**(203) 254-4000**
**www.fairfield.edu**
One of two higher education institutions
located in the town of Fairfield, Fairfield
University is a private Jesuit university
enrolling about 3,000 undergraduates and
1,000 graduate students each semester.
The school attracts local students, those
from other parts of the country, and international students with a 200-acre campus, eight dorms, apartments, and
financial aid programs. Fairfield's six colleges—Dolan School of Business, School
of Nursing, School of Engineering, University College, College of Arts and Sciences,
and the Graduate School of Education
and Allied Professions—offer more than 33
majors, including mechanical engineering,
communication, accounting, marine science, history, psychology, finance, computer engineering, nursing, marketing,
chemistry, and education. The school's
sports facilities support 19 varsity teams
playing at the Division I level. The on-site
Regina A. Quick Center for the Arts offers
two theaters and an art gallery for students and other community members.

**Housatonic Community**
**Technical College**
**900 Lafayette Boulevard, Bridgeport**
**(203) 332-5000**
**www.hctc.commnet.ed**
Accredited by the New England Association of Schools, Housatonic Community
College offers a wide variety of majors
and degree programs as well as noncredit
continuing education classes, seminars,
and forums for the general public.
Courses of study include management,
graphic design, human services, accounting, journalism, computer science, mathe-

matics, business administration, nursing, clinical laboratory sciences, and theater arts. Certificate programs are also available in criminal justice, business office technology, business administration, graphic design, and other areas. The downtown campus provides students with a library, a bookstore, computer labs, classrooms, art galleries, and a cafeteria. The school's Academic Support Center adds to the academic experience at Housatonic by providing tutoring services, study groups, a writing center, and disability support services.

### Norwalk Community Technical College
### 188 Richards Avenue, Norwalk
### (203) 857-7000
### www.nctc.commnet.edt

Often simply called Norwalk Community College, or NCC, this small but academically diverse school has eight departments: Engineering and Technology, Allied Health, Computer/Information Systems, Liberal Arts, Education and Social Science, Business, Communication Arts, and General Studies. Some students arrive here directly from high school; others return years later to freshen up their skills and learn new ones. Some programs of study include computer science, archaeology, culinary arts, marketing, criminal justice, accounting, education, and nursing. Students can also take advantage of NCC's Career Center, library, bookstore, financial aid programs, computer labs, Women's Center, and job-training programs. The school's new Center for Information Technology is home to the newest course of study: the Computer Security Institute and Degree Program.

### Sacred Heart University
### 5151 Park Avenue, Fairfield
### (203) 371-7999
### www.sacredheart.edu

Approximately 6,000 students from near and far enroll each year at Sacred Heart, a private Catholic University. The school offers 42 undergraduate and graduate degree programs in its College of Educa-

tion and Professions, College of Business, College of Arts and Sciences, and University College. Courses of study at Sacred Heart include sports management, computer science, English literature, nursing, economics, education, accounting, occupational therapy, biochemistry, criminal justice, illustration, psychology, environmental science, Spanish, media studies, sociology, and mathematics. For those who prefer to live on campus, dormitories and apartments provide a home away from home. Students can also join some of the 70 clubs and organizations on campus and cheer on one of the university's Division 1 athletic teams. Other university offerings include the Institute for Religious Education and Pastoral Studies, the Center for Christian-Jewish Understanding, the Edgerton Center for the Performing Arts, and the Gallery of Contemporary Art. Study-abroad programs and internships are also available to interested students.

### University of Bridgeport
### 126 Park Avenue, Bridgeport
### (203) 576-4552
### www.bridgeport.edu

More than one-third of the University of Bridgeport's students come from overseas locations, a statistic that has led the school to declare itself "America's most international university." The school's 26 undergraduate majors include such courses of study as industrial design, computer engineering, public relations, music education, history, journalism,

*The Fairfield County business community and local college students often work together by creating internships, work-study programs, and similar arrangements that can benefit both parties. To learn more, contact the individual departments (such as journalism, business management, or engineering) at each school, or call the main administrative telephone number and ask about internship or student-work programs.*

*The University of Bridgeport is owned by none other than the Reverend Sun Myung Moon of the Unification Church (known as the "Moonies" to nonmembers). The Unification Church's reputation and the school's large population of foreign students has led some locals to worry that the university is nothing more than a "cult" recruitment station designed to promote Moon's message. The conspiracy theories, however, remain pure speculation.*

dental hygiene, business administration, accounting, psychology, and biology. Master's degrees are also available in business administration, electrical engineering, human nutrition, and nine other subjects. On the doctoral level, students can pursue naturopathic medicine, chiropractic medicine, and education leadership. The campus experience includes four dormitories, a health center, a career center, a counseling center, a student congress, numerous student activities and clubs, an athletics program, and an interfaith center.

**University of Connecticut—Stamford Campus**
**1 University Place, Stamford**
**(203) 251–8400**
**www.stamford.uconn.edu**
Best known as UConn Stamford, this satellite campus of the University of Connecticut (based in Storrs) gives local residents the chance to take advantage of many of the large university's academic programs. The downtown "commuter" school offers bachelor's degrees in history, psychology, business administration, English, economics, sociology, political science, and general studies. MBA degrees are offered at the graduate level. Students can start a course of study in more than 90 other subjects at the Stamford campus and finish up their degree at the main campus in Storrs.

**Western Connecticut State University**
**181 White Street, Danbury**
**(203) 837–9411**
**www.wcsu.edu**
WestConn's dorms, athletic facilities, and classroom buildings are spread throughout two campuses in Danbury: the "main" Midtown Campus in the White Street area and the Westside Campus near exit 4 off I–84. The school has plenty of commuter students as well as those who live on-site while studying biology, social work, accounting, music, computer science, theater arts, comparative literature, management, history, physics, art, marketing, environmental science, nursing, and finance. An extensive athletics department supports football, soccer, volleyball, basketball, and other teams for women and men. For working adults and other nontraditional students, the university provides a good selection of evening classes as well as noncredit courses, seminars, and programs. Students can also take advantage of a career development center, health services, a counseling center, computer labs, a bookstore, media services, libraries, student centers, a child-care center, the Westside Nature Preserve, summer music programs, and financial aid. Study-abroad programs in London are also available.

# CHILD CARE

First, the good news: Connecticut ranks among the best in the nation when it comes to the quality of child care. In addition, Fairfield County offers myriad choices for parents seeking in-home care and day-care centers. All that quality doesn't come without cost, however. Child care is usually the most expensive aspect of raising children, an adventure that has never been cheap to begin with. And as more and more local households contain single parents or two working parents, more families are finding themselves in need of outside help when it comes to keeping an eye on the kids.

Experts suggest investigating child-care centers as soon as possible—even during pregnancy. Some of the more popular centers have waiting lists, so the sooner you make a decision, the sooner you'll be able to secure a spot. And if you do find yourself on a wait list, expect to pay some kind of deposit. More often than not, centers charge more for infant care than they do for the care of older children.

Child-care choices in the region primarily include day care, half-day preschools, full-day preschools, sitters, nannies, and au pairs. In-home caregivers, like au pairs and nannies, are the most convenient—and most expensive—option for parents. Au pairs generally hail from foreign countries, although most are required to speak English. The families that use their services are called "host families." Nannies are more typically Americans who care for their employers' children while living in the house full-time. Day-care centers and preschools, the most common types of child care, are also the most economical options. Parents using these centers drop their children off in the morning and pick them up at a designated time later in the day.

No matter which style of child care you choose, it is crucial that you request a tour of the facility and gather as much information as possible before signing up for any service. A listing in this chapter is not tantamount to a recommendation; for more detailed information about a company, including its past history and possible infractions, contact the Better Business Bureau (203-269-2700; www.connecticut.bbb.org) or the Connecticut Department of Public Health's Childcare Licensing Agency (860-509-8045).

## NANNIES AND AU PAIRS

**Absolute Best Care**
**Serving Connecticut, New York, New Jersey, and Pennsylvania**
**(212) 481-5705**
**www.absolutebestcare.com**
This agency helps families find nannies, babysitters, and newborn-care specialists throughout Connecticut, New York, New Jersey, and Pennsylvania. Clients can choose from full-time live-in help, full-time live-out help, or part-time assistance. Baby nurses specialize in caring for all types of newborns, including colicky infants, twins, triplets, and premature babies. The agency also has a large pool of babysitters and home-care companions, all of whom come with references.

**Adele Poston Domestic Agency**
**16 East 79th Street, New York, NY**
**(212) 879-7474**
**www.adelepostonagency.com**
Based in Manhattan, the Adele Poston agency matches clients with service professionals such as au pairs, nannies, governesses, babysitters, mother's helpers, chefs, chauffeurs, baby nurses, social secretaries, housekeepers, and butlers. All recommended professionals are screened and are fluent in English.

## All About Nannies Family Connection
**Serving Fairfield and Westchester Counties**
**(800) 269-9067**
www.allaboutnannies.net

Clients and nannies working with this agency meet and mutually agree to work together before any contracts are signed. Nannies typically perform such duties as housekeeping, child care, running errands, visiting the park, and helping with homework. Before being hired, a nanny must produce references and proof of American citizenship; most come from Utah and are placed in southwestern Fairfield County or Westchester County homes.

## Connecticut Cares Nanny Referral
**P.O. Box 11, Ivoryton 06442**
**(860) 227-2843**

This agency serves the whole state, providing full- and part-time and live-in and live-out home help workers. The referral service guarantees a placement of at least 90 days, interviews and screens each candidate, and conducts background checks on all applicants. Most nannies perform household duties and assume primary child-care duties.

## Cultural Care Au Pair
**1 Cultural Education Street**
**Cambridge, MA**
**(800) 333-6056**
www.efaupair.org

Au pair clients, called host families, can use Cultural Au Pair to locate a full-time child care professional for their home. Some just help out during summer; others stay year-round. Many come from countries other than the United States, including Argentina, Germany, New Zealand, Chile, Italy, Mexico and Lithuania.

## EurAuPair
**210 North Lee Street, Alexandria, VA**
**(800) 901-2002**
www.euraupair.com

Like au pairs at other agencies, those working through EurAuPair are usually young adults from foreign countries who are hoping to trade their services for a chance to live in and explore the United States. All the au pair professionals are considered "live-in," meaning the family provides room and board in addition to a salary. Host families are free to choose whichever professional they feel most comfortable with.

## Family Extensions
**45 Grove Street, New Canaan**
**(203) 966-9944**
www.familyextensions.com

Family Extensions specializes in matching client families with nannies. Some nannies live with the host family; others live outside the home but work full-time or part-time or even just during the summer season. Nannies are screened and come with references and a high-school diploma or equivalency certificate. Host families are expected to provide room and board (when applicable), a salary, contributions toward medical benefits, and a written job description.

## Hometown Nannies Plus
**125 Main Street, Westport**
**(203) 227-3924**

The carefully screened live-in nannies employed by Hometown Nannies are usually between 22 and 55 years of age an enjoy paid vacations, salaries with benefits, room and board, and use of the host family's car. Families can also opt for part-time of live-out nannies. All are high-school graduates, English speaking, nonsmoking, have good driving records, and are certified in CPR.

---

*Westport is home to the Saugatuck Outreach Nutrition Program, a nonprofit that helps child-care providers offer nutritious meals to the children in their care. Providers who qualify can be reimbursed for the cost of food. For more information call (203) 221–0853.*

---

**Katie Facey Agency**
**15 East Putnam Avenue, Greenwich**
**(203) 547-6188**
With locations in Greenwich, Beverly Hills, and McLean, Virginia, the Katie Facey Agency specializes in domestic staffing for families in need of child care and other household help. Ms. Facey herself worked as a nanny in her youth. Today her agency's nannies receive full benefits packages and work in warm home environments.

**The Sitting Service of Fairfield County**
**980 Post Road, Darien**
**(203) 655-9783**
This agency has been serving Fairfield County families for more than 60 years. In the realm of child care, the Sitting Service primarily matches families with babysitters (not au pairs or nannies). Most sitters are 40 to 60 years old. Pet- and house-sitters are also available. To take advantage of the services, clients first become members of the agency.

**Tri-State Nannies Referral Service**
**5 Cannon Brook Lane, Norwalk**
**(203) 847-3929**
**www.tsnnannies.com**
Tri-State Nannies works with families in Connecticut, New York, and New Jersey (the "tri-state area") to provide live-in nannies. The nannies typically work a Monday-through-Friday schedule and receive competitive salaries, benefits, and room and board. The agency's co-owner, Charlotte Schwartz, once worked as a nanny herself. She now runs Tri-State with her husband, Tom Schwartz.

## DAY-CARE CENTERS AND PRESCHOOLS

Many local day-care centers are independent, located inside private homes or storefronts. Some of the most popular programs are held at churches or synagogues. You don't have to be a member of the congregation to enroll your child, although preference is sometimes given to members if

enrollment is competitive. Within the county you'll also find a generous smattering of some of the larger child-care "chains," including the following companies:

**Bright Horizons**
**15 Parklawn Drive, Bethel**
**(203) 792-0078**

**60 Gregory Boulveard, Norwalk**
**(203) 854-6781**

**Three Corporate Drive, Shelton**
**(203) 926-1398**

**300 First Stamford Place, Stamford**
**(203) 323-1972**

**126 Monroe Turnpike, Trumbull**
**(203) 459-8610**

**7 Godfrey Place, Wilton**
**(203) 834-2616**
**www.brighthorizons.com**
Bright Horizons makes working parents' lives easier by teaming with companies to create employer-sponsored child-care programs, often within corporate parks or other convenient areas. Infants and toddlers through school-age kids can participate in creative play, skills classes, sensory expression programs, artistic endeavors, and outdoor experiences while Mom or Dad works nearby.

**KinderCare Learning Centers**
**174 Old Hawleyville Road, Bethel**
**(203) 792-6991**

**123 South King Street, Danbury**
**(203) 748-2480**

**304 Elm Street, Monroe**
**(203) 445-9548**

**1 Trap Falls Road, Shelton**
**(203) 944-0104**
**www.kindercare.com**
Founded in 1969, KinderCare has expanded to include more than 1,200 sites throughout the United States. The company offers programs for infants, toddlers, preschoolers, kindergarteners, and school-age children. Reading, singing, writing, counting, playing instruments, drawing,

and playing are all a part of the day-to-day experience at each center.

**Tutor Time Learning Centers**
**25 Valley Drive, Greenwich**
**(203) 861-6549**

**477 Main Street, Monroe**
**(203) 261-6330**

**466 Main Avenue, Norwalk**
**(203) 846-6046**
**www.tutortime.com**
Care and education are combined at Tutor Time, a child-care company with locations in 20 states. Infants receive attention and sensory stimulation throughout the day; toddlers learn and explore with toys and enjoy active play, snacks, and naps. Preschoolers engage in phonics, math, reading, writing, physical fitness, and music programs. Kindergarteners and school-age children continue to develop with supervised play and educational activities.

## OTHER DAY-CARE CENTERS AND NURSERY SCHOOLS

Following is a sampling of other day-care and nursery school options, grouped by location in Northern or Southern Fairfield County. There are literally hundreds of child-care centers throughout the region; check the Yellow Pages for a more thorough listing of the centers in your town.

*Late pickup fees can be very high at most day-care centers—some even charge by the minute. To avoid extra expenses, budget a few extra minutes into your schedule to make sure you arrive before the center's official closing time.*

# Southern Fairfield County

**A Child's Garden**
**100 Mona Terrace, Fairfield**
**(203) 259-1327**

**234 Greenfield Street, Fairfield**
**(203) 576-1041**
**www.achildsgarden.net**
The Mona Terrace location of A Child's Garden is a preschool where children learn through play. Highlighted activities include art, drama, language, music, and science. Children attending the preschool program can also enroll in the center's summer camp program, which emphasizes fun, outdoor activities, and socializing. The Greenfield Street location focuses on infant and toddler care, with a recently added kindergarten program. The centers do not follow the school-closing schedule on inclement days and are closed on major holidays. Hours of operation are 7:00 A.M. to 5:30 P.M. year-round.

**Care Around the Clock**
**500 State Street, Bridgeport**
**(203) 345-2104**
This child-care center offers a unique service in the industry. Catering to parents with nontraditional working hours, it is open literally around the clock. Enrolled children can take advantage of a computer center, a full-time nurse, indoor and outdoor play spaces, music and art rooms, and separate spaces for infant care. Parents (using a password) can peek in anytime using closed-circuit cameras via the Internet.

**Child Care Center, Inc.**
**Stamford (four locations)**
**(203) 961-8070, (203) 323-5944**
The four Stamford locations of Child Care Center provide guidance and care for hundreds of infants, toddlers, and young children. Some of the spaces are reserved for children from high-risk situations and for

the children of Stamford Health System employees. Head Start, Early Head Start, school readiness, nutrition, and family literacy programs are also available through all of the center's locations.

## Child Guidance Center
### 180 Fairfield Avenue, Bridgeport
### (203) 394-6529

Unlike most other child-care centers in the area, the Child Guidance Center has a special mission to care for local children who are struggling with emotional and psychological problems. Founded in 1925, the center serves families living in Bridgeport, Fairfield, Stratford, Monroe, Easton, and Trumbull; staff members speak Spanish as well as English. The Child Guidance Center also operates several outpatient clinics for children and is funded by public and private sources. Call for details about treatment and enrollment.

## Children's Community Daycare Center
### 90 Hillspoint Road, Westport
### (203) 226-8033
### www.myccdc.org

This nonprofit childhood education and day-care center (also known as CCDC) provides supportive care for infants, toddlers, and preschoolers in three- and five-day programs. Children are encouraged to develop their social, mental, and physical skills while playing with toys, singing, listening to stories, learning about music, and interacting with one another. The program is accredited by the National Academy of Early Childhood Programs.

## Community Nursery School
### 49 Weston Road, Westport
### (203) 227-7941

The Community Nursery School has been around for more than 45 years, providing nondenominational child care for toddlers, 3-year-olds, and 4-year-olds. The class for 1-year-olds meets once a week; 2-year-olds meet two or three times a week; and preschoolers meet up to five times a week. Extended-day programs are also available. The center's goal is to treat each

child as an individual with his or her own pace of learning and socializing and to promote healthy development in all areas.

## Cornerstone Children's Center
### 16 Hickory Street, Trumbull
### (203) 261-0499
### www.cornerstonekids.com

This early childhood education center aims to nuture and support infants, toddlers, preschoolers, and school-age children with a variety of programs and services. Infants receive plenty of social contact, exercise, and soothing. Toddlers explore their environment through play and group activities, while preschoolers learn and grow in a noncompetitive atmosphere. The center is open from 6:30 A.M. to 6:30 P.M. year-round, except major holidays.

## Fairfield YMCA Child Care
### 901 Kings Highway, Fairfield
### (203) 367-0729
### www.fairfieldymca.org

The YMCA of Fairfield offers an impressive array of child-care programs. In the center's Tiny Tot Nursery School, 3- and 4-year-olds take part in morning sessions two or three days per week. The Pre-K program offers 4- and 5-year-olds the opportunity to take part in a five-day program and an optional extended-day schedule. Kindergarteners can enjoy before-school and after-school classes. School-age care, vacation camps, and "play days" are also available. Parents must have a program membership in order to enroll a child in any child-care program.

## Family Centers, Inc.
### 40 Arch Street, Greenwich
### (203) 869-4848
### www.familycenters.org

With locations in Greenwich, Stamford, Darien, and New Canaan, this nonprofit human-service organization has been helping families in lower Fairfield County since 1891 with a variety of programs and services. Among those services is a full-day early childhood education program for 3- and 4-year-olds; Head Start preschools conducted in public housing facilities; the Joan Melber Warburg Early Childhood Center for infants and toddlers; the Den for Grieving Kids outreach program; and the TLC-Nurturing Families program, which helps new parents with parenting skills and information.

## Gray Farms Nursery School
**884 Newfield Avenue, Stamford**
**(203) 322-8787**

This licensed and accredited program provides three- and five-day programs for children ages 3 and 4. The daily schedule is 9:00 A.M. to noon, although extended-day program are also available. Children at Gray Farms enjoy a supportive environment in which to explore music, art, physical activity, language development, socialization, and other skills. The nursery school is run by St. John's Lutheran Church.

*The Connecticut Child Care Infoline (800-505-1000) is a good local resource for information about camps, nursery schools, and day-care providers in the state.*

## Hillel Academy
**1571 Stratfield Road, Fairfield**
**(203) 374-6147**
**www.hillelacademy.org**

The Hillel Academy is a private Hebrew school offering nursery school and kindergarten programs for young ones in the community. Enrolled children take part in story times, play times, art lessons, rudimentary math and science classes, and Hebrew lessons. They also learn about Jewish culture and traditions through music, stories, and fun activities. When the children graduate from these programs, parents have the option of continuing their education at Hillel Academy through the eighth grade.

## Hilltop Preschool
**257 Stanwich Road, Greenwich**
**(203) 629-0621**

Located at the Greenwich Reform Synagogue, the recently renovated Hilltop Preschool offers playgrounds, classrooms, and indoor playrooms. Enrolled children sing songs, paint, visit nearby museums and nature centers, learn about Jewish traditions, play music, explore science and math, listen to stories, cook, enjoy snack time, and make plenty of friends. Children of all religions are welcome.

## Italian Center Nursery School
**1620 Newfield Avenue, Stamford**
**(203) 322-6943**
**www.italiancenter.org**

Members of the Italian Center can enroll their children in the center's licensed nursery school for 3- and 4-year-olds. In addition to classroom activities, participants also enjoy group sports, music lessons, swimming lessons, and a variety of other activities. Other opportunities include a summer day camp for older children and a Kiddie Camp for children ages 3 to 6.

## Jesse Lee Nursery School
**25 Flat Rock Road, Easton**
**(203) 372-4178**

The Jesse Lee Nursery School caters to children under age 5, providing games, quiet time, and intellectual stimulation. Equal emphasis is given to physical and mental challenges. The school, which is nonprofit and nonsectarian, was founded in 1968 to provide a safe and nurturing environment for children. Call for updated classroom schedules and open enrollment.

## Methodist Family Center Preschool
**345 Middlesex Road, Darien**
**(203) 655-7407**

This private preschool is run by the Darien Methodist Church and a school board committee. Enrolled children take part in art, music, math, and writing classes, as well as programs that involve quiet play, physical activity, and outdoor adventures. An extended day program is also available. The school has separate curricula for toddlers, 3-year-olds, 4-year-olds, and 5-year-olds.

### Noroton Presbyterian Church Nursery School
**2011 Post Road, Darien**
**(203) 655-3223**
**www.norotonchurch.com**
Also known as NPC Nursery School, this nonprofit program offers team-teaching (two teachers per classroom) and small classes. The curriculum is based on a daily or weekly theme, which is then carried through activities involving math, reading, art, music, and other areas. The programs are designed to take into account the individual needs and congnitive abilities of each child. Most programs take place in the morning, with an extended-day option available. A prekindergarten program also meets five days a week. Enrollment preference is given to church members.

### Pumpkin Preschool
**449 Grasmere Avenue, Fairfield**
**(203) 255-7505**

**15 Burr Road, Westport**
**(203) 226-1277**
**www.pumpkinpreschool.com**
The Fairfield location serves as headquarters of Pumpkin Preschool, a child-care provider that also has offices in Westport and Shelton. (For more information on the Shelton location, see the Northern Fairfield County listings.) The preschool keeps children busy in a safe and stimulating atmosphere with arts and crafts projects, story times, physical activity, and rest periods. The Westport location has a new classroom wing; the Fairfield location offers large classrooms and several playgrounds.

### St. Luke's Parish School
**1864 Post Road, Darien**
**(203) 655-9783**
**www.saintlukesdarien.org**
St. Luke's is a large Episcopal parish, serving as headquarters for the nonprofit organization Person to Person and offer-

ing numerous other opportunities for Darien residents. One of those is the St. Luke's Parish Nursery School, a weekday program serving children ages 2 through 5. The schedule is flexible, including morning and afternoon programs and two-, three-, four-, and five-day programs. Slots open up periodically; call for the latest information.

### St. Mark's Nursery School
**111 Oenoke Ridge Road, New Canaan**
**(203) 966-4515**
Part of St. Mark's Episcopal Church, this nursery school was designed to provide care for parishioners' children as well as for children in the larger community. Emotional, intellectual, and physical learning are equally emphasized in the programs, which primarily cater to 3- and 4-year-olds, The values and faith of the Episcopal church are also a part of the day-to-day curriculum.

### Teddy Bear Corner
**273 Villa Avenue, Fairfield**
**(203) 330-0302**
This day-care facility has been welcoming young local residents since 1993. The staff provides a homelike environment and encourages children to play, explore, and learn at an age-appropriate level. Teddy Bear Corner accepts infants, toddlers, and children ages 3 to 5 in bright classrooms filled with books, snacks, toys, play mats, and music. Outside, children will find sandboxes, play areas, picnic tables, and even easels.

### YMCA Childcare
**500 West Avenue, Norwalk**
**(203) 866-1376**
Child care-options at this YMCA include Little Wonders, a two- or three-day-a-week morning program for 2-, 3-, and 4-year-olds; day care and preschool for children ages 6 weeks to 5 years; school vacation day-care programs; and school-age child care. All programs incorporate fitness and swimming into the schedule,

with morning and afternoon snacks provided. All participants pay tuition on a
monthly schedule.

# Northern Fairfield County

### A Child's Garden
### 20 Ivy Brook Road, Shelton
### (203) 402-0334
### www.achildsgarden.net
A Child's Garden has three locations within
the county; the Shelton site offers infant,
toddler, preschool, and kindergarten programs. The teacher-to-child ratio here is 1
to 3 for infants, 1 to 4 for toddlers, 1 to 8
for 3-year-olds, and 1 to 10 for 4-year-olds
and older children. A summer camp program is also available. The center is open
from 7:00 A.M. to 5:00 P.M. daily, except
major holidays. For more information
about the other Fairfield County Child's
Garden locations in Fairfield, see the listings under Southern Fairfield County.

### Boughton Street YMCA Children's Programs
### 12 Boughton Street, Danbuy
### (203) 744-1000
This YMCA location, part of the Regional
YMCA of Western Connecticut, provides
child care in addition to typical YMCA
offerings such as swimming, basketball,
and weight training. Child care is offered
for children ages 2 to 12, including toddler
programs, prekindergarten programs,
afterschool programs, and even help-with-
homework programs.

### Country Kids Play Farm
### 107 Old State Road, Brookfield
### (203) 775-2126
### www.countrykidsplayfarm.com
Infants, "mobile infants," toddlers,
preschoolers, and older children will all
find a home-away-from-home at Country
Kids Play Farm. Full-day and half-day care
are both offered. The on-site facilities

include playgrounds, a gymnasium, a
computer room, and colorful classrooms.
The center also has two heated swimming
pools (indoor and outdoor) and a summer
camp program that incorporates tennis,
field trips, scuba diving, art and crafts, and
other activities.

### Enchanted Garden
### 165 Danbury Road, Ridgefield
### (203) 431-3350
Parents of infants, toddlers, preschoolers,
kindergarteners, and school-age children
will all find thoughtfully designed child
care programs at the Enchanted Garden.
Teachers work with children to promote
self-esteem and independence through
programs in music, art, language, and simple play. Specializing in the performing
arts, this center also offers a wide range
of classes in dance, theater, and stagecraft
for all ages.

### Grassy Plain Children's Center
### Grassy Plain Street, Bethel
### (203) 744-4890
Managed by the Regional YMCA of Western Connecticut, this child-care center
offers programs for children ages 2
months to 12 years. For infants the center
has a 1 to 3 teacher-student ratio and individualized attention. Toddlers can enjoy
arts and crafts, instruments, and play time;
2-, 3-, and 4-year-olds learn to swim, play
music, draw, write, and perform other
skills. School-age children embark on age-
appropriate programs in cooking, Girl
Scouts, physical education, and word-
working.

### Greenknoll Children's Center
### 2 Huckleberry Hill Road, Brookfield
### (203) 740-3432
This child-care center, run by the Regional
YMCA of Western Connecticut, offers care
options for infants, toddlers, 4- and 5-
year-olds, and school-age children. Day
camp programs are also available. Older
children learn through crafts, music, field
trips, language lessons, swimming, cook-

ing, and other programs; infants and toddlers play and explore their world and their physical abilities.

### Kiddie Campus Preschool
### 515 Cutlers Farm Road, Monroe
### (203) 261-2296

Affiliated with the United Methodist Church, this day-care and preschool facility incorporates play times, art, writing, drama, music, and science into its day-to-day curriculum. Three-year-olds meet twice a week, 4-year-olds meet three times a week, and pre-K students meet five times a week. Kiddie Campus also recently added an extended-day program on designated days.

### Pumpkin Preschool of Shelton
### 100 Beard Sawmill Road, Shelton
### (203) 926-1800
### www.pumpkinpreschool.com

This preschool program has three locations in Fairfield County. The Shelton site is located within the Route 8 Corporate Center, making it ideal for working parents in that area. Tots can enjoy the center's brightly painted classrooms, story hours, play times, and arts programs, as well as separate playgrounds for infants/toddlers and preschoolers. For more information about Pumpkin Preschool's Westport and Fairfield locations, see the Southern Fairfield County listings.

### Ridgefield Academy Preschool
### (203) 894-1800

Long admired for its rigorous education through the eighth grade, Ridgefield Academy has recently added a preschool program to its academic offerings. The

*Parents who utilize day-care services can take advantage of a tax credit from the federal government. The exact amount will depend on your income, but you can expect a yearly credit between $480 and $720 for one child and between $960 and $1,440 for two children.*

early-childhood program was designed for 3- and 4-year-olds and provides an encouraging space for them to play, socialize, and learn. The preschool accepted its first students in fall 2004.

### St. Stephen's Nursery School
### 351 Main Street, Ridgefield
### (203) 438-3789

St. Stephen's Episcopal Church offers child-care programs for 3-, 4-, and 5-year-olds. Social, physical, and spiritual well-being is encouraged through varied exercises in play, movement, music, and creative arts. The school follows the Ridgefield Public School system for closings on holidays and during inclement weather. Scholarships are available for families who need tuition assistance; call for details.

### Wesley Learning Center
### 92 Church Hill Road, Newtown
### (203) 426-6149

Affiliated with the Methodist Church, the Wesley Learning Center is located in the Sandy Hook section of town. The school offers programs in physical, spiritual, mental, and social development in its early-childhood education and day-care center for preschoolers and kindergarteners. About 130 children are enrolled at any one time.

# HEALTH CARE

No one wants to encounter a health-care problem. But Fairfield County residents can rest assured that if they do find themselves in need of a doctor or hospital, they're living within short driving distance of some of the best facilities and practitioners in the United States. And if by chance one of the local doctors can't meet your needs, there are always the world-renowned researchers, facilities, and hospitals located just down the road in New York City.

There's no shortage of specialists here, from pediatricians and cardiologists to ultrasound technicians and surgeons. Of course your choice of a doctor will depend largely on your insurance (or lack thereof). In general you're likely to find your practitioner working out of a group health-care center or hospital, although a few still maintain individual, one-doctor practices. Most smaller health-care centers and group practices are affiliated with one of the nearby large hospitals and enjoy access to the hospital's facilities if the need arises.

Fairfield County also offers several assisted-living facilities, where senior citizens can enjoy independence, activities, and socialization while under the close watch of medical professionals. Although not inexpensive, these facilities offer a win-win situation that many local seniors are increasingly taking advantage of.

*Like so many other places in Bridgeport, the local hospital is affiliated with the legacy of P. T. Barnum: The showman helped establish Bridgeport Hospital in 1878 and served as its first hospital president.*

## HOSPITALS

**Bridgeport Hospital**
**267 Grant Street, Bridgeport**
**(203) 384-3000**
**www.bridgeporthospital.org**
A private, nonprofit facility, Bridgeport Hospital is affiliated with the Yale New Haven Health System and offers 500 attending physicians, 180 medical residents, 2,000 employees, and more than 400 volunteers. One of the hospital's best-known features is its Heart Institute, a cardiology and open-heart surgery center with inpatient and outpatient care. The Norma F. Pfriem Cancer Center provides transfusions, chemotherapy, biopsies, a resource library, and a satellite office of the American Cancer Society. Other hospital features include the Birthplace in the Women's Care Center, the Newborn Intensive Care Unit, the Joint Reconstruction Center, the Ambulatory Surgery Center, the Center for Sleep Medicine, a burn center, and units for emergencies, radiology, urology, rehabilitation, neurology, respiratory care, psychiatric care, and gastroenterology.

**Danbury Hospital**
**24 Hospital Avenue, Danbury**
**(203) 797-7000**
**www.danburyhospital.org**
More than 500 doctors, 67 medical residents, and 3,000 employees work at Danbury Hospital, a teaching facility located not far from I-84. In addition to serving as a Level II trauma center, this 371-bed hospital also offers the relatively new Praxair Cancer Center—a space where cancer patients can come for treatment, therapy, and comfort in a "homey" atmosphere. The hospital's Family Birth Center has

whirlpool tubs, private and semiprivate rooms, and a neonatal intensive care unit. Danbury Hospital also provides patients with a rehabilitation center, a center for ambulatory surgery, a sleep-disorders center, a community health center, and facilities for MRIs, ultrasounds, CAT and PET scans, and asthma management. The hospital's staff members also work in conjunction with Hospice of Western Connecticut, the Visiting Nurse Association, and Health Care Affiliates.

## Greenwich Hospital
### 5 Perryridge Road, Greenwich
### (203) 863-3000
### www.greenhosp.org

Greenwich Hospital is a 160-bed community medical center offering emergency services and outpatient care. In 1999 the hospital unveiled its Helmsley Medical Building, which is admired almost as much for its design as for its state-of-the-art equipment and care. The hospital's newest addition is the three-story Tom and Olive Watson Pavilion, due to be completed by 2005, which will provide diagnostic services and treatment for acute conditions. Other hospital features include the Bendheim Cancer Center, the Breast Care Center, wellness programs, surgical facilities, a sleep-disorders laboratory, and departments for maternity care, pain management, radiology, geriatrics, cardiology, cancer treatment, addiction and recovery, gastroenterology, neuroscience, occupational health, plastic surgery, and pediatric medicine.

## Norwalk Hospital
### Maple Street, Norwalk
### (203) 852-2000
### www.norwalkhosp.org

The Same-Day Surgery Center at Norwalk Hospital supports the bulk of surgeries—more than 75 percent—at this private, 100-year-old hospital. Although its history is long, its facilities are modern: Patients can take advantage of the Whittingham Can-

*AmeriCares, a nonprofit organization based in Stamford, offers two free health-care clinics in the county for the uninsured or underinsured. The hours are somewhat limited at each, but no appointments are necessary and all services are provided free of charge. To take advantage of the services, patients must have a total household income between 200 and 300 percent of the Federal Poverty Level. The clinics are located in Danbury (198 Main Street; 203-748-6188) and Norwalk (98 South Main Street; 203-899-2495).*

cer Center, a treatment and care facility with a holistic approach; the Newborn Intensive Care Unit, where neonatologists care for sick infants; and a Behavioral Health Services center that offers programs to treat depression, eating disorders, and addictions. The hospital also provides facilities and practitioners in the areas of emergency care, pediatrics, rehabilitation, obstetrics, prostate health, cardiology, nutrition, anesthesiology, and childbirth. Visitors can expect to find a pharmacy, religious services, valet parking, a coffee shop, and a gift shop.

## Stamford Hospital
### Shelburne Road at West Broad Street
### Stamford
### (203) 325-7000
### www.stamfordhospital.org

Part of the Stamford Health System, Stamford Hospital is a comprehensive teaching facility with 305 beds, 24 departments, and numerous community outreach programs. More than 45,000 patients per year visit the Emergency Department; parents-to-be utilize the prenatal diagnosis center; and cardiology patients take advantage of the latest testing equipment. One of the hospital's best-known features is the Carl & Dorothy

Bennett Cancer Center, which offers out-patient services, inpatient care, nutritional counseling, art therapy, and a wide variety of cancer-fighting treatments. Other Stamford Hospital departments include rehabilitation services, senior services, pediatrics, a diabetes management program, a neonatal intensive care unit, an infusion center, a center for sleep medicine, gynecology, maternal-fetal medicine, an infectious disease division, psychiatry, neurology, and pulmonary medicine.

### St. Vincent's Medical Center
### 2800 Main Street, Bridgeport
### (203) 576-6000

This acute-care facility is affiliated with the Columbia University College of Physicians and Surgeons and New York Medical College. The hospital's Wellness Services center provides health screenings, flu shots, and other preventive services. The Regional Heart and Vascular Center offers surgery, rehabilitation, diagnostics, and all-around cardiovascular care. The Family Birthing Center has private suites and a newborn Special Care Unit. Other departments include cancer services, behavioral health, women and family services, senior services, special needs services, orthopedics, community health, and ambulatory services. Special clubs and organizations at the hospital include Women at Heart for cardiovascular patients; Club 50, a wellness group for ages 50-plus; and the

---

ℹ️ *Residents of Brookfield, New Fairfield, and Sherman might want to consider heading out of the county when it's time to have a baby, mend a broken leg, or see a specialist: New Milford Hospital, located just north of the county line, offers rehabilitation services, a family birthing center, cancer treatment, an emergency room, laboratories, full surgical facilities, and even a sleep-medicine clinic. The hospital is located at 21 Elm Street (860-355-2611), not far from New Milford's town green.*

---

Vinny Club, a health-and-safety program aimed at children.

## GENERAL HEALTH-CARE CENTERS

These facilities often feature a mix of health-care services, including rehabilitation, immediate care, physical therapy, behavioral and mental health services, dieticians, wound care, and family medicine.

### Daniel and Grace Tully
### & Family Health Center
### 32 Strawberry Hill Court, Stamford
### (203) 967-5933

### Darien Medical Center
### 1500 Post Road, Darien
### (203) 655-7308

### Greenwich Convenient
### Medical Care Center
### 1200 East Putnam Avenue, Greenwich
### (203) 698-1419

### St. Joseph Medical Center
### 128 Strawberry Hill Avenue, Stamford
### (203) 353-2000

## URGENT-CARE CENTERS

### Brookfield Health Center of New Milford
### Hospital Walk-In Center
### 31 Old U.S. Route 7, Brookfield
### (203) 740-5111

### Doctors Center Immediate Medical Care
### 660 Bedford Street, Stamford
### (203) 324-8800

### First Aid Immediate Care
### Medical Center of Trumbull
### 900 White Plains Road, Trumbull
### (203) 261-6111

### Huntington Walk-In Medical Center
### 887 Bridgeport Avenue, Shelton
### (203) 225-6020

Immediate Medical Care of Monroe
388 Main Street, Monroe
(203) 459-0191

## COMMUNITY HEALTH CENTERS

Community health centers in Connecticut provide dental care, pediatric care, social services, adult care, and geriatric care to poor and underinsured residents of the state.

Bridgeport Community Health Center
471 Barnum Avenue, Bridgeport
(203) 333-6864

Norwalk Community Health Center
121 Water Street, Norwalk
(203) 899-1770

Southwest Community Health Center
743 South Avenue, Bridgeport
(203) 330-6010

Stratford Community Health Center
737 Honeyspot Road, Stratford
(203) 375-7242

Stamford Community Health Center
137 Henry Street, Stamford
(203) 327-5111

## MENTAL AND BEHAVIORAL HEALTH SERVICES

Connecticut PsyCare
225 Main Street, Westport
(203) 221-7415

Greater Bridgeport Community
Mental Health Center
1635 Central Avenue, Bridgeport
(203) 551-7400

Hall-Brooke Behavioral Health Services
47 Long Lots Road, Westport
(800) 543-3669

Southwest Connecticut
Mental Health Center
780 Summer Street, Stamford
(203) 388-1548

## REHABILITATION CENTERS

Advanced Center for
Rehabilitation Medicine
698 West Avenue, Norwalk
(203) 852-3400

Bishop Wicke Health and
Rehabilitation Center
584 Long Hill Avenue, Shelton
(203) 929-5321

Coleman Park Health and
Rehabilitation Center
62 Coleman Street, Bridgeport
(203) 367-8444

Healthsouth Rehabilitation Center
2260 Main Street, Bridgeport
(203) 366-3566

*Part hospital, part intermediate-care center, and part rehabilitation center, the Flora & Mary Hewitt Memorial Hospital in Shelton (45 Maltby Street; 203-924-4671) is specially designed to meet the needs of elderly patients. The hospital also became one of the first locations in the state to offer an adult day-care program.*

## NURSING HOMES

Bethel Health Care Center
13 Parklawn Drive, Bethel
(203) 830-4180

Bridgeport Health Care Center
and Bridgeport Manor
600 Bond Street, Bridgeport
(203) 384-6400

Cambridge Manor
2428 Easton Turnpike, Fairfield
(203) 372-0313

Centennial House
23 Prospect Avenue, Norwalk
(203) 853-0010

Courtland Gardens Health Center
53 Courtland Avenue, Stamford
(203) 351-8300

Greenwich Woods Health Care Center
1165 King Street, Greenwich
(203) 531-1335

---

**i**

*If possible, always verify that your doctor accepts your insurance before receiving treatment—especially if you haven't visited the office in a while. It's not uncommon for local practices to change their policies regarding certain insurance companies or for one doctor to accept your insurance while another doctor at the same practice doesn't.*

---

Harborside Healthcare
1 Glen Hill Road, Danbury
(203) 744-2840

Haven Health Center of Greenwich
1188 King Street, Greenwich
(203) 531-8300

Homestead Health Center
160 Glenbrook Road, Stamford
(203) 353-6151

Honey Hill Care Center
34 Midrocks Road, Norwalk
(203) 847-9686

Lourdes Health Care Center
345 Belden Hill Road, Wilton
(203) 762-3318

Maefair Health Care Center
21 Maefair Court, Trumbull
(203) 459-5152

Mediplex of Danbury
107 Osborne Street, Danbury
(203) 792-8102

Mediplex of Darien
599 Boston Post Road, Darien
(203) 655-7727

Mediplex of Stamford
710 Long Ridge Road, Stamford
(203) 329-4026

Mediplex of Westport
1 Burr Road, Westport
(203) 226-4201

Northbridge Health Care Center
2875 Main Street, Bridgeport
(203) 366-0232

Shelton Lakes Health Care Center
5 Lake Road, Shelton
(203) 924-2635

St. Camillus Health Center
494 Elm Street, Stamford
(203) 325-0200

St. Joseph's Manor
6448 Main Street, Trumbull
(203) 268-6204

3030 Park Fairfield Health Center
118 Jefferson Street, Fairfield
(203) 372-4501

Wilton Meadows Health Care Center
439 Danbury Road, Wilton
(203) 834-0199

## ASSISTED-LIVING FACILITIES

Atria Assisted Living of Stratford
6911 Main Street, Stratford
(203) 380-0006

Brighton Gardens of Stamford
59 Roxbury Road, Stamford
(203) 322–2100

Crosby Commons
580 Long Hill Road, Shelton
(203) 225–5000

Edgehill Continuing Care
Retirement Community
122 Palmers Hill Road, Stamford
(203) 325–5599

The Gardens
8 Glen Hill Road, Danbury
(203) 748–0506

Glen Crest-Harborside
3 Glen Hill Road, Danbury
(203) 790–9161

Greens at Cannondale
435 Danbury Road, Wilton
(203) 761–1191

Greens at Greenwich
1155 King Street, Greenwich
(203) 531–5500

Homesteads at Newtown
166 Mount Pleasant Road, Newtown
(203) 426–8118

Jewish Home for the Elderly
175 Jefferson Street, Fairfield
(203) 365–6400

Laurel Gardens of Trumbull
2750 Reservoir Avenue, Trumbull
(203) 268–2400

Lockwood Lodge at Ashlar of Newtown
Toddy Hill Road, Newtown
(203) 364–3179

The Marvin
60 Gregory Boulevard, Norwalk
(203) 854–4600

Meadow Ridge
100 Redding Road, Redding
(203) 544–1000

The Mews
Bolling Place, Greenwich
(203) 869–9448

New Canaan Inn
73 Oenoke Ridge Road, New Canaan
(203) 966–1272

Priority Care
999 Oronoque Lane, Stratford
(203) 381–1333

Ridgefield Crossings
640 Danbury Road, Ridgefield
(203) 431–2255

Spring Meadows of Trumbull
6949 Main Street, Trumbull
(203) 261–0006

Stony Brook Court
50 Ledge Road, Darien
(203) 662–1090

Sunrise Assisted Living of Stamford
251 Turn of River, Stamford
(203) 968–8393

Sunrise Assisted Living of Wilton
96 Danbury Road, Wilton
(203) 761–8999

Village at Brookfield Common
246 Federal Road, Brookfield
(203) 775–8696

Village at Waveny Care Center
3 Farm Road, New Canaan
(203) 966–8725

Westfield Court
77 Third Street, Stamford
(203) 327–4551

# MEDIA

From gossip to hard news, the county's newspapers have long been an invaluable source of information for local residents. The smaller weeklies tend to concentrate on in-town stories—the latest changes in zoning laws, for example, or the debate over repairs to the Town Hall roof. The larger dailies, meanwhile, work from a more regional point of view and often cover the affairs of numerous nearby towns and cities. Many residents find that subscribing to one of each helps them keep perspective on their local schools and town officials as well as the larger picture of life in the county and state. In addition to its newspapers, Fairfield County supports several glossy magazines that take a more lighthearted look at lifestyles with an emphasis on such topics as dining, fashion, entertainment, interior design, and gardening.

The region also has a fairly decent selection of radio stations, although persons moving here from larger metropolitan areas might not agree. It's important for locals to note that not all radio stations can be heard in all parts of the county. Those living in the southern regions can often pick up New York City and Long Island stations. For those living in the northern area, popular stations like 98Q

and I95 usually start to fade as you head south. If your commute or other daily travels typically include visits to both northern and southern county towns, you might want to program stations into your radio from both ends of the county.

## NEWSPAPERS

## Dailies

*Connecticut Post*
**410 State Street, Bridgeport**
**(203) 333-0161**
**www.connpost.com**
Covering the greater Bridgeport area, including the towns of Trumbull, Stratford, Fairfield, and Monroe, the *Connecticut Post* has a large staff and an emphasis on hard news. Home delivery of the *Post* costs $4.50 per week for Monday through Sunday service, $3.75 per week for Thursday through Sunday service, $3.25 per week for Friday through Sunday service, $2.75 per week for Saturday and Sunday service, and $2.25 per week for Sunday only service.

*Danbury News-Times*
**333 Main Street, Danbury**
**(203) 744-5100**
**www.newstimes.com**
Residents of Danbury, Bethel, Ridgefield, Bridgewater, Brookfield, New Milford, New Fairfield, Redding, Newtown, Washington, Southbury, and Sherman can all get daily updates on news, sports, weather, local politics, and arts and entertainment from the *News-Times*. Readers will also find extras like the Bridal Guide, *Jill Magazine*, recipes, a leisure guide, an extensive online edition, and a Senior Services Directory. A daily subscription to the paper costs $18.50 per month.

*The Hersam Acorn media company owns seven newspapers in Fairfield County, including the* Weston Forum, *the* Redding Pilot, *and the* Ridgefield Press, *which was established in 1875. The company made its newest acquisition in 2003, when it took over operations of the* Greenwich Post. *Other local newspaper chains include Hometown Publications and Brooks Community Newspapers.*

*Greenwich Time*
**20 East Elm Street, Greenwich**
**(203) 625-4400**
**www.greenwichtime.com**
Business, sports, community news, editorials, travel information, and world-events coverage are all part of the package at this daily newspaper, headquartered in Greenwich. Home delivery of the Greenwich Time costs $4.20 per week for Monday through Sunday service, $3.00 per week for Monday through Saturday service, and $2.50 per week for Monday through Friday service. Mail delivery is also available.

*Norwalk Hour*
**346 Main Avenue, Norwalk**
**(203) 354-1000**
**www.thehour.com**
This popular morning newspaper is published in full color seven days a week. The classifieds have listings for jobs, cars, and real estate; the main sections cover regional, national, and world news, local births, deaths, and weddings, entertainment and recreation options, government information, editorials, sports, and feature stories. Daily home delivery is available for $15.10 per month, $49.00 for 13 weeks, $94.25 for 26 weeks, or $181.00 for 52 weeks.

*Stamford Advocate*
**75 Tresser Boulevard**
**P.O. Box 9307, Stamford 06904**
**(203) 964-2200**
**www.stamfordadvocate.com**
Local, countywide, New York City, and world news are the focus at the *Advocate*, which also offers features, classifieds, editorials, business and sports sections, and community pages. Home delivery is available for $4.20 per week for Monday through Sunday service, $3.00 per week for Monday through Saturday service, $2.50 per week for Monday through Friday service, $1.95 per week for Saturday and Sunday service, and $1.50 per week for Sunday only service.

# Weeklies

*Darien News-Review*
**24 Old Kings Highway South, Darien**
**(203) 655-7476**
**www.dariennews-review.com**
The *News-Review* covers local news, regional happenings, and world events. It's also a good resource for job hunting, apartment hunting, weather forecasts, movie times, and more. The paper is part of Brooks Community Newspaper chain and comes out every Thursday. The subscription cost is $16.50 per year.

*Darien Times*
**4 Corbin Drive, Darien**
**(203) 656-4230**
Although small in area, Darien is home to more than 18,000 people, all of whom can stay up to date with local news, sporting events, and other happenings thanks to this weekly newspaper. The *Times* is free for all residents of Darien and $30 per year for those who live in nearby towns.

*Easton Courier*
**Hometown Publications**
**1000 Bridgeport Avenue, Shelton**
**(203) 926-2080**
A member of the Hometown Publications newspaper group, the *Easton Courier* keeps residents up to date with events in the local schools, government, and businesses. If you live within Fairfield County, a yearly subscription to the *Courier* costs $16. For those living outside county border, the cost is $37.50.

*Fairfield Citizen-News*
**220 Carter Henry Drive, Fairfield**
**(203) 255-4561**
**www.fairfieldcitizen-news.com**
This weekly paper keeps locals current on Fairfield's news, sports, and recreation opportunities. (At the time of this writing, the *Citizen-News* office was in the process of relocating; check your local telephone book or the Web site for updated contact

information.) An annual subscription costs $27.50.

### Fairfield County Weekly
**3 Quincy Street, Norwalk**
**(203) 838-1825**
**www.fairfieldweekly.com**
Irreverent and alternative, this free newspaper is circulated throughout the county. The staff aims to push buttons with hard-hitting exposés, straightforward language, and an unbashful look at local entertainment, politicians, and controversies. Restaurant reviews, music reviews, editorials, and an extensive classified section add to the paper's offerings. Readers can find the *Weekly* in sidewalk boxes and in restaurants and stores throughout the region.

---

*Although most local newspapers provide entertainment listings, the* **Fairfield County Weekly** *is the best resource for night owls and others looking for a fun time. The popular newspaper keeps its readers on top of the action with news about local band performances, nightclubs, and the alternative arts and entertainment scene.*

---

### Greenwich Post
**22 West Putnam Avenue, Greenwich**
**(203) 861-9191**
Columns, feature stories, news stories, movie listings, election news, and more are all part of the package at this weekly newspaper dedicated to covering its hometown. For residents of Greenwich, an annual subscription to the *Post* is free. Other Fairfield County residents can receive the paper for $24 per year.

### Monroe Courier
**Hometown Publications**
**1000 Bridgeport Avenue, Shelton**
**(203) 926-2080**
Monroe residents can peruse the editorial page, learn local school bus routes, read

movie reviews, and catch up on all the latest in-town news in this weekly paper. Within Fairfield County, a one-year subscription costs $16. If you live outside of the county, the cost rises to $37.50 per year.

### New Canaan Advertiser
**42 Vitti Street, New Canaan**
**(203) 966-9541**
The *Advertiser* has served New Canaan residents for nearly 100 years, providing all the latest information about local government, births, deaths, controversies, and entertainment. For New Canaan residents, a subscription to the paper costs $41.34 per year.

### Newtown Bee
**5 Church Hill Road, Newtown**
**(203) 426-3141**
**www.newtownbee.com**
The *Newtown Bee* provides community news, wedding and engagement announcements, equestrian news, columns, updates on school happenings, and much more. The paper also offers an online edition with lots of links and information. A one-year subscription costs $30, with discounts given to students.

### Norwalk Citizen-News
**542 Westport Avenue, Norwalk**
**(203) 750-0811**
**www.norwalkcitizen-news.com**
Part of the Brooks Community Newspapers company, the *Norwalk Citizen-News* competes with the city's daily paper to provide a unique look at life in the Norwalk community. The paper is free of charge for Norwalk residents; the cost for nonresidents is $25 per year.

### Redding Pilot
**P.O. Box 389, Georgetown 06829 (Redding)**
**(203) 544-9519**
This local paper is part of the Hersam Acorn newspaper group and shares offices with the *Weston Forum* at 3 Main Street in Georgetown. For those living within county borders, the yearly sub-

scription costs $39, with discounts given to students and military personnel.

## Ridgefield Press
**16 Bailey Avenue, Ridgefield**
**(203) 438-6544**
**www.theridgefieldpress.com**
News, sports, entertainment, the arts, election results, and other aspects of Ridgefield life are all chronicled in this historic newspaper, first established in the late 1800s. A one-year subscription costs $39 for addresses within the county. Discounts are given to students and military personnel.

## Trumbull Times
**Hometown Publications**
**1000 Bridgeport Avenue, Shelton**
**(203) 926-2080**
Trumbull politics, businesses, schools, births, sports, weddings, entertainment, and special events are all covered in the pages of this weekly paper, which is part of the Hometown Publications newspaper group. A one year, 52-issue subscription costs $16.00; or choose a two-year subscription for $26.50.

## Weston Forum
**P.O. Box 1185, Weston 06883**
**(203) 544-9990**
The *Forum* publishes every Wednesday morning, serving the town's 9,000 residents with all the latest local news. A yearly subscription is free for Weston residents. For those living in other Fairfield County towns, the cost is $24 per year.

## Westport News
**15 Myrtle Avenue, Westport**
**(203) 226-6311**
**www.westport-news.com**
The diverse offerings of this local newspaper include regular columnists, classified ads, a police report, local and regional perspectives on news stories, weather updates, sports scores, and an online edition that goes well beyond the headlines. An annual subscription to the *News* costs $32.

## Wilton Bulletin
**47 Old Ridgefield Road, Wilton**
**(203) 762-3866**
**www.acorn-online.com/wilton2**
Wilton residents depend on the *Bulletin* when it comes time to catch up on local news or submit obituaries, birth announcements, and classified ads. If you live within Fairfield County, a yearly subscription to the *Wilton Bulletin* will cost $30. Outside county lines, the cost jumps to $42 per year.

# MAGAZINES

## Connecticut Magazine
**35 Nutmeg Drive, Trumbull**
**(203) 380-6600**
**www.connecticutmag.com**
This monthly glossy magazine covers all aspects of life in the state, from dining out to politics, entertainment, family life, and periodic "Best of Connecticut" lists that rank towns, doctors, employers, and more. A 12-month subscription is available for $12.97. Individual copies of *Connecticut Magazine* are available at newsstands and other retailers for $3.95 each.

## Fairfield County Business Journal
**Westfair Communications**
**108 Corporate Park Drive**
**White Plains, NY**
**(914) 347-5200**
Published by Westfair Communications, this weekly trade journal keeps local business owners and business watchers up to date with all aspects of manufacturing, finance, corporate dealings, and other business-related topics in the region. A 52-week subscription is available for $48.

## Greenwich Magazine
**39 Lewis Street, Greenwich**
**(203) 869-0009**
**www.greenwichmag.com**
Owned by Moffly Publications, *Greenwich* is a glossy monthly with articles about noteworthy residents, outdoor activities,

fashion, local restaurants and businesses, sports, and other topics of interest. A one-year subscription is available for $27; or choose a two-year subscription for $45 or a three-year subscription for $63.

*New Canaan, Darien & Rowayton Magazine*
**14 Grove Street, New Canaan**
**(203) 966-0077**
**www.ncdmag.com**
This is another Moffly magazine offering glossy pages, 10 issues per year, and articles that focus on living, learning, dining, playing, shopping, and exploring in the greater New Canaan area. Subscribers can receive home delivery of *New Canaan, Darien & Rowayton* for $19.95 for one year, $29.95 for two years, or $39.95 for three years.

*Ridgefield Magazine*
**P.O. Box 608, Ridgefield 06877**
**(203) 894-8132**
**www.ridgefield-magazine.com**
Owned and operated in its namesake hometown, *Ridgefield Magazine* focuses on topics such as home and garden, dining and entertaining, local politics, antiques, and in-town happenings. The magazine is available at newsstands and other vendors in Ridgefield, Danbury, Darien, Redding, and Westport. You can also buy a six-issue subscription for $15.

*For those long commutes, no local radio station beats WSHU-FM (91.1) when it comes to news and talk. The station, broadcast out of Sacred Heart University in Fairfield, is a local affiliate of National Public Radio and includes complete coverage of state, national, and world events during prime drive times in the morning and evening.*

*Westport Magazine*
**205 Main Street, Westport**
**(203) 222-0600**
**www.westportmag.com**
Covering the towns of Westport, Weston, Fairfield, and Wilton, this monthly publication celebrates local residents, highlights special events, outlines entertainment and dining options, and explores regional politics. An annual subscription to *Westport* costs $19.95; a two-year subscription costs $29.95.

## TELEVISION

Local residents with cable or satellite television service can pick up all the major broadcast and cable channels. Local news broadcasts come from within Connecticut (Fox 61; News Channel 8; NBC 30; News Channel 12) or from New York City (CBS 2, NBC, ABC, Fox 5), depending on where in the county you live and what type of service you subscribe to, if any. (With some satellite services, for example, you won't be able to receive Connecticut stations.) WNET 13 New York is a PBS station that is accessible to most Fairfield County residents.

## RADIO

### ADULT CONTEMPORARY

WEZN-FM 99.9 (Star 99.9)
WEBE-FM 107.9 (WEBE 108)

### CURRENT HITS

WDAQ-FM 98 (98Q)
WKCI-FM 101 (KC 101)

### JAZZ

WKCR-FM 89.9
WPKN-FM 89.5

## NEWS/TALK/CLASSICAL MUSIC

WEDW–FM 88.5
WEFX–FM 95.9
WICC–AM 600
WGCH–AM 1490
WLAD–AM 800
WMNR–FM 88.1
WNLK–AM 1350
WQXR–FM 96.3
WSHU–FM 91.1
WSTC–AM 1400

## OLDIES

WKNL–FM 100.9 (Kool 101)
WREF–AM 850

## ROCK/CLASSIC ROCK

WEFX–FM 95.9 (The Fox)
WPLR–FM 99.1
WRKI–FM 95.1 (I-95)

# WORSHIP

N ew England's colonists, who came to these shores in search of religious freedom, would likely be pleased to find so many houses of worship in Fairfield County. Many of the region's oldest buildings are, in fact, its churches—not surprising when you consider Connecticut's long and religious history. Congregational churches were among the first to be built: The Trumbull Congregational Church, for example, has been a center of the community since 1730. Members of this parish, originally called the Parish of Unity, held their services outdoors until the church was built. The Second Congregational Church of Greenwich was first established in 1705, although the original building has been expanded over the years. And the stone foundation for the Congregational Church in West Redding was first laid in 1732.

Another New England tradition is the classic Meeting House, where members of all faiths can gather for wedding ceremonies, political meetings, and other assemblies. Newtown's Meeting House was built in 1792 in the classic Yankee style and still stands just across from the town's other famous landmark, the towering flagpole. Stamford's first Meeting House, built in 1641, served as both a town hall and church building for almost 100 years. (The building was later destroyed, probably by fire.)

As the years passed, Connecticut's Puritan history gave way to a plethora of religions, churches, and synagogues. Today you're likely to find a Greek Orthodox church down the road from a Congregational one. Many houses of worship are clustered around the traditional town green, creating picturesque scenes from town to town. Others are located in more unusual locales, including storefronts and shopping plazas.

Our county is home to virtually every type of denomination you might imagine.

Although some, such as Roman Catholic and Baptist, do seem to hold a majority, the region nonetheless offers numerous choices when it comes to finding a religious group or organization that adheres to your beliefs. That said, some chosen houses of worship will be more convenient than others: Jewish synagogues, for example, tend to be clustered in the southern part of the county, while Protestant churches have representation in nearly every town and city in the area.

The most common houses of worship in the region are Episcopal, Congregational, Roman Catholic, Baptist, and Lutheran. Slightly less prolific are synagogues—including Orthodox, Reform, and Conservative—and houses of worship for the Methodist, Pentecostal, Muslim, Presbyterian, Christian Science, Greek Orthodox, Eastern Orthodox, Apostolic, and Seventh-Day Adventist faiths. The county also harkens to New England's early history with two Quaker churches, located in Wilton and Stamford.

One of the most famous churches in the area is the First Presbyterian Church of Stamford, better known as "the fish church." Built in 1954, the wooden structure is literally shaped like a fish, a well-known symbol of Christianity. You can see the shape from the air, from the interior, and also in the profile, depending on where you're standing. Designed by Wallace K. Harrison, the church also boasts stained-glass windows made with more than 20,000 separate pieces of glass.

Fairfield County, of course, is not the only region in Connecticut to boast a long tradition of religious worship. If you have an interest in historic church buildings, step outside county borders to see some of the state's other religious and architectural treasures. Perhaps the best known is the Congregational Church of Litchfield, often referred to as the most-photographed church in New England. It stands near the beautiful town green as an example of the classic early New England style. The Roman Catholic Cathedral of St. Joseph in Hartford has a very different architectural style, calling to mind the grand cathedrals of Europe. Nearby, the Faith Congregational Church in Hartford is one of the earliest African-American churches in Connecticut and is a stop on the Connecticut Freedom Trail. The state's first synagogue, the Charter Oak Cultural Center, is also located in Hartford. In the town of Bethlehem, Gregorian chants are sung daily at the Abbey of Regina Laudis. And in New Haven, the green is surrounded by notable church buildings, at which many parishioners became involved with the now famous events of the *Amistad* mutiny of the 1800s.

*Many local churches celebrate the seasons and holidays with outdoor festivals, carnivals, and other special events throughout the year. (Some also double as fund-raisers.) In most cases, all members of the general public—not just church members—are welcome. Look for hand-painted signs along the roadways for information about impending fun fests.*

No matter what your interests or religious beliefs, Connecticut and Fairfield County offer a place to exercise your freedom to worship. To find the church or synagogue nearest you, consult the Yellow Pages of the phone book. The denominations are listed alphabetically, with addresses and phone numbers.

# INDEX

## A

Abis, 52
Absolute Best Care, 257
accommodations
 Northern Fairfield County, 43–47
 Southern Fairfield County, 38–43
Acoustic Cafe, 78
Acqua, 64
Acting Company of Greenwich, 152
Adam Broderick Salon and Spa, 106
Adams Rib at the Norwalk Inn & Conference Center, 57
Addessi of Ridgefield, 103
Adele Poston Domestic Agency, 257
Adirondack Store, 98
Adopt-A-Dog, 224
Agabhumi, 98
air travel, 21–25
Alberti Realty Associates, 234
Aldrich Museum of Contemporary Art, 144
All About Nannies Family Connection, 258
Allen's East, 62
All Fired Up, 133
Amberjacks: A Coastal Grill, 81
American Cancer Society, 224
American Classical Orchestra, 147
American Pie Company, 77
American Realty Associates, 234
American Red Cross, 224
AmeriCares, 224–25
Ameriland Real Estate, 234
And Company, Inc., 101
Anderson Associates Real Estate, 234
Animal Adoption Network, 225
Anne Fontaine, 93
Ann's Place, The Home of I CAN, 225
Annual Antiques Show and Open House, 158
Annual Book Sale, 161
Annual Easter Egg Hunt, 159
annual events, 156–74
Annual Greater Danbury Irish Festival, 168
Annual Juried Art Exhibition, 169
Annual Juried Spring Art Show, 161
Annual Labor Day Parade, 167
Annual Lego Contest, 159
Annual Memorial Day Strawberry Festival, 162
Annual 9-Ball Pool Classic, 156–57
Annual Redding Antiques Fair, 170
Annual Ridgefield Antiques Market, 163
Annual Rocking Rooster Run/Walk 5K, 163
Annual Taste of Greater Danbury, 168
Antiquarious Antiques Show, 171–72
Antique Auto Show, 160
Antiques and Collectibles Show, 157
Antiques and Treasures Sale, 166
antiques stores, 90–91
Antonio's, 50
Antonio's Italian Bistro, 70
Apple Festival, 170
Archie Moore's, 50–51, 79
Arena at Harbor Yard, 111, 129
Arthur Harris Linear Park, 186
Art in the Park, 167
Artisans Alliance Annual Applefest, 169
Artists' Market, 144
Art/Place, 144
arts
 centers and associations, 140–44
 for children, 134–36
 community theater, 152–54
 dance, 147
 film, 154–55
 museums and galleries, 144–47
 music, 147–50
 professional theater, 150–52
Art & Soul/The Bead Bar, 133
Ash Creek Saloon, 79
assisted-living facilities, 270–71
attractions
 for children, 129–30
 Christmas tree farms, 127
 farms, 125–27
 general, 111–13
 historical, 119–25
 museums, 113–16
 nature centers, 116–19
 vineyards, 127–28
Audubon Center of Greenwich, 116, 196
Augustyn's Blue Goose Restaurant, 62–63
au pairs and nannies, 257–59

## B

Baby and Toy Superstore, 92
Bailey's Backyard, 75
Balloon Parade Spectacular, 171
Ballpark at Harbor Yard, 129–30
Bangkok, 70
Barcelona Restaurant & Wine Bar, 79, 80, 81

Bar 11, 81
Barnum Festival, 162
Barnum Museum, 113–14
Bartlett Arboretum, 116
baseball, 206
basketball, 206–7
Bates-Scofield House Museum, 119
beaches
    Northern Fairfield County, 179
    Southern Fairfield County, 175–79
Beardsley Organic Farm, 125
Beardsley Park, 180–81
Bear Mountain Reservation, 186, 196
Belgian Huis, 101
Below Deck, 190
Bendheim Gallery at the Greenwich Arts
    Center, 145
Bernard's Inn at Ridgefield, 75
Best Western Berkshire Motor Inn,
    43–44
Best Western Stony Hill Inn, 44
Bethel, 12–13
Bethel Cycle & Fitness, 107
Bethel Historical Firefighters Museum, 114
Bethel Religious Store, 98
Betteridge, 103
Beval Saddlery, 107
biking, 188–89
Bisceglie-Scribner Pond Park, 181
Bistro Bonne Nuit, 55
Black Duck Cafe, 64
Black Rock & Blue, 78
Black Rock Castle, 48, 78–79
Blessings, 92
Bleu, 80
Bloodroot, 49
Bloomin' Metric Bicycle Tour, 162
Blue Jay Orchards, 125
Blue Moon Gifts, 98–99
Blue Sky Realty, 234
boating, 189–94
Bobby Valentine's, 83
Bob Tendler Real Estate, 234
Bombay, 64
Bone Jour, 105
Books on the Common, 91
bookstores, 91–92
Boothe Memorial Park and Museum,
    111–12, 181
Boston Billiards Club, 79, 86
Botticelli, 93

Boughton Street YMCA Children's
    Programs, 264
Bourbon Street, 83
Boxcar Cantina, 53
Boxing Cat Grill, 80
Bradley International Airport, 21–22
Bradley Park, 188, 196
Breath of Spring Craft Show, 158
Brewhouse Restaurant and Tasting Room,
    57, 81
Bridge Cafe, 64
Bridgeport, 3–4
Bridgeport Bluefish, 206
Bridgeport Hospital, 266
Bridgeport Sound Tigers, 207–8
Bright Horizons, 259
Brinsmaids, 103–4
Brock's Restaurant, 60
Brookfield, 13
Brookfield Craft Center, 140
Brotherhood & Higley Real Estate, 234
Bruce Museum of Arts and Science,
    114, 145
Buffalo Bill's Steakhouse, 87
Building with Books, 225
Burying Hill Beach, 175
buses, 26, 27
Bush-Holley Historic Site, 119–20

C
cable/satellite television, 240–41, 276
Cafe on the Green, 70–71
Cafe Tango, 60
Calf Pasture Beach, 175–76
CancerCare of Connecticut, 225
Candlewood East Marina Club, 193
Candlewood Lake, 180–81
Candlewood Town Park, 179
Cannon Grange Agricultural Fair, 167
Captain's Cove Seaport, 112
Captain's Cove Seaport Restaurant, 49
Care Around the Clock, 260
Cargo Bay, 93
Carolee, 104
Casa Bella, 101
casinos, 212–13
Center for Women and Families of Eastern
    Fairfield County, 225
Centro at the Mill, 53
Centro Ristorante & Bar, 50, 51
Century 21 Access America, 234–35

Century 21 Greengarden Realty, 235
chambers of commerce, 20, 245–46
Charles Ives Center for the Arts,
    140–41, 147
charter boats, 194–95
Charter Oak Gallery, 145
Chef's Table, 65
Cherry Lawn Park, 182
child care
    chain day-care centers and pre-
        schools, 259–60
    nannies and au pairs, 257–59
    Northern Fairfield County day-care
        centers and nursery schools,
        264–65
    Southern Fairfield County day-care
        centers and nursery schools,
        260–64
Child Care Center, Inc., 260–61
Child Guidance Center, 261
children, activities for. See kidstuff
children's clothing, furniture, toys, and
    accessories stores, 92–93
Children's Community Daycare Center, 261
Child's Garden, A, 260, 264
Ching's Table, 55
Choice Pet Supply, 105
Chola, 53
Christmas in July, 166
Christmas tree farms, 127
Chuck's Steak House, 50, 71
churches, 278–79
CityCenter Grand PRIX, 163
city halls, 242–44
Clarke Outdoors, 193
CLASP Homes, 225–26
Classic Rock Brew Pub, 86
clothing and accessories stores, 93–95
Coach's, 83
Coastal Atlantic Striper Hunters, 195
Coastal Charter Company, 194
Cobb's Mill Inn, 64
Coldwell Banker, 235
colleges and universities, 254–56
Collis P. Huntington State Park, 186,
    188, 196
Colonials, The, 206–7
Colorado Brewery, 71, 86
Comfort Suites Danbury, 44
Command Performance, 147–48
community health centers, 269

Community Holiday Celebration, 174
Community Nursery School, 261
Compo Beach, 176
Compo Beach Point-to-Point Swim,
    165–66
Connecticut Audubon Birdcraft
    Museum, 116
Connecticut Audubon Society at Fairfield,
    116–17
Connecticut Ballet, 147
Connecticut Cares Nanny Referral, 258
Connecticut Grand Opera & Orchestra, 148
Connecticut Magazine, 275
Connecticut Master Chorale, 148
Connecticut Post, 272
Connecticut's Beardsley Zoo, 112, 130
Conte's Fish Market and Grill, 65
Cornerstone Children's Center, 261
Coromandel Cuisine, 50
Country Kids Play Farm, 264
Country Living Associates, 235
Country Living Imports, 101
Country Touch, A, 98
Courtyard by Marriott Danbury, 44–45
Courtyard by Marriott Norwalk, 40
Cove Island Park, 176
Covenant to Care, 226
Crab Shell, 83
craft and needlepoint supplies stores, 95
Craft Basket, 95
Cranbury Park, 182
Creative Castle, 134–35
cruises, 194–95
Cultural Care Au Pair, 258
Cummings Park and Cummings Park
    West, 176
Curtain Call, 152
Curtiss & Crandon Realtors, 235
Cystic Fibrosis Bike Tour, 169–70

**D**

D. Fairchild-Wheeler Golf Course, 200
Danbury, 13–14
Danbury Animal Welfare Society
    (DAWS), 226
Danbury Fair Mall, 105–6
Danbury Flight School, 24
Danbury Hospital, 266–67
Danbury Ice Arena, 136, 198
Danbury Municipal Airport, 24
Danbury Music Centre, 148

*Danbury News-Times,* 272
Danbury Railway Museum, 114–15
dance, 147
Darien, 4
Darien Antiques Show, 158
Darien Book Aid Plan, 226
Darien Ice Rink, 198–99
Darien Nature Center, 117, 130–31
*Darien News-Review,* 273
Darien Sport Shop, 107–8
*Darien Times,* 273
Darien Windsurfing, 191
Darien YMCA, 136
David Northrup House Museum, 120
Davis & Hoyt Realtors, 235
day care. *See* child care
day trips and getaways
    Berkshires (MA), 214–15
    Block Island (RI), 222
    Boston (MA), 215
    Cape Cod (MA), 216–17
    Hudson Valley and Catskill Mountains
        (NY), 217–18
    Litchfield Hills (CT), 209–10
    Long Island (NY), 218–19
    Mystic (CT), 210–11
    New Haven (CT), 211–13
    Newport (RI), 222–23
    New York City (NY), 219–22
Delamar, The, 39
Derma Clinic, 106–7
Design Solutions, 101–2
Devil's Den Preserve, 182, 196
Devil's Glen Park, 182
Diane's Books, 91
DiGrazia Vineyards, 127–28
diners, 54
Discovery Center at Ridgefield, 117, 131
Discovery Museum, 115, 131
Dogwood Festival, 161
Domestic Violence Crisis Center, 226
Dorothy Hamill Skating Rink, 199
Down the Hatch, 86
Downtown Cabaret Theater, 135, 150–51
driver's licenses, 241–42
Dry Dock Cafe, 57

**E**
E. Gaynor Brennan Municipal Golf
    Course, 200
Earth Animal, 105

Earth Day Annual Celebration, 159
Earthplace: The Nature Discovery Center,
    117–18, 131–32
Easter Bunny Railyard, 159
Eastern Scrabble Championship, 157
Easton, 4–5
*Easton Courier,* 273
Easton Volunteer Fire Company
    Carnival, 166
Echo Bay Marina, 193
education. *See* colleges and universities;
    schools, private; schools, public
Edward Tunick, Men's Clothier, 93–94
Ego, 81
El Acapulco, 57–58
electricity service, 239
Elms Inn, 46
Elms Restaurant and Tavern, 75
Elm Street Books, 91
Emily's Gourmet Food & Gifts, 99
Emmanuel Church Country Fair, 168
Enchanted Forest Holiday Stroll, 171
Enchanted Garden, 133–34, 264
English Heritage Antiques, 90
ERA Shays Real Estate, 235
EurAuPair, 258
European's Furniture and Gifts, 102

**F**
Fairfield, 5–6
*Fairfield Citizen-News,* 273–74
*Fairfield County Business Journal,* 275
Fairfield County Chorale, 148–49
Fairfield County Home and Better
    Living Show, 158
Fairfield County Irish Festival, 164
Fairfield County Rambles, 188
Fairfield County Real Estate, 235
*Fairfield County Weekly,* 274
Fairfield Gallery & Frame, 96
Fairfield Historical Society, 120
Fairfield Lighting and Design, 102
Fairfield Road Races, 165
Fairfield University, 254
Fairfield YMCA, 136
Fairfield YMCA Child Care, 261
Fall Festival, 169
Family Britches, 94
Family Centers, Inc., 261–62
Family & Children's Agency, 226
Family Extensions, 258

Family Fall Festival, 170
Family ReEntry, 226
F&M Lighting Showroom, 102
farms, 125–27
FCI Danbury, 34–35
ferries, 26, 28
Festival of Lights, 174
festivals, 156–74
Figaro, 53
fine art and framing stores, 96–97
Firehouse Deli, 51
Fireside Inn, 88
First Americans' Festival, 164
First Night Danbury, 174
First Night Westport/Weston, 174
fishing, 195–96
5K Pancake Breakfast, 160
Fjord Catering and Charters, 194
football, 207
Four Points by Sheraton Norwalk, 40–41
Fourth of July Festivities, 165
framing and fine art stores, 96–97
Friends of Ferguson Library Bookstores,
    91–92
Friends of the Bethel Library Annual
    Book Sale, 165
Front Street Fish House and Cranky Fish
    Saloon, 69, 85

**G**
galleries, art, 144–47
Garbage Museum, 115, 132
gardening and landscaping supplies
    stores, 97–98
GarlicFest, 160
gas service, 239
Gates Restaurant & Bar, 56
Geary Gallery, 96
Georgetown Saloon, 88–89
getaways. See day trips and getaways
Gift Cottage, 99
gifts stores, 98–100
Giggles, 92
Giovanni's, 60
Giovanni's II, 50
golf courses
    private, 203–5
    public, 200–203
Golf Quest, 136–37
Good Friend, 227
Gotta Dance, 108

Gould Manor Park, 182
gourmet/specialty foods stores, 100–101
Governor's Horse Guard Annual Open
    House and Horse Show, 166
Gracious Home and Garden Show, 160
Graham Dickinson S.P.I.R.I.T. Skate
    Park, 137
Grand, 60–61
Grassy Plain Children's Center, 264
Gratzi, 63
Gray Farms Nursery School, 262
Great American Stamp Store, 95
Greater Bridgeport Symphony, 149
Great Hollow Lake, 188
Greek Festival, 164
Green, The, 182–83
Greenknoll Children's Center, 264–65
Greenwich, 6–7
Greenwich Arts Council, 141
Greenwich Bicycles, 108–9
Greenwich Community Sailing,
    137, 191–92
Greenwich Concours d'Elegance, 163–64
Greenwich Family YMCA, 137–38
Greenwich Film Festival, 169
Greenwich Golf, 109
Greenwich Hospital, 267
*Greenwich Magazine,* 275–76
Greenwich Point, 176–77
Greenwich Polo Club, 208
*Greenwich Post,* 274
Greenwich Rowing Club, 192
Greenwich Symphony Orchestra, 149
*Greenwich Time,* 273
Greenwich Workshop Gallery, 96
Greenwood Antiques and
    Consignments, 90
Greenwoods Restaurant and Pub, 69, 85
Griffith E. Harris Golf Club, 200–201
Gut Reaction, 109

**H**
H. Smith Richardson Golf Course, 201
Habitat for Humanity of Greater
    Bridgeport, 227
Halloween Costume Contest, 170
Halloween Parade, 170
Handwright Gallery and Framing, 96
Harbor House Inn, 39
Harbor Lights, 58
Harvest Festival, 169

Hat City Cyclists, 188–89
haunted places, 122–23
health care
    assisted-living facilities, 270–71
    community health centers, 269
    general health-care centers, 268
    hospitals, 266–68
    mental and behavioral health
      services, 269
    nursing homes, 269–70
    rehabilitation centers, 269
    urgent-care centers, 268–69
Helen Ainson, 94
Helen B. Charters, 195
Helga's, 69
Hidden Garden Tour, 163
Highstead Arboretum, 118
hiking, 196–97
Hillel Academy, 262
Hilltop Preschool, 262
historical attractions, 119–25
history, 32–37
hockey, 207–8
holiday craft fairs, 171, 172–73
holiday house tours, 121
Holiday Inn Bridgeport, 38
Holiday Inn Danbury-Bethel, 45
Holiday Inn Select Stamford, 41
Holiday Tree Lightings, 171
Hollandia Nurseries, 97
home furnishings stores, 101–3
Homestead Inn, 39
Hometown Nannies Plus, 258
horseback riding, 197–98
hospitals, 266–68
hotels. See accommodations
hotlines, 240
Hot Shots II Grille, 88
Hot Shots Sports Pub & Cafe, 88
Housatonic Community Technical
    College, 254–55
Housatonic Museum of Art, 145
Housatonic Valley Classic International
    Pro/Am Bicycle Race, 162
House and Garden Show, 159
Howard Johnson Inn Darien, 38–39
Hubbell Farm at French's Corner, 126
Hula Hank's Island Grille & Bar, 83
Hunan Cafe, 67
Hunan Gourmet, 53
Hyatt Regency Greenwich, 39–40

**I**

ice-cream shops, 65
ice-skating, 198–99
Il Falco Ristorante, 61
Image Arts of Greenwich, 96
IMAX Theater at the Maritime Aquarium at
    Norwalk, 112–13
Indian Ledge Park, 183
Indian Well State Park, 186, 193
Inn at Ethan Allen, 45
Inn at Longshore, 43
Inn at National Hall, 43
Inn at Newtown, 46, 73
inns. See accommodations
Interfaith AIDS Ministry, 227
Interlude, 227
International Festival, 159
International Institute of Connecticut, 227
Internet and telephone service
    providers, 240
Island Cruise Lines, 194
Italian Center Nursery School, 262
Ives, Charles, 142–43
Ivy Urn, 90

**J**

Jennings Beach, 177
Jeremiah Donovan's, 81
Jesse Lee Nursery School, 262
jewelry stores, 103–5
Jim Barbarie's Restaurant, 71
John F. Kennedy International Airport,
    22–23
Jones Family Farm, 126
Jubilee Yacht Charters, 194
Just Books, 92
Just Books, Too, 92

**K**

Kate's Paperie, 110
Katie Facey Agency, 259
Kayak Adventures, 192
Keeler Tavern Museum, 120–21
Kelly Associates Real Estate, 235–36
Kennedy Center, The, 227
Kiddie Campus Preschool, 265
Kids in Crisis, 227–28
Kid's Supply Co., 92
kidstuff
    arts, 134–36
    attractions, 129–30

museums and nature centers, 130–33
rainy-day activities, 133–34
sports and fitness, 136–39
KinderCare Learning Centers, 259–60
King & I, 49
Kitchen Corner, 102
Klaff's, 102
Klein Memorial Auditorium, 147, 149, 151
Knitting Niche, 95
Knobel Brothers, 99
Kotobuki, 61

**L**
Labriola Frame and Art Gallery, 96
La Colline Verte, 51
La Fortuna, 69
LaGuardia Airport, 23
Lake Kenosia, 193
Lake Lillionah, 193
Lake Mohegan Recreation Area, 183
Lakeside Pottery, 134
Lake Zoar, 193
Landmark Properties, 236
landscaping and gardening supplies
stores, 97–98
Lanphier Day Spa, 107
Larson's Amazing Corn Maze, 130
Larson's Farm Market, 126
Lattins Cove Boat Launch, 194
Lava Lounge, 83
La Zingara Ristorante, 69
L'escale, 53
Leslie's Jewelry Connection, 104
Levitt Pavilion for the Performing Arts, 141
Liana's Trattoria, 51
libraries, 244–45
Lime Restaurant, 58
limousines/shuttles, 25
Linda's Loveable Bears, 134
Liquid, 81–82
Literacy Volunteers of Southeastern
Fairfield County, 228
Lockwood-Mathews Mansion Museum, 121
Loft, The, 82
Lois Richards Galleries, 96–97
Lombardi Realtors, 236
Long Beach, 177
Long Ridge Tavern, 61
Longshore Club Park, 183, 201
Longshore Sailing School, 138, 192
Love in Bloom, 164

Luca's, 54
Luna Rossa, 61
Lux Bond & Green, 104
Lynnens, 102

**M**
magazines, 275–76
Make-A-Wish Foundation of
Connecticut, 228
malls, 105–6
Manfredi, 104
Marbella Restaurant and Tapas Bar, 63
Mario's Place, 65
Marisa's Ristorante & Lounge, 63
Maritime Aquarium at Norwalk, 113, 130
Mark's Tap Room, 88
Mark Twain Library Annual Art Show, 174
Match, 58, 82
Matthew Curtiss House, 121
McLaughlin Vineyards, 128
Mead Memorial Park, 183
Meals on Wheels of Stamford-Darien, 228
media. See news media
medical care. See health care
Mediterraneo, 54
Meigas Restaurant, 58
Memorial Day Parades, 162
Mendelssohn Choir of Connecticut, 149
mental and behavioral health services, 269
Methodist Family Center Preschool,
262–63
Metro Grille & Bar, 76, 89
Mexicali Rose, 73–74
Mianus River Park and Glen, 183, 189,
196–97
Microtel Inn and Suites, 44
Mid-Fairfield AIDS Project, 228
Milano Restaurant, 58
Military Museum of Southern New
England, 115
Mill River Park, 183–84
Minute Man Race, 160
Mitchells of Westport, 94
Mizak Realtors, 236
Molly Darcy's, 86
Mona Lisa, 74
Monroe, 14–15
*Monroe Courier,* 274
Morton's of Chicago, 61
motels. See accommodations
Mother Earth Mining Gallery, 134